Comprehensive COMPUTING

the GCSE course

Peter Bishop

Hodder & Stoughton

LONDON SYDNEY AUCKLAND TORONTO

The publishers would like to thank the following for their permission to reproduce copyright photographs:

Austin Rover 284; Banking Information Service 262; Barclays Bank 16 (top), 54; BASF United Kingdom Ltd 48, 193 (bottom left); BBC Radio Kent 16 (bottom); S G Brown (a division of Hawker Siddeley) 67; British Airports Services Ltd 189; British Caledonian Airways Ltd 263; British Museum 11 (middle); British Telecommunications plc 56 (top and bottom), 274 (top); The Burton Group 162; Centre-File Ltd. 281; Racal-Chubb Ltd 233, 269 (top); Cincinnati Milacron 13 (right, 64 (middle); Jez Coulson 201, 251; COI Crown Copyright 289, 292; Cray Research UK Ltd 36 (bottom); Daily Telegraph 243; Datasolve 26 (right) 47 (top), 141, 222, 274 (bottom), 282; Andrew Devic (Insight) 143; Digital Equipment Company Ltd 36 (top right), 85, 279; Economatics (Education) Ltd 239; Educational Electronics 66; Ferranti plc 31 (left), 51, 60, 156, 291; Fiat UK Ltd 13 (bottom Left), 64 (bottom); Vivien Fifield 8, 27; Fishing News International 208; GEC Computers Ltd 212; Sally and Richard Greenhill 108, 182, 214, 216, 225; Hewlett-Packard Ltd 9, 44 (left and right); Hitachi Electronic Component (UK) Ltd 14 (left and right), 31 (right), 32, 278; Hong Kong Tourist Association 228, 277; Sue Hyman Associates Ltd/Nobby Clark 236; IBM United Kingdom Ltd 26, 35; ICI Pharmaceuticals Division 172; ICL 18; Inmos Ltd 254; Kent County Library 107; Ladbroke Hotels 185; Lloyd's of London/Janet Gill 197 (bottom); Logica Ltd 200; Marconi Communications Systems Ltd 11, 40 (top), 56 (middle), 57 (top and bottom), 95, 193 (top) 198, 266; Adrian Meredith Photography 181, 249; Meteorological Office Crown Copyright 17; Metropolitan Police 115, 116, 118; Lawrence Migdale/Science Photo Library, cover; National Portrait Gallery 255; NCR Ltd 52, 165; The Newspaper Society 125, 126, 129; Northumbrian Water 177 (bottom); Pilkington plc 60 (left), 244; Pulse 10, 273; Chubb Safe Equipment Company 269 (bottom); Research Machines Ltd 53, 193 (right); Rolls Royce plc 64 (top), 94, 232, 248; St. Margarets Software Ltd 38; J Sainsbury 166 (bottom), 167, 168; The Science Museum 12, 13, 22; Science Photo Library 45 (top and bottom), 197 (top); Seagate Technology 47; Shell UK 93; Katie Sparkes 174; Thames Water 177 (top).

First published in Great Britain 1988
Fourth impression 1993

British Library Cataloguing in Publication Data

Bishop, Peter, *1949–*
    Comprehensive computing: a GCSE course.
    1. Computer sciences – For schools
    I. Title
    004

ISBN 07131 7669 5

Typeset in Century Schoolbook by Tradespools Ltd, Frome, Somerset.
Printed and bound in Great Britain for Edward Arnold, the educational, academic and medical publishing division of Hodder and Stoughton Limited, Mill Road, Dunton Green, Sevenoaks, Kent by Butler & Tanner Ltd, Frome and London.

Preface

The adoption of the General Certificate of Secondary Education (GCSE) course presents a new challenge to teachers of Computer Studies. Long accustomed to teaching a subject in which the content-matter advances on a daily basis, teachers have to come to terms with a new approach:

- What are the capabilities of a computer system?
- How are the capabilities of a computer system matched to the requirements of particular applications?
- Why is information technology (IT) proving to be so useful, and what are the effects of the widespread introduction of IT?

As far as possible, these questions are to be approached in a practical way. Pupils must acquire elementary skills in the use of computers, in ways which bear some resemblance to the way they are used in commerce and industry. This means a reduced emphasis on programming, and increased use of software packages on school micros. These packages—word processors, information retrieval software, spreadsheets and similar general-purpose packages—are simple versions of those in use in industry. The 'hands-on' experience gained by the pupils in using them provides a basis for the study of actual IT applications in commerce and industry.

The Structure of the Book

Comprehensive Computing presents a balance of theory, activities, applications, case studies and issues, in accordance with the requirements of the GCSE National Criteria for Computer Studies, and the syllabuses derived from these criteria. The book is in three main parts:

- Chapters 1 to 8 present the theory of computing in a non-technical way. Ideas of information and data, the nature of a computer, hardware and software, as well as the principles of data communications and control systems, are presented simply and clearly. The emphasis is on the suitability of various techniques and items of equipment for various types of application.
- Chapters 9 to 23 cover a wide range of applications of IT. Each application starts with at least one **activity** which the pupils can do on their school computers and which is relevant to their immediate experience. This gives a basis of hands-on experience with which to approach the **applications**, which are case studies of IT at work. If a particular **issue**, such as unemployment caused by robots, is raised in the chapter, then it is discussed in a section at the end of the chapter.
- Chapter 24 to the end of the book draw together the threads. These chapters review what it is like to live and work in a world of IT. There is a revision exercise, based entirely on specimen GCSE

examination papers. There is also a set of suggestions for GCSE projects, in addition to those given at the end of most applications chapters. There is a glossary of technical terms and an index.

- A separate **Teacher's Book** provides a list of suitable software which may be used in the applications chapters, some notes for the guidance of teachers suggesting alternative ways of using the book, and the answers to the questions and exercises.

The chapters are set out in a progression from theory to practice, but do not have to be taught in this sequence. Theory may be alternated with practice, or applications used to introduce theory if required. The presentation in the book is a logical sequence, and avoids the fragmentation and excessive cross-referencing which any other approach would have required. It should be borne in mind that an application of IT is an attempt to bring to bear **all** the resources of a computing system in order to perform a task as efficiently and cost-effectively as possible. It is misleading to associate particular capabilities of computers too closely with particular applications.

Activities, Questions and Exercises

The practical side of **Comprehensive Computing** takes the form of **activities** in each application chapter. These guide the pupils, step-by-step, through a practical activity, using a software package on a computer. These range from writing an introductory letter to a pen-friend using a word processor, to planning a school trip overseas using a viewdata system for the information and a spreadsheet for the budget. These activities provide a basis of hands-on experience to help the pupils understand the remaining material in these chapters, on how computers are used in similar ways in commerce and industry.

At the end of most sections of the book are sets of **questions** to check that the pupils have understood the section and to enable them to consolidate their knowledge. At the end of each chapter is an **exercise** containing a set of graded questions. In addition to straightforward comprehension and extension questions, there are **things to find out**, **points to discuss**, and, finally, **project starters**. Any questions of above average difficulty are marked*. The project starters are suggestions for substantial activities based on the material in the chapter which may form the basis of GCSE projects. There is also a separate chapter containing project suggestions which are based on material in more than one chapter.

The aim of the activities, questions and exercises is to provide as much as possible for the pupils to do (or for teachers to choose for them to do) during the course. In addition, an **Activity Pack** comprising a set of worksheets on copy master pages is available to complement the material in the book.

Software Packages

Comprehensive Computing makes extensive use of software in the practical introductions to each computer application. The software packages required are the types which most schools will already have: a word processor, a spreadsheet and an information retrieval package, etc. The book does not require any specific software packages; the instructions are all in general terms, assuming that a simple, conventional software package is being used. For schools which do not already have the required software, a comprehensive list of suitable software is provided in the Teacher's Book.

It is realised that there is a difficulty in matching the general instructions in the text with the specific commands to be given when using a particular software package. It is impossible to include specific instructions in a book of this nature; a glance at the list of accompanying software shows the range of software available at the time of writing, and this list is growing all the time.

It needs to be borne in mind that solving this problem—matching the capabilities of a software package to the requirements of a task—is an essential skill in computing. Pupils will need specific guidance from staff at first, but later might be able to use the software with minimal supervision. If so, an essential problem-solving skill will have been acquired. Some additional guidance for teachers in approaching this problem is given in the Teacher's Book.

Acknowledgements

A number of people have reviewed the initial outline and the drafts of this book. I am most grateful to them for their time and expertise, and for their useful comments. I am grateful to the Home Office, Pilkington Brothers plc, the Daily Telegraph and Today newspapers, Blue Bell (Wrangler) Limited, Building Design Partnership, Prestel Education, The Times Network for Schools and Rolls-Royce plc for information used in applications case studies. My thanks go to Sarah Bishop for much of the administrative work and checking involved in a book of this nature.

Specimen GCSE examination questions have been reproduced with permission from the examining groups:

LEAG   London and East Anglian Group
MEG   Midland Examining Group
NISEC Northern Ireland Schools Examinations Council
SEG   Southern Examining Group

The text for this book was prepared on an RM Nimbus computer, using the Wordstar word processing program

Peter Bishop

Contents

1

Introduction

Theolonius Colby and two assistants in his office. Note the paperwork on his desk and the large number of ledgers and reference books on the shelves.

MESSRS. COLBY and CO. respectfully give notice that they are now offering for SALE the finest SILK from CHINA, recently imported. Not previously available in England.

250 pieces fine silk, suitable for Evening, Dinner and Ball dresses. A range of shades for every combination, 7s. 6d. per yard.

The Fabric is on show at the Premises of the above, Limehouse Basin.

Inspection respectfully invited.

The advertisement in *The Times*, 1887.

Theolonius Colby felt pleased with himself. He looked out of the window of his office and, through the smog, saw gangs of workmen bringing goods from the docks to the many warehouses in the East End of London. It was 1887, and the Empire was prospering.

The previous evening he had been at a masked ball. One of the ladies, recently arrived from Paris, had been wearing a dress made from a most unusual fabric. He had managed to find out that it was a silk from China, of a type that had not been seen in Europe before.

Theolonius Colby was an importer of fabrics from the East. His experienced eye told him that the dress he had seen the previous night was going to be the talk of the town. If he could import the fabric before his rivals, he would do very well...

He summoned Oliver, his new clerk, to take a letter to his agent in Hong Kong. Oliver was only fourteen, but had the makings of one who could go far. Mr Colby dictated the letter slowly, while Oliver set it out as neatly as he could with his quill pen. Afterwards Mr Colby made Oliver read it back to him (he did not like to admit that he could not read too well himself). Oliver was sent at speed to the Post Office, to make sure that the letter caught the next steamer.

Seven weeks later, the agent's reply arrived. He had found a source of the fabric, and enclosed a sample. He also quoted a price for the shipment Mr Colby required. Mr Colby called his accounts clerk, young Matthew. Together they looked at the large, leather-bound ledger of accounts. As Matthew read out the figures, Mr Colby pondered. He decided that he could afford an even larger quantity than he had first ordered. He was sure that his agent in Hong Kong could get a discount for the larger quantity.

Mr Colby called on his banker to get a banker's draft for the money. He then got Oliver to write out an order for the goods, and enter it in the order book. He personally sealed the order and the banker's draft in a large envelope, and sent one of the boys to post it. Matthew made an entry in the ledger to record the banker's draft.

Nine weeks later, a messenger from the steamship company called to say that the shipment of fabrics had arrived. Mr Colby instructed his storeman, one Alfred Sykes, to organise some lads to bring it from the docks. When the shipping documents were brought to the office, Matthew entered the shipping charges in his ledger, and arranged the payment to the shipping company. Alfred Sykes told his assistant, young Steven, to make an entry in the stock book for the new fabric.

Mr Colby summoned his seller, James Tyburn, to his office. Together they drafted an advertisement for *The Times* to announce that the new fabric had arrived and was for sale. After a fair amount of crossing out, they eventually decided that the wording was right. James Tyburn got his assistant, young Theodore, to make a neat copy and then take it to the newspaper offices.

Joanna Cameron using her desktop microcomputer. It is showing a graph of her company's sales on the screen. She is able to print the graph on the laser printer.

One hundred years later, Joanna Cameron sat in the same office. The grime of the previous century had been removed from the outside of the building, but it was otherwise the same. However, the inside had changed beyond all recognition.

Joanna had arrived for work early, because of something she had seen on television the previous night. The singer of a band on *Top of the Pops* had been wearing a jumpsuit made from a most unusual fabric, not at present available in Europe. Her experienced eye as a fabric importer told her that thousands of young girls would soon be wanting outfits made from that material. She had telephoned the band's agent, and found that the fabric was being produced in Hong Kong.

As the painting of Theolonius Colby stared down at her from the wall of her office, Joanna switched on her desktop computer. She had a quick look at the company's finances while she telephoned her agent in Hong Kong. Although it was late afternoon there, he agreed to work into the evening while he made some calls to get a quote for the fabric.

Two hours later, her agent called back. He gave a quote for a large consignment of the fabric. Joanna entered some figures on her desktop computer as she spoke on the phone. After a few minutes, they had agreed the price, quantity and delivery date. Joanna drafted a telex to confirm the order. Her secretary typed it at the telex machine; it was printed in Hong Kong as soon as she finished it.

Four days later a telex arrived to say that the fabric had been dispatched by airfreight. Joanna telephoned her clearing agent at Heathrow to advise him that the goods were on the way. It took three more days for the consignment to reach her company's warehouse because of a delay in clearing customs. The warehouse manager entered details of the consignment into the stock control computer system.

The advertisement in a trade magazine, 1987.

Joanna looked at the documents which arrived with the goods, printed by the computers of the airfreight company and the supplier. She asked her accountant to enter the figures into the accounts system on her company's computer. He did so, and telephoned the bank to authorise the payments by electronic funds transfer.

Joanna took a sample of the fabric to her marketing manager, Edward Colby. He used the graphics program on his desktop computer to prepare an advertisement for the fabric. Joanna looked at the advertisement on the computer screen. When she was satisfied, Edward printed a copy on the laser printer, and posted it to a trade magazine.

Questions

1   How were orders placed for the fabric in the two stories? Estimate the times taken for the orders to be received.
2   In each story, how long did it take for the orders to be supplied?
3   What items of information are common to both stories? In each story, how was this information decided on?
4   List all the uses of computers in the second story. For each use, state what was used in the first story to do the same task.
5   What methods of communication were used in the two stories? List the advantages and disadvantages of each method.
6   Describe the differences in working conditions between the two stories. To what extent do you think these changes have been due to the new technology which has been introduced in the last hundred years?

1A Information and Technology

Paper records at a doctor's surgery. Note the large number of filing cabinets needed to store all this information.

Almost everything we do needs information. Doctors and hospitals keep records of patients, shops keep records of sales, governments keep records of taxes, banks keep records of money in accounts, every school subject has bookfuls of information, to name just a few examples. Many years ago, when life was simpler, less information was needed. With society as complex as it is today, and changing as rapidly, the need for information becomes greater all the time.

We need to store large amounts of information, but we also need to do things with it. Information needs to be kept up-to-date and accurate. Information needs to be sorted, the items of information which are needed must be selected, decisions need to be made on the basis of information, and calculations need to be done on the information. For example, when someone makes a reservation for a flight, the information about the flight is located from the records of all the flights for which bookings are being made. If there are seats available, then one can be booked. The amount for the fare is added to the total amount received from flight bookings that day.

We need to get the right information to the right place at the right time. For this, methods of communication are required. For example, every edition of a newspaper carries a large amount of information. This is gathered from all over the world, and must reach the newspaper office as quickly as possible. The information is in the form of words and pictures. In a similar way, a television news broadcast uses pictures and sound which have been sent from all over the world.

Much of the equipment we use to make things needs to be controlled in some way. Some equipment is entirely automatic, such as the robots which do assembly jobs on cars. Other equipment, such

A library—a large store of useful information. This is carefully arranged to make it easy to find what you want.

as that used in chemical plants, is partly automatic. Information is needed to control things; for example the control system in a chemical plant needs information like the temperature and pressure of the chemical reaction.

The equipment used for the three things which can be done with information—processing, communicating and controlling—is known as **information technology** or **IT** for short. The aim of information technology is to help people store and process information, send it from place to place, and use it to control equipment, as efficiently as possible. Information technology has developed gradually over the centuries, but the speed of development is now rapid. Information technology used to be based on paper and mechanical devices; now it is based on electronics. The most important item of IT equipment is the computer.

Questions

1 List the most important items of information which are needed in each of the following activities:
   (a) choosing optional subjects at school
   (b) revising for an examination
   (c) running a small grocery shop
   (d) planning a family holiday
   (e) designing a house.
2 What must be done with information in order for it to be of practical use?
3 List some of the ways in which information can be processed.
4 What are the *three* aspects of information technology?

1B Storing and Communicating Information

Top: A Sumerian clay tablet—one of the earliest permanent records of information which we still have. *Bottom:* A modern telephone, which can reach hundreds of millions of people all over the world quickly and cheaply.

For many centuries, permanent records have been kept of information. The ancient Sumerians used clay tablets; the Romans were the first large-scale users of paper. It has been said that the Roman Empire could not have spread over most of Western Europe without paper to keep records and to carry messages and instructions. Modern societies create a huge demand for stored information: more and more information is created all the time, and much less is thrown away.

Paper is still widely used to store information, but it is very bulky, and information on paper can be hard to find. Other storage media are also used: microfilm, magnetic tape, video tape and optical disks, as well as the disks and tapes used by computers.

There has always been a need for communications. For many centuries, messengers carried news, stories and warnings. At first they remembered their messages as best they could; centuries later the information was written on paper. Nearly one hundred and fifty years ago came the telegraph, which used pulses of electricity along a wire. By the end of the 1800s there was a worldwide telegraph network. For the first time, messages could travel faster than messengers. Messages were sent in codes such as the Morse code which consisted of dots and dashes. The telegraph system led to the telex network which is still in use today.

The telephone was invented in 1876, and over the last hundred years the worldwide telephone network has grown to become the largest man-made system in existence. It is still growing rapidly, and now carries many other signals in addition to voice messages. The introduction of fibre optics cables has reduced the costs of telephone links, and greatly increased the amount of information they can carry.

Radio and television are technologies of this century. They enable sound and pictures to be sent as waves, over long distances if necessary. The coming of satellites has meant that radio and television signals can be sent from one continent to another by orbiting satellites more than thirty thousand kilometres up.

Communications networks are becoming interlinked: telephone signals are sent by radio over long distances, and radio and television signals can be sent over short distances by telephone cables if necessary. Telephone cables and radio channels are used to carry information between computers.

1C Processing Information

Punched card equipment from around 1900.

Processing information can be a tedious job. Imagine working in a bank and having to write down every transaction and work out all the totals, entirely by hand! The most tedious job of all is doing calculations, particularly adding up long columns of figures. Business accounting systems contain built-in checks, and accounts do not work out unless every calculation in them is correct. Many hours are spent, even today when computers are used, looking for mistakes in business accounts.

Over the centuries, people have looked for devices to help them process information, and in particular to do calculations. Mechanical calculators have been with us for several centuries, and have only been replaced by electronic calculators in the last twenty years. They were used for business and scientific calculations, and, particularly in the early days, to work out taxes.

But calculating is only one part of information processing. Towards the end of the last century, equipment came into use which used punched cards to store information, and mechanical devices called tabulators to read and sort the cards and to perform calculations on the information on them. Tabulators were first used in the USA Census of 1890, and were then rapidly accepted for business use. Other accounting systems which combined information storage with mechanical calculators and printers were also used during this period. Punched card equipment and mechanical office systems were displaced by computers after the Second World War.

Computers are now the commonest items of equipment used for information processing. Computers work very fast, and can store and process large quantities of information. The important thing about a computer is that it can be **programmed**. It is given a set of instructions (a program) for a particular task. Once the program is running, the computer carries out the task by itself. It does not need someone to supervise the step-by-step work that is required. When one task is complete, another program can be loaded into the computer to set it to work on another information processing task.

Questions

1. What are the main uses of calculating machines?
2. How was the information stored in some early automated office systems?
3. Find out more about some of the early information processing systems mentioned in this section.
4. When did computers first come into use?
5. Why is it important for computers to be able to be programmed?

1D   Controlling Equipment

Above: A Jacquard loom. *Below right:* An automatic metal workshop with a number of workstations, all controlled by computer. *Below left:* A robot welding a car body.

The Industrial Revolution of the 1800s was based on machines. These were more powerful, and could work much faster, than people working with simple hand tools. One of the problems to be solved in the design of machines is ways of controlling them. The first machines simply carried out repeated sequences of operations, without any variations. They pressed metal, wove cloth, rolled paper and performed similar tasks. Their control systems were mechanical: rods and levers which opened and closed valves and engaged wheels in a fixed cycle. The machines could not cope with much variation in the product they produced, and resetting them was a slow process, requiring a fair amount of skill.

The idea of programming a machine to produce a specific product, and varying the program to vary the product, began in the design of weaving looms. In the early 1800s, Joseph Jacquard, a French textile manufacturer, devised a method of controlling a weaving loom by a set of punched cards. A new set of punched cards produced a new pattern of cloth. The Jacquard system soon became very popular, but the principles were not applied to other types of machinery.

As machines began to be powered by electricity, so electricity was used to control them. But for a long time there was no change in the method of control: the machines carried out a fixed cycle of operations, with little variation. It is only in the last few decades that the demand for variety has made many fixed-cycle machines obsolete. Most of the new machines are controlled electronically, either by

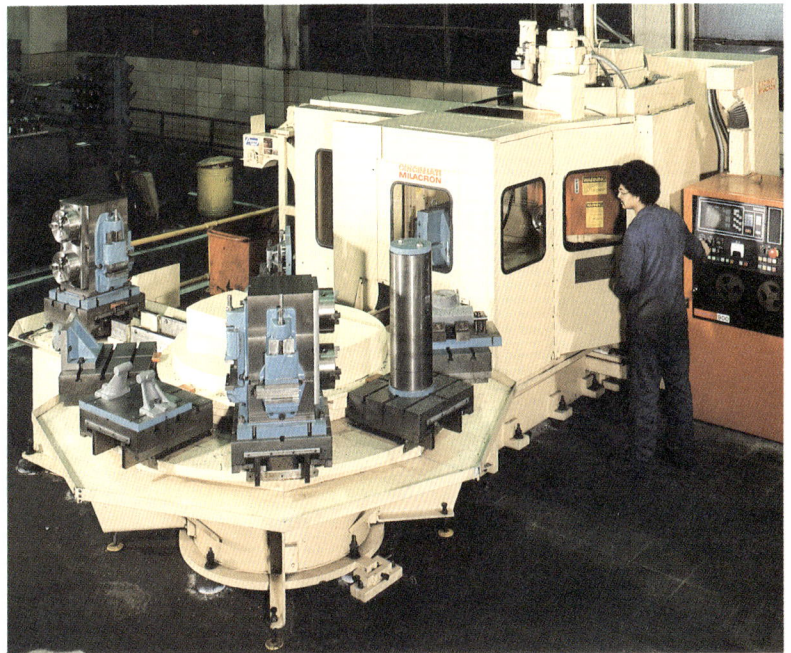

built-in microprocessors or by connections from a separate computer. Robots are machines with sophisticated control systems: they can be programmed to do a wide range of tasks, and some of them can make decisions about their work as they are doing it.

The use of robots and computers to control machines is bringing about great improvements in productivity, and reducing costs. A small set of machines which produce a variety of products can replace a much larger set of fixed-cycle machines. Flexible manufacturing means that production can be matched closely to demand, and therefore reduces waste.

Questions

1 How were early industrial machines controlled?
2 What are the disadvantages of fixed-cycle control systems?
3 How are Jacquard looms controlled? Suggest some reasons why this technique of control was not used for other equipment.
4 How are modern machines controlled? What are the advantages of this type of control system?

1E Microchips: a Technology for Information

The great advances in methods of storing, processing and communicating information, and in control systems for machinery, have been made possible by the availability of cheap, powerful **microchips**. Microchips are small, contain no moving parts, and are made largely from silicon. Silicon is found in sand, and is one of the most plentiful elements on Earth.

Microchips contain large numbers of very small electric circuits. They can be used for all types of operations to do with information: storing, processing, sending and receiving, and controlling equipment. Designing microchips is a difficult process, because they are so complex. But once they are being produced in large numbers, microchips are cheap, and getting cheaper all the time. Their speed, processing power and the amount of information they can store are increasing as well.

Below left: A high-capacity memory chip in its case. The two banks of memory cells can be seen inside the case. *Below right:* A processing chip, without its case. The processing elements are laid out in rows, with large numbers of connections running between them.

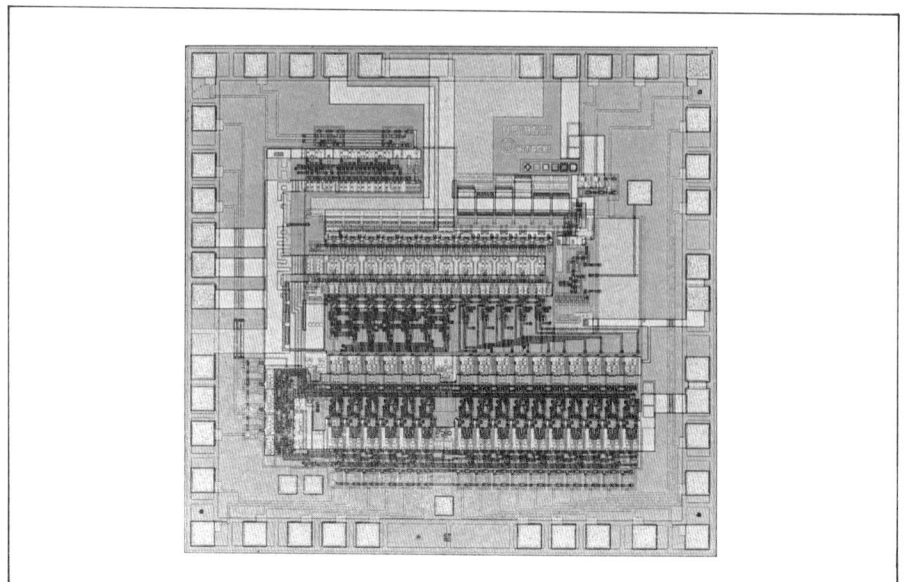

14

1   From what material are microchips made? Is it very rare?
2   Why is it difficult to design microchips?
3   Are microchips expensive? Suggest some reasons for their price.
4   Make a list of all the items of equipment you can think of which contain microchips.
5   In what ways have microchips contributed to the rapid spread of information technology?

1F End-of-Chapter Summary

The main points of this chapter are as follows:

- Information, often in large quantities, is needed for almost everything we do.
- To be of any use, information needs to be stored properly and kept up-to-date. It may also need to be sorted, required items may need to be selected, and decisions may need to be made on the basis of the information.
- Information technology is the use of computers and other electronic equipment to store, process and communicate information, and to control equipment.
- For many centuries, paper has been the main storage medium for information. It is now being replaced by media which can be read by computer.
- Over the last hundred years, the worldwide telephone network has grown to become the largest man-made system in existence.
- A computer is an information processing device which can be programmed.
- Early machines had mechanical control systems, and operated on a fixed cycle. Modern machines are more flexible in operation.
- The basic technology of computers, robots and other electronic equipment is microchips.

Exercise 1

1   Choose the correct word from the list for each of the following spaces:

satellites; flags; Morse code; sonar; radio; voice; radar; signal lamps.

Until the invention of ____, the only methods of communication between ships at sea were ____ and ____. A modern ship has a number of communications channels: radio, using ____ and ____, communications ____ for telephone calls, ____ to watch for other ships, and ____ to detect undersea rocks.

2   Thousands of years ago, most people lived in villages or small towns and lived directly off the produce from the surrounding land. Make a list of the most important information which a small community of this nature would need. Suggest ways which would have been available to store this information.

3   What is one of the most important factors in the spread of information technology throughout commerce and industry in most parts of the world?

4   Write two short stories, similar to those at the start of this chapter, to show the changes in technology which have taken place over the last hundred years in any of the following:
(a) banking   (b) police work
(c) travel   (d) the home.

Things to find out

1   A few items of IT equipment which have been very influential in their time are listed below. Select one of these, and find out when it was first introduced, what technology (if any) it superseded, and what the effects were of its introduction.
(a) printing press   (b) typewriter
(c) factory robot   (d) video recorder

2 Information and Data

Information is the raw material of computers. However, computers cannot handle all types of information, nor can they deal with it in any form. This chapter describes how information is represented on computers, and some of the ways computers manipulate it.

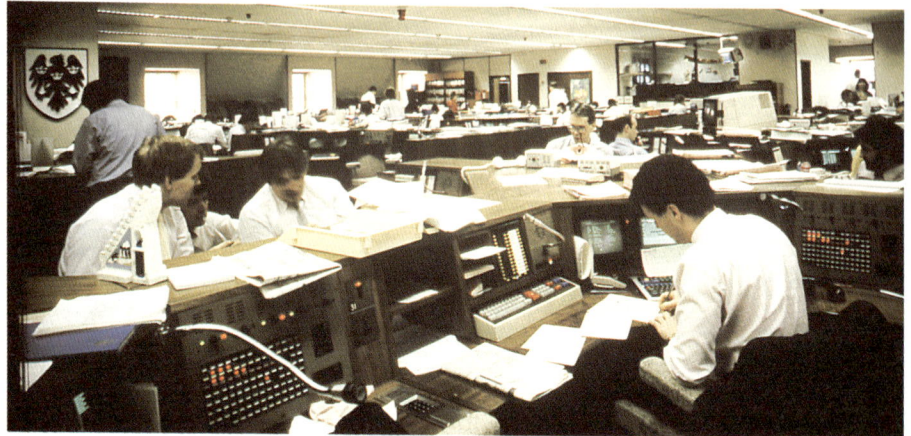

Financial transactions being carried out at a bank. A number of computers and electronic communications systems are used to transfer funds.

2A Information, Data and Codes

A radio reporter doing an interview in the street.

A local radio station wanted to find out how popular one of its programmes was. It sent out a reporter with a tape recorder to interview people in the street. The comments he received were something like this:

'It's great, but the presenter talks too much.'

'Some days I like it; other days I don't.'

'I hardly ever listen to it.'

'It is an excellent example of edification, elucidation and enlightenment, and entertaining in the extreme.'

'It's awful!'

This information is splendid for broadcasting, but is not very precise, and so it is not much use for getting an accurate measure of the popularity of the programme. Accordingly, a questionnaire was devised for people to fill in. Two of the questions were as follows:

1   How often do you listen to the programme?

A   never   D   most of the time
B   occasionally   E   every day
C   about half the time

2 Do you enjoy listening to the programme?

A dislike it strongly
B dislike it
C indifferent to it
D quite like it
E like it very much

People were asked to tick the nearest response to their own opinion.

In the second case, the information is gathered in a specific way. Numbers can be allocated to the responses, and averages of the numbers worked out. When information is represented in this form, it is **data**. Data is information which has a precise meaning, and can be analysed in various ways.

When information is represented as data it becomes more specific, but a certain amount of information is lost in the process. This can be seen by comparing the original statements above with the data obtained from them.

Because data has a precise meaning, it can almost always be written in a concise way. For example, the responses to the above questions have been given letters. If a person chose the third reply to question 1, and the fifth to question 2, their reply could be represented as 1C2F. The data is now in **code**: the characters 1C2F are a brief way of representing the responses to the questionnaire, but they only make sense if the method of coding is known.

Computers work with data rather than information. Although the first set of replies above could be typed into a computer, using a word processing system, they would just be a set of characters, and very little could be done with them on the computer. The second set of data, in its code, could be stored and processed in a variety of ways. However, the computer does not know what the data means—it is just a set of codes.

Computers store and process data, but it is the people who use the data who interpret it and turn it into information. For example, one of the most powerful computers in Britain does the calculations which form the basis of weather forecasts. However, the results produced by this computer are just tables of numbers and lines on maps. These are interpreted by the staff at the weather centre, who produce the forecasts from them.

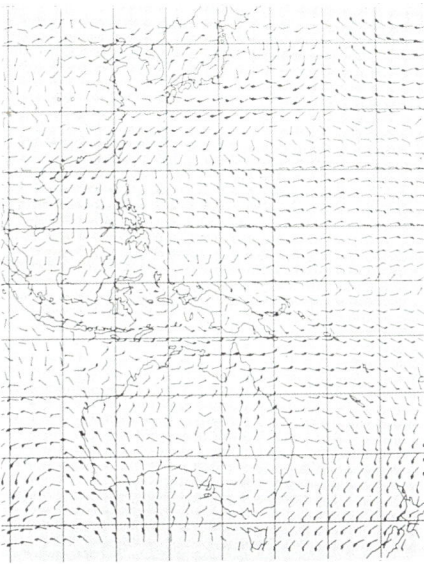

A weather map produced by computer. It is one of the items of information used in making weather forecasts.

Questions

1 What is the difference between information and data?

2 A British motor vehicle registration mark is an example of data in code. For example, the registration A319HGT is interpreted as follows:

A indicates the year (starting in August) of manufacture
319 is the number within the area code
HGT indicates the area where the vehicle was registered.

(a) Make a list of other data which is in code.
(b) For each item in the list explain what the letters or digits in the code mean.

3 A school club needs the following information about each member: name, sex, date of birth, form, hobbies.

(a) Devise a suitable method of coding this information so that it can be stored concisely.
(b) Design a form for members to fill in, with simple instructions for the codes used.

4 Conduct a survey of the pupils in the class to find out their attitudes to a topic such as violence on television.

(a) Ask the question 'What do you think of violence on TV?'. Write down the answers, and try to analyse them.
(b) Devise a set of structured questions, as in the above example. Get the pupils in the class to answer the structured questions. Count up the numbers choosing each answer, and present the results as a graph.
(c) Comment on the effectiveness of the two methods of conducting the survey.

5 A computer used for weather forecasting produces the following figures for the next day's weather at a coastal town in Britain:

max temp: 15 deg C   rainfall: 5 mm
wind speed: 5 m/sec   wind direction: SW
humidity: 78%   pressure: 1012 mm
                                           falling

Use these figures, and your general knowledge of the weather, to produce a weather forecast in words for the town.

6 One use of codes is to keep information secret. A message is sent in a secret code so that anyone who intercepts it cannot find out what the message is. However, most codes have some pattern to them which makes it possible, with a lot of patience and skill, to work out what they are.

(a) See if you can work out the following two codes (they are not the same for each message):

20 8 5   17 21 9 3 11   2 18 15 14
6 15 24   10 21 13 16 5 4   15 22 5 18
20 8 5   12 1 26 25· 4 15 7

20 9 7   6 5 25   25 8 28   24 24
5 20 18   27 16 10

(b) Devise a secret code of your own. Encode a few short messages in it, and exchange them with messages from other pupils. Try to break the code by looking for patterns in the messages.

(c) One of the earliest uses of electronic computers was to work out codes. Find out more about this work, and its importance.

2B Characters in Bits

Computers work with data which, to them, is no more than strings of symbols. These symbols are letters, numbers, other characters, and, to an increasing extent, graphs and pictures. Inside a computer (and out of sight from the people using the computer) all the data is represented in the computer's own codes. These codes are based on two symbols only, the digits 0 and 1. The digits 0 and 1 are also those used in the binary (base two) number system. They are given the names **bits**, short for binary digits.

The reasons for using bits as the basis of computer codes have to do with the way computers are constructed. The electronic circuits which process the data, and the magnetic disks and tapes which store it, can handle data much more easily as bits than in any other form of coding. The use of bits simplifies the design of computers, and therefore helps to keep their costs down.

A single bit can only have one of two values: 0 or 1. On its own, a bit can represent an answer 'yes' or 'no', or a switch being open or

The control panel of a large mainframe computer. In some computers, the control panel includes lights which show the bits in certain parts of the computer.

closed. Most data has more than two possible values, and so more than one bit is used to encode it. For example, a common code for characters is the seven-bit **ASCII** code. A few letters in this code are as follows:

a	1	1	0	0	0	0	1
b	1	1	0	0	0	1	0
c	1	1	0	0	0	1	1
. . .							
y	1	1	1	1	0	0	1
z	1	1	1	1	0	1	0

A convenient grouping of bits inside a computer is in sets of eight. A **set** of eight bits is called a **byte**. Most computer memories are partitioned into bytes, and small microcomputers process one byte of data in one operation. A byte can store an ASCII character with one bit to spare.

It must be emphasised that the coding of data using bits is done inside a computer, to suit its internal workings. When data is entered into a computer, and when it is printed or displayed by a computer, it is in a form which people can interpret: characters, numbers or graphics. The conversion to and from the internal codes is done by the computer, without the person using the computer needing to know anything about it.

Questions

1 Why is data represented inside a computer in the form of bits?
2 One bit can have two possible values: 0 or 1. Two bits can have four values: 0 0, 0 1, 1 0 or 1 1. How many possible values can the following have:
   (a) three bits
   (b) four bits
   (c) one byte?
3 A switch is a device which has two **states** only: it is either on or off. Make a list of other devices which can only have two states.
4 Decode the following word, which is in ASCII code:

   1100011 1100001 1110100

5 Make up a secret code of your own, using bits to represent letters. Use the smallest number of bits needed to represent the letters of the alphabet.

2C Numbers in Bits

Because computers use binary digits (bits) to represent data, the code used for numbers is based on the binary (base two) number system. Using six bits, the first four positive whole numbers are as follows:

base ten	base two
1	0 0 0 0 0 1
2	0 0 0 0 1 0
3	0 0 0 0 1 1
4	0 0 0 1 0 0

When they represent numbers, the binary digits have **place values**, like the hundreds, tens and units in ordinary (base ten) numbers. Looking at the above numbers, the place values can be seen to be, from the right, units, twos, fours, eights, etc:

base two							base ten	
32	16	8	4	2	1		10	1
0	1	1	0	1	1	=	2	7

The commonest way of representing negative integers is to make the bit with the highest place value (the **most significant** bit) represent a negative quantity. This is to simplify the subtraction of numbers, as explained in the next section. The technique is known as **twos complements**. Below are some numbers in six-bit, twos complement form:

base two							base ten	
-32	16	8	4	2	1		10	1
0	1	0	0	0	1	$=$	1	7
1	0	1	1	1	1	$=-$	1	7
0	0	1	1	0	0	$=$	1	2
1	1	0	1	0	0	$=-$	1	2
0	1	1	1	1	1	$=$	3	1
1	0	0	0	0	1	$=-$	3	1

Looking at the first pair of numbers, 17 and -17, the rule for changing from a positive number to the corresponding twos complement negative number can be seen: change the 0s to 1s and the 1s to 0s, and add 1. This can be done very easily by the electronic circuits inside a computer, which is one of the reasons for using twos complements.

Although it is not so obvious, this rule applies to the other pairs of numbers in the table as well. It also works when changing from a negative number to the corresponding positive number. Try it for yourself.

The above table also shows the range of numbers that can be represented as six-bit, twos complement integers. It is -32 to 31, not a very wide range. If an attempt is made to represent a number outside this range in the way described above, an error occurs: an **overflow error**. Using more bits increases the range of numbers that can be represented, but it is always limited, and overflow errors can still occur.

In order to increase the range of numbers that can be represented on a computer, and to deal with fractions, other ways of storing numbers are used. They are all based on the binary system. Such numbers are beyond the scope of computing courses at this level.

Questions

1 (a) Why are numbers stored on computers in codes based on the binary system?
(b) What is the advantage of twos complements?

2 Convert the following decimal numbers to six-bit, twos complement form: 13, -9, 10, -21, 30.

3 Write the following decimal numbers as six-bit, twos complement numbers. Then obtain the corresponding negative number in twos complements, and convert it back to a decimal number as a check: 19, 11, 30, 7, 2.

4 (a) What are the place values for four-bit, twos complement numbers?
(b) Convert the following decimal numbers into four-bit, twos complement form: 3, -3, 5, -7, 6.
(c) What is the rule for changing from a positive number to the corresponding negative number in four-bit, twos complement numbers?
(d) What is the range of numbers which can be represented in four-bit, twos complement form?

5* If a byte is used to store integers in twos complement form:
(a) Write down the place values.
(b) What is the range of numbers which can be represented?
(c) Encode the following decimal numbers: 19, -19, 30, -30, -15, 12, 24, 48, 96.
(d) Compare the first four answers from part (c) with the results from question 3. Comment on the similarities and differences.
(e) Write down the rule which explains the last four results in part (c).

2D* Computer Arithmetic

Twos complement binary numbers are added in the normal way:

	−32	16	8	4	2	1			10	1
	0	1	0	0	0	1			1	7
+	0	0	1	1	0	1		+	1	3
	0	1	1	1	1	0		=	3	0

carry   1

The result is correct, as long as there is no 'carry' into the most significant place, which represents a negative quantity. The following example shows the consequences of this happening:

	−32	16	8	4	2	1			10	1
	0	1	0	1	1	0			2	2
+	0	0	1	1	0	0		+	1	2
	1	0	0	0	1	0		=	− 3	0

carry   1   1

The result is not correct. The reason is that the correct answer (34) is outside the range of numbers which can be represented in six-bit, twos complement form. This is an example of **overflow** during an arithmetic operation.

Subtraction is based on the idea that it is the same as adding a negative number. For example, $19 - 11$ is the same as $19 + (-11)$. Doing this calculation in six-bit, twos complements is as follows:

		−32	16	8	4	2	1			10	1
code 11:		0	0	1	0	1	1	=		1	1
reverse bits:		1	1	0	1	0	0				
add 1:	+						1				
gives −11:		1	1	0	1	0	1	= −		1	1
code 19:	+	0	1	0	0	1	1		+	1	9
add −11 and 19:		0	0	1	0	0	0	=			8

carry: 1

The carry from the most significant place is ignored.

Questions

1 How is subtraction performed using twos complement numbers?
2 Do the following calculations using six-bit, twos complement numbers. Convert the result back to a decimal number as a check.
  (a) $9 + 7$ (b) $18 - 5$
  (c) $20 + 11$ (d) $12 - 23$
  (e) $17 + 18$

Explain why the result is not correct in every case.
3* Repeat question 2, but this time use eight-bit, twos complement numbers. Comment on any differences between the results you get this time and the previous ones.

2E Computer Logic

Computers represent data in codes based on the binary digits 0 and 1 only. Data is processed in terms of operations on these digits. The electronic circuits inside a computer which do the processing may be thought of as **gates** which the bits pass through and are transformed on the way. The operations performed by the gates are **logical** operations following simple rules.

Four of the commonest types of **logic gates** are described in this section. The working of each is expressed using an **operation table** (or **truth table**) which describes how the bit produced by the gate (the **output**) relates to the bit or bits which enter the gate (the **inputs**).

NOT gate

The simplest type of gate is the NOT gate, shown in Figure 2.1. It reverses an input bit to produce an output bit. Its operation table is as follows:

input A	output B
0	1
1	0

A = NOT (B)

AND gate

An AND gate takes two (or more) inputs and produces a single output. The output is 1 if one input AND the other input are 1; otherwise it is 0. Figure 2.2 shows a two-input AND gate. The operation table is as follows:

input A	B	output C
0	0	0
0	1	0
1	0	0
1	1	1

C = A AND B

OR gate

An OR gate takes two (or more) inputs and produces a single output. The output is 1 if one input OR the other input (or both) are 1; otherwise it is 0. Figure 2.3 shows a two-input OR gate. The operation table is as follows:

input A	B	output C
0	0	0
0	1	1
1	0	1
1	1	1

C = A OR B

Exclusive OR gate

The exclusive OR (XOR) gate, also known as a non-equivalence (NEQ) gate, has two inputs and produces a single output. The output is 1 if one input OR the other input (but not both) are 1. Figure 2.4 shows an exclusive OR gate. The operation table is as follows:

George Boole (1815 to 1864), the founder of mathematical logic. Boole's theory is the basis of the design of electronic computers.

Figure 2.1   NOT gate

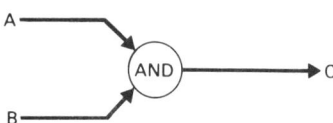

Figure 2.2   AND gate

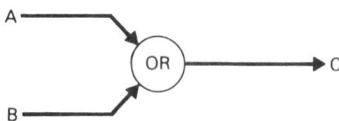

Figure 2.3   OR gate

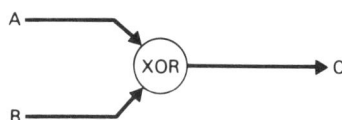

Figure 2.4   Exclusive OR gate

input		output	
A	B	C	
0	0	0	
0	1	1	
1	0	1	
1	1	0	

$$C = A \text{ XOR } B$$

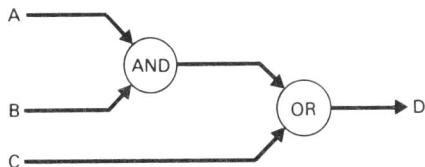

Figure 2.5   Logic circuit example

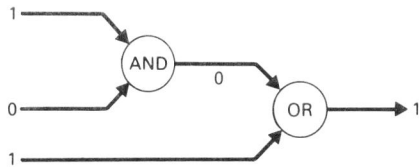

Figure 2.6   Inputs followed through logic circuit example

From the operation table it can be seen that the output is 1 if the inputs are different. This is why this gate is called a non-equivalence gate.

Logic circuits

The processing circuits in a computer are constructed by connecting logic gates together so that the output from one gate connects to the input of other gates. Some control systems are also built up in this way, as described in chapter 21. The operation of the combined circuit can be described by a truth table, like the ones above.

Example

Figure 2.5 shows a logic circuit with three inputs, an AND gate and an OR gate. This circuit may be written as:

$$D = (A \text{ AND } B) \text{ OR } C$$

The truth table for the circuit may be worked out by following each set of inputs through the gates, and writing down the output produced. Figure 2.6 shows how this is done for the sixth row of the operation table. The operation table has eight rows, because there are eight possible combinations of 0s and 1s from three inputs.

inputs			output
A	B	C	D
0	0	0	0
0	0	1	1
0	1	0	0
0	1	1	1
1	0	0	0
1	0	1	1
1	1	0	1
1	1	1	1

... as shown in Figure 2.6

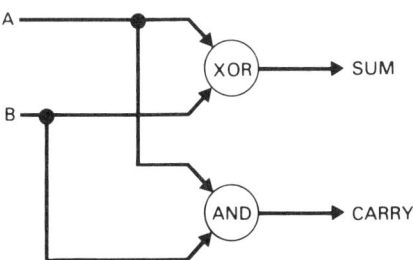

Figure 2.7   Half adder

Half adder

When two binary digits are added, the result is a digit for the sum, and one for the carry. A table for the operation is as follows:

input		output		
A	B	sum	carry	
0	0	0	0	0 + 0 = 0 carry 0
0	1	1	0	0 + 1 = 1 carry 0
1	0	1	0	1 + 0 = 1 carry 0
1	1	0	1	1 + 1 = 0 carry 1

Comparing this with the truth table for AND, OR and exclusive OR, it can be seen that the sum bit can be produced by an exclusive OR gate, and the carry bit by an AND gate. A logic circuit which adds up two bits is shown in Figure 2.7. It is known as a **half adder**—it does not include a carry from an addition in another column.

Questions

1 Follow the inputs shown in Figures 2.8, 2.9 and 2.10 through the gates in the logic circuits, and write down the outputs produced.

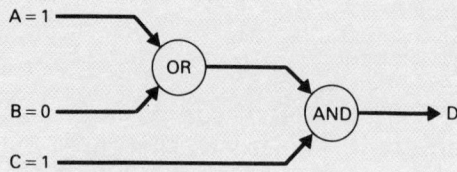

Figure 2.8

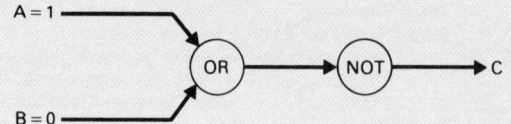

Figure 2.10

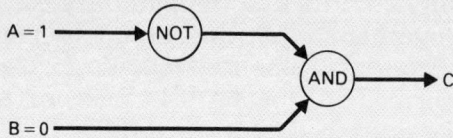

Figure 2.9

2 Write down the operation tables for the logic circuits shown in Figures 2.11, 2.12 and 2.13.

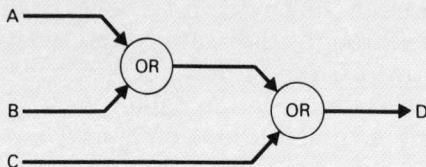

Figure 2.11

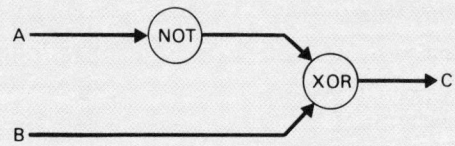

Figure 2.13

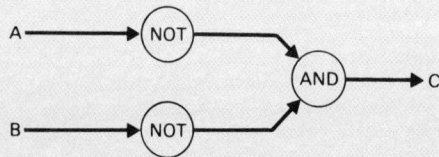

Figure 2.12

3 Design logic circuits for the following operation tables:

(a)
inputs		output
A	B	C
0	0	0
0	1	1
1	0	0
1	0	0

(b)
inputs		output
A	B	C
0	0	1
0	1	0
1	0	0
1	1	1

4* Draw a diagram showing how two half adders and a gate may be combined to form a logic circuit which adds two bits and a carry from a previous column to produce a sum and a carry bit. Also draw up the operation table for the circuit, known as a **full adder.**

2F End-of-Chapter Summary

The main points of this chapter are as follows:

- Data is information in a precise form. It is often written in a code.
- Computers process data, rather than information. A computer regards data as a set of symbols, and does not know what the data means.
- The people who use computers interpret the data produced by the computer and turn it into information.
- Computers represent data in codes based on the binary digits (bits) 0 and 1 only.
- a byte is a group of eight bits.
- Integers are commonly represented on computers as twos complement binary numbers.
- Logic circuits process data represented as binary digits.

Exercise 2

1 Choose the correct word from the list for each of the following spaces:

data; analysed; measuring; information.

The residents in the area near an airport were complaining about the noise of the aircraft. Using the ____ in the letters sent in, a team of engineers equipped with sound ____ equipment was sent to gather ____ in the people's homes. The measurements were ____ by computer in order to find out how serious the problem actually was.

2 Perform the following calculations using six-bit, twos complement numbers. In each case, convert the result to decimal and check whether or not it is correct.
(a) $24 - 17$ (b) $17 - 24$
(c) $24 + 17$ (d) $-17 - 24$

3 An alternative method of representing whole numbers on a computer is to encode each decimal digit separately in binary. Four bits are used for each decimal digit. For example:

$$39 = 0\ 0\ 1\ 1\quad 1\ 0\ 0\ 1$$
$$75 = 0\ 1\ 1\ 1\quad 0\ 1\ 0\ 1$$

This technique is called **binary coded decimal (BCD)**.
(a) Change the following decimal numbers into binary coded decimal: 29, 48, 139.
(b) Convert the following BCD numbers to decimal:
1 0 0 1 0 1 1 1, 0 1 1 0 1 0 0 0.
(c) What is a benefit of using BCD to represent numbers in a computer?
(d) Does BCD use more bits than twos complements to store numbers of the same size? Give some examples to illustrate your answer.

4* Design a logic circuit with three inputs and one output so that the output is 1 if any one of the inputs is 1 and the other two are 0. The output is 0 for all other input combinations. (Use three-input AND and OR gates.)

5* The place values for decimal fractions are tenths, hundredths, thousandths, etc. Similarly, the place values for binary fractions are halves, quarters, eighths, etc. For example:

	binary				decimal	
$\frac{1}{2}$	$\frac{1}{4}$	$\frac{1}{8}$		$\frac{1}{10}$	$\frac{1}{100}$	$\frac{1}{1000}$
. 1	0	1	=	. 6	2	5
. 0	1	0	=	. 2	5	0

(a) Change the following decimal fractions to binary: .5, .375, .875
(b) Change the following binary fractions to decimal: .1, .1 1, .0 0 1
(c) Change the following fractions to decimal and to binary. If they cannot be represented exactly, express them correct to four binary or decimal places:

$$\frac{3}{4}\quad \frac{1}{8}\quad \frac{1}{5}\quad \frac{1}{3}\quad \frac{7}{16}$$

(The method of conversion is the same in both cases: divide the bottom number into the top number. For the binary fractions, first convert the two numbers from decimal to binary.)
(d) If fractions are represented on computers in binary form, will the numbers always be correct? If the result of a calculation is a fraction, will it always be correctly represented?

3 Computer Structure

Above left: An IBM Personal Computer (PC). The PC was the most popular desktop microcomputer during the early 1980s.
Above right: The units of a large mainframe computer. A computer of this type has separate units for input, output, storage and processing.

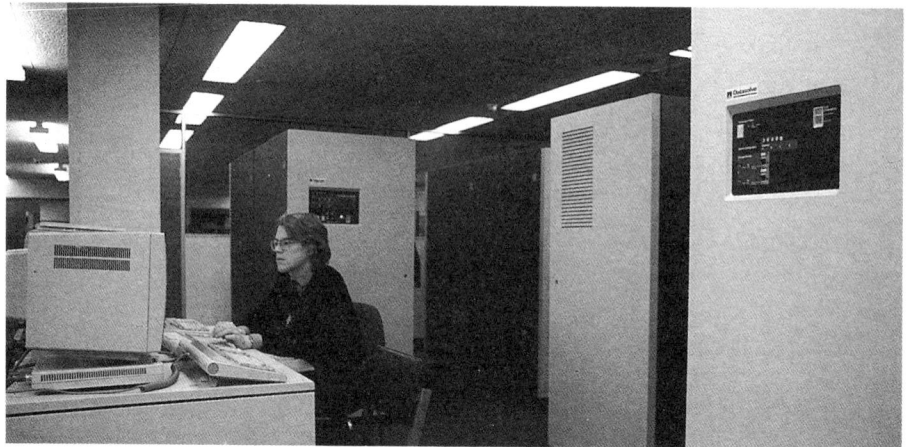

It took from 1946 to 1982 for the first million computers to be produced. Now there are many millions in operation. Most are desktop microcomputers like the IBM Personal Computer (PC) and its many imitators. At the other end of the scale are large computer installations which occupy specially built air-conditioned rooms and require skilled operators to run them. Computers are used for almost every type of work, and their numbers are growing all the time.

3A What is a computer?

The point was made in chapter 1 that a computer is an information processing machine which can be programmed. This section investigates this idea in more detail.

A fuller description of a computer is as follows:

A computer is a digital electronic information processing machine which can be programmed.

Looking at each term in this description:

- **Digital** describes the way in which data is represented in a computer. Computers store data in codes which are based on binary **digits**. These codes can only represent characters and whole numbers, or fractions to a certain precision.
- **Electronic** describes the technology used by computers to store and process data. Computers are made from **microchips** which are electronic devices. They have no moving parts, and operate by the movement of electrons through the tiny circuits inside them.
- **Information processing** is a general term describing the work done by a computer. More details are given below.

Charles Babbage's Analytical Engine—an unsuccessful attempt to build a mechanical computer during the late 1800s.

- **Machine** reminds us that computers can be grouped together with washing machines, sewing machines, lathes and metal presses. Machines are devices which do useful work. They need regular maintenance, and can break down from time to time. Although computers are more reliable than many other types of machine, there is nothing magic about them.
- A **program** is a set of instructions which control the operation of a computer. Once a program for a task has been loaded into a computer and starts running, the computer will carry out all the steps of the task automatically. The physical components of a computer—the chips, keyboard, screen, disks, etc.—are the **hardware**; the programs which control the hardware are the **software** of a computer system. In order to do useful work, a computer system needs hardware and a number of items of software.

3B The Work Done by a Computer

A computer can perform seven types of operation, all involving data. They are **input**, **output**, **storage**, **retrieval**, **sending**, **receiving** and **processing**:

- **Input** is the action of getting data into a computer. The commonest method of input is via a keyboard like a typewriter keyboard.
- **Output** is the action of getting data out of a computer. The commonest methods are to display the information on a screen or to print it.
- **Storage** is the action of making a permanent copy of data that the computer can use again later. The commonest methods of storage are to write the data on a magnetic disk or a magnetic tape.
- **Retrieval** is the action of reading data back from the magnetic disk or tape on which it has been stored.
- **Sending** is transferring data to another computer. The other computer may be in the same building, or hundreds of kilometres away.
- **Receiving** is accepting data sent by another computer.
- **Processing** is what the computer does to the data. Processing includes sorting, selecting, combining and rearranging data, as well as doing calculations. Computers are also able to make decisions on the basis of data, and draw conclusions from the data. Processing is the most complicated of all the operations carried out by a computer, but it is usually the fastest.

In spite of its calculating and decision-making powers, a computer cannot think for itself. A computer does not understand what it is doing. Its capacity for behaviour which we would regard as intelligent is limited. A computer cannot take initiatives or make moral judgements. It cannot go beyond the data at its disposal and the instructions it has for processing the data. An example of the limitations of computers is their inability to interpret continuous passages of text in a natural language like English. A computer can respond to individual words or phrases, but anything more complicated is beyond it. The question of the degree of intelligence of computers is examined in chapter 22.

1   What *seven* types of operation can a computer perform?
2   List *six* types of information processing.
3   To what extent are computers capable of intelligent behaviour?
4   Would a present-day computer be able to:
    (a) Forecast tomorrow's weather fairly accurately?
    (b) Forecast the result of a horse race?
    (c) Decide whether or not war is a bad thing?
    (d) Translate a passage from one language to another?
    (e) Correct the spelling mistakes in a passage?
5   Computers are not the only devices which can be programmed. (Automatic washing machines are another programmable device.) Make a list of other equipment which can be programmed.
6   What are the differences between a pocket calculator and a computer?

3C The Parts of a Computer

The structure of a computer is based on the operations which it performs, as described in the previous section. Whatever the size of a computer, it is made up of the components shown in Figure 3.1. In large computers, these components are separate units; in small computers most of them are contained in a single unit. The components are as follows:

- **Input devices** such as a keyboard, which enable data to be supplied to a computer.
- **Output devices** such as a display screen and printer, which enable data to be output by the computer.
- **Backing store** such as disk drives and magnetic tape units, on which programs and data are stored for access by the computer whenever they are required.
- **Data communication links** for sending data to and receiving it from other computers.
- The **processor** and **memory**. In large computers, these are housed together in the **central processing unit (CPU)**. The memory stores the programs and data the computer is using at the

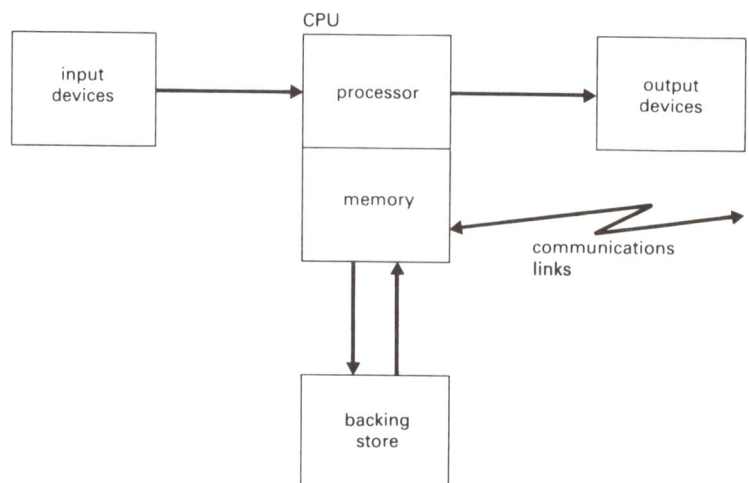

Figure 3.1   Components of a computer

A modern desktop microcomputer, with (from the top) graphics display screen, Winchester disk storage, processor with disk drives and keyboard. The printer and mouse are on the left.

time. The processor is the hardware which carries out the processing operations described in the previous section.

An important point about the way computers are constructed is that the components are **modular**. This means that a unit can be unplugged and replaced by another one without affecting the computer system as a whole. For example, if the disk drives on a computer system do not have sufficient capacity for new work planned for the computer, they can be unplugged and replaced by larger ones. Many computer manufacturers make ranges of central processing units. The CPU of a computer in such a range can be unplugged and replaced by a more powerful one in the same range if this becomes necessary.

Questions

1   Where are programs and data stored while the computer is using them? Where are they stored when not in use at the time?
2   What two components of a large computer are in the CPU?
3   A computer manufacturer sells a CPU with three different memory capacities. If a company buys the one with the small memory, what can the company do if this memory later becomes too small?
4   Which is the fastest component of most computer systems?
5   Look at the photographs of computers in this book, and other photographs of computers you have. Identify the input, output, backing store and processing units in the photographs.
6   A modular system is one where the components fit together by means of standard connections, and components can be unplugged and replaced without affecting the system as a whole. A railway is an example of a modular system.
(a) Write down some other examples of modular systems.
(b) Discuss the advantages of modular construction of systems.

The memory (or **main store**) of a computer is where instructions and data are stored while the computer is using them. The memory consists of a number of **cells**, each of which can contain one data item or one instruction (or a part of these). The contents of each cell can be read or written individually. In most small computers, one cell contains one byte (eight bits). Larger computers have 16, 32 or 64 bits per memory cell. The capacities of computer memories vary between about 500K (1K, short for kilobyte, is 1024 bytes) and 500 **megabytes** (1 megabyte is 1024K, or approximately one million bytes). At present, the usual memory capacity of a small business microcomputer is 1 megabyte.

Each cell in a computer memory is identified by a number, the **address** of the cell. The idea is like that of an address of a house: the address of a house contains a number which locates the house in the street. The address of a cell is a number which locates the cell in the computer memory. See Figure 3.2. Instructions to the processor make use of addresses, for example:

Fetch the character at address 15786.

Store the next character input at the keyboard at address 78954.

Like the processor, the memory of a computer is constructed entirely from microchips. There are two types of these, **RAM** and **ROM**:

RAM (for random access memory) chips make up the working memory of the computer. They store whatever instructions and data the computer needs at the time. Each cell in a RAM chip may have its contents read or replaced by something else whenever required. The contents of RAM are changing all the time; as soon as the computer has finished with the contents of a cell in RAM, it may write something else into the cell. When a computer is switched off, the contents of RAM chips are lost.

ROM (for read-only memory) chips are used for storing permanent data and instructions. The contents of a ROM chip may be read

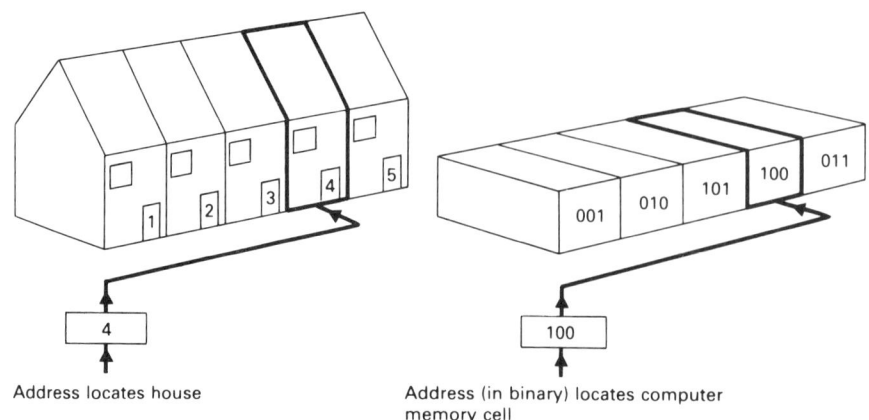

Address locates house

Address (in binary) locates computer memory cell

Figure 3.2   Addressing memory cells

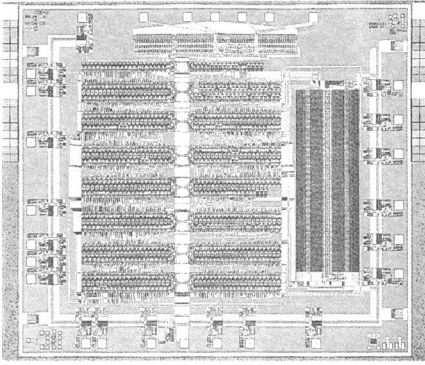
An enlarged chip without its case. The banks of memory cells can be seen on the right.

whenever needed, but cannot be altered. The instructions and data in ROM are not lost when the computer is switched off. ROM chips have a number of uses. These include storing the instructions and data needed to get a computer going when it is switched on, and the patterns of dots needed to form characters on the screen. Special-purpose computers, such as those in a missile, have all their programs in ROM, and have only a small proportion of their memory as RAM. ROM chips are also used for backing store—see section 4J.

A special type of ROM is **PROM** chips. ROM chips are made with their contents already stored in them. PROM (for programmable read-only memory) chips are made as blanks, and their contents are 'burned into' them by a special device, controlled by a program. **EPROM** chips are PROM chips whose contents may be erased and replaced with something else. Once in use in a computer, neither PROM nor EPROM chips can have their contents altered. They retain their data and instructions while the computer is switched off.

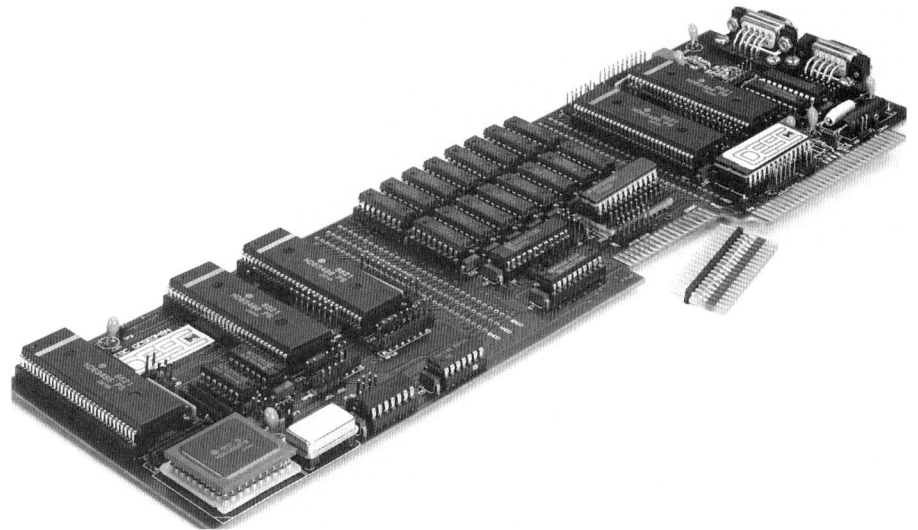
A printed circuit board, forming part of a computer. The chips are mounted in rows on the board, connected by metal tracks.

Questions

1   (a) What are the differences between RAM and ROM?
(b) State some uses for RAM and ROM chips.
(c) Can a computer have its entire memory made from ROM chips?
(d) Can a computer have its entire memory made from RAM chips?
(e)* Find out how computers were started up before ROM was available to store programs for this purpose. List the advantages of ROM over previous methods of getting a computer started when it is first switched on.

2   Small computers have memories which hold eight bits per cell. This means that characters occupy one cell each, but numbers (which need about 32 bits) take four cells. Large computers can store an entire number in one cell, but if the cell is not used for several characters much of it is wasted.
(a) What are the advantages and disadvantages of storing only eight bits in a memory cell?
(b) What are the advantages and disadvantages of storing a larger number of bits in a memory cell?

3   An address is a number used to locate a cell in a computer memory. A bank account number is a number which identifies one bank account. Make a list of other situations where a number is used to identify or locate something.

4   Five memory cells in a computer store characters as follows:

address	contents
12	u
13	n
14	i
15	p
16	t

If the computer runs the following program, what is the output?

Display the character at address 14
Display the character at address 13
Display the character at address 15
Display the character at address 12
Display the character at address 16

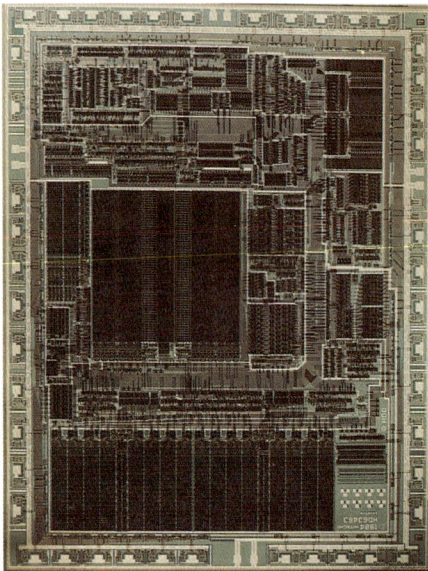

A microprocessor chip, showing the groups of processing circuits. The chip includes two blocks of memory cells.

The processor is the hardware item in a computer where data is processed. In the past, most computers had only one processor; today it is quite common for computers to have several. Processors differ widely in the speeds at which they operate and the types of operation they can perform, but they all follow the same overall pattern of working.

A processor has a number of **registers** which store the data and instruction which the computer is working on at the time. The most important registers are the **program counter**, the **instruction register** and the **accumulator**.

- The program counter holds the address of the instruction the computer is carrying out. Also called the **sequence control register**, it 'keeps the computer's place' in the program.
- The instruction register holds the program instruction the computer is carrying out at the time.
- The accumulator holds the item of data that is being processed at the time. After a processing operation, it holds the result of that operation.

These registers, and their connections to the computer memory, are shown in Figure 3.3.

A processor has a **cycle** of steps which it repeats all the time the computer is running. The commonest steps are as follows:

- Fetch an instruction from memory. The program counter locates the instruction, which is copied into the instruction register.
- Carry out the instruction, processing data in some way. Most instructions refer to a data item in memory, or the one in the accumulator. The result is usually placed in the accumulator.
- Adjust the contents of the program counter, so that it holds the address of the next instruction.

This **fetch-execute** cycle is repeated millions of times per second.

Processors are made from logic circuits as described in section 2E. They have no moving parts. They are constructed as one or more microchips, which contain hundreds of thousands of logic gates on a 5 mm square of silicon. The processor in a microcomputer is a single chip, the **microprocessor** chip.

Although it is the most important component in a computer system, a microprocessor chip costs only a few pence, uses hardly any electricity, and will work without breaking down for many years. The availability of cheap, reliable microprocessor chips has been one of the main reasons for the rapid spread of computers in recent years.

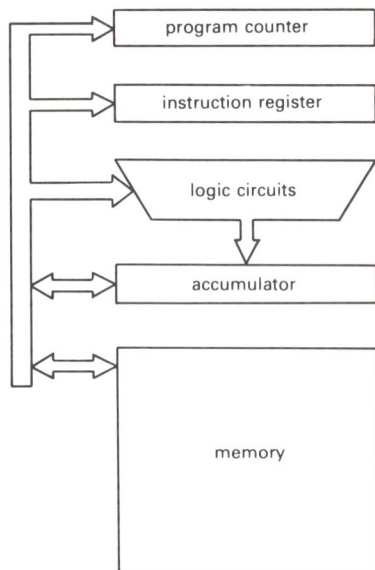

Figure 3.3   Registers in a computer processor

1 A computer program includes the following two instructions, located in memory starting at address 105:

Address	Instruction or Data
105	Load the number at address 200 to the accumulator.
107	Add the number at address 204 to the number in the accumulator, and place the result in the accumlator.
...	
200	12
204	17

Describe the sequence of steps in the fetch-execute cycles for these two instructions.

2 (a) From what components are computer processors made?
(b) Find out how the processors of the first computers, in the late 1940s, were made.
(c) What are the benefits of the changes in the construction of computer processors since those days?

3 Microprocessors are not only used in computers. Make a list of other devices in which they are to be found.

4 A microprocessor chip is an example of modular construction. What are the benefits of modular construction of computer processors?

3F Input and Output

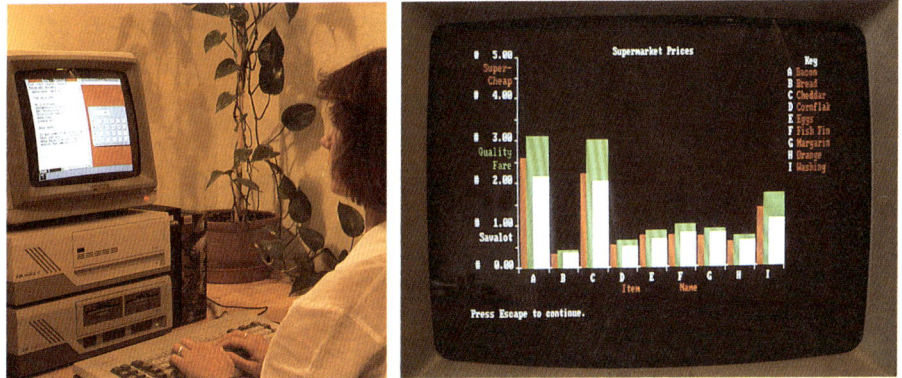

Left: A person typing at a computer keyboard. *Right:* A graphics display on a computer screen.

The memory and processing elements of all computers are based on the same principles. This is not the case for input and output devices. There is a large, and increasing, number of input and output devices in use. Some can be used for a variety of purposes; others are specialised. They are connected to the computer processor as shown in Figure 3.1.

Broadly speaking, there are two types of input: data read directly from documents or labels, and input from a person. An example of the first type is **bar codes**. These are read by special readers, which check the code as it is input, and change the data into an internal code which the computer can work with. The commonest method of input by a person is by means of a **keyboard**. A computer keyboard is like a typewriter keyboard, with a few extra keys for control purposes.

Data is output either in printed form (known as **hard copy**) or as screen displays. Most modern computers can display or print data as characters and as **graphics**. Graphics includes pictures, technical drawings, graphs and pie charts. Graphics enables data to be presented more clearly than as tables of text or figures.

More details about the input and output of data are given in chapter 4.

3G Backing Store

A word processing program disk and a set of data disks—the disks on which the text of this book was produced.

Backing store is permanent storage for programs and data in a form which a computer can read quickly. The most common backing store media are magnetic disks and tapes. Capacities of backing store media are generally higher than those of computer memories: small disks can store a few hundred kilobytes; the largest disks used by mainframe computers can hold hundreds of megabytes. A typical disk capacity for a small business computer is one megabyte.

Most backing store media are **exchangeable**: computers transfer data to and from a tape or disk while it is in use. When the tape or disk is finished with, it is removed. The data remains on the tape or disk until it is needed again. This creates a **filing system** for the computer. For example, this book is written using a word processing system. There is a disk for the word processing program, which is loaded into the computer whenever it is needed. There are two other disks for the text of the book (and backup copies of each of these). The required chapter is loaded into the computer from one of the disks when the book is being worked on. The set of data disks for the word processing program forms the filing system for the word processor documents.

Disks and tapes written by one computer can be read by other computers of the same type. They are used to transfer programs and data from one computer to another.

More details about backing store are to be found in chapter 4.

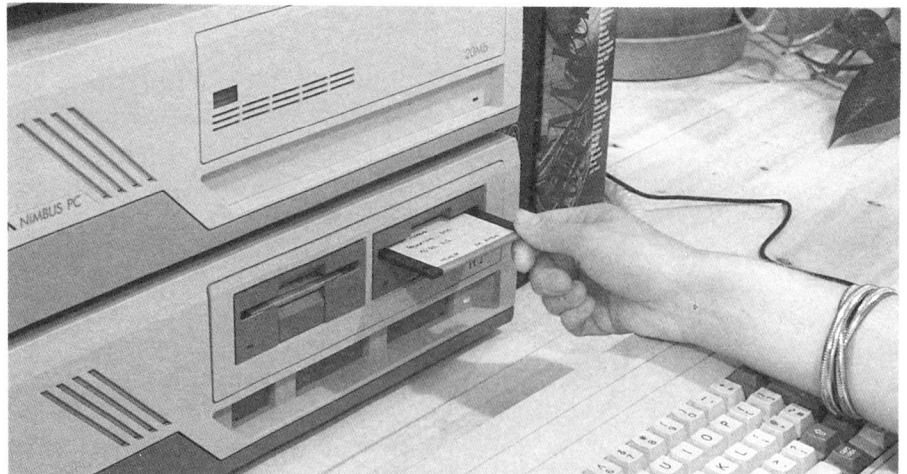

A magnetic disk being inserted into a disk drive.

3H Micros, Minis, Mainframes and Supercomputers

Computers are made in all shapes and sizes. The smallest fit comfortably on a desktop; the biggest occupy a large room. Broadly speaking, computers can be classified into four groups, according to their size and processing power:

* **Microcomputers** are small computers based on a single microprocessor chip. They fit on a desktop, and cost between a few hundred and a few thousand pounds. Most microcomputers can only be used by one person at a time. There are now millions of

microcomputers in use, and their numbers are growing rapidly. A typical business microcomputer costs in the region of a thousand pounds.

- **Minicomputers** are about the size of a filing cabinet. They are used in offices, colleges, factories and warehouses, and are generally housed in their own rooms. They can do a number of tasks at once. A minicomputer costs tens or hundreds of thousands of pounds.
- **Mainframe computers** are large and powerful, and require special air-conditioned rooms. They can do most of the information processing of a large company, university or bank. A mainframe computer costs hundreds of thousands or millions of pounds.
- **Supercomputers** are used for scientific and engineering work, and have multiple processors. They work very fast, and have large memories. There are only a few hundred supercomputers in existence, each costing tens of millions of pounds.

Not included in this classification are the special-purpose computers which are built into other devices. These include machines in factories, ships, aircraft, missiles and other modern weapons systems and many household devices such as video recorders. These computers are made from microprocessors with their software stored permanently in ROM.

An IBM mainframe computer. IBM is the world's leading manufacturer of computers and other IT products.

Questions

These questions cover sections 3F, 3G and 3H.

1 (a) What *two* main types of input are there?
   (b) What *two* main types of output are there?
2 (a) Can a computer have only one type of input device, and one type of output?
   (b) What are the benefits of a range of input and output devices?
3 List some uses of backing store.
4 A typical letter produced on a word processor occupies five kilobytes on disk. How many of such letters could be stored on a floppy disk for a typical business microcomputer?
5 What is the distinguishing feature of a microcomputer?
6 Approximately how many small business microcomputers can be bought for the cost of a supercomputer?

A popular desktop microcomputer, the Research Machines Nimbus.

A popular minicomputer, the Digital Equipment Corporation VAX.

A Cray 2 supercomputer, one of the most powerful computers ever produced.

3I End-of-Chapter Summary

The main points of this chapter are as follows:

- A computer is a digital electronic information processing machine which can be programmed.
- A computer can do seven types of operation, all involving data: input, output, storage, retrieval, sending, receiving and processing.

- A computer can process data and make decisions on the basis of the data, but it cannot think for itself.
- A computer system comprises input devices, output devices, backing store, communications links, processor and memory. In large computers, the processor and memory together make up the central processing unit (CPU).
- Units of a computer system are modular: they can be unplugged and replaced, without affecting the system as a whole.
- The cells in a computer memory are located by their addresses.
- Computer memories are made from RAM (random access memory) and ROM (read-only memory) chips.
- Memory and backing store capacities are measured in K (1K = 1024 bytes) or megabytes (1 megabyte = 1024K).
- A processor contains a number of registers which hold data items and instructions while the computer is working with them.
- A processor operates on a fixed cycle of fetching an instruction, and applying the instruction to a data item.
- A microprocessor is an entire processor on a single chip.
- Computers can be classified by size as microcomputers, minicomputers, mainframe computers and supercomputers.

Exercise 3

1 Choose the correct word from the list for each of the following spaces:

disk drives; hard copy; megabyte; 600; minicomputer; memory.

A few years ago, a small travel company bought a ____ with a CPU, 1 ____ of memory, two 300 megabyte ____ as backing store, a printer for ____ output and a number of terminals for input. After a while, this computer installation became too small. The company replaced the disk drives with ones storing ____ megabytes, upgraded the ____ to 4 megabytes and bought a second printer.

2 (a) Describe the function of the program counter in a processor.
(b) Describe the cycle of steps whereby a processor carries out a program instruction. Mention the tasks of the program counter, instruction register and accumulator in the cycle.

3 The owner of a small business has a desktop microcomputer with two disk drives. He has the following software and data:

An accounts program, and all his accounts

A word processing program, and all his correspondence

A stock control program, and his stock records

A spreadsheet program, and his business plans.

Suggest a way of arranging this software and data on disks to form a simple filing system. Two copies of every data disk are required; a master and a backup copy. Devise a code to identify the disks, using letters and numbers, so that each disk is immediately recognisable.

4 Would a microcomputer, minicomputer, mainframe computer or supercomputer be the most suitable for each of the following applications:
(a) All the data processing at a large insurance company,
(b) Processing student programs at a polytechnic,
(c) Keeping accounts and doing bookings at a small travel agency,
(d) Controlling a set of robots in a factory,
(e) Calculating the positions of spacecraft on journeys to distant planets,
(f) Doing letters and keeping accounts at home?

Things to find out

1 Look at the photographs in this book, and some obtained from other sources, showing computer output on the display screen. Compare those which show data as tables of numbers with those which show data as graphics.
(a) List the advantages of graphics over the display of data as tables.
(b) Under what circumstances might it be better to present data as tables?
(c) Make a list of some uses of computers where graphics is essential.

2 At present a small business microcomputer with a single processor, 1 megabyte of memory, screen, keyboard and a disk drive with a 1 megabyte capacity can be bought for less than £1000.
(a) Find out the costs of a computer system with a similar capacity 5 years ago and 10 years ago.
(b) Give the reasons for the changes in cost over the last ten years.
(c) List and discuss some of the effects of the change in price during this period.

4 Peripheral Devices

A severely disabled person controlling a microcomputer by movements of his head. Computers have opened up a new way of life for many disabled people.

Getting data into and out of a computer system, and storing it in a convenient way, are three of the most important aspects of computing. They often take more time than processing the data. The aim of input, output and storage systems is to make it easy for people to use computers, to reduce errors during the input and output of data, and to allow large quantities of data to be stored cheaply and efficiently.

This chapter describes the commonest methods of input, output and data storage in use at present, and their suitability for various computer applications. It also describes the link or **interface** between processors and the **peripheral devices** used for input, output and storage. Input and output devices used for control purposes are discussed in chapter 6.

4A Communicating with a Computer

At the centre of a computer system is the processor, or CPU. Around it are the devices for the input, output and storage of data. These are the **peripheral** devices: see Figure 4.1. One of their tasks is to enable people to communicate with a computer system. In the early days of computing, there were only a few types of peripherals. Users of computers had to make do with what was available. Now there are many, and the important thing is to choose the most suitable peripherals for a particular application. The peripherals are the most expensive part of the hardware of a computer system, and must be chosen with care so that the money spent on them is not wasted.

The problem of communication between a person and a computer system is more than just the choice of the right peripherals. For

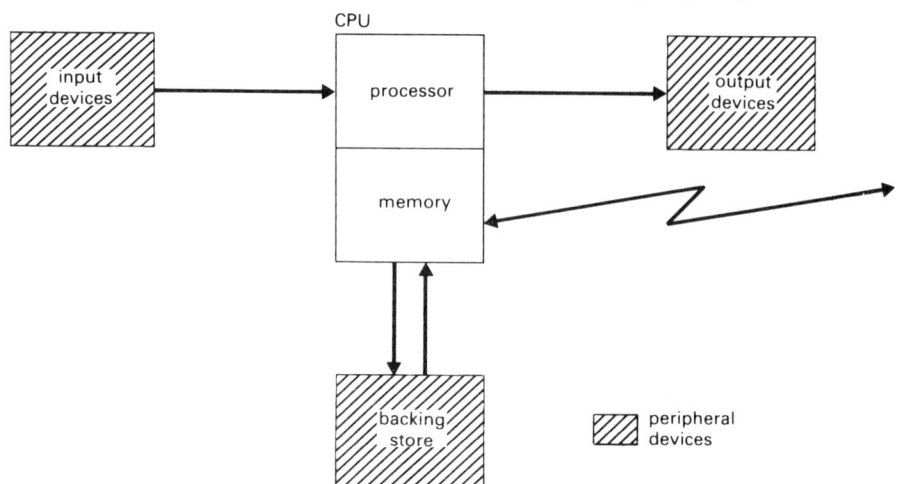

Figure 4.1   Peripheral devices

many years, computer systems were not designed with the needs of the user in mind. The methods of input and output were chosen to make things simple for the computer, not for the person using it. Many people found it difficult to use computers.

Now things are beginning to change. The importance of good communications between user and computer is being recognised. New peripheral devices, such as the cash terminals used by banks, are being designed to suit the needs of the people using them. Many computer programs are being revised, or new programs written to replace old ones, with the aim of improving the **user interface**. Much of the work in the Fifth Generation computer project is devoted to better communication between user and computer: see chapter 22.

4B Input from a Person

Many computer systems require input from a person. Most are **interactive**, in the sense that there is a conversation between the person and the computer. The person enters data, and the computer responds immediately.

If the computer system deals mainly with text or figures, the most suitable input device is a **keyboard**. For example, a keyboard is the ideal input device for a word processing program. A computer keyboard is set out like a typewriter keyboard, with a few extra keys for control purposes. People who have learned to type on a typewriter seldom find much difficulty in using a computer keyboard.

Many computer applications work on large batches of data which are processed in one operation. The input data for these systems is typed at a keyboard and copied onto a magnetic tape or disk, an operation known as **direct data entry (DDE)**. The data is only processed when all the input is complete.

Some applications need fewer characters than those on a keyboard. These include control systems where there are only a small number of control options, and educational software for use by disabled pupils. A **keypad** is the most suitable input device for these applications. A keypad has a small number of specially selected keys. A **touch-sensitive screen** is used in a similar way. The characters or symbols are displayed on the computer screen, and the required one is touched by the user.

The speed of input using a keyboard or keypad is limited by the speed at which a person can type. This is generally between 100 and 500 characters per minute. In some applications, such as word processing, this limits the speed of the whole operation. In other applications where input is less frequent, the speed of input does not affect the process very much.

If input data is not in the form of characters, then a number of input devices are more suitable than a keyboard or keypad. Many modern computers use a **mouse** for input. This is a small object with a 'tail' consisting of a cable connected to the computer. The mouse is moved around on the surface of a desk and, as it moves, a **pointer** moves on the computer screen. The pointer may be used to draw shapes, move objects on the screen, and select control options in a program.

Drawings, designs and architects' plans are best input using a **digitiser**. This is a round object which is moved by hand on a pad. As

A simple way of controlling a computer is by means of a mouse moved over the surface of a desk.

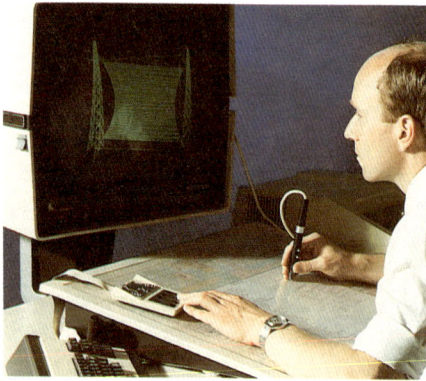

An engineer using a digitiser to enter a drawing into a computer.

it moves, a pointer moves on the screen in the corresponding position. A digitiser is more precise (and more expensive) than a mouse. An alternative form of input for these applications is a **light pen**. This enables the user to draw directly on the computer screen. The advantage of a light pen is that you can see where you are drawing. The disadvantages are that a light pen is not very precise, and it is tiring to hold up against a screen for a long time. Light pens are becoming less popular than digitisers.

Computer games are controlled by **games paddles** and **joysticks**. Both are based on small levers which can be moved in various directions. A joystick is a small version of the control stick used on aircraft. It allows any combination of movement: forwards, backwards or sideways. A games paddle has a more restricted range of movement.

Questions

1 Which method of input is the most suitable for each of the following? Give reasons in each case.
   (a) word processing
   (b) producing engineering drawings on a computer
   (c) controlling a machine by computer
   (d) playing space invaders
   (e) controlling a program with a limited number of options at each stage
   (f) entering the data for a payroll program.
2 What are the advantages of a digitiser over a light pen for graphics input?
3 For what purposes is a mouse used?
4 List some computer applications where the speed of input determines the speed of the whole process.

4C Input from a Document

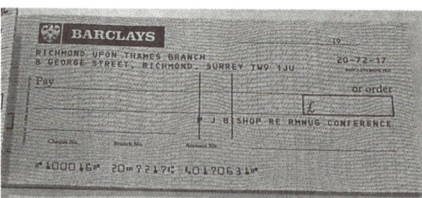

Top: A telephone bill, showing the row of OCR characters along the bottom. *Bottom:* A cheque, showing the row of magnetic ink characters along the bottom.

Typing input data at a keyboard is slow and a source of errors. It is to be avoided in all applications where it is not essential. These include applications where the data is already printed, on a price tag, cheque, gas bill, etc. Input devices are used to read the data from these documents directly, without it having to be retyped. This is much quicker, and most of the input techniques include automatic checks. These detect errors in the data as it is input and signal to the operator to read it again.

The commonest method of reading data from a document into a computer system is **optical character recognition (OCR)**. The characters are printed in a special typeface, and read by a scanner. OCR scanners are fast, and the error rate is low. Optical character recognition is used to read the return slips on gas, water, electricity and telephone bills, bank deposit forms, and in a number of similar applications. It is ideal when there is a large volume of data to be read from the same type of document.

Similar to OCR, but less widely used, is **magnetic ink character recognition (MICR)**. MICR is used to read the characters printed on the bottom of cheques. A special magnetic ink is used to print the characters, which are read by a scanner. They show the cheque number, account number, bank branch code and amount. The advantage of MICR is its low error rate. Millions of cheques are sorted and cleared automatically every day in the UK, with hardly any errors.

Mark sense documents are used when a small amount of input data needs to be recorded by hand, away from a computer system. They are used, for example, to record gas and electricity meter

A collection of groceries with bar coded labels.

readings, and in some examinations to record the answers to multiple-choice questions. A mark sense document has a number of small areas which may be marked by shading them with a soft pencil. A scanner reads the document, and registers the shaded areas. The disadvantage of mark sensing is the higher error rate than some of the other methods of input.

Bar codes are used to identify goods sold in shops and supermarkets, books, and other products. A bar code consists of a pattern of wide and narrow stripes, which encodes a number. Most bar codes used in Europe follow the **European Article Numbering (EAN)** system. This has twelve digits, and no two types of product have the same code. A bar code can be in any dark colour on a light background. One benefit is that they can be printed on goods as part of the label, and therefore do not cost any extra.

Bar code readers detect the pattern of stripes, and change them into a number. Most bar code readers look like pens, and are moved across a bar code to read it. There are a number of built-in checks to ensure that the code is read correctly. Some readers make a sound when a bar code is read successfully; others read the code repeatedly until it is input correctly.

An older type of input from product labels is **Kimball tags**. These have codes in the form of patterns of holes. When an item is sold, its Kimball tag is removed and sent in a batch of tags to the computer system. The data on the tag is read from the pattern of holes. The disadvantages of Kimball tags are that they cannot be read in the shops when the goods are sold, and that they are easy to damage. They are now being replaced by bar codes and magnetic strips.

Magnetic strips are used on credit cards and some product labels. They store a small amount of data encoded in a piece of magnetic tape stuck to the card or label. A magnetic strip can store more data than

Two credit cards and a British Rail train ticket, showing the magnetic strips on the reverse side.

41

a bar code, and the data cannot be read by eye. This is an advantage in some cases, for example if the credit limit is stored on the magnetic strip on a credit card. The data on a magnetic strip can be altered at any time, unlike the other input media described here.

Questions

1 Which method of input is the most suitable for each of the following? Give reasons in each case.
   (a) electricity meter readings
   (b) the return slips on electricity bills
   (c) the article code on goods in a shop
   (d) the article code, description and price on goods in a shop
   (e) the data on a cheque
   (f) the card number and other details on a credit card
   (g) the identification on a container of goods.

2 (a) Which of the methods of input described in this section can be read by eye as well as by the computer input device, and which ones cannot?
   (b) What are the advantages and disadvantages of each of these types of input?

3 What are the advantages of entering data directly from source documents over typing it at a keyboard?

4D Output to a Screen

The main output device of almost all computer systems is a **display screen**. This looks like a television screen, and can display text and, in most cases, **graphics**. Many computers have display screens in colour.

Text display screens are ideal for word processing and similar applications. They show the text in the same layout as it will appear when printed. As the text is entered or corrected, it appears on the screen.

Graphics displays are made up of a large number of small **pixels** (picture elements) on the screen. The more pixels, the higher the **resolution** of the graphics. High-resolution graphics images are sharper and can show more detail. Graphics displays are essential for applications such as computer-aided design (CAD), and programs which produce graphs, pie charts and similar displays.

Many modern applications require a combination of text and graphics. Some computers can break their screens up into a number of **windows**: each window shows the output from a different program. Some may show text; others graphics. Programs are coming into use which enable a complete page of a book or magazine to be made up on the computer screen. A page many include text, photographs and illustrations.

Below right: A word processor document showing on a computer screen. *Below left:* A graphics display on a computer screen.

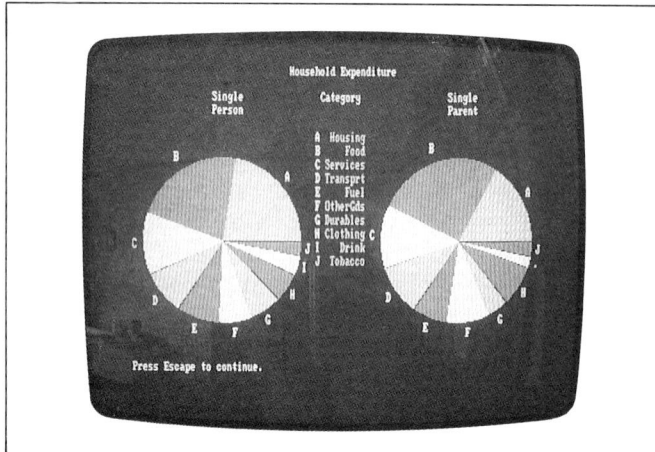

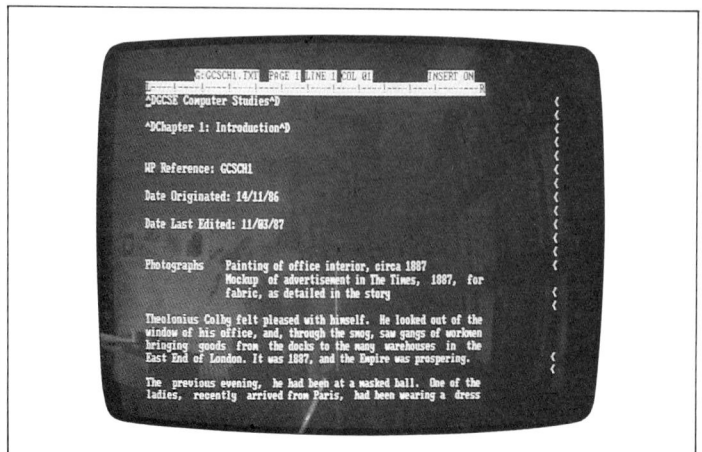

A dot matrix printer.

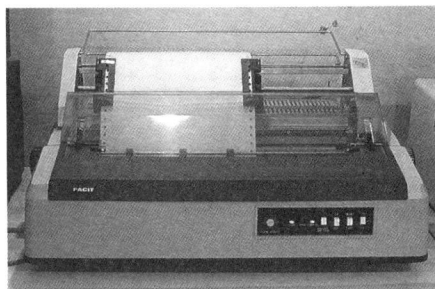

A daisy wheel printer.

Output can be displayed on a screen immediately, and can be visually very attractive. But many applications require a permanent record of output—**hard copy**. A range of **printers** is available to produce hard copy, the type depending on the type of application.

The smallest and cheapest printers are **dot matrix** printers. They form characters as a pattern of small dots, produced by fine, inked needles. They are somewhat noisy, and the quality of the output is not high. Their main use is printing drafts of documents and program listings. More expensive (and noisier) are **daisy wheel** printers, which use a rotating wheel with characters mounted on flexible 'petals'. The output produced by a daisy wheel printer is as good as that produced by an electric typewriter. Daisy wheel printers are most commonly used for word processing.

Ink jet printers are a newer technology. They are quiet, producing characters by fine jets of ink in a dot matrix pattern. Some work in colour. The newest (and most expensive) types of printers are **laser printers**, which use a laser beam and dry, powdered ink (as used by photocopiers) to produce images. They also work to a dot matrix pattern, but the resolution is so high that the dots can hardly be seen. The disadvantages of these high-resolution laser printers is their relatively slow speed. (Other types of laser printers, which print characters only, work very fast.)

Line printers are used by mini and mainframe computers. They print a whole line at a time, and work much faster than the other types. The fastest of all are the character laser printers, mentioned above.

Dot matrix printers, ink jet printers and high-resolution laser printers can produce graphics as well as character output. Laser printers are particularly well suited to the page make-up software referred to in the previous section, which produces pages containing text, photographs and illustrations.

Digital plotters are used to produce graphs, plans and engineering drawings. Some are able to work in colour. They are expensive and somewhat slow, but the quality of their output is high.

In spite of the wide range of printers available, there are only a small number of **interfaces** between processors and printers. The interface is the way the printer is linked to the processor: it determines the speed at which data is transferred, and the way the processor controls the printer. If a computer has a particular printer interface, then any printer which is controlled by that interface may be linked to it. For example, a microcomputer may use a standard interface to control a dot matrix printer. This may be replaced by a daisy wheel printer which uses the same interface without any modification to the microcomputer.

When printing large batches of documents such as gas bills, the background data, which is the same on all the bills, is pre-printed. This stationery is then lined up in the printer so that the computer output is printed in the correct places. These bills and similar documents contain tear-off slips which are returned with the payment. These **turnaround documents** are read by the computer program which deals with payments.

Printed output can use large quantities of paper. An alternative is

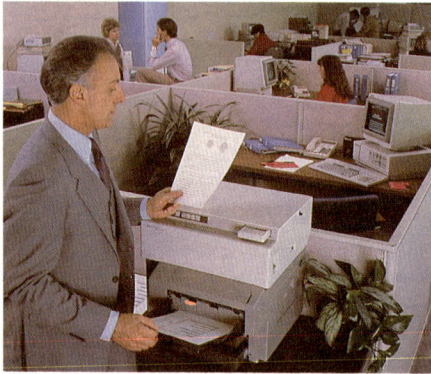

A digital plotter in use.

computer output on microfiche (COM). The output is displayed on screen and photographed with a special camera. The image of the screen is small: about five millimetres square. The images from approximately one hundred screens are developed onto a single microfiche. The major application of COM is printing the balances of bank accounts every night. This saves large amounts of paper, and reduces transport costs.

A laser printer in use.

Questions

These questions cover sections 4D and 4E.

1 What are the *two* general methods of computer output? Give some examples of the use of each type.

2 (a) How are the graphics images formed on a computer screen?
(b) List some uses for computer graphics.

3 Which output device is the most suitable for hard copy for each of the following? Give reasons in each case.
(a) word processing
(b) magazine pages
(c) engineering drawings
(d) bank statements
(e) gas bills
(f) an advertisement in colour
(g) rough drafts of documents
(h) listings of programs written by school pupils.

4 (a) Which of the types of printers described above can work in colour?
(b) What are the advantages of output printed in colour?

5 What are the benefits of a small number of standard interfaces between processors and printers?

6 (a) List some uses of turnaround documents, in addition to those described in the text.
(b) What are the advantages of turnaround documents?

4F Voice Input and Output

Dr Frederick Jelinek, pioneer of voice recognition and speech synthesis, at the terminal of one of his experimental speech systems.

People have written science fiction stories about computers which are able to understand the spoken word, and speak themselves, for many years. The reality is less spectacular. Computers are not able to understand continuous passages of a natural language, whether spoken or written, and still find it hard to make out even a small number of single words from a known speaker.

In a few situations, such as controlling ships or submarines, a small number of words from a known speaker is all the computer will have to cope with. Voice recognition systems are coming into use for applications like these. However, the rate of development remains slow. Voice recognition is one of the main tasks of Fifth Generation computers, at present under development. See chapter 22.

Spoken output is a little easier, and a number of computer systems can produce a limited range of speech. The speaking clock, which tells the time over the telephone, is now the output of a computer system. Computers can store digital versions of the elementary sounds which make up speech, and join them to form words. The difficulty is to produce a flow of speech and a variation of tone which sounds natural.

A number of computer terminals being used for financial transactions in a stockbroker's office.

4G Terminals

The most popular device for input and output on all computers larger than micros is the **terminal**. A terminal consists of a keyboard and a display screen which shows text and, in some cases, graphics. A terminal is also known as a **visual display unit (VDU)**. A mainframe computer can support hundreds of terminals, all operating at the same time. Terminals may be in the same building as the computer (**local terminals**) or connected to it from a distance (**remote terminals**). Remote terminals are connected to computers via telephone lines.

Terminals are versatile devices. They can be used for direct data entry (see section 4B), or to run a computer program interactively. They are also used to develop programs. Special types of terminal are used, for example, in shops to record sales and in banks to dispense cash. Terminals were the first devices which brought computing power out of computer rooms onto people's desks, and onto the counters of shops and travel companies. They enabled people who were not computer specialists to work with computers directly. Terminals and desktop microcomputers have done much to make information technology accessible to a large number of people.

Questions

These questions cover sections 4F and 4G.

1 How are remote terminals connected to computers?
2 Make a list of some uses of computer terminals. Include those mentioned in section 4G, and others you know about.
3 (a) Find out how people had access to computers before terminals were widely available.

(b) What are the benefits of the use of terminals?
4 List some applications of voice recognition systems, bearing in mind the limitations of voice recognition technology at present.
5 Make a list of some applications for speech synthesis, including some not mentioned in section 4F.

4H Backing Store: Magnetic Disks

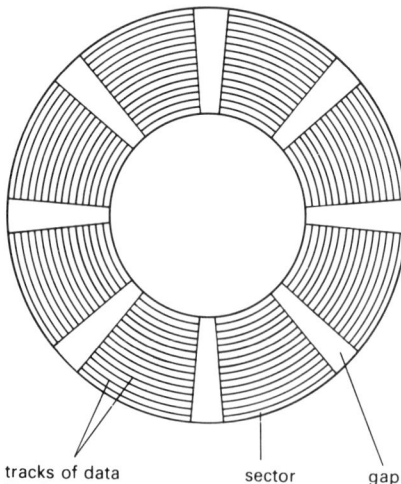

tracks of data
(far fewer than the
actual number)   sector   gap

Figure 4.2   Data layout on a disk

Magnetic disks are the commonest backing store media. Those used by microcomputers consist of a single disk, with both surfaces coated with a magnetic substance. These disks are flexible, hence their name, **floppy disks**. Larger computers use **disk packs**, which have a number of rigid disks mounted on a common shaft. Data is stored in a binary code in terms of small, magnetised spots. The spots are arranged in circular **tracks**, each of which is divided into a number of **sectors**. See Figure 4.2. Data is transferred to and from a disk one sector at a time. A sector generally stores about 1K of data.

Disk drives read data from disks, and write data to them. Microcomputers have one or two disk drives; mainframe computers generally have between four and sixteen. Disk drives have **read/write heads** which move over the surface of the disk to locate the required track of data. One of the reasons for having gaps between sectors is to allow for the movement of read/write heads. Data is transferred to and from a disk at rates of up to a million bytes per second.

Most disks can be removed from their drives and used to create a filing system, as described in section 3G. An exception is **Winchester disks**, which are high-capacity disks permanently mounted in their drives. The main advantages of Winchester disks are their low cost and fast access to data.

One of the benefits of disk drives is that any sector of data can be read or written whenever it is needed. The time taken to locate the data is more or less independent of the position of the data on the disk. A magnetic disk is a **random access medium**. This is very important for all applications which need to locate any item of data they have stored on disk quickly.

Note the difference between the terms **medium** and **device**. A medium, such as a magnetic disk, stores data. A device, such as a disk drive, transfers data to and from a medium.

An exchangeable disk pack being inserted into the disk drive of a mainframe computer.

Below left: A 5.25 inch floppy disk and drive, as used by many microcomputers. Below right: A Winchester disk with its protective case removed.

4I Backing Store: Magnetic Tape

Magnetic tape is the cheapest way of storing large amounts of data, and the most convenient for certain applications. Magnetic tape used to be the most popular backing store medium; now it is disks.

Magnetic tape is made in the same way as sound recording tape. A reel is several hundred metres long, and stores between ten and one hundred megabytes. Data is stored in a binary code as magnetised spots. The spots are in **tracks** along the tape, with one data item contained in a **frame** across the width of the tape. The data is divided into **blocks**, separated by gaps. See Figure 4.3. One block of data is read from tape or written to tape in one operation. A block generally contains about 1K of data.

Magnetic tape drives transfer data to and from tape. The tape is wound at high speed between two reels, passing over a **read/write head**. Most magnetic tape drives can transfer data with the tape running in either direction. One reason for the gaps between the blocks is to allow the tape to be started, stopped or reversed.

Magnetic tape is a **serial access medium**. The most convenient way of reading the data on tape is in the same order as it was written. If a block of data is required out of sequence, it takes some time to wind the tape forwards or backwards to locate it. Serial access is

Magnetic tapes being manufactured in a clean environment.

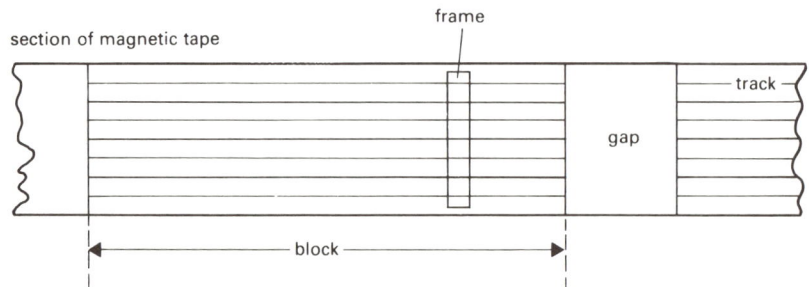

Figure 4.3 Data layout on a tape

ideal for applications where the data is processed in large batches, such as payroll systems. In these applications, the data is processed in the same order as it is written to the tape. No time is wasted winding the tapes forwards and backwards.

Another use for magnetic tape is making backup copies of the data on disks, particularly Winchester disks. The data is copied from the disk, track by track. If the disk develops a fault, the data can be copied back from the tape. This happens only rarely, and the slow speed of the tape is not a problem.

4J Silicon Disks, Optical Disks and ROM Cartridges

Magnetic disks and tapes are by far the most popular backing store media, but a small number of others are coming into use. One of the original reasons for having backing store on computers was the high price of memory. Part of the backing store was used as a secondary memory, with data transferred to and from it as required. Now memory is much cheaper, and the reverse trend is occurring: a portion of memory is being used as backing store on some computers. This memory is regarded as a **silicon disk**. It holds copies of the data files which the computer is using at the time. Silicon disk is a random access medium. The transfer of data to and from silicon disk is much faster than to and from magnetic disk. This speeds up many applications which spend much of their time transferring data to and from disk. When data on silicon disk is finished with, it is copied to a magnetic disk—otherwise it will be lost when the computer is switched off.

ROM cartridges are exchangeable portions of read-only memory. They are normally used to store software rather than data. Programs can be plugged straight into memory when they are wanted, and unplugged and replaced by other programs whenever necessary. This reduces the time taken to load software from disk. ROM cartridges are popular on certain types of microcomputers. They are more expensive than disks for the same storage capacity, and their uses are somewhat limited.

Another read-only medium is **optical disks**. Optical disks use the same technology as compact disks for sound recording. Software and data is stored in a binary coding as small indentations on the surface of a disk, and is read by laser beam. The advantage of optical disks is their high capacity, measured in **gigabytes** (1 gigabyte is 1024 megabytes, approximately one thousand million bytes). The current capacity of an optical disk is approximately 50 gigabytes, at a cost of a few pounds. Optical disks are used to store archives of data, and for training material which combines video sequences with software and data.

Questions

These questions cover sections 4H, 4I and 4J.

1 Suggest the most suitable backing store medium for each of the following. Give reasons in each case.
(a) the data for a payroll program
(b) a computer game
(c) a company's trading records for the previous year
(d) a file containing current stock exchange prices
(e) the documents for a word processing program
(f) the data for a stock control program, which is updated once a day as a batch
(g) the data for airline bookings, which are taken all the time.

2 What is the advantage of magnetic tape over magnetic disks?

3 (a) What are the benefits of silicon disks?

(b) State a disadvantage of silicon disks, compared with magnetic disks.

4 What is the unit of data transferred to and from:
(a) a magnetic disk
(b) a magnetic tape?

5 A small business computer system includes a 20 megabyte Winchester disk, two floppy disk drives each holding a disk with 750K capacity, a 500K silicon disk and a 20 megabyte magnetic tape cartridge. The main use of the magnetic tape cartridge is to make backup copies of the Winchester disk. Suggest some uses for:
(a) the Winchester disk
(b) the floppy disk
(c) the silicon disk.

6 List some applications of optical disks, in addition to those mentioned in section 4J.

4K End-of-Chapter Summary

The main points of this chapter are as follows:

- Peripherals are devices for the input, output and storage of data.
- It is important to choose the most suitable peripherals for each computer application, and to make it as simple as possible for people to communicate with computers.
- Input by a person to a computer can be by keyboard, keypad, touch-sensitive screen, mouse, digitiser, light pen, games paddle or joystick.
- Data can be input from a source document by optical character recognition (OCR), magnetic ink character recognition (MICR), mark sensing, bar codes, magnetic strips or Kimball tags.
- Computer output is either displayed on a screen or printed.
- Graphics displays are made up of pixels. The more pixels, the higher the resolution of the graphics.

- Some computer systems can show windows on their display screens, with the output from a different program in each window.
- Hard copy is produced by printers. Types of printer include dot matrix printers, daisy wheel printers, ink jet printers, laser printers and line printers.
- Graphics output may be produced by dot matrix, ink jet or laser printers, or by digital plotters.
- Turnaround documents are the output from one stage of a computerised process which forms the input for the next stage of the process.
- Voice recognition input and speech synthesis output are at present limited in their capabilities.
- Terminals are general-purpose input/output devices, used very widely with mini and mainframe computers.
- Magnetic disks are the commonest backing store medium; magnetic tapes are the cheapest.
- Magnetic disks are a random access medium; magnetic tapes are serial access.
- New techniques of backing store include silicon disks, optical disks and ROM cartridges.

Exercise 4

1 Choose the correct word from the list for each of the following spaces:

Winchester; filing; daisy wheel; graphics; mouse; tape; floppy; laser; silicon; memory.

The manager of a small business was choosing a microcomputer system. The microcomputer was supplied with a keyboard and high-resolution ____ screen. He needed a large, fast backing store. Accordingly, he selected a model with a large ____ so that part of it could be used as a ____ disk. He chose a ____ disk to store all the data and programs he used most of the time. He also selected a drive for a ____ disk so that programs and data could be exchanged with his disk ____ system. He added a ____ drive for backing up the Winchester disk. For hard copy output, he chose a ____ printer, as he needed facilities for text and graphics. To control programs quickly without using the keyboard, he chose a ____.

Things to find out

1 Find out the cost of the equipment mentioned in question 1. Discuss whether this equipment represents good value for money.
2 The arrangement of keys on a computer keyboard follows that of a typewriter. This **Qwerty** layout (named after the first six letters on the top row of keys) is more than a century old, and is not very efficient.
   (a) Find out why the Qwerty layout was chosen in the first place.
   (b) Why is the Qwerty layout not very efficient?

Points to discuss

1 If it becomes possible to recognise continuous passages of speech by computer, list some potential applications for voice systems.

2 What peripheral devices are needed by a computer designed for games?
3 Suggest some uses for a computer with the capability for screen windows.
4 Suggest the peripheral devices needed by the following computer systems:
   (a) A large mainframe computer system used by a bank to keep its accounts. The accounts are brought up-to-date every night from data sent in by the branches at the end of the day's trading. Summaries of the balances are produced.
   (b) A minicomputer at a polytechnic used for running programs written by students.
   (c) A microcomputer used to keep records and control the stock levels in a warehouse.
   (d) A computer at a travel agent, used for bookings and keeping accounts.
   (e) A microcomputer used in the home for word processing and keeping household accounts.

   (c) Suggest some more efficient layouts for keys.
   (d) Discuss the reasons for the continued popularity of the Qwerty layout.
3 **Magnetic bubble memory** looked like being a very cheap, high-capacity backing store medium a few years ago, but has not been implemented. Find out how magnetic bubble memory works, and its advantages over other backing store media. Also find out why it has not been used.

Discuss the effects of the introduction of these systems.

5

Communications Networks

The aim of information technology is to provide the right information at the right place and at the right time. Computers can be used to provide the right information; communications networks are needed to get it to the right place at the right time.

The most important telecommunications network in the world is the telephone system. It connects hundreds of millions of users on a single, worldwide network. It is no longer used just for voice signals. It now carries data between computers, television signals and other types of signals. The telephone system is changing into an **integrated services digital network (ISDN)** for high-speed communications of all types, all over the world.

5A Computer Terminal Networks

A mobile satellite ground station, able to establish communications, via satellite, with any other point on earth.

The very first computers could only be used by people in the computer room itself. This limited their use, and ways of gaining access to computers from a distance were soon tried. The most popular method is via a network of **terminals**. A terminal is a general-purpose device for input and output, as described in section 4G. A minicomputer can support tens of terminals; a mainframe can support hundreds. A network of terminals connected to a computer is shown in Figure 5.1.

Terminals can be in the same building or on the same site as the computer to which they are connected. In this case, they are connected directly by cables. This is common, for example, in universities, where there are terminals in various buildings on the campus connected to a central computer.

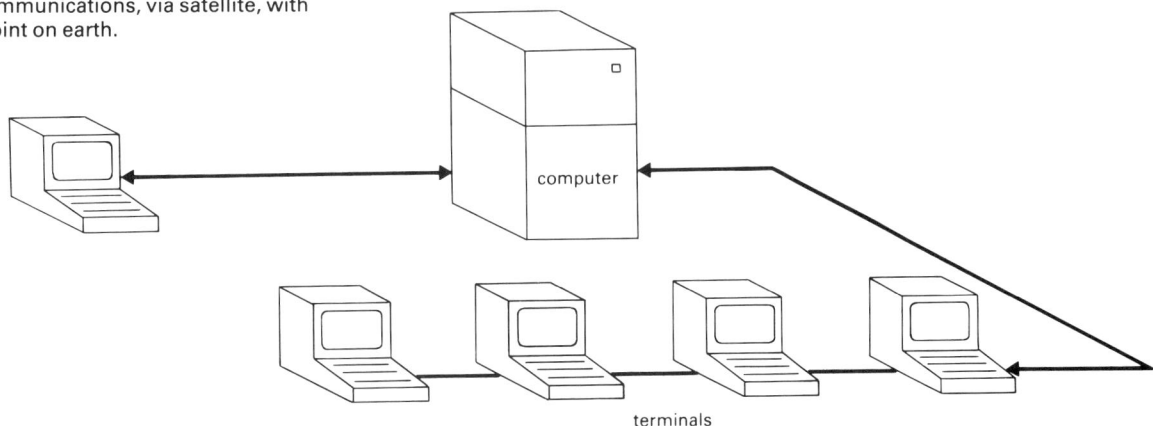

computer

terminals

Figure 5.1   Network of computer terminals

A point-of-sale terminal in use at a supermarket.

Terminals can also be connected to a computer over long distances. These **remote access** terminals are linked by telephone lines to the computer. Because the signals used to send data inside a computer do not travel well over long distances, a device known as a **modem** is used to connect a terminal to a telephone line. The modem changes the signals into a form which can be sent over long distances without distortion. At the computer, there is another modem which changes the signals back to the form used by the computer. See Figure 5.2.

In many applications, a number of remote access terminals share the same telephone line. For example, many shops have a number of cash terminals which are linked to a computer at head office. To allow several terminals to share a single communications link, a **multiplexer** is used. See Figure 5.3. Using a single communications link is cheaper than separate links for each terminal. (A multiplexer is also used when a computer is connected to several communications links.)

Some computer terminals can do a certain amount of processing themselves. Examples include the cash terminals used by banks, and the terminals used in shops and supermarkets. These **intelligent terminals** share the processing load with the central computer. They handle the details of the processing, saving the time of the main processor and reducing the amount of data which is transferred between them.

Simpler than computer terminals are **remote input devices**, which are used to supply limited amounts of data to some computers. For example, the weather forecasting computers in Britain are connected to input devices all over the world, which send in weather reports. A **viewdata** network uses a special type of terminal, as described in chapter 19.

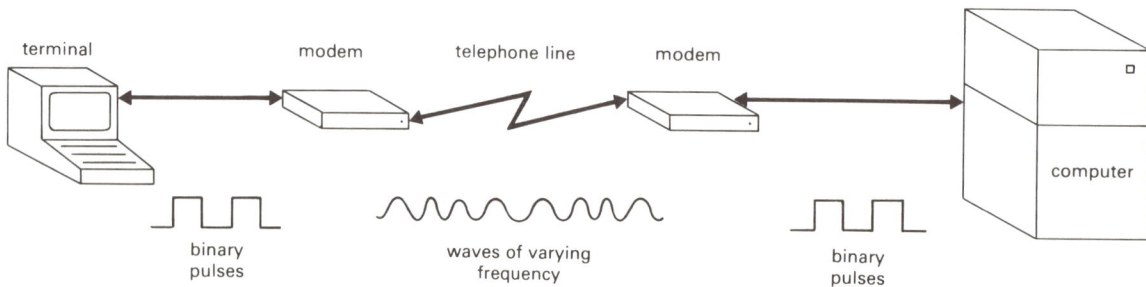

Figure 5.2   The operation of a modem

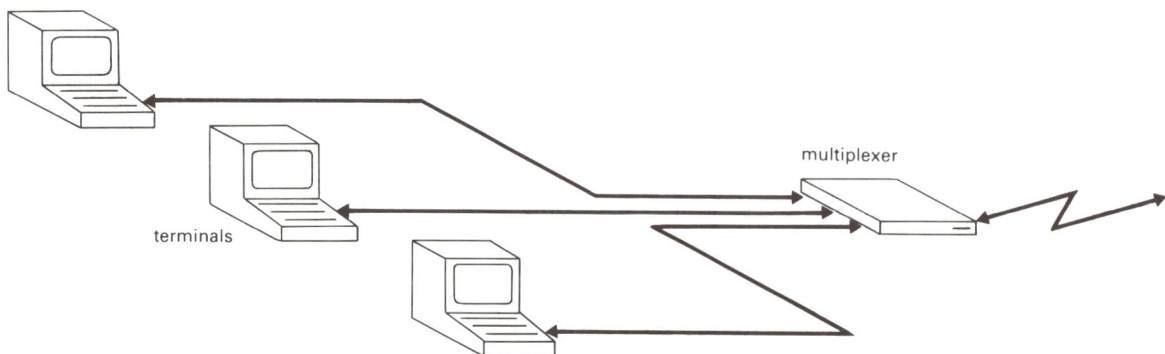

Figure 5.3   The operation of a multiplexer

Questions

1. (a) List some of the benefits of computer terminals.
   (b) Make a list of some computer applications which use computer terminals.
2. (a) What does a modem do?
   (b) Why is it necessary to have modems?
   (c) What is the reason for using multiplexers in a network of terminals?
3. (a) What is an intelligent terminal?
   (b) Give some examples of intelligent terminals. Include those mentioned in the text, and others.
   (c) What are the advantages of intelligent terminals over ordinary terminals?

5B Local Computer Networks

A local network of microcomputers in use in a school computer laboratory.

Networks of computer terminals originated in the days when computers were large and expensive. These days, when microcomputers are cheap and powerful, an alternative method of providing information processing power where it is needed is **networks** of computers. The commonest type of computer network has microcomputers as **workstations**, linked to each other and to a central **fileserver**. The fileserver is a computer which controls the running of the network, and gives all the workstations access to a central backing store device, which they share. The shared backing store device is usually a Winchester disk. The fileserver also controls the use of a shared printer, if there is one. See Figure 5.4. Networks of this nature are generally local: they are in a single room or a single building.

When a person at a workstation wants to run a program, the program is loaded from the shared backing store into the memory of the workstation. While the program is running, it can use data from files on the shared backing store. Some of these files are accessible to all users; others are private, and can only be used by one user. Results are sent to the shared printer for output.

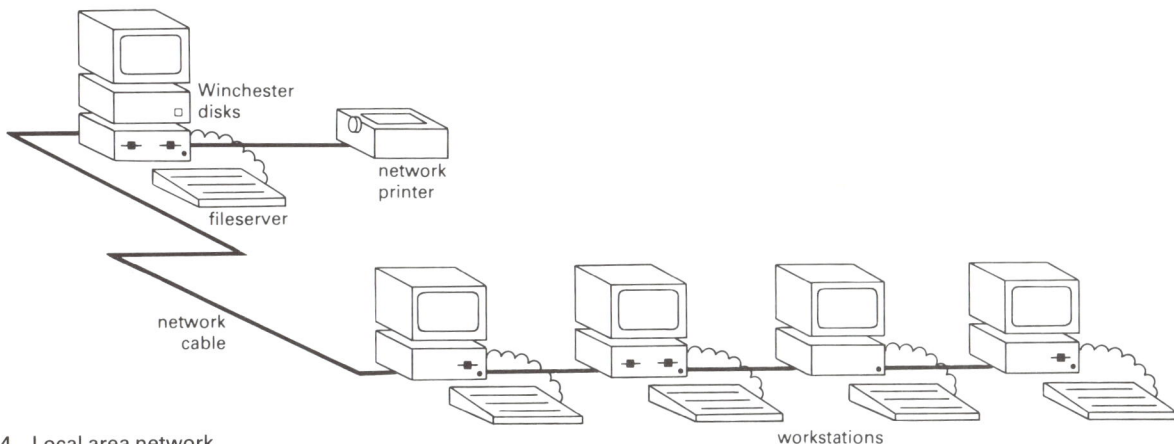

Figure 5.4   Local area network

Workstations may have their own backing store; silicon disks are a popular choice. They may also have a **local printer**, which can only be used by the workstation to which it is attached. These local peripherals allow workstations to operate more independently, and reduce the data traffic on the network. Because of the modular construction of computer systems, more workstations can be added to a network, and more peripherals added to existing workstations, whenever required.

Local computer networks are used widely in schools and colleges,

53

and are gaining popularity in businesses. They make good use of the cheap processing power of microcomputers, while enabling users to share programs, data and expensive peripherals such as Winchester disks. In many situations, a network of microcomputers is cheaper but more powerful than a central computer with terminals.

5C Long-distance Computer Networks

Networks linking large computers over long distances are becoming increasingly common. Some link the computers in the same organisation; others are between computers in different organisations. As an example of the first type, a company might have a computer at its head office for order processing, administration and management work. It might have a number of production plants, each with its own computer for stock control, controlling machinery, etc. The communications network linking these computers allows reports to be sent from the production plants to the head office, and instructions to be sent from the head office to the production plants. A network of this type is shown in Figure 5.5. Note that there are also links between the head office computer and computers belonging to the company's customers. These enable orders, invoices and payments to be sent directly from one computer system to another.

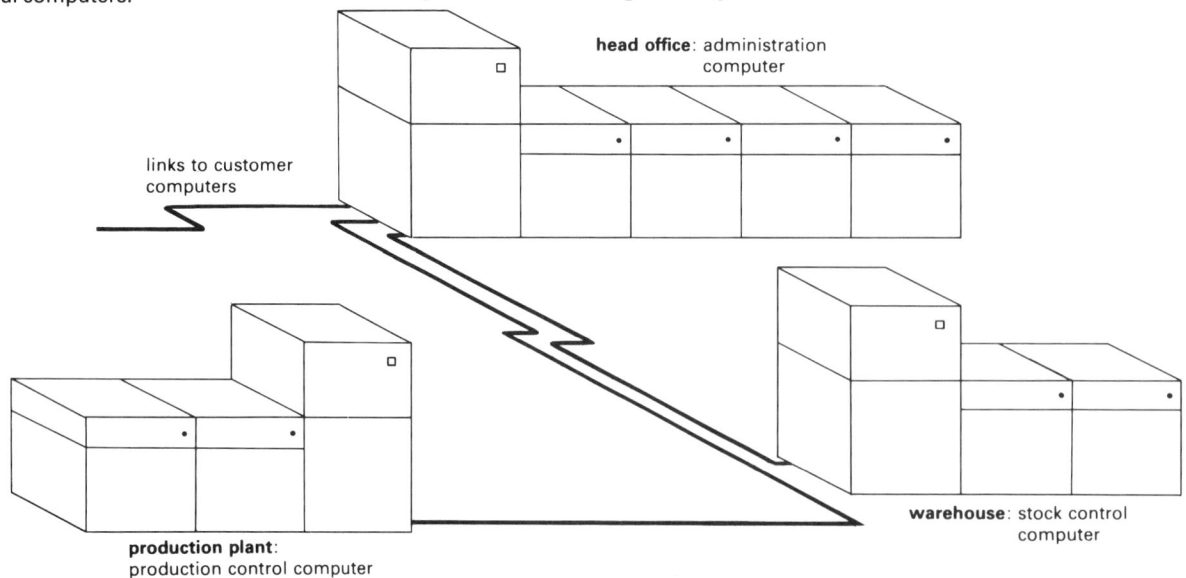

A cash terminal in use. Banks have networks of cash terminals, connected over telephone lines to central computers.

head office: administration computer

links to customer computers

warehouse: stock control computer

production plant: production control computer

Figure 5.5   Company computer network

An example of a computer network linking computers of different organisations is the system for handling payments from one bank to another: **electronic funds transfer**. The network links the computers of a number of banks throughout the world. There are central

54

computers which act as exchanges. They route messages to the computer to which they are addressed, and store messages in transit if necessary. See Figure 5.6. Many people have their salaries paid directly into their bank accounts by the organisations for whom they work. These payments are handled by the communications network which links the banks' computers. See section 20B for more details.

A second type of long-distance network is when a number of computers can link to a single central computer which has a large store of information about a particular subject. Networks of this sort are more common in the USA than the UK. They are used by home computer users to look up information in electronic encyclopaedias, and by professional people such as lawyers to look up legal documents or reports of cases.

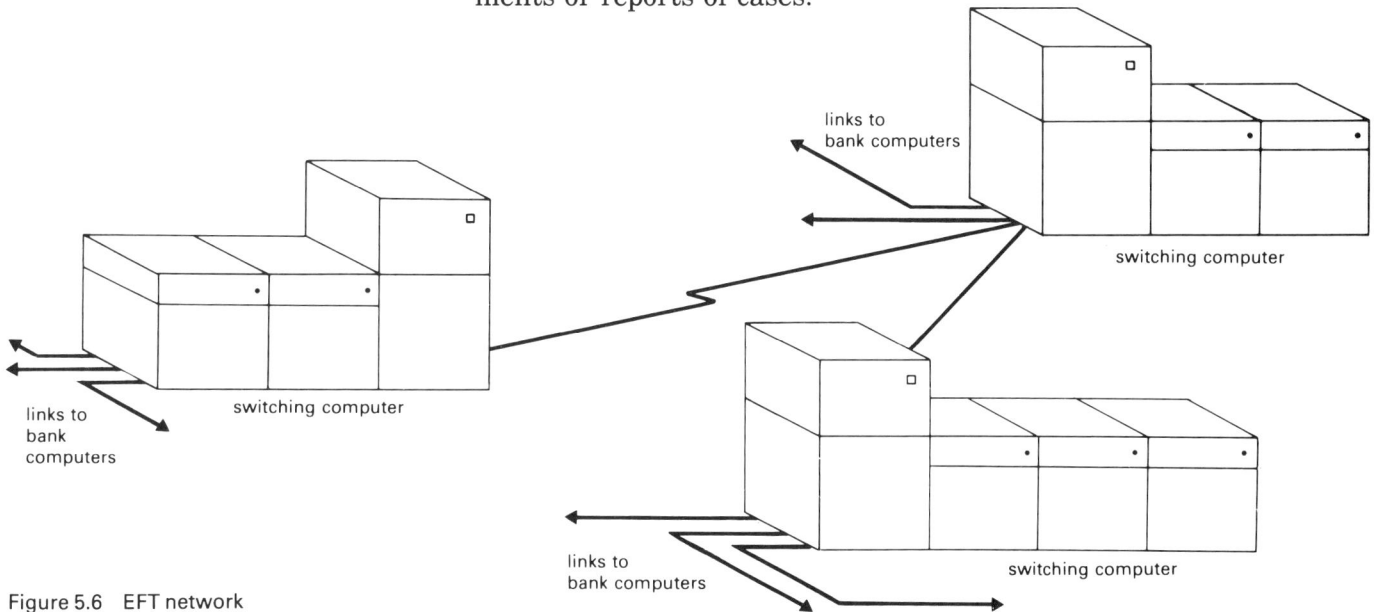

links to
bank computers

switching computer

links to
bank
computers

switching computer

links to
bank computers

switching computer

Figure 5.6   EFT network

Because the computers on a long-distance network are of different types, there must be some standard way of sending and receiving messages so that all the computers can deal with them. One method often used is to send messages as **packets** of data of a standard structure. The network is a **packet switching network**, and the computers which act as exchanges handle all the data in packets. The data is sent on high-speed lines leased from telephone companies and which are not used for any other purposes.

Questions	1 Give some examples of uses of long-distance networks of computers. Include those from the text, and others you know of. 2 (a) What problem must be overcome when linking computers of different types?	(b) Describe one way in which this problem is overcome. 3 What *two* tasks do switching computers perform?

5D Communications Technology

Until fairly recently, the telephone system was based on the same communications technology that it used when it was first built: metal cables for connections, and mechanical exchanges to switch calls to their destinations. As the volume of calls grew, and the telephone

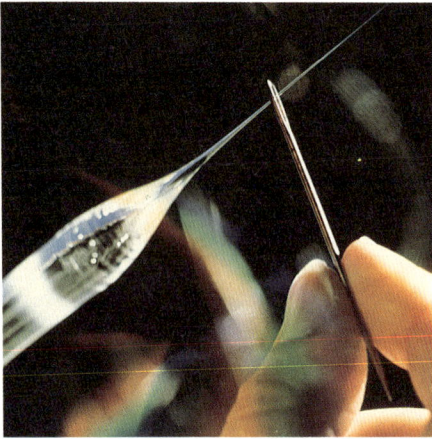
A glass rod being drawn out to form a fibre optics cable.

A microwave radio link set up for military use.

A communications satellite in orbit. The dishes send and receive the signals. The large panels are batteries powered by the Sun.

network was used to carry data between computers, these technologies became too slow and expensive. Metal cable made from copper or aluminium is expensive, and can only carry a limited number of channels. Mechanical switches in exchanges are slow, cost a lot to maintain, and often break down.

Fibre optics cable is now used for short-distance communications links. A fibre optics cable is made from a highly purified type of glass, drawn out into thin strands. Signals are carried as pulses of light. A fibre optics cable can handle far more telephone calls or data links than a metal cable, and data can be sent much more quickly along it. There is less interference on a fibre optics cable than on a metal cable.

For trunk lines over medium distances, **microwave radio** links are used. These are sent and received by dishes mounted on towers within sight of each other. See Figure 5.7. A microwave radio link can carry a large number of telephone lines, and avoids the cost of running cables between the centres. Microwave radio is hardly affected by the weather. However, as fibre optics cable becomes cheaper and its carrying capacity increases, fibre optics is becoming an alternative to microwave radio for medium distances.

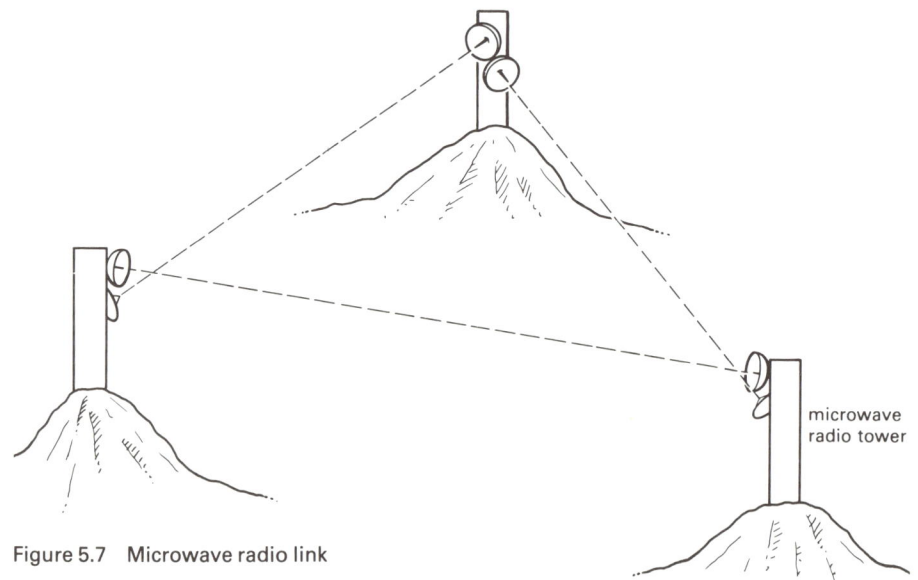

microwave radio tower

Figure 5.7   Microwave radio link

Long-distance telephone lines were first carried on cables laid on the sea-bed between continents. Some calls are still carried in this way, but the capacity of such links is limited. If an undersea cable develops a fault, it is difficult and expensive to bring it up from the sea-bed for repair. The modern method is to use **communications satellites**. These are in special orbits so that they appear to remain in fixed positions above points on the equator. Most are over the centres of oceans. Data is sent to and from the satellites from **ground stations** which use radio dishes pointed at the satellites. See Figure 5.8.

Mechanical telephone exchanges are being replaced by **electronic exchanges**, which use microchips like computer chips. They have no moving parts, and can handle far more telephone calls than the previous types. Although electronic exchanges are expensive to install, their running costs are much lower than those for mechanical exchanges. They also provide a number of new features, such as the ability to reroute calls to alternative numbers.

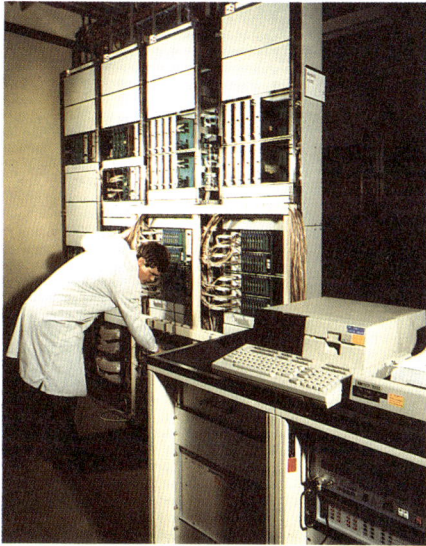
An engineer attending to a digital telephone exchange. Note the racks of printed circuit boards, each containing the switching chips.

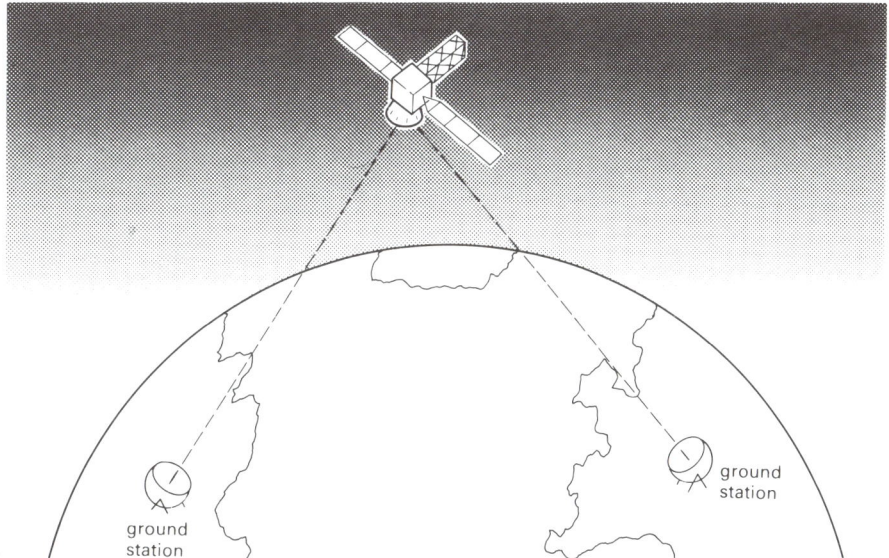
Figure 5.8 Communications satellite link

Electronic exchanges and fibre optics cables handle telephone calls and computer data in **digital** form, similar to the way it is stored and processed by computer. The telecommunications network is gradually changing from the old methods of transmitting messages to digital techniques. This has a number of advantages: transmission is faster, signals are less distorted, and less conversion is required to link computers to the network.

Questions

1 (a) What were the two original technologies used in telephone networks?
    (b) What are the disadvantages of these traditional technologies?
2 (a) What are the uses of fibre optics cable?
    (b) What are the advantages of fibre optics cable over traditional types of cable?
3 (a) What are the advantages of microwave radio links?
    (b) Why are fibre optics links becoming an alternative to microwave radio for medium-distance communications?

4 (a) Explain how communications satellites are used to carry long-distance data.
    (b) What is the minimum number of communications satellites needed to reach all points on Earth (apart from areas very close to the poles)? Draw a diagram to illustrate your answer.
5 What are the benefits of digital communications?

5E Integrated Networks: Speech, Data and Pictures

An integrated office workstation, including a modem for data communications.

Communications is the biggest growth area in information technology. On the one hand, new equipment is coming into use which greatly increases the capacity of telecommunications networks and provides new services. On the other hand, demand is growing as the benefits of the new systems become apparent. The trend is towards **integrated services digital networks (ISDN)**, which combine voice, data, video and other signals.

In an organisation which has computerised all of its internal operations and is linked to an ISDN, the combined facilities are very powerful. People can talk to each other by telephone, and use the same telephone line to send data between their desktop computers. Meetings can be held with people at different places able to talk to each other, see each other via video screens, and at the same time exchange computer data. Commercial documents such as orders and invoices are not sent by post but by electronic mail, and payments are made by electronic funds transfer (see chapter 20). The result is a great saving of time and money, and many new business opportunities.

5F End-of-Chapter Summary

The main points of this chapter are as follows:

- Communications networks are the biggest growth area in information technology.
- The telephone system is becoming an integrated services digital network (ISDN), providing a range of voice, data and video links.
- Networks of terminals are the traditional way of gaining access to a computer from a distance.
- A modem is used to link a computer to a telephone line.
- Networks of microcomputers provide computing power where users need it, and give access to shared software and data.
- Long-distance links between mainframe computers enable these computers to exchange data and messages, and are used for electronic funds transfer.
- New communications technology includes fibre optics cable for short and medium distances, microwave radio for medium distances, and communications satellites for long distances.
- Mechanical telephone exchanges are being replaced by digital electronic exchanges which use microchips and work like computers.

Exercise 5

1 Choose the correct word from the list for each of the following spaces:

Winchester; modem; line; telephone; workstations; accounts; data; software; word processor; fileserver; network; local; floppy.

The director of a small company decides to install a local ____ of microcomputers to use for order processing, word processing and keeping ____. The network has a central ____ using a ____ disk. This holds all the ____ and the data files to be shared. Some of the ____ have local ____ disk drives. These are for ____ which is not to be shared, such as management reports. There is a ____ printer on the fileserver for invoices, orders and statements. Two of the workstations have ____ daisy wheel printers for ____ documents. There is a ____ on one of the workstations so that the network can be connected to other computer systems via a ____ line.

2 In what way do communications systems help to fulfil the general aims of information technology?

3 Suggest a suitable set of equipment for a local computer network to be used at a research laboratory. There are five scientists and nine technicians, all doing experiments. The laboratory is managed by a director, who has a secretary.

The computer system is used to record and analyse the results of the experiments and to produce reports and papers based on the work, and for correspondence. The director keeps the accounts of the laboratory on the computer system, and one of the technicians does the stock control on the equipment and materials they use.

Make a list of the hardware and software required, and find out or estimate the cost of each item. Work out the total cost of the whole system.

4 Look at the map in Figure 5.9. It shows the local and regional exchanges in a telephone network connecting five towns.

(a) Either trace the map, or make a copy of it as accurately as you can.

(b) Draw in a suitable network of links between the exchanges, choosing fibre optics cable or microwave links as appropriate. Keep the total length of the connections to a minimum.

(c) Choose a suitable site for a satellite ground station for long-distance communications. It must be outside all the towns, and have at least two connections to the rest of the network. Mark the position of the ground station, and draw in the connections.

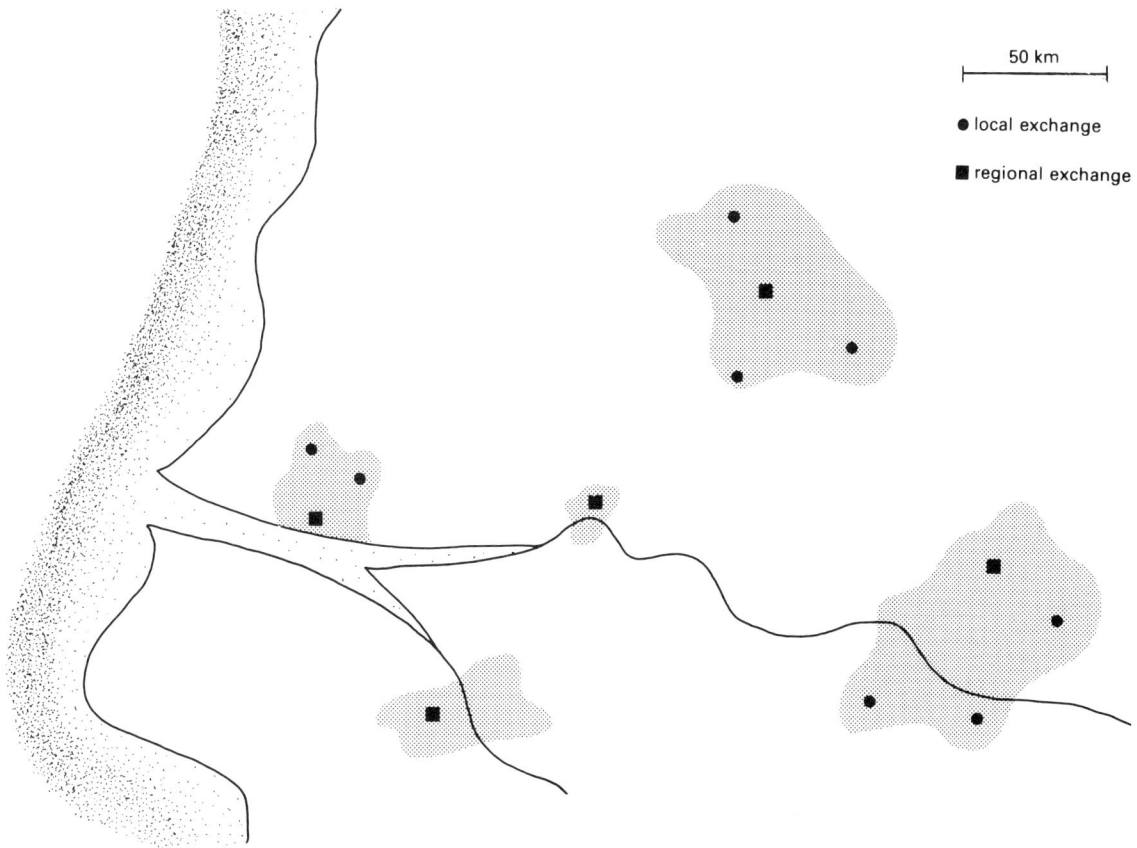

Figure 5.9

Things to find out

1 A computer system which controls the traffic-lights in a town is an example of **distributed processing**. Some processing is done at the central computer, and some by the microcomputer at each junction.
(a) Find out, or work out from the information in this chapter, what processing is done by the central computer, and what by the local microcomputers.
(b) Find out some other examples of computer networks where distributed processing is done. In each case, state how the processing load is shared.

Points to discuss

1 The view is sometimes expressed that information technology is developing towards a global telecommunications network, with computers as no more than 'lumps in the network'.

2 (a) Find out what progress has been made in the UK towards an integrated services digital network. (There are two telecommunications networks in the UK: British Telecom and Mercury.)
(b) What are the advantages of an integrated services digital network for a company?
3 There is a project at present under way to lay a series of undersea fibre optics cables to link Europe, North America and the Far East. Find out how far this project has progressed, and what effect it is having on satellite communications.

(a) What evidence is there of this happening already?
(b) Give your opinion on the likelihood of this happening in the near future.
(c) Comment on the effects of this trend.

6 Control Systems

Control systems are used in a range of equipment from microwave ovens to nuclear reactors. The details of the way the systems work vary, but they are all based on a few general principles. This chapter introduces these general principles. The theory discussed here is put into practice in chapter 21, which describes some applications of control systems.

The end of the Pilkington float glass production line. Some of the electronic control equipment can be seen in the foreground.

A modern camera, showing the electronic control circuits in the top of the case.

6A Control Systems: Sense, Decide and Act

The simplest control device we use all the time is a light switch. We move the switch by hand to turn a light on or off. This is an example of **direct** or **manual** control. Manual control is used on a great many devices, but is of limited use compared with **automatic** control, where devices control themselves to some extent.

One of the commonest devices which is controlled automatically is the refrigerator. It has a motor which pumps liquid through a network of pipes to cool the inside of the refrigerator. The motor is controlled by a **sensor** which measures the temperature in the refrigerator. The required temperature is set by a dial. See Figure 6.1.

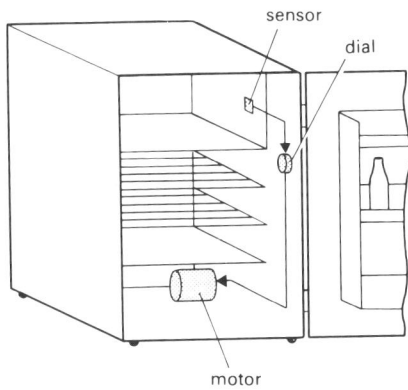

Figure 6.1 Control system for a refrigerator

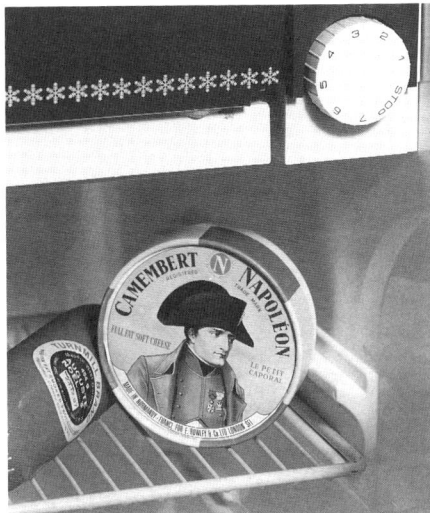

The controls on a refrigerator.

The operation of the refrigerator is as follows:

- The sensor measures the temperature inside the refrigerator.
- The temperature is compared with the setting on the dial. If it is above the setting, the motor is switched on.
- The motor pumps the cooling liquid, which causes the temperature in the refrigerator to drop.
- When the temperature falls below the required level, the motor is switched off.

The first three stages illustrate the general operation of a control system:

$$\text{sense} \rightarrow \text{decide} \rightarrow \text{act}$$

These stages are illustrated in Figure 6.2. All control systems have these three stages:

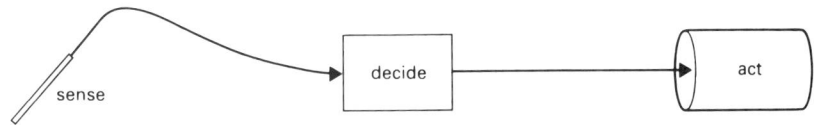

Figure 6.2 Control system: sense, decide, act

- The **sensors**, such as the temperature sensor in the refrigerator, take some kind of measurement. They measure quantities such as temperature, pressure, the height of a liquid in a tank, the acidity of a solution or the loudness of a sound. The measurements are either taken continuously, or at regular intervals.
- The control system **decides** what to do on the basis of the data from the sensors and other data it may have. The control system of the refrigerator decides whether or not to switch on the motor. It does this by comparing the data from the temperature sensor with the setting on the dial, which may be altered as required.
- The control system **acts** according to the decision. In the case of the fridge, the act is switching the motor on or off. Other control systems open and close valves, switch lights on or off, or alter the angles of the control surfaces on an aircraft.

A refrigerator is an example of **hard-wired control**. It is controlled by wires and switches, and control can only be varied in one way; by setting the required temperature. If more flexible control is required, then **programmed control** is used. Control is done by software—a control program—rather than hardware. A control program is a set of control instructions to be followed in sequence. For example, some central heating systems have programmed control. They can be set to follow a cycle of operation, depending on the time of the day. Washing machines, video recorders and microwave ovens are other examples of devices in the home which are under programmed control. Many modern machines and industrial processes are under programmed control.

A **robot** is a device which can perform a range of tasks under programmed control. For example, robots are used for painting in factories. A robot of this type has a spray nozzle and can switch the flow of paint on and off. The nozzle can be moved on an 'arm' in a number of directions in order to reach all the surfaces of the object being painted. A program directs the robot to follow the sequence of steps needed to paint a particular shape. If a different object is to be painted, a different program is used to control the robot.

Questions

1 Describe the **sense**, **decide** and **act** stages of each of the following control systems.

Example: Domestic hot water tank

Sense: The temperature in the tank

Decide: If the water is below the preset temperature

then Switch the water on

else Switch the water heater off

Act: Switch the water heater on or off

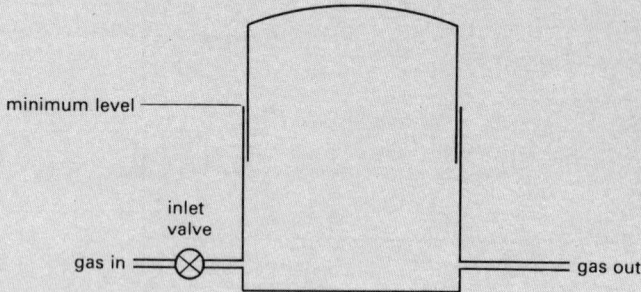

Figure 6.3 Gas storage drum

(a) central heating system
(b) automatic door
(c) lift
(d) flexible gas storage drum, as shown in Figure 6.3. The volume of gas must not be allowed to fall below the minimum level shown.
(e) An automatic pilot on a ship. This keeps the ship pointing in a preset direction.

2 What is a control program?

3 Make a list of some systems which are controlled automatically, other than those mentioned in section 6A and question 1. For each system, state whether or not it is controlled by a program.

4 (a) Would it be possible to run a refrigerator without an automatic control system?
(b) Make a list of some systems in the home which are now controlled automatically, but were not in years gone by. In each case, list the advantages of automatic control.
(c) Suggest some systems in the home which are at present operated manually which might be controlled automatically in the future. In each case, list the possible advantages (and disadvantages) of changing to automatic control.

6B Logic Circuits for Control

Logic circuits of the type described in section 2E can be used in hard-wired control systems. They combine signals from sensors in order to carry out the decisions of the control system.

Example: refrigerator control

The temperature sensor in a refrigerator sends out a signal if the temperature is higher than the set level, and no signal if it is lower. This signal can be connected to the control switch of the motor, as shown in Figure 6.4. If the switch which turns the refrigerator on or off is included, an AND gate could be used, as shown in Figure 6.5. The on/off switch sends a signal when it is on, and no signal when it is off. The operation of the control system is shown in the following table:

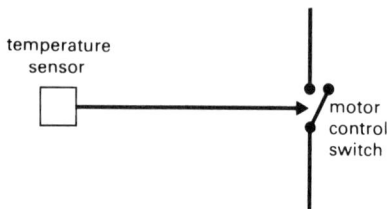

Figure 6.4 Refrigerator control signal

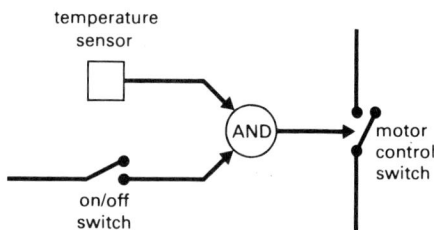

Figure 6.5 Refrigerator control with on/off switch

Inputs: On/off Switch	Temperature Sensor	Output: Motor Control
0 (off)	0 (off)	0 (off)
0 (off)	1 (on)	0 (off)
1 (on)	0 (off)	0 (off)
1 (on)	1 (on)	1 (on)

The motor is on if the on/off switch is on AND the temperature sensor is sending a signal to indicate that the temperature is too high.

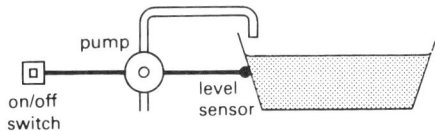

Figure 6.6   Water reservoir

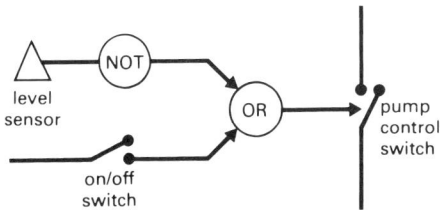

Figure 6.7   Logic circuit for water reservoir control

Example: water reservoir

The water reservoir in Figure 6.6 is supplied from a pump. The pump is switched on if the water falls below the minimum level or if a manual switch is switched on. There is a sensor which sends a signal if the water level is above the minimum level.

The logic circuit for the control of the pump is shown in Figure 6.7. The signal from the water level sensor passes through a NOT gate, as a signal is required when the water is below the minimum level. It is combined with the signal from the switch with an OR gate. The truth table is as follows:

Inputs: Water Level Sensor	On/off Switch	Output: Pump Control
0	0	1
0	1	1
1	0	0
1	1	1

The pump is switched on when the water level sensor sends no signal OR when the on/off switch is on.

Questions

1   Draw a logic circuit and a truth table for each of the following control systems:
(a) An automatic door which opens when someone stands on a pressure sensor on one side or the other side of the door.
(b) A kettle with an automatic cut-off switch, which switches it off when the temperature goes above boiling point. It also has an on/off switch.
(c) A central heating system which has a time switch, an on/off switch and a temperature sensor. The time switch sends a signal during the times when the system should be on, and no signal when it should be off. The temperature sensor sends a signal when the room temperature is above the preset level.

2   (a) Suggest some other uses for control systems which use logic circuits.
(b) What are the limitations of control systems made from logic circuits?

6C   Programmed Control

A control program is a set of instructions to control a device. The instructions are carried out in sequence. Devices which can be controlled by a program are much more versatile than those under hard-wired control.

Example: drilling machine

As a simple example of programmed control, a drilling machine drills holes in flat plates of metal. It can move the drill left, right, forwards and backwards above the plate, and drill a hole at the current position. The diameter of the hole can be selected from the drill bits available.

The program on page 64 will drill the holes shown in Figure 6.8. The drill starts from the home position, at the bottom left of the metal plate. All dimensions are in millimetres.

Right	20
Forward	15
Drill	3
Forward	15
Drill	3
Forward	15
Drill	3
Right	50
Drill	10
Backward	30
Drill	10
Home	

Top: The control centre for the Rolls-Royce integrated manufacturing system for jet engine components. *Bottom:* A computer-controlled lathe and drilling machine in operation. Once the operator has set the machine to work, it runs unattended.

The last instruction moves the drill back to the home position.

This program is run every time the drill works on a plate like the one shown in Figure 6.8. If a different arrangement of holes is required, a different program is used. Many **numerically-controlled (NC)** machines are in use which are operated by programs like this. In the old types of machine, the programs are punched on paper tape. Modern NC machines are linked to microcomputers, or have microprocessors built into them.

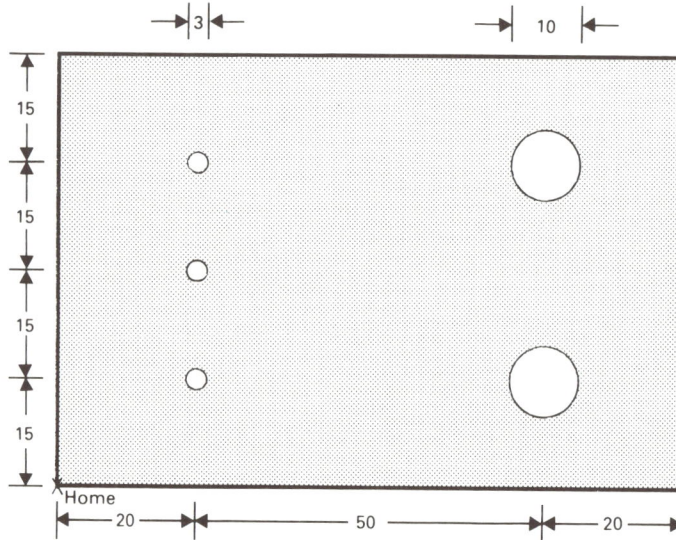

Figure 6.8   Holes made by drilling machine

In the classroom, simple control programs of this sort can be written in the programming language **Logo**. This controls a 'turtle' which moves across the computer screen. A mechanical floor turtle can be attached to the computer. This moves across a desk or the floor in response to control instructions from the computer.

Example: potato weighing machine

The previous program has no input from sensors. It performs a fixed cycle of control. A control program which includes inputs from sensors, for a machine which grades potatoes, is given below. A diagram of the machine is shown in Figure 6.9. The potatoes are fed by a conveyor belt onto a weighing platform. They are weighed automatically (in grams), and then tipped off the platform into one of the three channels, according to their weight. There is a light beam which shows when there is a potato on the platform.

A robot arm about to lift a part of a motor car engine.

Repeat
    Wait for light signal
    Get weight
    If weight > = 500 then Open gate A
    If weight < = 500 and weight > = 250 then Open gate B
    If weight < 250 then Open gate C
    Tip platform
    Close gates

Note that the program is written as a **loop** which is repeated for as long as the machine is switched on.

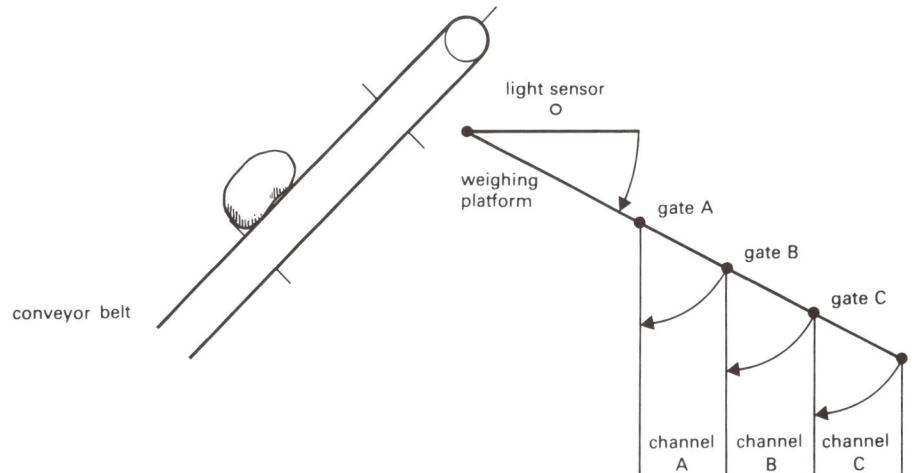

Figure 6.9 Potato weighing machine

Questions

1 Write a program for the drilling machine in the example, to drill a set of holes as shown in Figure 6.10.

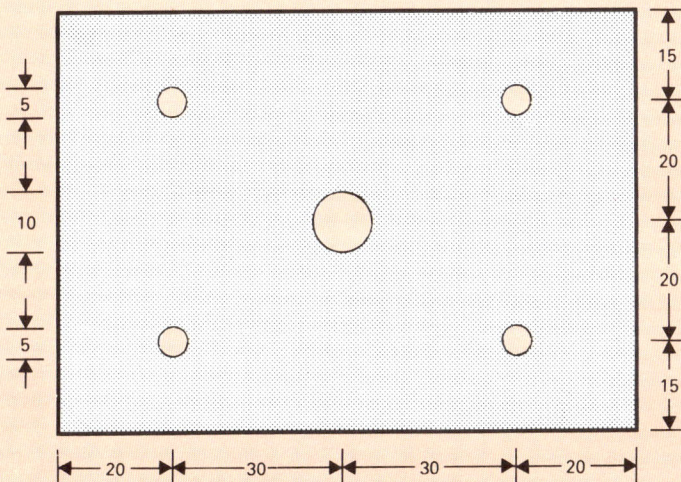

Figure 6.10

2 Draw the pattern of holes produced by the following program. It contains a loop which is repeated three times.

```
Right       10
Repeat      3
    Forward     20
    Drill       5
Right       10
Backward    30
Drill       10
Home
```

3 (a) Write a version of the example program for the potato weighing machine if the categories of weight are:

A   over 300 grams
B   between 100 and 300 grams
C   less than 100 grams.

(b) Modify the program so that there is an inlet gate which makes sure that only one potato at a time reaches the weighing platform. The gate is opened at the start of the cycle, and closed as soon as a potato is detected on the weighing platform.

4 A washing machine and a central heating system are examples of devices in the home which may be controlled by a program.
(a) Make a list of other devices in the home which can be programmed.
(b) What are the advantages of being able to program the control of devices in the home?
(c) Make a list of some items of equipment found in factories which can be programmed.
(d) What are the advantages of being able to program factory equipment?

6D Analogue and Digital Signals

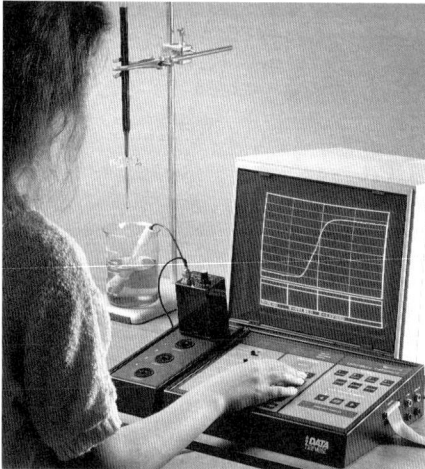

An analogue-to-digital converter in use with an acidity (pH) meter.

The sensors in the control systems described in sections 6A and 6B can do only one of two things: either send a signal or not send a signal. More sophisticated sensors (such as the weight sensor in section 6C) measure quantities more accurately. For example, instead of signalling whether a temperature is above or below a preset level, they send a signal which gives an indication of what the temperature is.

The signals sent by sensors of this sort are almost always electrical voltages. They are proportional to the quantity being measured: the higher the temperature, the higher the voltage. They are **analogue** devices. Sensors of this sort have many more uses than those which can only send on/off signals.

As explained in section 3A, computers are **digital** devices. They handle data in bits, which represent numbers in binary code. They cannot cope with data in analogue form.

In order to connect an analogue sensor to a digital computer or microprocessor, an **analogue-to-digital converter (ADC)** is used. This is a box with connections on one side for the analogue signal from the sensor and connections on the other side to the digital computer. The ADC **samples** the analogue signal at regular intervals, changes the voltage to a binary number, and sends the bits to the computer. See Figure 6.11. Some ADCs can take a number of analogue inputs. The computer selects the one to sample at any time. In some control systems, the control outputs must be changed from a digital signal to an analogue signal for the device being controlled. A digital-to-analogue converter (or an ADC which can work in both directions) is used.

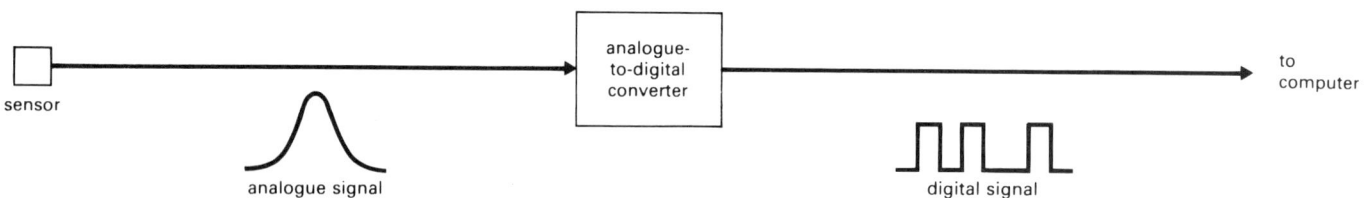

Figure 6.11   Analogue-to-digital converter

Questions

1   A mercury thermometer is an example of a sensor which produces a signal that is proportional to the quantity which is being measured. Make a list of other analogue sensors of this sort which are found:
   (a) in the home
   (b) in motor cars, ships and aircraft
   (c) in factories and offices
   (d) in hospitals.

2   An automatic weather station has sensors which measure temperature, air pressure, humidity and wind speed. These are sampled in turn, one at a time, by a microcomputer, and the data from them is stored on disk. Draw a diagram showing how the probes are connected to the computer.

3   A number of automatic noise monitoring stations are set up around a busy airport. These are connected to a computer at the airport via telephone lines. Draw a diagram showing all the interfacing devices between the monitoring equipment and the computer.

4   Copy and extend the table below. Where possible write down pairs of similar devices, one analogue and one digital. Otherwise, classify as many devices as you can think of as analogue or digital.

Analogue Devices	Digital Devices
traditional watch	digital watch
slide rule	calculator

6E* Feedback

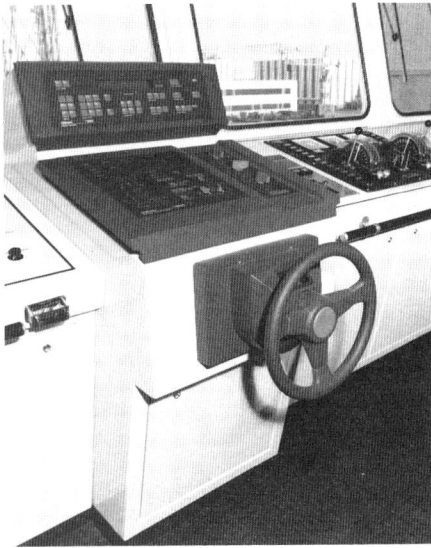

The automatic pilot on a ship. Once a course has been set, the ship is steered on this course without anyone at the helm.

The operation of the automatic pilot on a ship may be described by the following algorithm:

Repeat indefinitely

Sense the direction of the ship

If the ship is off course

then Send a control signal to the rudder

Change the direction of the ship

The action of the control system—changing the direction of the ship—is measured by the sensors of the control system. It is an example of **feedback**. Feedback occurs whenever the output of a control system affects the inputs of the system. Most control systems which aim to keep something at a steady level or travelling in a fixed direction make use of feedback.

Feedback always involves a reversal of the direction of control—**negative feedback**. For example, if the ship is veering to port (left), it is turned to starboard (right). If a refrigerator is too warm, it is cooled down.

One of the limitations of most of the factory robots in use at present is that they have no feedback mechanisms. In other words, they cannot sense whether what they are doing is right. For example, a robot makes welds along the edges of two sheets of metal on a car body. It is programmed to make a sequence of welds at precise positions along the edges of the metal sheets. However, if the car body is not quite in the right position the robot makes the welds in the wrong places, but it has no way of sensing this. A new generation of robots is at present under development with sensors, including video cameras, to overcome these problems.

Questions

1 (a) Make a list of all the control systems mentioned in this chapter which make use of feedback. In each case, state how the system reverses the control.
(b) Make a list of other control systems you know of which make use of feedback.

2* A number of the control systems in the human body are based on feedback. Find out what some of the simpler ones are. Describe them in terms of sensing, deciding and acting, and explain how the feedback works.

3 If the speaker of a public address system is placed so that the sound can be detected by the microphone, then a sound can build up all by itself. Explain what is happening in terms of the idea of feedback.

6F End-of-Chapter Summary

The main points of this chapter are as follows:

- Control systems are based on the cycle:

$$\text{sense} \rightarrow \text{decide} \rightarrow \text{act}$$

- Automatic control systems can use hard-wired control or programmed control. Programmed control systems are more flexible than hard-wired control systems.

- A control program is a set of instructions to control the operation of a device. The instructions are carried out in sequence.
- A robot is a device which can perform a range of physical tasks under programmed control.
- Logic circuits can be used in hard-wired control systems.
- Most sensors send signals as voltages which are proportional to the quantity being measured. These analogue signals are converted to digital signals for the computer to process by an analogue-to-digital converter (ADC).
- Feedback is when the output of a control system affects its inputs.

Exercise 6

1 Choose the correct word from the list in each of the following spaces:

quantities; analogue-to-digital; signal; valves; program; analogue; sensors; outputs.

The control system for a chemical reaction includes three ____ attached to the tank. They measure the temperature, pressure and volume of liquid in the tank. The volume sensor sends a ____ if the level exceeds the maximum level. The other two are ____ sensors: they send signals which are proportional to the ____ they are measuring. They are connected via an ____ converter to the control computer. This runs a control ____ for the reaction. The control ____ are to the heating element in the tank, and the ____ which control the flow of liquids into and out of the tank.

2 A canal lock is shown in Figure 6.12. It has two gates which can be opened only if the water level on each side of them is the same. It has two valves which control the flow of water into and out of the lock, as shown. It has two level sensors: one sends a signal when the lock is at the upper level and the other sends a signal when the lock is at the lower level. It also has a button which the lock-keeper pushes when a boat has entered or left the lock.

Write a control program for the lock. It starts with the water at the upper level, and the upper gate and valve open. The lower gate and valve are closed. It allows a ship to pass through it in the downward direction, and then one in the upward direction. It ends in its original state.

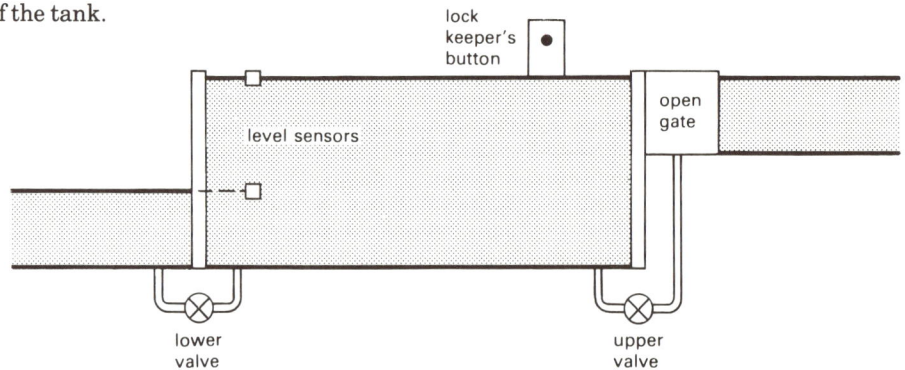

Figure 6.12 Canal lock

Things to find out

1 Some railway crossings are operated by hard-wired control: the train passes a sensor which switches on the warning lights and then closes the barriers. However, there have been some accidents at crossings of this sort.

(a) Find out what alternative methods of control are used, and the reasons for their use.
(b) Discuss the advantages and disadvantages of hard-wired control for railway crossings.

Points to discuss

1 Automatic drilling machines of the type described in section 6C replaced manual machines where the holes had to be positioned by eye and the drill bits inserted by hand. The automatic machines have a feeder which takes the next sheet of metal from a pile and, after it has been drilled, places it on another pile.

The manual machines each required a trained operator. The automatic machines require one minder for a whole group of machines. The minder wheels the piles of plates in and out, and changes the control tapes when required.

(a) Discuss the advantages of the automatic machines from the point of view of productivity.
(b) Discuss the consequences of having automatic machines for employment at the factories where they are installed.
(c) Is the standard of work produced by the automatic machines likely to be better or worse than that produced by the manual machines? Give your reasons for your opinion.

7 Computer Software

The hardware of a computer, as described in chapter 3, enables it to input, output and process information, and to transfer it to and from backing store. In order to do useful work with these capabilities, **software** is required. Software is sets of instructions which the computer carries out automatically to enable it to do specific tasks. Software transforms the general-purpose hardware of the computer into a device which is dedicated to a particular task. Each task has its own software: the **program** for the task.

7A What is a Program?

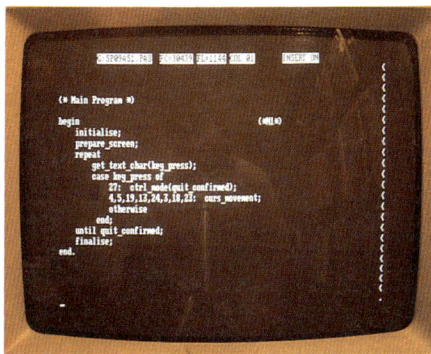

A module of a computer program on a display screen.

As discussed in section 3A, a program is a set of instructions which control the operation of a computer. The program is stored in the memory of the computer while it is being run. The computer works its way through the instructions one at a time. Computers can process millions of instructions in one second.

Most programs are long: they contain tens of thousands of instructions. The instructions are grouped in **modules**, each of which carries out a specific task. For example, a program may have a module which asks the user for the date, and another to check that the reply is a valid date. A program has hundreds of such modules. The modules of a program are put together in a precise structure. The module which controls the overall running of the program is at the top of the structure. Modules which carry out detailed operations are at the bottom. See Figure 7.1 for an example of modular program structure.

Figure 7.1   Modular program structure

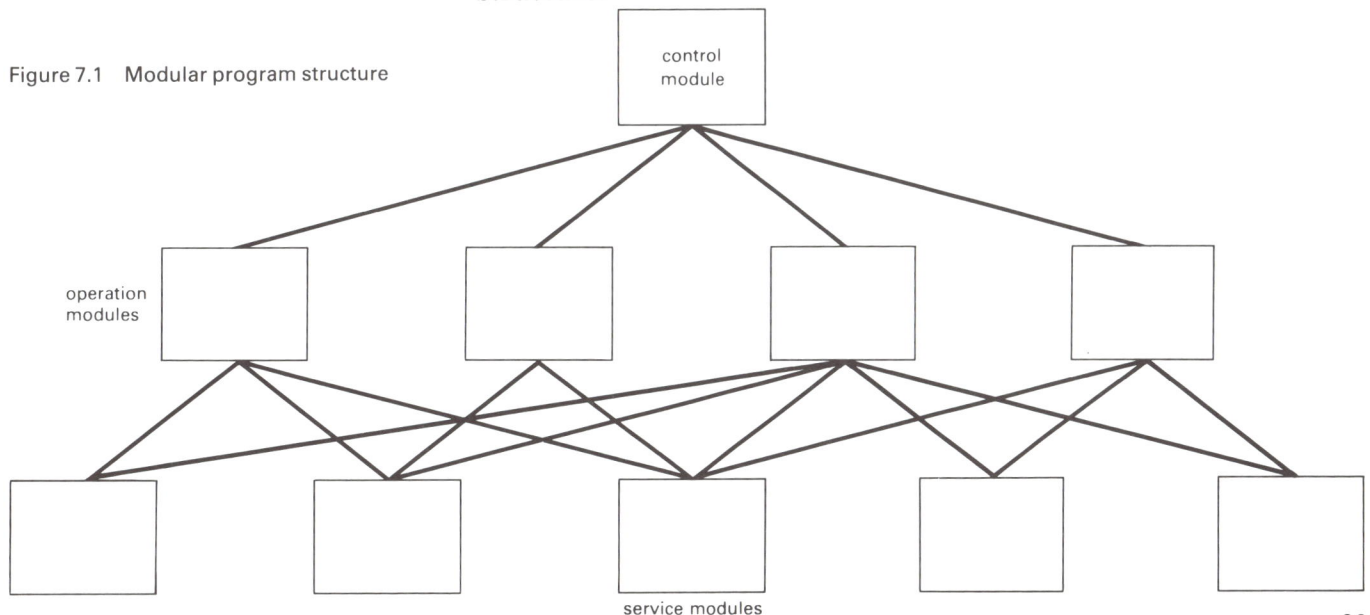

control module

operation modules

service modules

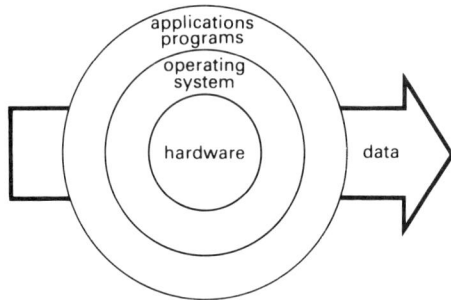

Figure 7.2 Layers of software

A computer requires several programs to make it do useful work. These may be imagined as **layers** of software on top of the hardware of the computer. See Figure 7.2. The lowest layer is the **operating system**. This program runs all the time that the computer is switched on. It deals with the operations which are common to all the work done by the computer. For example, the operating system transfers blocks of data to and from magnetic disk or tape. It gets characters from the keyboard, and deals with the details of putting data onto the screen. See chapter 8.

Supported by the operating system are the **applications programs**. An applications program does a particular type of work, such as word processing. Most microcomputers can only run one applications program at a time; minicomputers and mainframes can be running several at any time.

Computer programs can be in a number of programming **languages**. Some programming languages refer directly to the hardware of the computer. These **low-level languages** (sections 7B and 7C) are difficult for people to understand. Other languages refer directly to the task the computer is doing. Programs in these **high-level languages** (section 7E) are easier to write and to understand. It is not necessary to be able to program a computer in order to be able to use one.

Questions

1 What is the difference between an operating system and an applications program?
2 (a) How are most computer programs constructed?
(b) Why is it important for programs to be properly structured?
3 What does the module at the top of a program structure do?
4 State whether each of the following tasks would be done by an operating system or an applications program:
(a) Transferring a block of data from memory to a magnetic tape.
(b) Calculating the amount of income tax to pay on a wage.
(c) Getting a character from the computer keyboard.
(d) Sorting the data in a file.
(e) Checking whether a number typed by a user is valid.

7B Machine Code

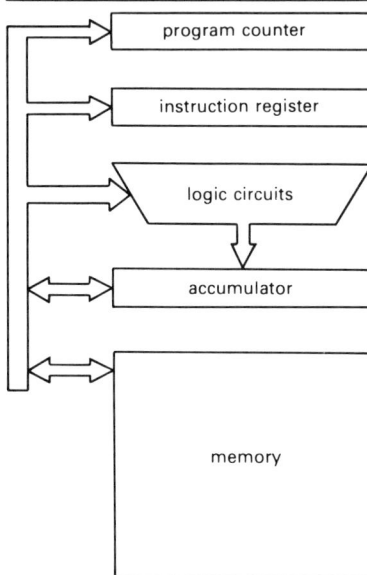

Figure 7.3 Registers in a computer processor

The hardware of a computer consists of memory cells, registers which store data during processing, and logic circuits to carry out the processing. The instructions which a computer carries out are in terms of these hardware items. These **machine instructions** refer directly to the computer hardware. They are in **machine language**, or **machine code**. Each type of computer has its own machine code to match its own hardware.

Section 3E discusses the most important registers in a computer processor and how they are connected to the memory. For convenience, Figure 7.3 shows a copy of Figure 3.3. (This diagram leaves out most of the details: actual processors are much more complicated than Figure 7.3.) The registers shown are:

- The **program counter**, which holds the address of the current machine instruction.
- The **instruction register**, which holds a copy of the machine instruction which the computer is carrying out at the time.
- The **accumulator** which holds the data item which is being processed at the time. It also stores the results of operations performed by the logic circuits.

Data items (and machine instructions) are stored in memory cells ready for use by the processor. Each cell in memory is identified by an **address**, as discussed in section 3D.

Machine instructions, items of data and addresses are all stored and processed in binary codes (chapter 2). For simplicity, all the data items, instructions and memory addresses in this chapter have eight bits (one byte). In practice, most computers use 16, 32 or 64 bits for data, instructions and addresses.

A machine instruction consists of two parts. The **operation code** states the type of operation, and the **memory address** identifies the memory cell from which the data item is obtained. For example:

	Operation Code	Memory Address
binary:	0 0 0 1 0 0 1 1	0 0 0 0 0 1 0 1
meaning:	Add to Accumulator.	Number at address 5.

This instruction adds the number in memory cell 5 to the number in the Accumulator, and places the result in the Accumulator.

A few common machine instructions are given in the table below. To avoid having to write them out in binary, they are written as **base sixteen** (**hexadecimal**) numbers. Conversion between binary and hexadecimal numbers is shown in Figure 7.4.

Decimal	Binary	Hexadecimal
1	1	1
2	10	2
3	11	3
4	100	4
5	101	5
6	110	6
7	111	7
8	1000	8
9	1001	9
10	1010	A
11	1011	B
12	1100	C
13	1101	D
14	1110	E
15	1111	F
16	10000	10

Figure 7.4   Decimal, binary and hexadecimal numbers

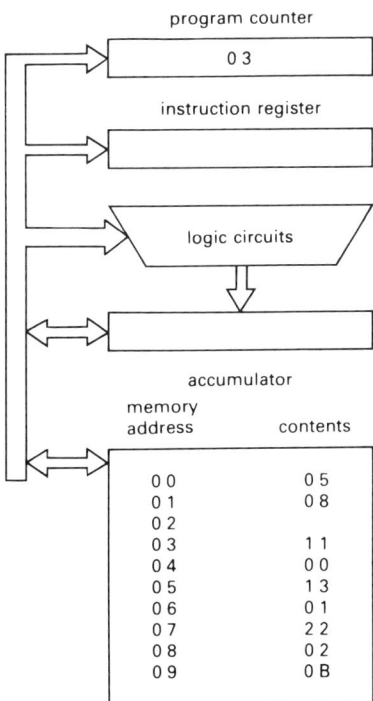

Figure 7.5   Processor registers at the start of example program

Operation Code (Hexadecimal)	Interpretation
11	Load data item from memory to Accumulator.
12	Store Accumulator contents in memory.
13	Add data item in memory to Accumulator.
31	NOT accumulator.
33	Increase Accumulator by 1.
52	Input data item to Accumulator.
54	Output contents of Accumulator.
0B	Halt.

Example program

The machine code program below adds two numbers from memory and stores the result in memory. The data is stored in cells at addresses 00, 01 and 02; the program starts at address 03. Note that most machine instructions occupy two bytes of memory.

71

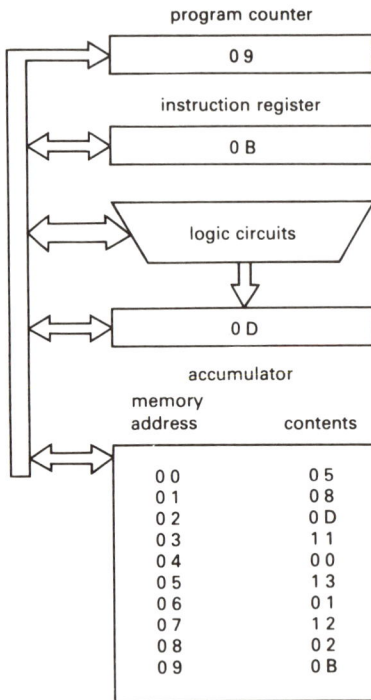

program counter
09

instruction register
0 B

logic circuits

0 D

accumulator

memory address	contents
0 0	0 5
0 1	0 8
0 2	0 D
0 3	1 1
0 4	0 0
0 5	1 3
0 6	0 1
0 7	1 2
0 8	0 2
0 9	0 B

Figure 7.6   Processor registers at the end of example program

Address	Machine Instruction		Interpretation
00	05		First number.
01	08		Second number.
02			Result.
03	11	00	Load the number at address 0 to Accumulator.
05	13	01	Add the number at address 1 to the number in the Accumulator.
07	12	02	Store the result at address 2.
09	0B		Halt.

The computer at the start of the program is shown in Figure 7.5. Following the steps of the program (known as a **dry run**), the contents of the registers and memory cells are as follows:

Program Counter	Instr. Register		Accumulator	Memory Cell 0	Cell 1	Cell 2	
03	11	00	05	05	08	00	Load number at address 0.
05	13	01	0D	05	08	00	Add number at address 1.
07	12	02	0D	05	08	0D	Store result at address 2.
09	0B		0D	05	08	0D	Halt.

The computer at the end of the program is shown in Figure 7.6.

Questions

1 What are the main characteristics of machine code?
2 Why are programs hardly ever written directly in machine code?
3 (a) Write down the interpretation of each instruction in the following machine language program:

Address	Machine Instruction	
00		Data
01		Data
02	52	
03	12	00
05	33	
06	12	01
08	54	
09	0B	

(b) Dry run the program, using suitable input data.
4 Write a program in machine code to add up three numbers. The numbers are already in cells 00, 01 and 02, and the sum is to go in cell 03. The program starts in cell 04. Dry run your program with suitable data.
5 A memory cell contains the binary equivalent of the hexadecimal number 12. Suggest *three* possible interpretations for this number. Comment on the consequences of these different interpretations.

7C Assembly Language

For a computer to be able to run a program, it must be in machine language. However, machine language is not a convenient language in which to write programs. A machine code program is just a set of numbers. It is difficult to understand, and even more difficult to correct if there is something wrong.

A type of programming language which is easier to use than machine language, but still refers directly to the hardware of a computer, is **assembly language**. There are four main differences between machine language and assembly language:

- In an assembly language, the numeric operation code of each machine instruction is replaced by a simple word, such as ADD, NOT, etc. These **mnemonic operation codes** are easier to recognise and remember than hexadecimal numbers.
- Addresses are also short words—**symbolic addresses**—chosen by the programmer. These symbolic addresses are also used as **labels** at the locations to which they refer.
- Numbers in an assembly language program may be in base ten, rather than in base sixteen as for machine code. Non-numeric data is represented as characters.
- There are a few additional instructions, known as **directives**, which have no equivalent in machine language.

Assembly languages and machine languages are closely related to the hardware of the computer which runs them. For this reason, they are known as **low-level languages**. Programs in assembly language are changed into machine language by **assemblers**, discussed in section 7D.

The assembly language versions of the machine instructions introduced in section 7B are as follows:

Mnemonic Operation Code	Interpretation
LOA	Load data item from memory to Accumulator.
STO	Store Accumulator contents in memory.
ADD	Add data item in memory to Accumulator.
NOT	NOT accumulator.
INC	Increase Accumulator by 1.
INP	Input data item to Accumulator.
OUP	Output contents of Accumulator.
HLT	Halt.

Two directives are sufficient to introduce the idea:

DTA	Reserve a byte of memory for a data item.
END	End of program.

Example program

The program below subtracts two numbers taken from the computer memory, and returns the result to memory. It uses the method of complementing and addition, described in section 2D.

Assembly Language Instruction			Interpretation
NM1	DTA	13	Reserve a byte for a data item with the label NM1. The value of the data item is 13.
NM2	DTA	9	Reserve a byte with label NM2 for a data item, value 9.
NM3	DTA		Reserve a byte of memory for the result.
	LOA	NM2	Load the number at address NM2 to Accumulator.

NOT		Apply the NOT operation to the binary code of the number in the Accumulator.			
INC		Add 1 to the number in the Accumulator. This produces the twos complement negative of the original number.			
ADD	NM1	Add the number at address NM1 to the number in the Accumulator.			
STO	NM3	Store the result at address NM3.			
HLT		Halt.			
END		End of program.			

A dry run of this program is as follows:

Instruction		Accumulator	Memory Cell NM1	Cell NM2	Cell NM3	
LOA	NM2	9	13	9		Load the number at address NM2 to Accumulator.
NOT		−10	13	9		Apply the NOT operation to the number in the Accumulator.
INC		−9	13	9		Add 1 to the number in the Accumulator.
ADD	NM1	4	13	9		Add the number at address NM1 to the number in the Accumulator.
STO	NM3	4	13	9	4	Store the result at address NM3.
HLT		4	13	9	4	Halt.

This is a very roundabout way of subtracting two numbers! It illustrates the strengths and weaknesses of assembly languages: each instruction is fairly easy to follow, but a program as a whole can be long and complicated, even for a simple operation.

7D Assemblers

An **assembler** is a program which converts from assembly language to machine code. It works through each assembly language instruction, and replaces it by its equivalent machine instruction. Data items are converted from decimal numbers to binary, or from character form to their ASCII codes. Addresses are converted from the symbolic form used in assembly language to the numbers required for machine language. Directives are carried out immediately.

For example, the result of assembling the example program from section 7C is as follows:

Address	Machine Code	Assembly Language Instruction			Interpretation
00	0D	NM1	DTA	13	Reserve a byte for a data item with the label NM1. The value of the data item is 13.
01	09	NM2	DTA	9	Reserve a byte with label NM2 for a data item, value 9.

Address	Machine Code	Assembly Language Instruction		Interpretation
02		NM3	DTA	Reserve a byte of memory for the result.
03	11 01	LOA	NM2	Load the number at address NM2 to Accumulator.
05	31	NOT		Apply the NOT operation to the binary code of the number in the Accumulator.
06	33	INC		Add 1 to the number in the Accumulator. This produces the twos complement negative of the original number.
07	13 00	ADD	NM1	Add the number at address NM1 to the number in the Accumulator.
09	12 02	STO	NM3	Store the result at address NM3.
0B	0B	HLT		Halt.
		END		End of program.

If the assembly language program contains errors, the assembler identifies them and gives **error messages** which indicate the type of error. These **diagnostic error messages** help the programmer to correct the errors. See section 7H for more details.

Questions

These questions cover sections 7C and 7D.

1 What are the advantages of writing programs in assembly language instead of machine language?

2 In what ways are assembly languages similar to machine languages?

3 (a) Write down the interpretation of each instruction in the following assembly language program:

```
X   DTA
Y   DTA
    INP
    STO  X
    INP
    STO  Y
    LOA  X
    ADD  Y
    OUP
    HLT
    END
```

(b) Dry run the program, using suitable input data.

4 Write a program in assembly language which inputs three numbers, adds them up and outputs the total. Dry run the program using suitable input data.

5 Write an assembly language program which inputs a number and outputs the corresponding negative number. For example, if the input is 5, the output is −5. Dry run the program using a suitable input number.

6 What *five* tasks does an assembler do?

7 Make a copy of the program from question 4. Next to each assembly language instruction, write the corresponding machine instruction. Assume that the first data item is in cell 0.

7E High-level Language

To make it possible for large numbers of people to write computer programs, programming languages have been developed which are suited to the task rather than to the hardware of the computer. These **high-level languages** have two main features:

- A high-level language is a natural way of setting out the steps required to perform a particular task.
- A high-level language is independent of the computer on which it runs. A program written in a high-level language can, with only minor modifications, run on a number of different types of computer.

Most high-level languages include short English words and use ordinary arithmetic for calculations. Programs in high-level languages are changed into machine code by **compilers**, discussed in the next section.

High-level languages were first used in 1957 and are the most popular type of programming language in use at present. There are hundreds of different high-level languages. Some are for particular types of task, for example commercial programs; others are general-purpose. A few of the commonest ones are as follows:

Fortran is the oldest high-level language. It is used for scientific and engineering programs.

Cobol is a commercial programming language. It is used for business programs of all kinds. It is one of the most widely used programming languages.

Pascal is a popular programming language at universities. It is a general-purpose programming language, also used in commerce and industry.

Logo is a programming language used in schools for a variety of purposes, including teaching about graphics. Logo controls a 'turtle' which moves on the computer screen under the control of a program.

Basic is an introductory programming language also taught in schools. It is a general-purpose language.

Prolog is a programming language for solving logical problems. It is taught in some schools, and also used in research into Fifth Generation computers (chapter 22).

Example program

A program in Basic which subtracts two numbers is shown below. The numbers are input at the keyboard and the result is displayed on the computer screen. Note that each line starts with a line number, followed by an instruction word.

```
10   INPUT A, B
20   LET    C = B – A
30   PRINT  C
40   END
```

Line 20 of this program is equivalent to the entire example program in assembly language (section 7C)! The program in high-level language is shorter and much easier to follow than the equivalent program in a low-level language. A dry run of the program is as follows:

			A	B	C
10	INPUT	A, B	9	13	
20	LET	C = B – A	9	13	4
30	PRINT	C	9	13	4
40	END				

7F Compilers and Interpreters

High-level languages are suited to the task being done on the computer, and are independent of the hardware of the computer. A machine language refers directly to the hardware of the computer on which it runs. This makes translation from a high-level language to a machine language difficult. There are two methods of doing this translation: **compilation** and **interpretation**.

A **compiler** is a program which takes a program in a high-level language and produces an equivalent program in machine language. The translation process is complicated and can take a long time. A number of stages are required. A large program is usually compiled as a number of separate modules. These are then linked together to give the complete machine code program. See Figure 7.7.

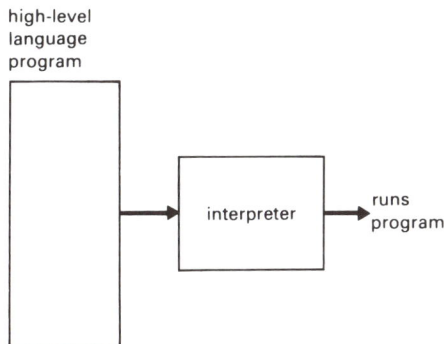

Figure 7.7 Compiling and linking program modules

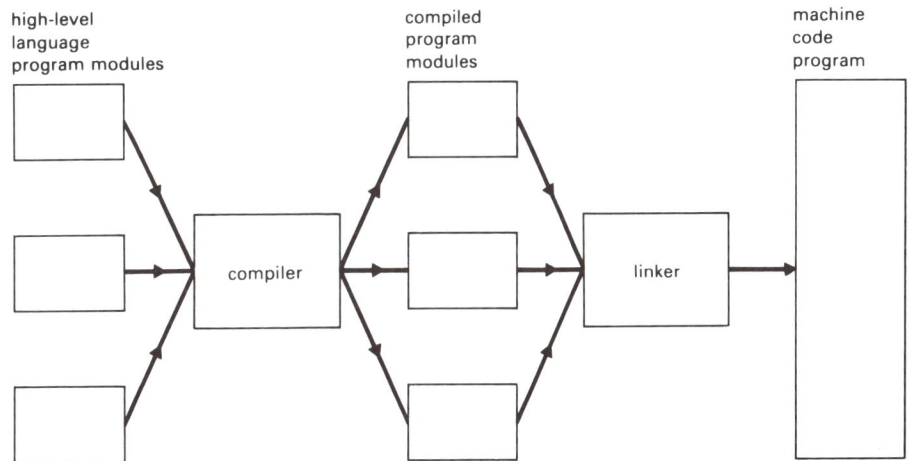

Figure 7.8 Interpreting a program

An **interpreter** scans the code of a high-level language program and carries out each instruction directly. A machine code version of the program is not produced. This process is simpler than compilation and is popular on introductory languages like Basic and Logo. See Figure 7.8.

77

Compiling a program is a slow process. However, the resulting machine code program can be run as often as required. Most compilers produce machine code which runs quickly and makes good use of the hardware of the computer. If an interpreter is used, it is needed every time the program is run. A program run by an interpreter is generally much slower than the equivalent machine code produced by a compiler. An interpreter has to share the computer memory with the program it is running, thus reducing the size of the programs which can be run. An interpreter cannot cope with a program written in separate modules.

Interpreters are useful while a program is being developed. They enable a version of a program to be run immediately, without waiting for compilation. They are used on small microcomputers, such as those found in schools. These computers are often too small to be able to run compilers. Interpreters are seldom used for commercial or industrial software.

Compilers and interpreters deal with errors in programs. See section 7H for details.

Example program

The result of compiling the example program from section 7E is shown below. To make it easier to read, it is shown in assembly language rather than machine language. Each assembly language instruction corresponds to a machine language instruction.

Basic		**Assembly Language**	
		A	DTA
		B	DTA
		C	DTA
10	INPUT A, B	INP	
		STO	A
		INP	
		STO	B
20	LET C = B − A	LOA	B
		NOT	
		INC	
		ADD	A
		STO	C
30	PRINT C	LOA	C
		OUP	
40	END	HLT	
		END	

Questions

1 (a) What are the advantages of compilers over interpreters?
(b) What are the advantages of interpreters over compilers?
(c) If both a compiler and an interpreter are available during the development of a program, explain how they can both be used.
2 Write down the assembly language program equivalent to the following Basic program:

```
10  INPUT   A, B, C
20  LET     T = A + B + C
30  PRINT   T
40  END
```

3 Look at the assembly language version of the example program in section 7F. There are at least two instructions which are not essential.
(a) Rewrite the assembly language version of the program using only the essential instructions.
(b) Repeat this process using the assembly language program from question 2 above.
(c) Removing instructions which are not essential in the code produced by a compiler is one aspect of **optimisation**. By examining the results from parts (a) and (b), state *two* advantages which optimised code has over code which is not optimised.

4   A program is written as a number of separate modules, as described in section 7A. Can an interpreter be used on each module separately? How does this limit the usefulness of interpreters?

5   Why are compilers long and complex programs? What are the consequences of this?

7G Utility Programs and Library Modules

On most computer systems, there are often a number of 'odd jobs' which have to be done. These include backing up disks, preparing new disks to be used (**formatting** the disks), sorting the records in a file, etc. These tasks are done by **utility programs**. Sets of utility programs are supplied with the operating system of the computer (chapter 8) for use whenever they are required.

In some cases, 'odd jobs' of this nature need to be included in applications programs. For example, a program may need to sort a file before combining it with another file. Rather than stop the program and run a separate utility program to do the job, a **library module** for the sort routine is linked into the application program. This is done as part of the compilation process—see Figure 7.9. A set of library routines is often supplied with the compiler for a particular programming language. As applications programs are written, modules for common tasks are included from the library and new ones added to it. In this way, the code for common tasks does not have to be duplicated. However, library routines can only be used if a program is written with a clear overall structure: see section 7A.

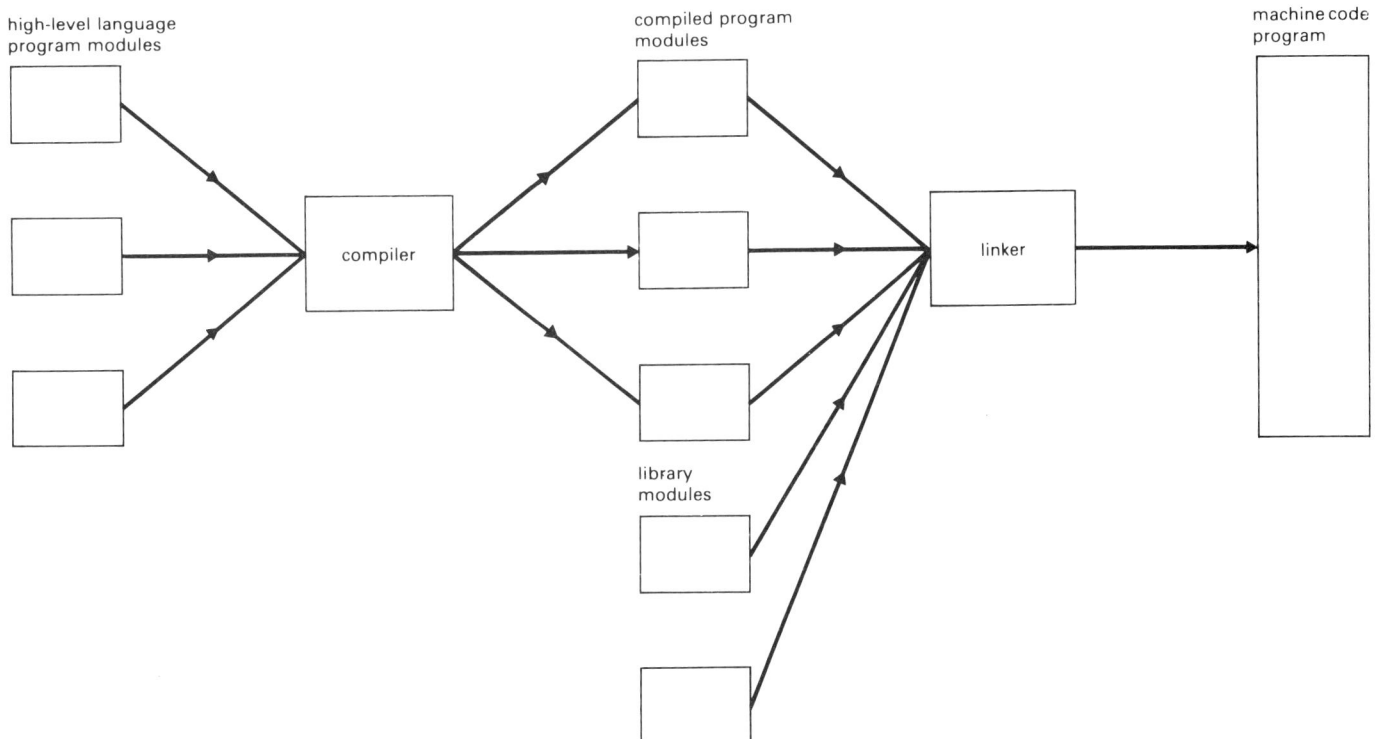

Figure 7.9   Linking library modules

79

Locating and correcting errors in a program is one of the most time-consuming parts of developing a computer application. Once a new program has been taken into use, further errors occasionally come to light. Corrections to these errors are included in revised versions of the software.

Broadly speaking, there are three types of program error; syntax errors, run-time errors and specification errors.

Syntax errors

Syntax errors are mistakes in the program language. They are detected by the assembler, compiler or interpreter, which is unable to translate the program into machine code. The language translator gives a **diagnostic error message** which indicates where the error is and the nature of the error. An example of a syntax error in the Basic program from section 7E, and the corresponding diagnostic error message, is as follows:

```
10   IMPUT A, B
```

Syntax Error: Mistake in instruction word

Because errors of this sort are detected by compilers, they are also known as **compilation errors**.

Run-time errors

Run-time errors cause a program to halt while it is running. The commonest causes are an attempt to divide by zero, or when a program tries to use a data item which has had no value given to it. A version of the example program from section 7E with an error of this sort is as follows:

```
10   INPUT  A, B
20   LET    C = B − D
30   PRINT  C
40   END
```

The run-time error message produced by this program would look something like this:

Execution Error: Line 20—Undefined variable D

Specification errors

Specification errors (or **logical errors**) are mistakes which give rise to wrong results when the program is running. They arise from a misunderstanding of what the program is intended to do. If the example program from section 7E were written as follows, then an error of this sort would result:

```
10   INPUT  A, B
20   LET    C = A − B
30   PRINT  C
40   END
```

The intention of the program is to subtract the first number from the second. However, line 20 sets out the subtraction in the wrong order. There is no syntax error or run-time error in the program, but it will produce the wrong result. Specification errors are the most difficult types of error to detect and correct. They generally occur during the design of the program, before any code is written.

Questions

These questions cover sections 7G and 7H

1 A program is designed to do three tasks:

    input a set of data and store it in a file

    sort the file in order

    print a summary of the contents of the file.

On a particular computer, both a utility program and a library routine are available for sorting files.
(a) State, with reasons, which is preferred in this case.
(b) If the other were used, how would it affect the running of the program?

2 List and discuss the benefits of library routines in the development of software.

3 The Basic program below is intended to accept the price of an item and a VAT rate. It calculates the VAT on the item, and outputs the price, VAT and price plus VAT.

Variables:
P	price
R	VAT rate (at present 15%)
V	VAT
T	price plus VAT

```
10  INPUT  P, R
20  LOT    V = P*R / 100
30  LET    T = P − V
40  PRINT  "Price"; P, "VAT"; U, "Price
           plus VAT"; T
50  END
```

Note that the symbol * is used for multiplication and / is used for division.

The program contains one syntax error, one run-time error and one specification error. Identify and correct each of these.

4 What are diagnostic error messages, and why are they useful to a programmer?

5 Write a few short programs in Basic or another language which runs on your school computer. Type each program and run it to make sure that there are no errors. Then deliberately introduce a single error into each program. Run each program again, and write down the diagnostic error messages you get. Compare these messages with the error you introduced. Do the messages identify and describe each error correctly? Comment on the results.

7I Software Development Tools

The development of computer software is now more time-consuming and expensive than the design and manufacture of hardware. Programs are expensive to design and write, and expensive to maintain. If a program has been written badly in the first place, correcting errors and making minor improvements is slow and difficult. Programmers earn high wages, making work of this sort expensive.

High-level languages helped speed up the process of software development and made it possible for people with no knowledge of computer hardware to write programs. However, the process of developing software using a high-level language is still slow and error prone, and every step is carried out by hand. Furthermore, many programs, especially those for commercial applications, are very similar. There are now large numbers of highly-paid programmers spending their time developing and maintaining large numbers of programs which do the same sort of work.

During the 1980s, various **software development tools** have come into use for the development of certain types of computer programs, especially those for commercial applications. These tools take over much of the production of the code. They increase the productivity of programmers, and enable the people who are to use the software to have more say in its development.

Most software development tools are based on a **data dictionary**. This holds the designs of the data files used by the programs. It enables these files to be set up quickly and easily, and also to be modified easily. There are **screen design** modules which allow the display screens for the input and output of data to be designed easily. The processing of the data is specified by **program generators**. These enable the processing operations to be set out in a simple language. They make use of the data dictionary for the file structures, and the screen design modules for input and output. The overall structure of a set of software development tools is shown in Figure 7.10.

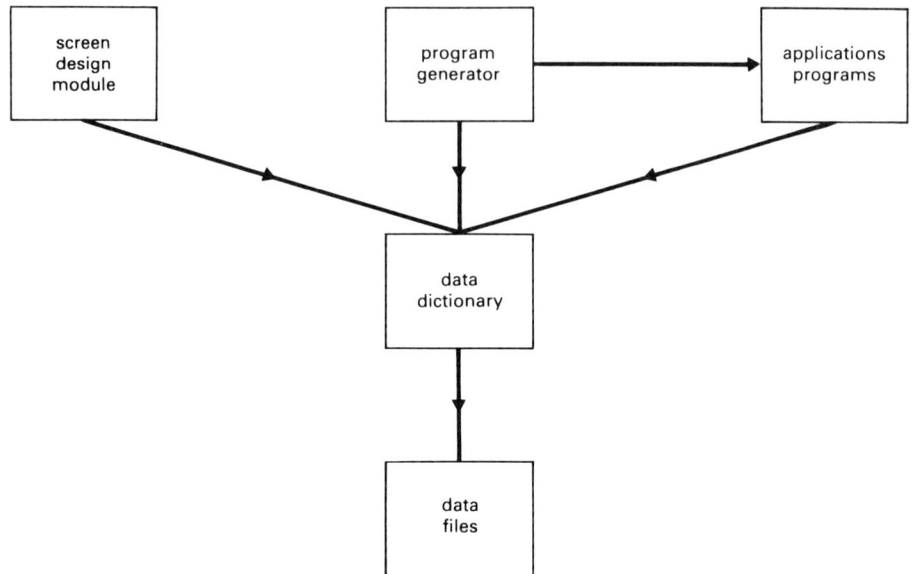

Figure 7.10   Software development tools

Software development tools, or **fourth generation languages (4GLs)** as they are sometimes called, have a number of advantages over high-level languages. They enable a **prototype** of a new piece of software to be put together quickly. This is a 'rough draft' of the software, but gives some idea of what the final version will look like. The prototype can be shown to the people who are to use the software. This reduces the chances of specification errors, and enables changes to be made before too much time has been spent on the software. Software development tools reduce the time and cost of software development, and make programs easier to maintain.

7J Software Packages

There are a number of computer applications which are common to a great many users. Word processing is the best example: it is the most popular use of computers. There are millions of word processing systems in use, all doing the same type of work. A word processing program is long and complex, and there is no point in each user

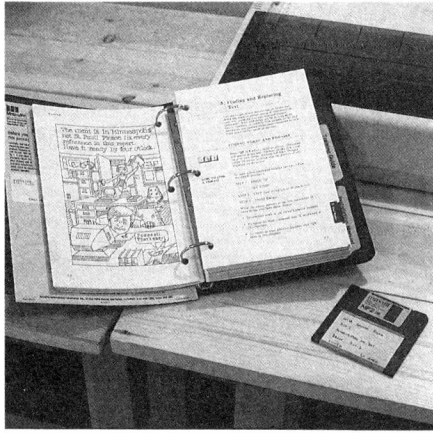

Wordstar word processing system manual and disk.

organisation developing its own word processing software. Instead, they purchase a software **package** from a software company.

Software packages are much cheaper to purchase than the cost of developing the software. They also have fewer errors than internally-developed software, as each version takes into account the experience of a large number of users of earlier versions. Most software packages have been carefully designed to be easy to use, particularly by people who are not computer experts. The disadvantage of software packages is that they may not suit the precise requirements of the organisations which use them.

Software packages are now available for a variety of applications. As well as word processing, there are software packages for spreadsheets, accounting systems, database systems, computer-aided design and a number of educational uses of computers. Most of the applications discussed in chapters 10 to 20 are based on software packages.

Software packages are particularly popular for microcomputers. Many small businesses now use a microcomputer for their administration. A set of software packages for word processing, accounting, payroll preparation and stock control, for example, allows all this work to be done at a reasonable cost with no computer experts in the company. The combination of a cheap, powerful microcomputer and a set of software packages has brought information technology within reach of many organisations which previously could not take advantage of it.

Questions

These questions cover sections 7I and 7J.

1 (a) What are the advantages of software development tools over high-level languages?
(b) For what types of application are software development tools used at present? Why are they suited to these applications?

2 A program is to be written to enable readers at a library to look up books on the library's catalogue. The catalogue is on a file on disk. Without going into detail, explain how a set of software development tools could be used to develop the program for this task.

3 Make a list of some types of computer application for which software packages are used, in addition to those mentioned in section 7J.

4 List and discuss some of the effects of the availability of cheap, powerful microcomputers and a wide range of software packages.

5 A small business needs software to do a certain task. The task is slightly different from the way it is done by most other companies. State the advantages and disadvantages of:
(a) using a software development system to develop the software,
(b) buying a software package for the required application.

7K End-of-Chapter Summary

The main points of this chapter are as follows:

- Software can be thought of as a series of layers between the hardware of a computer and the person using it.
- The lowest layer of software is the operating system. At higher levels are applications programs.
- A program is constructed as a set of modules. Each module performs a specific task, and has a specific relationship to the rest of the program.

- Machine code is the program language which controls the hardware of a computer directly. A machine instruction consists of an operation code and a memory address.
- An assembly language has one instruction for each machine instruction. Each instruction consists of a mnemonic operation code and a symbolic address.
- Machine and assembly languages are together known as low-level languages.
- An assembler translates a program from an assembly language into machine language.
- A high-level language is application oriented, and independent of the hardware of any particular computer.
- A compiler translates a program from a high-level language into machine language. An interpreter runs programs in a high-level language.
- Utility programs perform housekeeping tasks such as backing up disks. Library modules are program modules for common tasks such as sorting which are built into applications programs.
- There are three types of program error: syntax errors, run-time errors and specification errors. Compilers, interpreters and assemblers produce diagnostic error messages to identify syntax errors.
- Software development tools use data dictionaries, screen design facilities and program generators.
- A software package is a ready-to-run applications program for a common information processing task.
- Software development tools reduce the time and cost of software development. Software packages eliminate the need for software development altogether.

Exercise 7

1 Choose the correct word from the list for each of the following spaces:

machine; module; run-time; compiled; test; high level; specification; syntax; control.

A program to analyse the results of an experiment was written in a scientific ____ language. Each calculation was written as a separate ____. There was a ____ module at the top of the program structure. Each module was ____ separately. After the ____ errors had been detected and corrected, the modules were linked to form a single program in ____ code. The first few runs of this program stopped because of ____ errors. When these had been corrected, a simple set of ____ data was used to check the results of the calculations. Some of these were wrong because of ____errors. When these errors had been corrected, the program was put into use.

2 Which is the only type of program language that a computer can run directly?

3 A company has three different types of desktop microcomputers in use.

(a) What type of programming language must be used to develop software which will run on all three types of microcomputer?

(b)* After a program has been running for some time, it is decided to make a change to it. Without going into detail, describe the stages of making the change on all three versions. Describe some of the errors which might arise in the process.

4 Explain the difference between utility routines and library modules. Give an example of the use of each.

5 A certain type of camera includes a microprocessor which controls all aspects of its operation. The microprocessor is designed specially for use in the camera.

(a) What type of programming language would the software for the microprocessor be written in? Give reasons for your answer.

(b) Where would the software for the microprocessor be stored?

(c)* List and discuss some of the problems which might be encountered during the development of the software to control the camera.

8 Computers in Operation

A large mainframe computer installation in operation. In the foreground is an operator's console.

The hardware of a computer, even a small microcomputer, is complex. Transferring data to and from backing store, displaying data on the screen, accepting it from input devices and sending it to printers are especially complicated. Each peripheral device has its own way of working, and they all operate at different speeds.

On a large computer, the central processor is a valuable resource which needs to be kept fully occupied. The CPU should not waste time waiting for slower peripherals. Programs must be run according to their priorities, and the computer must be able to work on a number of programs at the same time. If errors occur, they must be limited to the program in which they arose, and the computer as a whole must carry on.

Problems of this nature—handling the transfer of data to and from peripherals, allocating work to the processor, and recovering from errors—are taken care of by the **operating system** of the computer. The operating system handles the detailed operation of the computer, and allows applications programs to be written simply.

8A What is an Operating System?

An operating system is a program which runs all the time a computer is switched on. It drives the 'raw' hardware of the computer, and provides a simple interface for applications programs. Most computers can only run one type of operating system, as there is a close connection between the operating system and the hardware of the computer. For this reason, operating systems are known as **systems software**, as they are an integral part of a computer system.

The operating system manages all the parts of a computer system:

- It schedules the running of programs on the central processing unit.
- It allocates memory to programs.
- It deals with the details of transferring data between the memory of the computer and peripheral devices.

Applications programs communicate with the operating system in two ways:

- If they require the operating system to perform a task such as reading data from disk, they **call** the module of the operating system which performs the task.
- If something happens 'outside' the running of the program, such as a character being typed at the keyboard or a program with a higher priority needing to be run, the running of the applications

85

A manual and disk for the Microsoft Windows operating system.

program is **interrupted** and the operating system takes over. After the interrupt has been dealt with, the applications program continues from where it left off.

Operating systems are large, complex programs and are extremely difficult to write. They must run as efficiently as possible because the time spent in 'housekeeping' tasks performed by the operating system is wasted computer time. Since at least part of an operating system is in memory all the time, an operating system should be as small as possible. It should be as free of errors as can possibly be managed, because an error in an operating system can cripple a computer.

8B Memory Management

Computers, with the exception of small microcomputers, are able to work on more than one program at a time. There is only one program actually running in the processor at any one time, but the processor switches between programs rapidly. This gives the impression that several programs are running at once.

At least part of each program which is at some stage of execution is held in memory. One of the tasks of the operating system is to partition the memory between programs and make quite sure that one program does not interfere with another, particularly if the program encounters a run-time error.

In most computers, the memory is too small to hold all the programs and data which are being worked on at the time. Many operating systems overcome this problem by creating a **virtual memory**. This is the memory of the computer as it appears to each program. The virtual memory is much bigger than the actual memory. Programs and data which are in the virtual memory but which cannot be fitted into the real memory are held on backing store. The portion of virtual memory which is required at any time is swapped into real memory automatically by the operating system. The idea of virtual memory is illustrated in Figure 8.1.

The benefit of virtual memory is that large programs can be written without the programmer needing to worry that they are too large for the computer memory. This is far more efficient than the alternative, which is for the programmer to break a program up into a number of **overlays**, each of which is small enough to fit into the computer memory. See Figure 8.2.

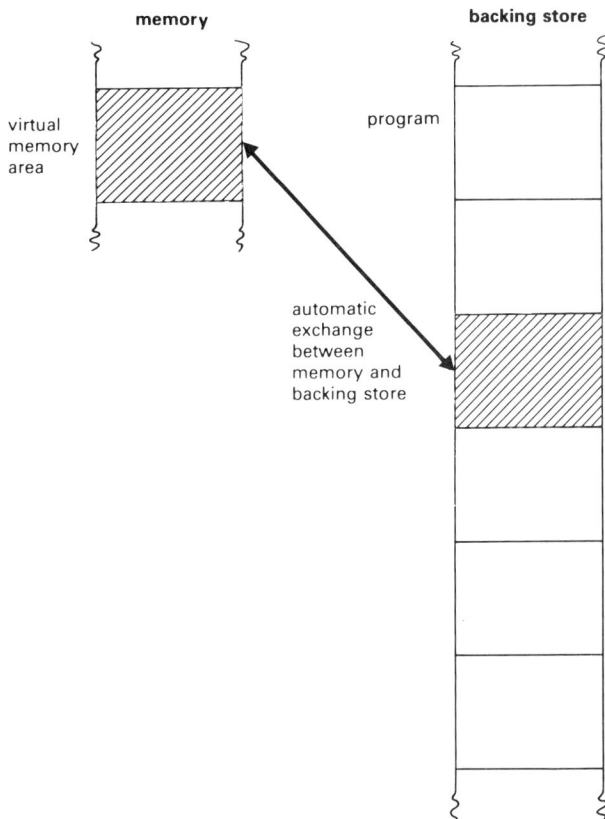

Figure 8.1   Virtual memory

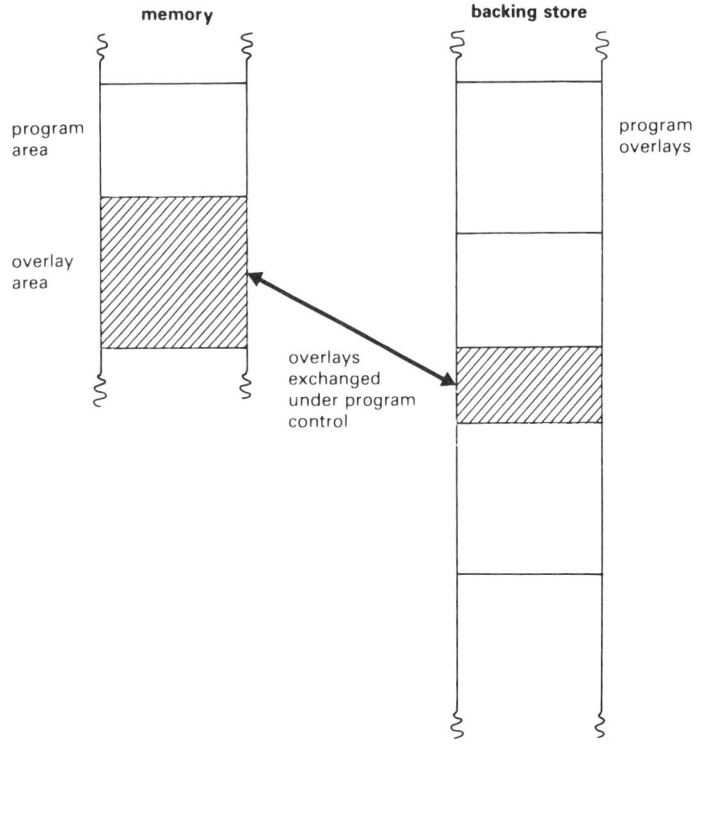

Figure 8.2   Program overlays

Questions

1   What are the *two* main tasks that an operating system does in order to manage the memory of a computer?

2   A particular computer has 24-bit addresses. Its main memory has a capacity of 4 megabytes.
(a) What is the size of the address space of the computer?
(b) How many times larger is this address space than the memory of the computer?
(c) Explain how the operating system runs programs which use more memory than the computer actually has.

3   A program works on an array of data containing 1024 items. This array is stored in memory after the code of the program. It is the last data item in the memory space used by the program. During the running of the program, an error occurs, and the loop counter accessing the array continues beyond 1024.
(a) What action should the operating system take when this happens?
(b) What type of program error is reported?
(c) Why is it essential for the operating system to stop the program immediately this error occurs?

8C   Input/Output Control

The control of input and output is one of the most important tasks of all operating systems, even those for small computers. Input/output devices work at different speeds and have different characteristics. The operating system makes all the peripherals of a computer system appear to an applications program to work in the same way.

For example, the keyboard of a computer works one character at a time. The process of getting a single character from the keyboard is

87

surprisingly complicated. Applications programs call the operating system to get a character from the keyboard; a module in the operating system does the rest. Alternatively, when a character is typed at the keyboard, an interrupt is generated.

Printers cause even bigger problems. They are slow, and can accept different numbers of characters at a time. Most have a **buffer** which the computer fills with characters. The printer works its way through the buffer, and asks for more characters when it has printed them all. It is a waste of time for the computer to have to wait while this is happening.

Most operating systems use **spooling** to overcome this problem. Data to be printed is first copied to backing store where it joins a queue of items waiting for the printer. See Figure 8.3. The printer works its way through each set of output from the spool on backing store. This requires only occasional use of the processor, to transfer a set of characters from the spool to the printer buffer.

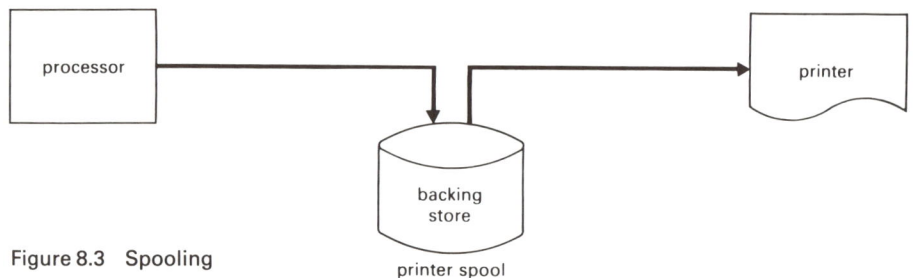

Figure 8.3   Spooling

Questions

1 (a) In what way does an operating system assist applications programs in the handling of input and output?
    (b) Why is this assistance necessary?
2 (a) For what purpose is the technique of spooling used?
    (b) What are the benefits of the use of spooling?
    (c) Why is it essential to have spooling on the central printer shared by all the workstations on a computer network?
3 A microcomputer uses a daisy wheel printer for hard copy output. The printer operates at a fairly slow speed, and has a small buffer to hold characters during printing. After some time, this printer is replaced by a laser printer. This works much more quickly, and has a large print buffer.
    (a) What changes need to be made to the operating system of the computer to enable it to use the new printer?
    (b) What changes need to be made to the applications programs running on the computer?

8D File Management

From a hardware point of view, magnetic tapes and disks are partitioned into blocks or sectors. Data is transferred to and from backing store as complete blocks or sectors. From an applications point of view, data on backing store is structured in **files**. Files are used for a variety of purposes. They have different structures and some are much larger than others. For example, each document on a word processing system is a file. A set of names and addresses of customers could also be a file.

The task of transforming from the structure of a file (as used by an applications program) to the structure of data on backing store, in blocks and sectors, is part of the **file management** facilities of an operating system. See Figure 8.4. Many operating systems treat all data being transferred to and from peripheral devices as if it were in files.

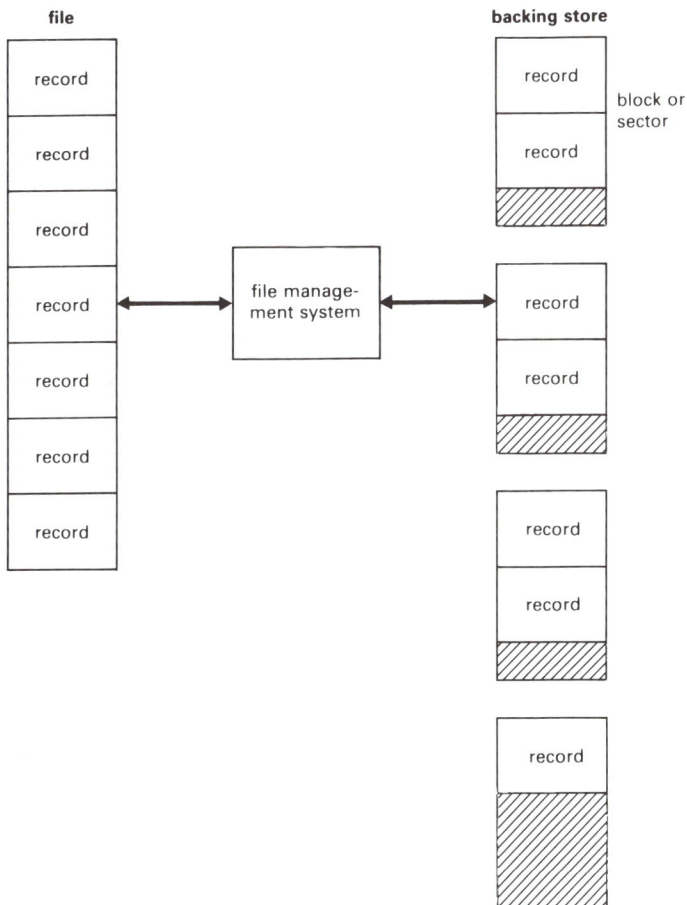

Figure 8.4   File management

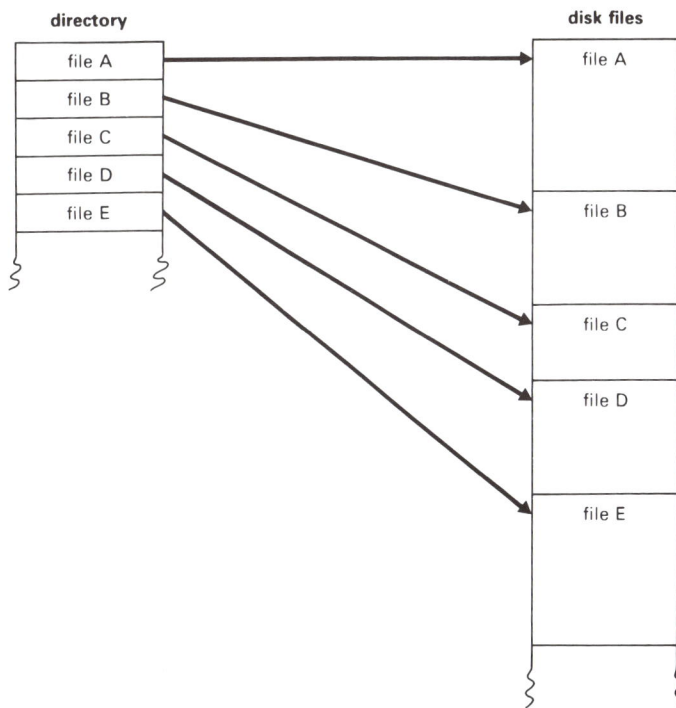

Figure 8.5   Disk directory

Operating systems have facilities to create files, read data from them, write data to them, make copies of them, and delete them. On each disk there is a **directory** of the files on the disk. See Figure 8.5. This allows users to see what files are on the disk, and also enables the operating system to find the file. The operating system keeps each directory up-to-date automatically as data is transferred to and from backing store.

Questions

1 (a) Write down all the steps which must be carried out by an operating system when it receives a call from an applications program to write a file to disk.
   (b) List some of the things which can go wrong during the process of writing the file to disk.

2 What are the advantages of transferring all data to and from peripheral devices as if it were in files?

3 At the end of a working day, a computer operator backs up all the disks which have been used during the day. A copy of each file on each disk is made on magnetic tape. This is done by a utility program which is part of the operating system.

   Describe the steps carried out by the operating system utility in backing up the files on a disk. (Assume that the size of a disk sector is the same as that of a block of data on magnetic tape.)

8E Program Scheduling

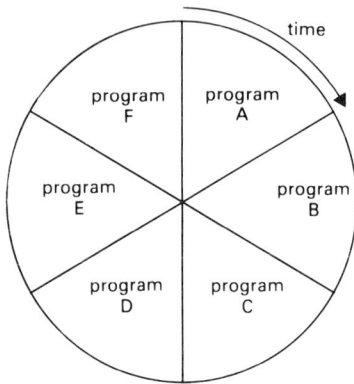

Figure 8.6 Time sharing

Most microcomputers can only run one program at a time. On larger computers the processor can be working on several programs at any time, a process known as **multitasking**. The work of the processor is scheduled so that all the programs are completed as quickly as possible. If programs have different priorities, then higher priority programs take precedence over lower priority ones.

A common method of sharing processor time between programs is **time slicing**. The operating system allocates short time intervals (less than a second) to each active program in turn. See Figure 8.6. If a program is not completed during its time slice, it waits its turn for another. If the program is being held up, for example waiting for a character from the keyboard, it misses its turn until it can proceed again. A large computer can run several programs under time slicing so quickly that each one appears to be running continuously.

Questions

1 A word processing program is based on the cycle:

Repeat

   Wait for a keystroke

   Process the keystroke

Even if the person using the word processing program is typing quickly, most of the computer's time is spent waiting for the keystroke. If a keystroke is not dealt with, it goes into the keyboard buffer.

Five people are doing word processing at terminals attached to a multitasking computer. Explain how the computer runs the programs so that none of the users is noticeably delayed.

2 Two programs are running at the same time under a multitasking operating system. One is in the middle of printing and needs to read some data from a file in order to continue printing. The other program is half way through writing data to the same file and is waiting for the printer to be free so that it can print a report.
(a) What happens to the two programs?
(b) Suggest some ways in which an operating system could prevent this situation from arising, or recover from it if it does happen.

3 A certain computer running a multitasking operating system takes one millisecond to change from one program to another. Programs are allocated time slices of 20 milliseconds, unless they are interrupted before their time slice is finished. Dealing with an interrupt takes a further millisecond before multitasking continues.

What percentage of the processor time is spent in running applications programs:
(a) if programs are not interrupted at all
(b) if programs are interrupted, on average, when they have completed half of their time slice
(c) if, on average, programs only run for one millisecond before they are interrupted? Comment on your results.

8F Types of Operating System

There are several types of operating system. The one chosen for an application depends on the size of the computer and the type of work.

Small microcomputers run **single-program** operating systems. These load and run one applications program at a time, and supervise the input, output, storage and retrieval of data. Single-program operating systems are relatively small and simple programs.

Larger microcomputers have operating systems which create **windows** on the screen. There is one program running in each window. The person using the computer can only interact with one program at a time but can transfer data from one window to another.

If microcomputers are connected on a network, each runs its own single-program or windows operating system. There is a **network** operating system which runs on the fileserver. This controls access to the fileserver, and operates a spooling system for the network printer. Some of the shared files are **read-only**. These can generally be read by more than one workstation at a time. Common files which are **read/write** can only be accessed from one workstation at a time.

Minicomputers and mainframe computers have operating systems which are capable of **batch processing**, **multiprogramming**, and **real-time processing**, or, in many cases, a combination of these.

Batch processing is when an operating system works its way through a series of programs which are kept in a queue. Although only one program in the batch is running at a time, the input and output from the programs can overlap, particularly if spooling is used for printed output. Batch processing is used, for example, at college computer centres to compile and run programs written by students.

Multiprogramming (or **multitasking**) is when a number of programs are being worked on at the same time. Each program is at a different stage of execution, and processor time is shared among them so that they all appear to be running simultaneously. **Multi-access** is when the programs which are running in this way are interactive. People are working at terminals on the programs as they run. Multi-access systems are used, for example, by airlines for bookings. The computers are attached to a large network of terminals which are all used to take bookings at the same time.

Real-time processing is when the computer system must keep up with another process. For example, the computer controlling a rocket must receive information from the rocket, process it, and return guidance instructions to the rocket fast enough to keep it on course. Real-time operating systems must take account of the fact that certain operations cannot be interrupted for any reason.

This classification of operating systems is similar to the classification of types of computer applications in section 23A.

Questions

1 What type of operating system is the most suitable for each of the following computer systems?
(a) A small microcomputer used for games.
(b) The desktop microcomputer of a manager who uses a spreadsheet and a word processing program.
(c) A computer for stock control, on which the stock file is brought up-to-date every night.

(d) The computer which controls the nuclear reactor at a power station.
(e) A computer used by a travel company, with bookings made at a number of terminals.

2 What are the benefits to a user of an operating system with a windows facility?

3 Explain in your own words how a multi-access operating system works.

8G End-of-Chapter Summary

The main points of this chapter are as follows:

- An operating system is a program which drives the 'raw' hardware of a computer system, and presents a simple interface for applications programs.

- An operating system is an integral part of a computer system. For this reason it is known as systems software.
- An operating system schedules the running of programs on the central processing unit, allocates memory space to programs, and deals with the transfer of data to and from peripheral devices.
- Applications programs call operating system routines when required, or they are interrupted by external events, after which the operating system takes over.
- Some operating systems create a virtual memory which is much larger than the physical memory of the computer.
- Data is transferred to slow peripherals like printers by the technique of spooling.
- Operating systems create a filing system to handle the data on backing store.
- Time slicing is a common technique for multitasking. Each active program is given, in turn, a short interval of processor time.
- Types of operating system include single-program operation, window environments, network operating systems, batch processing, multiprogramming, multi-access and real-time processing.

Exercise 8

1 Choose the correct word from the list for each of the following spaces:

mainframe; multitasking; spool; updated; batch processing; virtual; time slicing; backing; terminal; network; multi-access.

A mail order company has a ____ computer connected to a ____ of terminals. Orders are received by telephone or through the post. The operators enter the information for an order at a ____. The order is processed immediately: an invoice and packing note are printed, and the stock files and account files are ____.

The computer uses a ____ operating system. There is a ____ memory, with a space allocated as the working area for each terminal. Portions of the program being run from the terminal at any time are swapped in from ____ store as required. Documents to be printed are sent to a print ____ on disk. ____ is used to give each terminal a fair share of processor time.

2 A program searches a file on disk and prints selected records from it. List all the ways in which this program uses operating system facilities as it runs.

3 A file consists of 256 records, each 160 bytes long. When the operating system places the file on disk, it is written into disk sectors, each containing 1K bytes.
(a) What is the total length of the file, in bytes?
(b) If records cannot be split over disk sectors, how many records can be placed in a sector?
(c) How many sectors does the file take up?
(d) What percentage of the disk space allocated by the operating system is actually taken up by the data in the file?
(e) Comment on these results.

Things to find out

1 Find out what type of operating system each of the following are. Note any special features.

CP/M; MSDOS; MS Windows; Unix; VMS; Cics; VME/B

Points to discuss

1 Mainframe computers are large, powerful and expensive. They have complex operating systems which ensure that the hardware of the computer is used as efficiently as possible. However, these computers spend quite a lot of their processing time running their operating system.

Microcomputers are small, of limited power, and cheap. They have simple operating systems which take up hardly any processing time on 'housekeeping' tasks.

There is a debate in the computing industry whether it is better to have a single mainframe computer or a number of microcomputers for certain types of application. For example, multi-access computer systems are being challenged by networks of microcomputers for use in large offices.
(a) Give some arguments in favour of each type of computer.
(b) Give some arguments against the use of each type of computer.
(c) State your own preference, with reasons, for the type of computer system for a large office, with workstations of various types on everyone's desk.

Computers Going to Work

Information technology is becoming an essential tool in almost every aspect of work. It brings many benefits: better quality products and higher standards of work, speed, efficiency and a wide range of new products and services. All this is done at a lower cost than was previously possible.

This chapter introduces the areas of use of IT, and outlines the steps needed to set up a computer system to do a particular task. It provides the general ideas which form the basis of the next thirteen chapters, each of which covers one type of application. The ideas introduced in this chapter are followed up in more detail in chapter 23: Applications Review.

9A How Information Technology is Used

The commonest ways in which information technology is used are outlined below. Many of these applications are described in more detail in subsequent chapters.

Commercial Applications

The Shell Oil refinery at Stanlow. Computers are used to control all the chemical processes which take place here.

Banks, insurance companies and other financial institutions depend on information technology for every aspect of their business. All financial transactions are recorded on computers, and many are carried out by electronic messages sent from one computer system to another. The prices of stocks and shares, and the rates of exchange of foreign currencies are quoted on viewdata systems. The efficient way in which computers can handle the large quantities of information needed for financial transactions makes them essential for this type of work.

Businesses use computers for their accounts, stock control, payroll processing and forecasting. Shops use point-of-sale terminals to record sales. These link to computers which manage the ordering and distribution of stock, and keep accounts. Computers reduce the amount of paperwork, enable records to be more up-to-date, and are cheaper than other ways of doing these tasks. Most business correspondence is produced on word processors, and exchanged to an increasing extent via electronic mail.

Travel agents, hotels, airlines and shipping companies use computers for reservations. Computers mean that bookings can be made as soon as they are requested, and the communications system which links the computers enables bookings to be made all over the world. Viewdata systems are used to provide a central source of information on available holidays and hotel rooms.

Industrial Applications

The Rolls-Royce aircraft engine factory in Derby where computers are used to control manufacturing processes.

Complex industrial processes such as oil refining, steelmaking, chemical manufacture and glassmaking are carried out on equipment which is controlled to a great extent by computers. The control systems of nuclear reactors are electronic, and partially automated. The distribution of gas, electricity and water is supervised by computer systems. These control systems are more flexible, more precise and can respond much more quickly to an emergency than previous types.

Aircraft, motor vehicles and the chips and printed circuit boards used in computers are designed with the aid of computers. Computer-aided design (CAD) systems replace drawing-boards and paper plans: CAD is faster, and allows designers to make modifications without having to re-draw entire plans. Some CAD systems have facilities to simulate the operation of designs so that they can be tested; others enable quantities of materials to be estimated from designs. A few have direct links to manufacturing equipment.

Motor vehicles and other manufactured goods are assembled, welded and painted by robots. The overall management of the production process is under the control of computers. These ensure that the right components are supplied at each stage, and that production matches orders for the goods. Robots have revolutionised manufacturing: they are faster, more flexible and cheaper than assembly workers, and produce work of a more consistent quality.

Factories also use computers for stock control in their components warehouses, and for order processing, payroll and other administrative tasks.

Administrative Applications

In Britain, the administration of VAT, television licences and driver and vehicle licences is computerised. The police have a national computer network with information on stolen cars and wanted or missing persons. Regional police forces have computers which handle the information on major crimes. Income tax and Social Security benefits are administered partially by computer. Both are in the process of being transferred onto totally automated systems. These will be some of the largest computer applications in Britain.

Much of the administration of the National Health Service is done on computer: bulk ordering of supplies, keeping records of epidemics, etc. Some hospitals have all their records on computer systems, and a few general practices have computerised medical records systems.

Administrative computer systems can cope with large volumes of data quickly and efficiently. They need fewer staff to operate than systems based on paper records, and information is less likely to get lost.

Educational, Scientific and Research Applications

Computers are used in schools and colleges for teaching purposes. Computer-assisted learning (CAL) is used in subjects such as geography for information retrieval, and science subjects to process experimental results. School and university students are also taught to use and program computers. Most of the research at universities and industrial laboratories requires computers to record and analyse results. The experiments in such fields as nuclear physics and biochemistry generate masses of results which cannot be analysed without some of the most powerful computers in existence.

The weather forecasts in Britain, the USA and a number of other countries are based on simulations of the behaviour of the earth's atmosphere, run on large computers. These forecasts are vital to aviation, shipping, agriculture, the construction industry and the tourist trade as well as being of great interest to the general public. The forecasts are based on weather reports from large numbers of weather stations all over the world. The information must be processed very rapidly to produce forecasts in time—a task which would be impossible without some of the largest computers in the world.

Military Applications

Modern warfare relies heavily on electronic systems. Missiles have on-board guidance systems; ships, aircraft, submarines and tanks all carry computers. These are used for navigation, tracking and identifying targets, and defence against incoming missiles. The speed of computers makes them indispensable for these tasks. Electronic warfare is the conflict between the computerised radar systems of attackers and those of their targets: the side which wins effectively 'blinds' the other side. Large computer systems are used for tactical and strategic planning, and for the administration of supplies.

Questions

1 (a) Select at least *three* of the above applications of information technology. Give the main reasons for the introduction of IT in each application.
(b) For each of the above types of computer use, find out at least *one* application of IT which is *not* mentioned in this section.

2 Write down at least *three* areas of work where, in your opinion information technology is *not* likely to be introduced. Give reasons for your choices.

3 Choose any *three* of the applications listed above, and for each one comment on the effects of a shut-down of the IT systems on the operation of the process.

9B Setting up a Computer System

Setting up a computer system to perform a particular task is a complex process. A large computer system takes years to design and implement, and costs millions of pounds. Even an application such as an accounts system for a small business takes a few weeks to get going. In all cases, the process is difficult and mistakes can be expensive.

A number of people are involved in the process. There are the **users** for whom the system is being designed. In most organisations managers at various levels are involved, with a senior manager approving each stage (and granting funds). The work of the people who design computer systems is described in chapter 24. Decisions on the design of the computer system can be made by users or designers, and normally have to be approved by the others before things can go ahead.

The approach, when setting up a computer system, is to identify what is required of the system, and design one to meet these requirements. It is a **top-down** approach: the design is first expressed in general terms and details are added in an orderly way. Checks are carried out at every stage. If an aspect of the design is found to be wrong, it is redesigned before any more details are added.

Computer programmers at work, entering test data for a program which controls a digital telephone exchange.

Finding out what is wanted from a computer system is much more difficult than it first appears. The problem is trying to imagine what a computer system will do and how it will work before it is constructed. Although the general requirements of a task are usually obvious, the specific facilities required are not. In many cases, different people in the organisation have different ideas of what the computer system should do, and cannot communicate these ideas very clearly. Communication between users and computer specialists can also be a problem: users do not understand computer jargon, and computer specialists do not understand the work of the users. Methods of designing computer systems do their best to take these difficulties into account.

The first step is to do a **feasibility study**. This investigates the general requirements of the system, and recommends whether or not a computer system should be designed to meet these requirements. It also gives an estimate of the cost of developing the computer system. The feasibility study is presented to the managers, who decide whether or not to proceed with the design of the system.

Example: club membership records

As a simple example (which is developed through the remaining sections of this chapter) consider the task of setting up a computer system to keep the membership records of a club. It could be a school club, a sports club or a youth club. A feasibility study might identify the general requirements of the membership system as follows:

- To store all the relevant details of each member of the club, and enable this information to be kept up-to-date easily.
- To be used to produce membership lists and sets of address labels as required.
- To keep records of membership subscriptions, and enable these to be collected when they are due.
- To be simple, efficient and cheap to operate.

Questions   These questions cover sections 9B and 9C.

1 (a) How long does it take to develop a large computer application?
(b) What are the main difficulties in the design of a computer application?
(c) What steps are taken to deal with these difficulties?
2 (a) What is the aim of a feasibility study?
(b) By whom is a feasibility study normally undertaken?

(c) What are the *two* possible outcomes of a feasibility study?
3 Choose a simple application of computers, such as recording pupils' coursework marks or booking seats for a school play. Make a list of the general requirements of the computer system, like the one for the club membership system above.

Project starter   1 Using the requirements of the club membership system set out above, carry out a study of the feasibility of implementing such a system, using one of your school's computers.

Present a report, recommending whether or not to go ahead with the application and giving the reasons for your recommendation.

9D Designing a Computer System

The development of a computer system goes through a number of stages: **functional specification, implementation, testing, documentation** and **maintenance**. Each stage consists of a number of steps, depending to some extent on the type of application and how it is to be implemented. The stages are introduced in the remaining sections of this chapter, and discussed in the chapters on particular types of computer application.

Functional Specification

The first stage of the design of a computer system is to produce a **functional specification**. This is a document which describes the tasks carried out by the computer system in order to satisfy the aims identified in the previous section. In many cases, several versions of the functional specification are produced, with each version adding more detail once the previous version has been approved.

The functional specification describes:

* the output required from the computer system
* the input data which is necessary
* the structure of any files which store the data
* the processing carried out on the data.

For the club membership system, a brief functional specification is as follows:

Outputs
The outputs are:

Membership lists, showing in a table:

Name	Address	Telephone No	Membership No

Address labels, showing:

	Example:	
Name		Anne Jones
Address Line 1		21 Cedar Close
Address Line 2		Newport
Address Line 3		Gwent
Postcode		GW4 6TD

These may be produced for all members, or for subsets of the membership list selected on various conditions.

Inputs
Membership details are input, as shown in the file structure on page 98.

File structure
There is a record for each member, containing:

Note that a number of the data items—Sex, Postcode, Subs Month and Subs Paid—are in **code**. These reduce the size of the record and make processing easier. The length is the maximum number of characters which may be in a field.

Field	Type	Length	Example
Membership No	Numeric	5 digits	86073
Surname	Alphabetic	20 characters	Jones
First Name	Alphabetic	20 characters	Anne
Title	Alphabetic	4 characters	Miss
Sex	Alphabetic	1 characters	F
Address Line 1	Alphabetic	20 characters	21 Cedar Close
Address Line 2	Alphabetic	20 characters	Newport
Address Line 3	Alphabetic	20 characters	Gwent
Postcode	Alphabetic	8 charactes	GW4 6TD
Telephone No	Numeric	7 digits	7568344
Subs Month	Alphabetic	3 characters	Jan
Subs Paid	Alphabetic	1 character	Y

File Processing
Algorithms

Algorithms may be used to set out the processing steps. An algorithm is a written description of the steps of a task, set out in a structured way. For example, at the beginning of each month, all the members whose subscriptions are due that month have the Subs Paid field in their records set to N. An algorithm for this process is:

Enter code for Current Month (e.g. Feb)

For all records in the file, repeat

  If Subs Month = Current Month

    then Set Subs Paid to N

Note that the steps of the process are written on separate lines. If one line controls a subsequent line (such as the 'repeat' and 'if' lines above), the subsequent line is written further to the right. (It is **indented**.)

Decision tables

Decision tables may be used to indicate under what circumstances different processing options are selected. They can make difficult parts of the processing clearer. For example, the actions taken by the membership secretary when subscriptions are due or overdue can be set out in a table as follows:

Condition	Action 1st Reminder	2nd Reminder	Investigate	Delete
Subs due this month	*			
Subs due last month		*		
Subs due two months ago			*	
Valid reason for lateness		*		
No valid reason for lateness				*

The asterisks in the table show which conditions are linked to which actions. For example, members whose subs were due two months ago are investigated. If a valid reason is found for the late payment, a second reminder is sent again. If not, the member is deleted.

System Diagram

The system as a whole may be described by a **system diagram**. This shows the main parts of the system, and the flows of data. Figure 9.1 shows the common symbols used in system diagrams; Figure 9.2 is a system diagram for the club membership system.

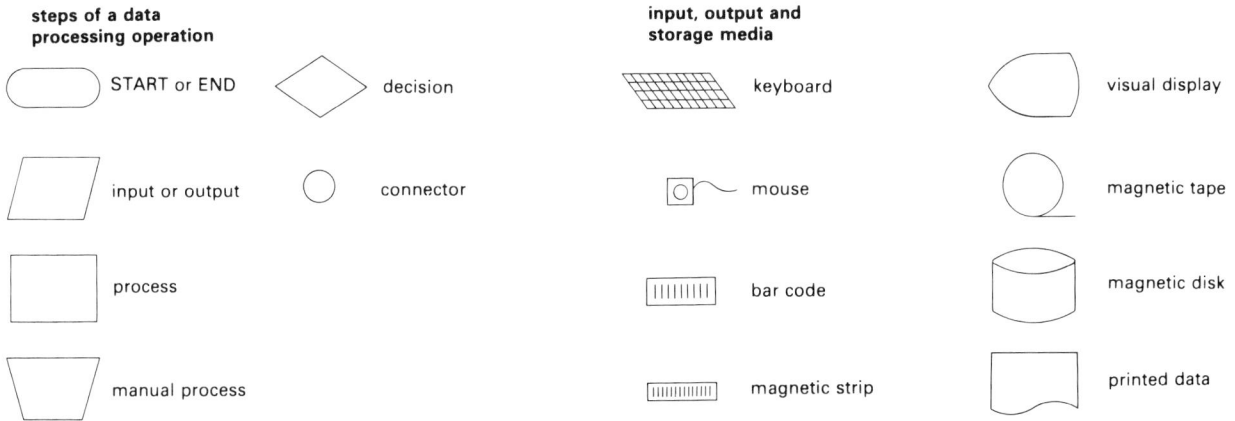

steps of a data processing operation

START or END   decision

input or output   connector

process

manual process

input, output and storage media

keyboard   visual display

mouse   magnetic tape

bar code   magnetic disk

magnetic strip   printed data

Figure 9.1   Systems diagram symbols

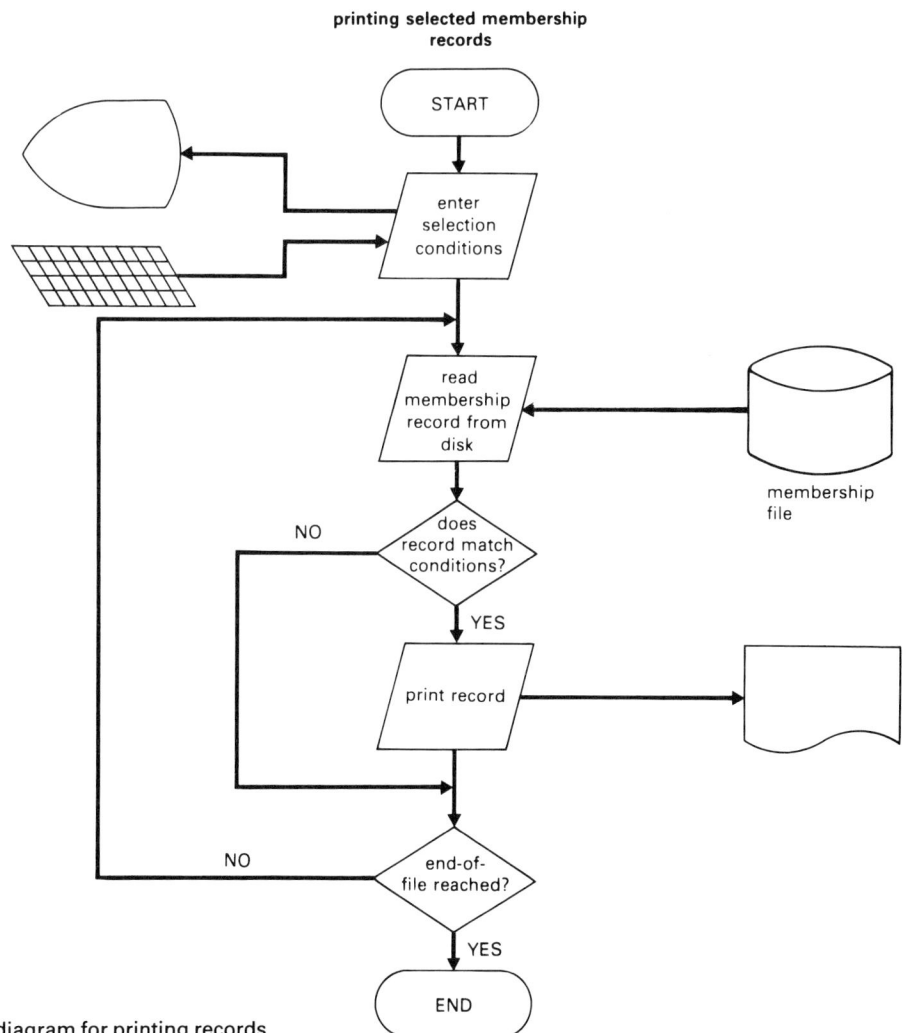

printing selected membership records

START → enter selection conditions → read membership record from disk → does record match conditions? → YES → print record → end-of-file reached? → YES → END

membership file

Figure 9.2   Club membership system: system diagram for printing records

1 Using the file structure of the club membership system above, write an algorithm for each of the following:
(a) Printing a list of names and addresses.
(b) Finding if a certain person is in the file of members.
(c) Printing a list of the names of all the members who joined in 1987.

2 It is found that the club membership file as described above will be too large for the computer on which it is to be implemented. Draw up a simpler file structure, taking fewer characters per record but still keeping the most important information.

3 An algorithm for adding up the total of a set of numbers is shown below. The set ends with the number 0.

> Set total T to 0
>
> Input number N
>
> While N>0 repeat
>
>   Add N to T
>
>   Input number N
>
> Output T

A **dry run** of this algorithm with the numbers 3, 5, 0 is as follows:

	First N T	Second N T	Third N T
Set total T to 0	0		
Input number N	3 0		
While N>0 repeat	True	True	False
Add N to T	3 3	5 8	
Input number N	5 3	0 8	
Output T			8

The condition N>0 is true for the first two numbers and false the third time. The repetition stops at this point with the total at 8, as required.
(a) Dry run this algorithm with the numbers 2, 6, 3, 5, 0.
(b) Dry run the algorithm with the numbers 4, 7, −1, 3, 8, 0. Explain why the total is not correct.
(c) Modify the algorithm so that it gives a correct answer with the test data from part (b).

4 (a) The decision table below shows the conditions and actions of a program which allocates discounts on the sale of goods.

Condition	Action No Discount	5% Discount	10% Discount
Sale < £100			
. . . .			

Copy and complete the table so that sales of less than £100 get no discount, sales between £100 and £1000 get 5% discount and sales of over £1000 get 10% discount.
(b) Draw up a decision table to determine whether a candidate gets a grade A, B or C in an examination based on two papers, as follows:

Average greater than 75%, grade A.
Average greater than 50% and one paper greater than 80%, grade A.
Average greater than 50% and neither paper greater than 80%, grade B.
Average between 30% and 50%, grade C.
Average less than 30%, ungraded.

9E Implementing the Design

When the final version of the functional specification has been approved, the implementation of the design of a computer system begins. There are two aspects to this: selecting the hardware for the task, and developing (or choosing) the software.

Choosing the Hardware

Many new computer systems are designed to run on the user's existing computers. Sometimes these need to be **upgraded** by purchasing additional memory or backing store; in other cases the hardware is adequate as it is. If new hardware is required, the equipment is selected on the basis of its suitability for the task, reliability, compatibility with existing equipment, and cost. A few applications, notably process control systems, require special-purpose hardware items to be constructed.

Hardware can be bought or rented. Renting means that there is no high initial cost, but the user does not own the equipment. Over a period of years, the total rent can be more than the cost of the equipment. Rental is not as common today as it used to be. Buying the equipment can mean spending a large sum of money (or raising a loan) straight away. There are also annual maintenance charges and insurance to be considered. However, buying gives the user the freedom to combine hardware from several suppliers in order to get the most suitable system at the lowest price.

There is also a choice between using a computer on the premises, or renting time on another computer. Renting time means that data preparation and input is done at the user site, and terminals are used to communicate with the remote computer. **Time-sharing** is useful if a small amount of time on a powerful computer is needed.

A final alternative is to use a **computer bureau** to do the data preparation, input, processing and production of output. This is common for payroll processing, even when a company uses computers for other purposes. Using a computer bureau frees the user from all aspects of the running of a computer system. The decision whether or not to use a bureau, if one is available for the task, is based mostly on cost.

Developing the Software

In most applications, the time-consuming and expensive part of the implementation is developing the software. There are three approaches: using an existing **software package** and modifying it to suit the particular needs of the system, using **software development tools** (including a **program generator**), or writing the software from scratch. See chapter 7 for the technical aspects of these methods.

In all cases, development of the software proceeds in a top-down manner. First the overall structure of the software is planned. **Structure diagrams** may be drawn to illustrate this structure. See Figure 9.3 for a structure diagram of the program for the club membership system. It shows the program **modules** which make up the software. Each module performs a specific task, and has a clear link to other modules.

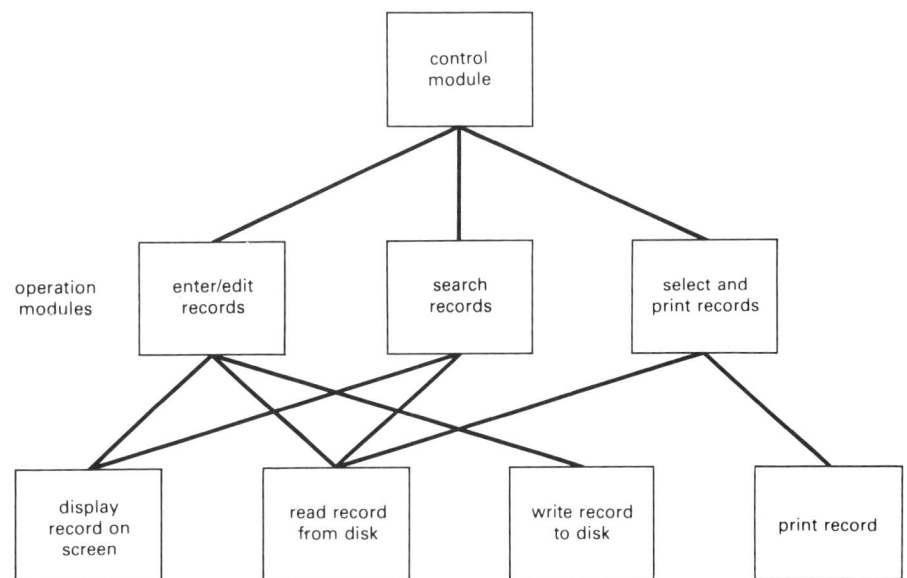

Figure 9.3   Club membership system: program structure diagram

Using a Software Package

General-purpose software packages are available for many information processing tasks. These include information storage and retrieval, stock control, payroll systems, accounting systems and word processing. These are described in the chapters on specific applications.

If a software package is to be adapted for the task, the file structures are entered into the package, and commands are written to carry out the required operations. The layout of the screens for the input and output of data and the format of printed output are specified if necessary. Figure 9.4. shows the screen for the entry of club membership details.

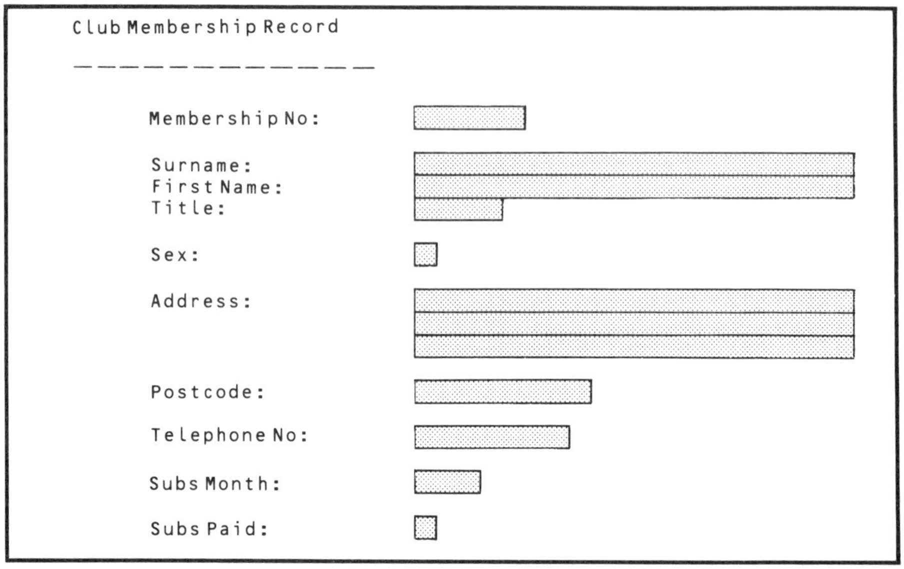

Figure 9.4   Club membership system: screen for data entry

Using a general-purpose software package is quicker than writing special software for the task. It also has the benefits of lower cost and the fact that the software package has been tried and tested by other users. Simple applications can be implemented on a general-purpose software package directly by users, without professional assistance. The main disadvantage of a standard software package is that it may not be able to do everything that is required for the particular application. The design of the system may have to be modified to match the capabilities of the software package.

Using Software Development Tools

Software development tools, including a program generator, may be used for conventional applications using common data processing operations. Program generators are used mainly for commercial systems such as order processing, stock control and accounting. The program generator is used to specify the structure of the data files, the format of the input and output data, and the operations needed to process the data. It then produces a program according to the specifications. Trained programmers are needed to operate the software development tools, but they can work closely with users as they specify and modify the program.

The benefits of software development tools include the speed of development of the program, a reduced chance of errors, and the ability to check and modify the implementation according to the users' comments.

Writing the software

Print selected membership records is
    Enter selection conditions
    Open membership file
    Repeat until end-of-file
        Read membership record from disk
        If record matches conditions
            then Print record
    Close membership file

Figure 9.5   Club membership system: algorithm for program module

If the software for the application is written from scratch, this task falls to the programming staff of the user organisation, or to a software house commissioned to do the work. In either case, it is a slow and expensive process. The usual approach is to break the modules in the structure diagram down into smaller, more detailed modules, and then write the program code, in a suitable programming language, for each of these. Figure 9.5 shows a detailed algorithm for one of the modules from Figure 9.3.

The benefit of software written specially for an application is that, at the end of the development work, the software does (or should do) precisely what the design requires it to do. If the application is complex or unusual, or is the first of its kind, then there is no alternative to developing the software from scratch.

Questions

1   Which method of software development (a software package, a program generator or a programming language) is the most suitable for each of the following?
(a) word processing
(b) an information retrieval system for a company's customers
(c) an order processing system for a mail order company
(d) the software to control the operation of a robot
(e) a program to produce examination certificates
(f) a program to control a chemical reaction.

2   Make a table summarising the advantages and disadvantages of the three methods of implementing software:

	Advantages	Disadvantages
Software package		
Program generator		
Programming language		

3   The owner of a small business computer wants to set up a system to keep her accounts. At present the accounts are written in a ledger. She has details of three software packages for business accounts. Describe the steps she might take in deciding which (if any) of the packages to purchase.

Project Starter

1   Using the information retrieval software package on your school microcomputer, implement the club membership system described in this chapter.

9F   Testing

The software is tested at almost every stage of development. Algorithms and drafts of programs are **dry run** by working through them manually, stage by stage, with simple data. Whether a software package is being adapted or new software written, modules are tested separately as soon as they are complete. As the overall system is built up, larger and larger parts are tested. Specially designed **test data** is used. This tests the normal running of the system and extreme cases, and includes data which tries to make the system fail. For example, a difficult set of test data for the club membership system would be for someone with the name Viscount Albert Brassington-Templethwaite, and who lived at three different addresses!

When all the corrections have been made and retested, the entire computer system, including any custom-built hardware, is assembled and tested as a whole.

When the development team is satisfied with the system, it is handed over to the users for **acceptance testing**. The system is run in the way that it is intended to be used, with test data which includes copies of operational data. The people who are to operate the system are sent on training courses if necessary.

When the users are satisfied, the new system is formally accepted. If necessary, data files are converted from a previous computer system to run on the new system. The new system is often run in parallel with the previous system for a while before becoming fully operational on its own. A year or more may have gone by since work started on the design of the system.

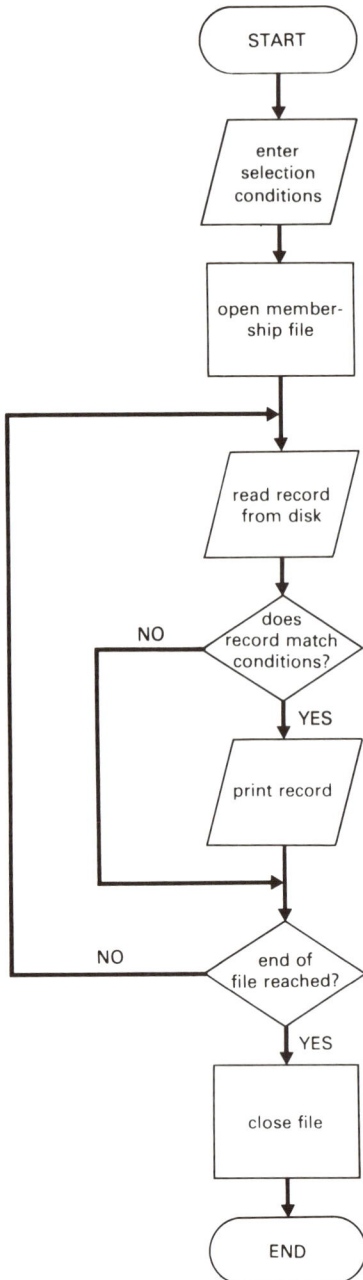

Figure 9.6   Flow diagram for Figure 9.5

Questions

1   Design a set of test data for the club membership file described earlier in this chapter. Include correct records, and ones which test whether incorrect data is rejected. If you have implemented the system, use this data to test it.
2   What are the benefits of running new and old computer systems in parallel during the changeover to a new system?
3   In a small company, the two separate computer programs used for keeping orders and stock control are being replaced by a single program which does both operations. Describe how the new program should be tested before taking over from the other two.

9G Documentation

A number of documents are produced during the development of a new computer application. The design is expressed as a **functional specification**, which may include a **system diagram**, as described above. The **program documentation** includes a **structure diagram**, and the algorithms and decision tables for the program modules. **Flow diagrams** may be drawn to illustrate the flow of control of program modules. Figure 9.6 shows a flow diagram for the program module described in Figure 9.5. If the software has been written from scratch, there is a **listing** of each module, with comments which explain how the module works. The program documentation is for the use of programmers when they locate and correct errors, and modify the software at a later stage.

User guides are written to explain the workings of the program to users. These are written in plain English, rather than the technical language used in the system and program documentation. They describe how to run the program and how to enter data, and explain the format of output data. They include a list of error messages, and advice on what to do if something goes wrong.

Operator documentation sets out the procedures to be followed by the people operating the computer when the application is running. They state what stationery is needed for the printer, what data disks and tapes must be loaded, and describe the recovery procedures for corrupted files.

Questions 1 (a) What are the requirements of a good user guide for a program?
(b) Look at the user guides for one or two programs that you use. State, with reasons, whether each of these satisfies the requirements of a good user guide.

2 What items of documentation are produced during the development of a program, and what are written after the program is complete? For each item, state by whom it is written, and for whom it is intended.

Project starter 1 Write a user guide for the club membership system described in this chapter. Use clear, concise English, and set it out so that it is easy to follow.

9H Maintenance

Once a new computer system is in operation, **maintenance** work is required to keep it running properly. Errors which come to light need to be corrected, and modifications are made in the light of experience. If new hardware becomes available, the system needs to be adapted to use it. Changes in business practice or changes in the law (such as laws about sick pay or income tax) may require modifications to the computer system.

Questions 1 After a while, it is decided to include an extra field in the file of the club membership system to include the members' interests. Briefly describe *all* the changes to the software and documentation needed to implement this change.
2 A payroll program calculates wages, income tax, National Insurance contributions, etc.

Make a list of some of the reasons that this program will have to be modified from time to time.
3 A programmer is asked to modify a program module, and finds that there is no documentation for the module. What are the difficulties that this will cause, and what further problems could arise?

9I End-of-Chapter Summary

The main points of the chapter are as follows:

- Information technology is used extensively in commerce, industry, administration and education, and for scientific, military and research applications.
- The main steps in the development of a computer system are:
    analysing the requirements of a task
    designing a computer system to match the requirements
    implementing the design
    testing the implementation
    documenting the system.
- Hardware can be purchased or rented, or data processing can be done by a computer bureau.
- There are three alternative ways of developing software: using a software package, using software development tools or using a programming language.
- A number of items of documentation are produced during the development of a new computer application. These include the functional specification, program documentation, user guide and operator documentation.

Exercise 9

1. Choose the correct word from the list for each of the following spaces:

   test data; functional specification; management; acceptance testing; feasibility study; system diagram; users; software package.

   The _____ approved the _____ which recommended that the proposed computer system should be developed. The systems analysts were instructed to do a _____ with a _____ to clarify the design. As the application was a common one, a _____ was chosen to implement the system. The programming staff ran a set of _____ on the package before handing it over to the _____ for _____.

2. (a) What *four* types of testing does a computer system undergo during development?

   (b) List *three* types of test data, and explain why each is necessary.

Points to discuss

1. (a) What are the options open to most users in choosing the hardware for a new computer system? Discuss the advantages and disadvantages of each option.

Project starters

1. Set out the steps for the design of a computer system for *one* of the following, or a similar system of your own choice. Use the club membership system as an example. Keep your description as brief as possible, use clear English, and use technical terms only when necessary. (Do *not* attempt to write any of the programs.)

   (i) A system which stores friends' names, addresses and telephone numbers on a home computer.
   (ii) A system for a personal diary on a home computer.
   (iii) A system to keep a record of a bank or building society account on a home computer.

3. Would each of the following normally be found in a functional specification, program documentation, operator documentation or a user guide?
   (a) an annotated listing of a program module
   (b) a description of the input data
   (c) a list of recovery procedures for corrupted files
   (d) a system diagram
   (e) a flow diagram
   (f) a description of the aims of the system
   (g) a list of the data disks needed to run the system
   (h) a description of how to run the program.

4.* The method of designing a new computer application is described in this chapter as 'top-down'.
   (a) State the main steps of the design of a computer system, and explain why they are in a top-down sequence.
   (b) Give reasons for the importance of a top-down approach to the design of computer systems.

   (b) Name *three* ways in which the software for a new system can be developed. Briefly discuss the advantages and disadvantages of each method.

   (a) Write down the aims of the system.
   (b) Draw up a functional specification, as described in section 9D. Include a system diagram, and write algorithms for the most important processes. Draw up any decision tables which are required.
   (c) Specify the type of file required, and set out a suitable record structure.
   (d) Specify the type of computer needed, and describe the peripheral devices required.
   (e) State whether a software package, software development system or a programming language is the most suitable for implementing the software.

10 Information Storage and Retrieval

The card index system which enables people to look up details of books at a library.

card index a set of cards containing an organised collection of information.
Dewey Decimal System a system of numbers to identify the subject of books in a library.
vendor a person selling a house or other property.

Computers are ideal for storing large quantities of information and retrieving it quickly. The information can be kept up-to-date easily. Information retrieval systems are interactive, displaying or printing information as it is requested. In this type of application, computers have replaced manual systems which used large card indexes. Computers are faster, cheaper and can store much more information than manual systems. In manual systems, the arrangement of the cards means that the information can only be accessed in one way, whereas computer systems can be searched in many ways. For example, most card indexes in libraries are arranged in order of authors' surnames. It is almost impossible to find the card for a book if its title is known, but not the author.

Information storage and retrieval systems are used in schools, universities and libraries, as well as in commerce and industry. In France, telephone directories are kept on an information retrieval system; a change to such a system is planned in the UK.

This chapter outlines the design of an information retrieval system for a school library, and describes two applications of such systems: by estate agents to keep lists of properties, and the Police National Computer system which keeps information about stolen cars. It puts into practice some of the general ideas introduced in chapter 9.

10A Activity: School Library Book Records

This section outlines the design of a computer system to store information about the books in a school library. It follows the general steps discussed in chapter 9. You are expected to implement the design using an information retrieval software package on your school's computer.

The Requirements of the Task

A computer system in a school library is intended to be used by library staff and pupils. It must:

- Keep up-to-date records of all books in the library.
- Store all the necessary details on each book.
- Be able to be searched in several ways: by title, author, subject, etc.
- Be simple to use, and respond quickly to requests.

Computer System Design

Outputs
A screen display shows all the details for one book. A copy of this may be printed.

Browsing through books at a library.

The system must be able to print tables showing all books or selected books under appropriate headings. For example:

Author	Title	Subject Code
William Golding	Lord of the Flies	820
....	....	....

Inputs

When the system is being set up or new books added, the information shown below is entered for each book.

When a search is made for a book, any item of information about the book may be entered: the author's surname, all or part of the title of the book, etc. Similar inputs are required when categories of books are to be selected.

File structure

A record for each book, showing:

Field	Type	Length	Example
Accession No	Alpha	10	86074
Author Surname	Alpha	20	Golding
Author First Name	Alpha	20	William
Title	Alpha	40	Lord of the Flies
Edition	Numeric	2	1
Publisher	Alpha	20	Faber
Date of Publication	Numeric	4	1954
Subject Category	Numeric	10	820
Subject Keywords	Alpha	60	boy, island, conch

The accession number is a number given to each book when it is received by the library. The usual number system starts with two digits identifying the year the book was received: 86001 is the first book received in 1986.

The subject category normally follows the **Dewey Decimal System** of classification. This is an international standard, with general subject areas being identified by whole numbers, and subdivisions of these areas identified by decimal places. For example, English Literature has the code 820.

The keywords are a set of words which describe the subject matter of the book. They greatly assist searches for a book by subject, when the author and title are not known. For example, a book on the social effects of information technology would have the keywords computer, information technology, social effects.

File processing

When the file is set up, it is created with the required record structure. As new records are entered, they are added to the end of the file. When corrections are made, the required records are found and updated. Records may be deleted from any point in the file when books are removed from the library.

Readers use the file to search for books by entering some information about the books they want: the title, author's name, etc. If a book is found, its full record is displayed or printed.

Library staff will want to display or print tables showing selected information about some or all of the books. For example, they might want to print the titles of all the books written by a certain author.

System Diagram

Figure 10.1 shows a system diagram for the library records system, assuming that it is implemented on a single microcomputer.

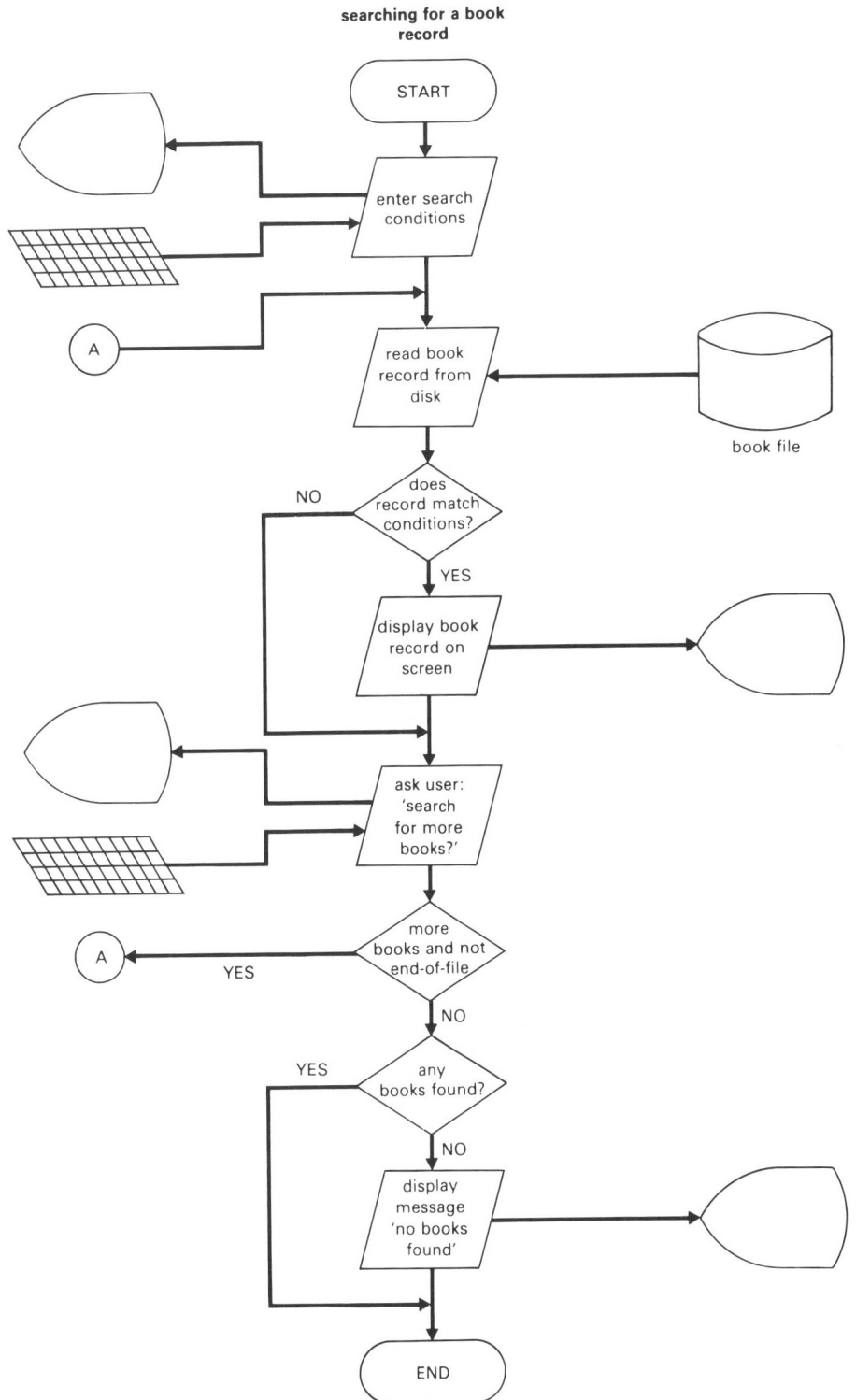

searching for a book
record

START

enter search
conditions

A

read book
record from
disk

book file

does
record match
conditions?

NO

YES

display book
record on
screen

ask user:
'search
for more
books?'

more
books and not
end-of-file

A

YES

NO

any
books found?

YES

NO

display
message
'no books
found'

END

Figure 10.1 Library records system: system diagram

Implementation

It is best to start by visiting the school library or a local library and looking at the record system. Then borrow a suitable set of books (between ten and twenty books to a group of five pupils) to get the

109

information for your own library records system. Include a variety of subjects in your set, but also include at least two books by the same author.

Use the information retrieval package on your school microcomputer to set up a library records system as designed above. Information retrieval packages have facilities to create data files and to enter, edit and delete records. It is possible to view records on screen and print them, and to print tables of certain fields from selected records.

- Look at the user guide for the information retrieval system you are going to use to find out how to carry out each operation.
- Create a data file with the fields given above.
- If the information retrieval system does not do so automatically, design a suitable screen layout for one record.
- Design a data input form for a book. See Figure 10.2 for an example. Set out the fields clearly, with spaces for the correct number of characters. Copy the form, and fill in copies for your selection of books.
- Using the facilities of the information retrieval system, enter records from the input forms. Check them carefully, and amend any which have errors. Save the file on disk, if this is not done automatically.
- Search for a book, using the author's surname to identify it. Most searches require the entry of a **condition** such as:

    Author Surname = Hardy

    If there is more than one book by this author, check that the computer system finds them all.

    Now search for a book using one of the subject keywords. For example:

    Subject Keyword $ cookery

    The $ symbol (or another symbol used for the same purpose) indicates that a field *includes* a word. It is particularly useful when searching for books by keyword.
- Instruct the computer to display the records of any books found in the search on the screen, and to print them.
- Select a category of books, and display and print tables of some fields for these books. For example, print a table of the authors and titles of all the books in the English Literature category.
- Make a backup copy of the file of books on another disk.

Documentation

- Write a user guide for readers who use the system to search for book references and select categories of books. Use simple, clear English. Give step-by-step instructions to carry out each operation. Include examples where appropriate. List the errors which can arise: explain the error messages which might appear, and how to correct mistakes.
- Write a clear description of the implementation of the system, intended for anyone who needs to understand how it works and who may wish to extend or modify it. Include a description of the file structure, and the procedures for creating the file, entering, amending and deleting records, and for backing up disks.

10B Application: Estate Agent Property List

Some estate agents are using information retrieval systems to store particulars of the properties which they have for sale. These systems enable them to search for and select properties according to the requirements of their clients. The information retrieval systems do not usually store all the details about the properties; the details are kept on documents produced on a word processor.

The Requirements of the Task

A computer system for property details will run on a microcomputer in an estate agent's office. The aims of the system are:

- To keep an up-to-date list of properties for sale.
- To hold brief details of each property.
- To enable properties to be selected quickly according to the requirements of people who want to buy.

Computer System Design

Outputs

For each property, details (as shown in the file structure on page 112) are displayed on screen or printed.

Summaries of properties are selected under certain conditions. These are displayed or printed as tables, for example:

Three-bedroomed terraced properties

Address	Vendor Name	Price
23 Lanark Way	Mr M J Smith	£55000
....	....	....

Figure 10.2 Estate agent records system: data input form

Looking at details of properties at an estate agent.

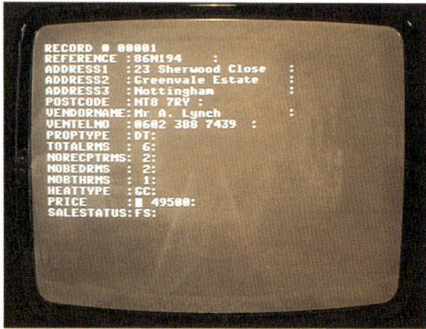
A property record on a computer screen.

Inputs

When someone asks the estate agent to put his or her property up for sale, the details given below for the property are entered. (This person is the **vendor** of the property.)

When someone wanting to buy a property visits the agents, details of their requirements are entered in order to search for suitable properties for them.

The estate agents can enter conditions in order to select categories of properties. For example, the estate agents might wish to know how many properties priced between £50 000 and £75 000 they have for sale. Brief details of the properties in this category are printed and included in a report. Reports like this help the estate agents to run their business.

File structure

A record contains the information for each property, as follows. The field lengths are the maximum number of characters the field may have.

Field	Type	Length	Example
Reference	Alpha	10	86M194
Address 1	Alpha	20	23 Sherwood Close
Address 2	Alpha	20	Greenvale Estate
Address 3	Alpha	20	Nottingham
Postcode	Alpha	8	NT8 7RY
Vendor Name	Alpha	20	Mr A Lynch
Vendor Tel No	Alpha	15	0602 388 7439
Property Type	Alpha	2	DT
Total Rooms	Numeric	2	6
No Reception Rooms	Numeric	2	2
No Bedrooms	Numeric	2	2
No Bathrooms	Numeric	2	1
Heating Type	Alpha	2	GC
Asking Price	Currency	7	49 500
Sale Status	Alpha	2	FS

Note that several of the fields are in code: Reference, Postcode, Property Type, Heating Type, and Sale Status. These codes shorten the record, and makes selection easier. For example, a set of codes for the Property Type is:

DT detached
SD semi-detached
TR terraced
ET end terrace
FT flat

The Sale Status codes show how far the sale has progressed:

FS for sale
UO under offer
CX contracts exchanged
SC sale complete

File processing

Data capture and entry

Data is normally written on data entry forms from information given by vendors and obtained from inspections of the properties. The layout of such a form is shown in Figure 10.2. The data is typed from these forms into the information retrieval system, using the built-in input facilities.

Updating and deletion
Records are updated as sales progress to show the current status of the sale. Some time after the sale has been completed, the record is deleted.

Searching
When someone calls at the estate agents looking for a property, their requirements are entered as a series of conditions. The file is searched for properties which match these requirements. For example, for a purchaser who wants a three-bedroomed, detached house costing up to £75 000, the conditions are:

No Bedrooms = 3
Property Type = DT
Asking Price <= 75 000

Depending on the computer program, these are entered as three separate conditions, or as a single condition using AND:

No Bedrooms = 3 AND Property Type = DT AND Asking Price <= 75 000

The records of the properties which match these conditions are displayed on screen and may be printed.

System Diagram

See Figure 10.3.

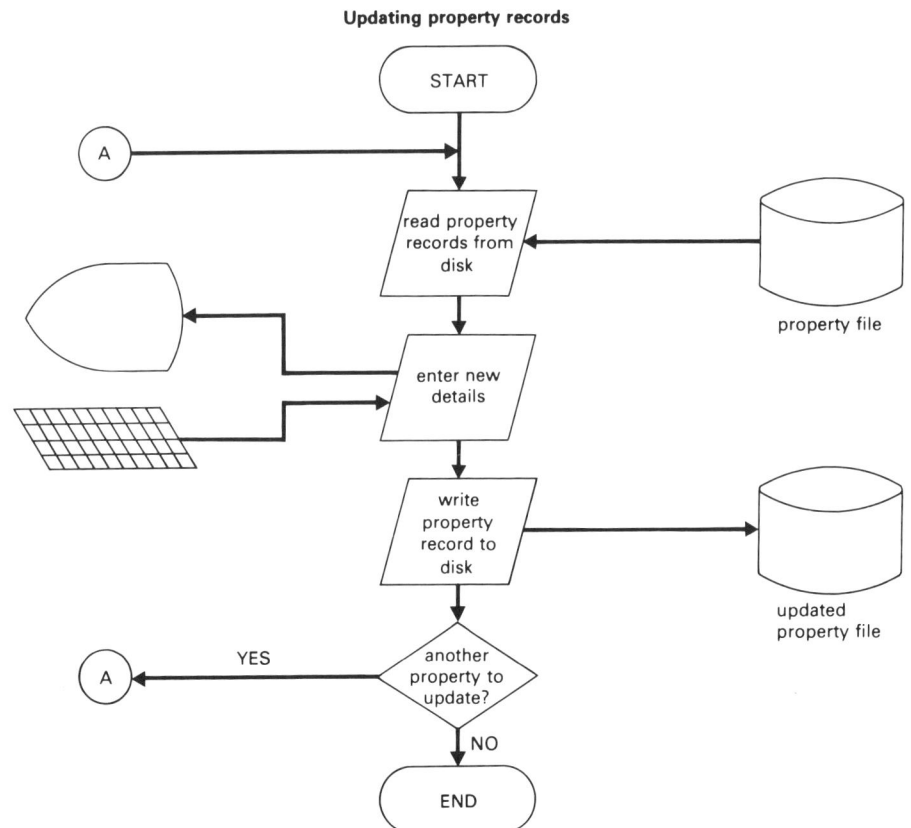

Figure 10.3 Estate agent records system: system diagram

Implementation

An estate agent's property information system is implemented using a standard commercial information retrieval package. It runs on a small business microcomputer.

To set up the system, a file is created with the record structure described above. The standard facilities of the software package are used to enter, amend and delete records and to search the file.

The file is backed up at the end of each day. The data entry forms are normally kept so that a day's entries can be repeated if the file is corrupted and the backup copy has to be used.

Testing

A varied selection of details of existing properties is used as test data. The new system is run in parallel with the existing card index until the errors have been eliminated.

Documentation

The user guide for the software package sets out the procedures for entering and editing data, searching the file, and printing records. Once the estate agents have got used to the system, it is hardly ever necessary to consult the user guide.

Questions

1 List the items of computer hardware needed for an estate agent's property information system.
2 Devise suitable codes for the Heating Type field in the property file.
3 Make a copy of the data entry form in Figure 10.2, and enter the details of your own home in it.
4 (a) What backup and security procedures are used in the estate agent's property information system?
(b) In your opinion, are these sufficient for the importance of the information? Give reasons for your answer.

Project starters

1 Design an information system for the estate agent to use to hold details of people wanting to buy a property. Use the steps of this section as examples, and design a file structure which is similar to the one given.

2 Implement the estate agent's property information system or the purchaser's system from the previous question on your school's microcomputer. Follow the steps of section 10A.

10C Application: Police National Computer—Vehicle Records

The theft of motor vehicles is a common type of crime in Britain. Hundreds of cars are stolen every day, and often driven long distances to avoid detection. Stolen vehicles are often used as transport for more serious crimes.

Years ago, the police force in each area kept its own records of stolen vehicles. These were on paper files, and there was no co-ordination between the police force in one area, and that in the next. Tracing a stolen vehicle was a slow process, and few were ever found.

Today, one of the tasks of the **Police National Computer (PNC)** is to assist in the tracing of stolen vehicles. The PNC is a central computer system, based in Hendon, just north of London. It is accessed from terminals in police stations throughout Britain.

The Requirements of the System

The aims of the PNC vehicle information system are as follows:

- To provide details of any vehicle reported to it from a terminal. The vehicle is identified by its registration mark, make, model, colour or any combination of these. The computer gives a full description of the vehicle and the name and address of its owner.

- To confirm whether or not a particular vehicle has been reported as stolen or missing.
- To cope with a large volume of such queries in a very short time. The response time must be fast enough for the information to be radioed from the police station to an officer who is questioning the driver of a vehicle.
- To keep the information up-to-date and accurate.

Computer System Design

A police car on patrol. The officers in the car can be put in touch with the Police National Computer via their radio.

Outputs
A full vehicle record (see below) is displayed on screen.

Inputs
The details of all new vehicles registered in Britain and amendments to existing details are sent on magnetic tape by the **Driver and Vehicle Licensing Centre (DVLC)** in Swansea every night. These details are input directly from the tapes into the Vehicle Owners File.

The information on stolen vehicles is entered at the PNC terminals by police officers all over the country.

When an enquiry is made, the commonest input is the registration mark of the vehicle. This may or may not be complete. However, any other combination of particulars, such as the make, model or colour, may be entered.

File structure
The Vehicle Owners File contains a record for each vehicle, including the following fields:

Field	Type	Length	Example
Registration Mark	Alpha	8	D869 RGY
Chassis No	Alpha	12	RX89665B
Engine No	Alpha	12	SEM865G
Make	Alpha	20	Jaguar
Model	Alpha	20	X40
Colour	Alpha	20	red
Year of Registration	Numeric	4	1986
Keeper Surname	Alpha	20	Williams
Keeper First Name	Alpha	20	Paul
Keeper Second Name	Alpha	20	Irving
Keeper Address 1	Alpha	20	483 Millbank Towers
Keeper Address 2	Alpha	20	Pimlico
Keeper Address 3	Alpha	20	London
Keeper Postcode	Alpha	8	SW1P 4RD

Note that the chassis and engine numbers are entered as alphabetic fields, as they often include letters.

There are more than 30 million records in the Vehicle Owners File. The records of stolen vehicles are kept on a separate file, with a structure similar to the main file.

File processing
The nightly update of the file is done as a **batch processing** operation. The file of new vehicles, deleted vehicles and amendments to registration details from the DVLC is the **transaction file**. It is already in the same order as the records on the PNC file. It produces an updated vehicle file, as shown in Figure 10.4.

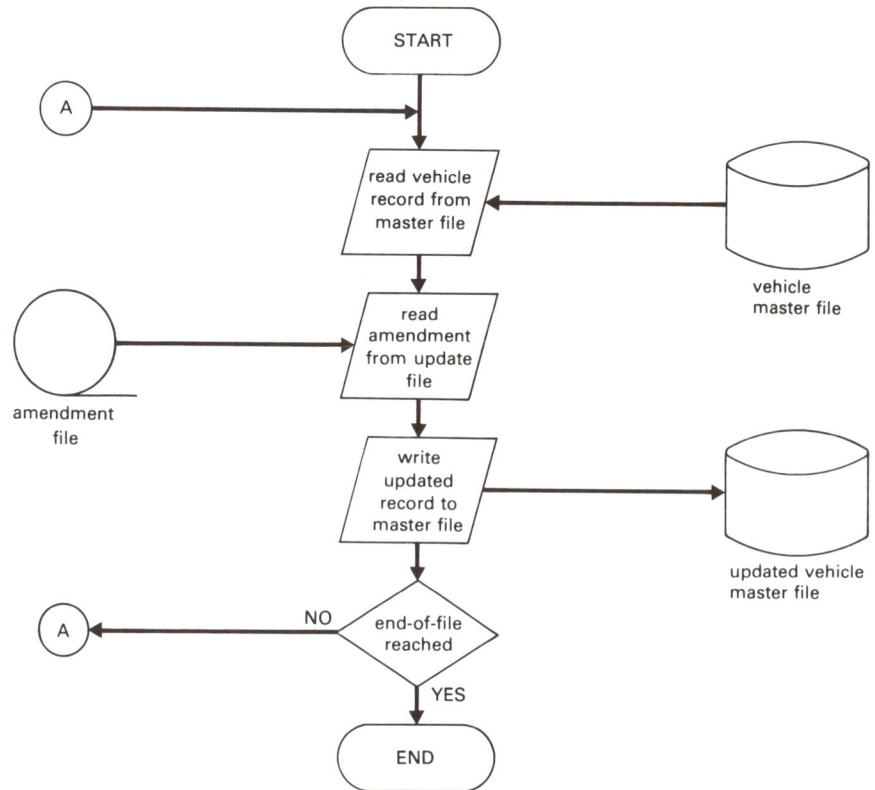

Figure 10.4 Police National Computer—
vehicle records: file updating

A police officer at a PNC terminal. He also
has telephone and radio communications
facilities.

System Diagram

Implementation

Enquiries are handled interactively, in **real time**. The filing
system is designed for multiple access to the files, and can deal with a
large number of such accesses in a short time. The sequence of events
is as follows:

- An officer enters a query at a terminal. Whatever details of the
  vehicle are known are entered. For example, if a witness to a hit-
  and-run accident reports a registration mark "starting with CN,
  ending with Y and including a 7 in the number", the registration
  mark is entered as CN? ?7?Y. A question mark indicates an
  unknown character.
- The information which has been entered is used to search the file,
  using **indexes** (see chapter 23) for rapid access.
- The number of records which match the query is reported to the
  terminal. The officer can choose to look at all of them, or enter
  additional information if there are too many.
- The matching records are sent to the terminal and displayed on
  the screen.

See Figure 10.5.

The vehicle information system is one of the systems running on a
large mainframe computer with three central processing units, 35
high-capacity disk drives and 15 magnetic tape units. There are four
high-speed data communications processors to link the computer to
the terminals. The terminals are on a network using special
telephone lines which links all police forces in the UK. The system

116

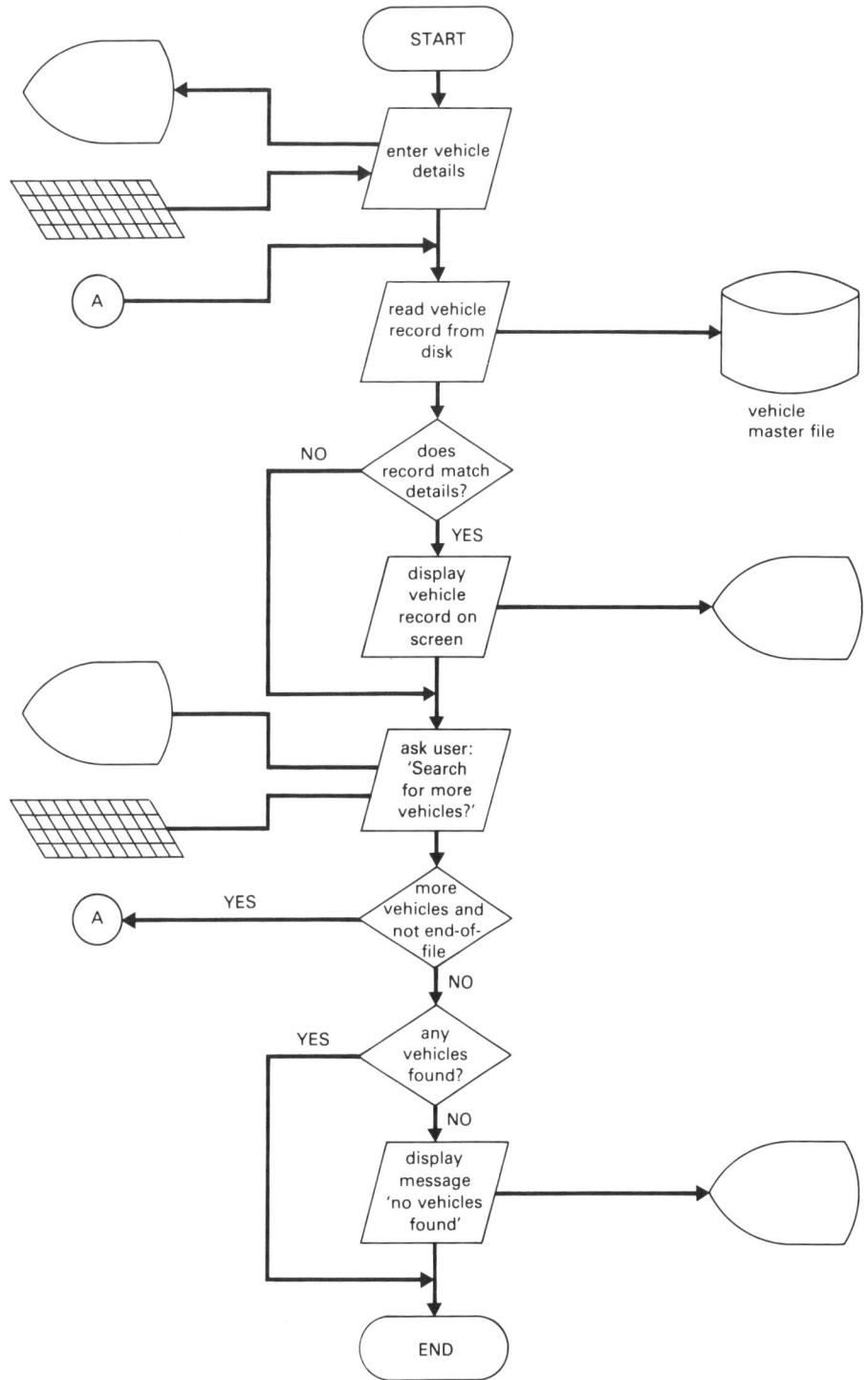

Figure 10.5 Police National Computer—
vehicle records: system diagram

operates continuously, even while units are disconnected for servicing. The hardware was chosen for its reliability and high speed of operation.

The software was designed specifically for the application. The main objective was to make the best use of the hardware, ensuring rapid access to the files and handling the large volume of requests.

Strict security measures are in force. Access to the computer installation is restricted, and passwords are needed by all officers who use it. Backup copies of the files are made every time they are updated: the computer switches to these immediately if the master files are corrupted. Most hardware devices of the computer system are duplicated. If any one fails, the system is re-configured to carry on without it.

Documentation

Detailed (and highly confidential) system documentation describes the overall operation of the hardware and software of the system and the structure of the files and indexes to them. The workings of the programs are also described in detail. This documentation is kept up-to-date all the time as the system is maintained.

Operator documentation describes the procedures to be followed by the staff who operate the computer installation.

There is a brief guide to the operation of terminals, written in non-technical language. Police officers are given a short training course before they use the equipment.

Questions

1 Write down in your own words the sequence of events that takes place when a car is stopped by a police officer.
2 Why is it important to trace stolen vehicles as quickly as possible?
3 In what ways has the PNC improved the ability of the police to trace stolen vehicles?
4 What factors were taken into consideration when selecting the hardware for the PNC system?
5 What usually happens if one of the units of the PNC breaks down?

10D Issue: Computers and the Police

Computers are used by police forces in the UK and other countries for an increasing number of purposes. In addition to the files on motor vehicles discussed in section 10C, the Police National Computer has files of all persons wanted by the police or reported missing, an index to the national criminal records file, and an index to the Metropolitan Police fingerprint file.

These files mean that, for example, if the driver of a car behaves suspiciously and is stopped and questioned by a police officer, the officer can contact the police station by radio with details of the car. The officer at the station can enter these details on a PNC terminal and find out:

- whether the person driving the car is its registered owner
- whether the car has been reported stolen
- whether the car has false number plates
- whether the driver is wanted by the police.

This information is reported back to the officer on the scene. The person driving the car may be arrested on the basis of any of the above information from the computer. A number of people who have committed serious crimes have been apprehended in this way. These include the Yorkshire Ripper, Peter Sutcliffe. However, it is possible that in spite of all the checks built into the system the information on the computer is out-of-date or incorrect. This could lead to someone being wrongfully arrested.

Police forces throughout Britain have computers which help them to control the way they use their resources. These **command and control** computers help to select which vehicle to send in answer to

Police officers interviewing a driver.

an emergency call. They also help in planning the police response to serious disturbances. These computers help the police respond rapidly to calls, and to make the best use of the officers, vehicles and equipment at their disposal. They are essential in co-ordinating the response to a major incident such as a bomb explosion.

Forces are beginning to install computers to help in the investigation of major crimes. Each force is implementing a computer system to its own design, but all follow the **Holmes** guidelines set out by the Home Office. They store and index large amounts of information and evidence, and allow it to be searched in a number of ways.

Although the computers do not take any active part in the solving of crimes, they store bodies of information in which police officers detect patterns and from which they draw conclusions. The information on the computer may not be used directly in court, but it can make the case for the prosecution stronger by its detail, and the strength of the apparent links between items.

The first serious crime to be solved in Britain with the aid of a computer system of this sort was the series of offences committed by the Bedfordshire Fox, Malcolm Fairley, in 1984. A number of other major crimes have been investigated with the aid of computers. Claims have been made that the lack of computer facilities in earlier cases, notably that of the Yorkshire Ripper, delayed the apprehension of the criminal. However, although no such cases have occurred yet, it is possible that wrong information on the computer could lead police officers to draw wrong conclusions and to present their evidence strongly enough in court for a person to be wrongly convicted.

Questions

1 What problems could be caused by errors in the information on a police computer system?

2 In what ways are computers being used to help police forces in Britain deal with serious crimes?

3 Can information from a computer be used directly as evidence in court in Britain?

4 For what purposes are command and control computers used?

10E End-of-Chapter Summary

The main points of this chapter are as follows:

- Information retrieval systems on computers are replacing card indexes in libraries, police stations, schools, colleges and businesses.
- Information retrieval systems are interactive and operate in real time.
- A school library information retrieval system stores details of all the books in the library. It can be searched on any field to find the reference of a required book.
- Some estate agents use information retrieval systems to store details of the properties they have for sale. These can be searched according to the requirements of purchasers.
- The UK Police National Computer has files of vehicles and their owners, stolen vehicles, missing or wanted persons, a fingerprint index and an index to the UK criminal records file. Information can be retrieved rapidly from these files from any of the PNC terminals at police stations.

Exercise 10

1   Choose the correct word from the list for each of the following spaces:

records; screen; input; output; searched; fields; terminal.

A request for information is entered at a PNC ____. Details about a vehicle are ____ and the vehicle file is ____. Any ____ which match the input ____ are ____ on the ____ of the terminal.

2   A person runs a small interior decoration business. She is based at her home, and travels in the local area to do painting, decorating and repair work. She has bought a desktop microcomputer and a software package for information retrieval.
(a) Suggest some ways in which the information retrieval system could be used.
(b) Select *one* of the suggested uses, and design the system in outline, stating the outputs, inputs and file structure.

3   Make a list of as many computer applications you can think of which involve information storage and retrieval.

Things to find out

1   Television licences in the UK are recorded on an information retrieval system. It is used to record the payment of the licence fees, and also by the detector vans which look for unlicenced televisions in use. Find out more about the system, and write a report on it. Include in your report:
(a) the aims of the system
(b) a description of the file of information which is used
(c) notes on how the information is input, output and processed
(d) your opinion on the advantages and any disadvantages of the system compared with a manual system.

2   Find out more about the way computers are used by police forces for the investigation of crimes:
(a) Find out what computer systems are used by the police force in your area, and whether any new ones are planned.
(b) Look for reports on any cases which have been cleared up with the aid of a computer.
(c) Look for reports of cases where a computer was not used and there were complaints about the lack of a computer.
(d) Write a brief report on your findings.

Points to discuss

1   Discuss the advantages and disadvantages that a computer system of the sort described in section 10B might have for an estate agent. Start by discussing the importance of information for the work of estate agents.

2   Discuss the advantages and disadvantages of the way in which computers are used by the police from the point of view of:
(a) senior police officers who are responsible for the rate of detection of crimes, and the way in which police forces spend the money allocated to them;
(b) people accused of crimes, and the lawyers who represent them in court;
(c) the general public.

Project starters

1   Using the library book information system as an example, design and implement *one* of the following systems or a similar one of your choice. This may form your GCSE project.
(a) An index for a record, slide, video cassette or stamp collection, running on a home computer.
(b) An inventory of home equipment such as washing machine, television, video recorder, etc. for insurance purposes, and so that maintenance of the equipment can be arranged.
(c) A garden information base, containing records of popular types of flowers and shrubs. For each species, information is stored about the type of soil, amount of light and amount of water it needs, and the months for planting, pruning, flowering, etc.
(d) An information base of local employment opportunities for school leavers. Each record contains the details of one job currently available.

11   Word Processing

Word processing is one of the commonest applications of computers. It is the use of computers to handle text, a task very different from the 'number crunching' work for which computers were originally designed. A word processing program allows the person using it to enter and edit documents, to store them on disk and retrieve them later, and to print all or part of a document whenever required. A word processor is interactive and responds immediately to each keystroke.

Word processors are used in the legal profession for contracts, in education to prepare texts and worksheets, by authors and translators, and, above all, in business for correspondence. In all these fields, they are taking over from typewriters as their benefits become more apparent, and the price of a word processor continues to fall. Word processors are the basis of electronic newspaper production systems which are replacing traditional methods in most newspapers.

This chapter introduces the use of word processors to produce a letter to a pen-friend and a business report, and discusses their use in newspaper production. It shows some further ways in which the general ideas of chapter 9 are put into practice.

11A   Activity: Letter to a Pen-friend

In this section you will use a word processor to produce a letter introducing yourself to a pen-friend. It can be to an imaginary pen-friend or, if your school has an exchange system based on electronic mail, to someone with whom you are going to correspond via electronic mail (chapter 20).

The Requirements of the Task

The aim is to produce a letter, two or three pages long, about yourself: your family, your work at school, your interests and hobbies, your views on things, and something about the place where you live—what it is like, and what there is to do.

The letter is to be produced in three stages: an **outline**, a **first draft**, and a **final copy**. The outline is first written on paper and then typed on the word processor; the other stages are done entirely on the word processor. Many important business documents are produced in these three stages—outline, draft and final copy (or **top copy**)—using word processors.

Computer System Design

Outputs

The outputs are printed copies of the three stages of the letter: the outline, the first draft and the final copy.

The text of a letter on a computer screen. The layout of the letter on the screen is the same as the layout when it is printed.

System Diagram

Inputs

The text of the outline of the letter is entered at the keyboard. This forms the basis of the first draft. The corrections to the first draft are entered to give the final copy.

File structure

The letter is stored on disk as a **text file**. This is a sequence of characters with no record structure. Some of the characters are text, others are control characters which specify how the text is set out.

File processing

The word processing program creates a text file for the letter when the outline is typed. Text is inserted, amended or deleted at any point in the file as the other versions are produced. Most word processors keep the only portion of the file which is being worked on at the time in memory; the rest is on disk. Text is transferred to and from the disk automatically as you work through the document.

When you finish working on the letter, the text is stored on disk. Most word processors do this automatically as you close down the letter; a few ask you whether you want to save the letter on disk (you do!). The next time you work on the letter, you call it up from disk. When the revised version is saved on disk, it overwrites the previous version. Some word processors keep the previous version as a **backup** file.

See Figure 11.1.

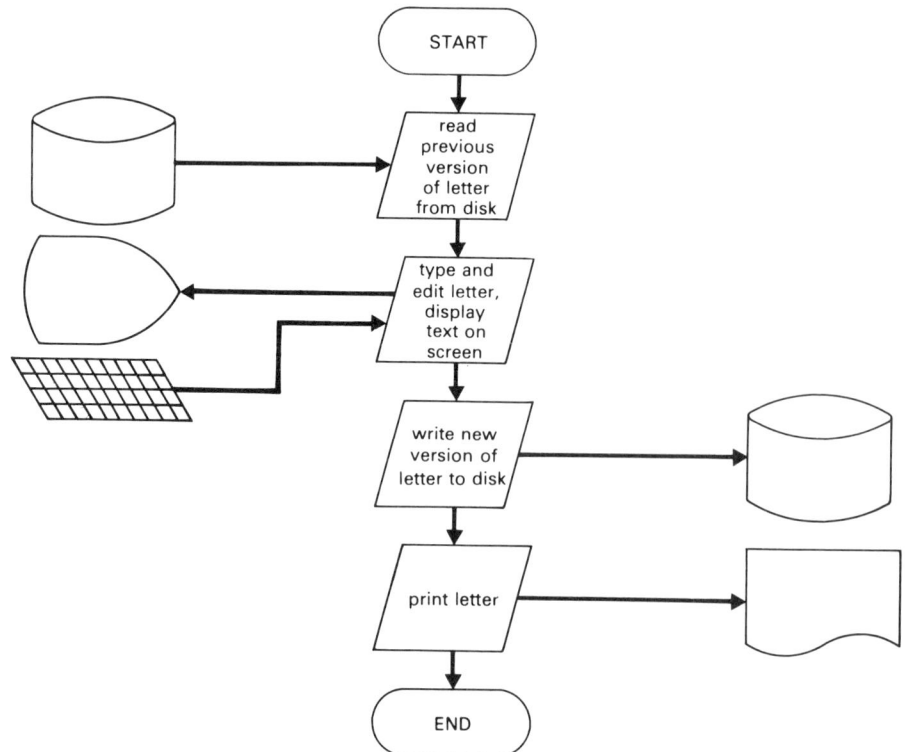

Figure 11.1   Word processor: system diagram

Implementation

First write the outline of the letter on paper: write headings for each topic you want to tell your pen-friend about, and list a few main points under each heading. Check your outline carefully, making sure that the points are all relevant and interesting and that they are in a sensible order.

Use the word processing program on your school computer to produce your letter:

- Look at the user guide for the word processor, and find out how to carry out each operation you require. (Most word processors can do far more than the things you need to do—try not to get lost in all the details.)

The outline

- Open up a new document for your letter. If necessary, give the document a **reference** to identify it on disk.
- You will see a blank area on your computer screen which will contain the text of your letter. At the top corner is a bright square or underline symbol which may be flashing on and off. This is the **cursor**, which shows where your next typed character will appear.
- Type the outline of the letter, copying it from your paper. The cursor moves along the line as you type. If you make a mistake, move the cursor back to the wrong character and delete it. Type the correct character in its place.
- When you have finished, move the cursor back to the start of the outline and check it carefully. Correct any errors you find.
- Save the outline on disk and print it. While someone else is having a turn at the word processor, check the printed copy of the outline, and mark any mistakes you find.

The first draft

- Call up the document containing the outline of your letter. You will see it on the screen, exactly as it was before you last closed it down.
- Correct any mistakes you found on the printed copy.
- Type each paragraph of the letter under the heading from the outline. When you have finished with the points from the outline, delete the headings.
- Set the paragraphs out as neatly as possible, using the facilities of the word processor to move the text on the screen.
- When you have finished, move the cursor to the start of the letter, and check it. Correct any mistakes you find.
- Save the first draft of the letter on disk, and print it.
- While someone else is having a turn at the word processor, check the printed copy of the first draft very carefully. Mark all the spelling and grammar mistakes, and mark any places where the sentences sound awkward.

The top copy

- Call up the draft of your letter on the word processor.
- Move the cursor through the text, and make all the corrections you have marked on the draft. Be very careful not to introduce any new errors.
- Move the cursor back to the top of the letter and give it one final check.
- Print the top copy of the letter, and save it on disk.

11B Application: Business Report

At least once a year, companies have to produce a report on their activities. The report is for the owners or shareholders of the company, and a copy of it is made public. This section describes the steps involved in producing such a report in a typical company, using word processing.

The Requirements of the Task

The aim is to produce the annual report of a company, covering its various activities. Sections are written by the various directors:

- the managing director writes the general section
- the accounts director describes the finances
- the marketing director describes the market for the company's products, and how they are being presented to the market
- the sales director reports on sales
- the personnel director discusses staff issues.

These sections need to be edited so that they have a similar style and do not duplicate information (or contradict each other!). Drafts of the report must be approved by all the directors. The final version must be ready for the company's annual meeting. Usually, about two weeks are allowed from the time of the first drafts to the time when the final version is sent to be printed.

Implementation

The secretary to the managing director is responsible for coordinating the production of the report. The steps are as follows:

- At a meeting, the directors agree on the overall structure of the report and on the main points to be made.
- The secretary enters an outline of the report on her word processor, based on her notes from the meeting, and sends a copy to all directors.
- Each director dictates a draft of his or her section of the report. The directors' secretaries enter these sections on their word processors.
- The accounts director copies a summary of the company's accounts from the accounting program to a word processor document.
- The managing director's secretary collects the disks from the other secretaries with the various sections of the report. She creates a document for the report, and copies the sections into it, in order. She includes the summary of the accounts at the appropriate place.
- The secretary works through the entire document, correcting errors and editing the style (but not the contents!). She saves the revised document on disk, and prints a copy for each director.
- The directors study the draft and mark their amendments on their copies. The managing director's secretary collects all the drafts and copies all the amendments onto a fresh printout.
- The managing director looks at the single marked copy and decides which amendments should be made. His secretary enters the amendments on her word processor, checks the whole document very carefully, and prints another draft.
- When the last few errors have been corrected the final version is printed. It is given to the managing director for his approval, and then sent to the printer.

The pages of a company's annual report.

1 How are the documents transferred from one word processor to another in this application?
2 How often is the material on the company report printed? Comment on your answer.
3 (a) Write down an equivalent series of steps for the production of a company annual report, assuming that all the work is done on typewriters.
(b) Comment on the benefits of using word processors for this task.

Project starter

1 Present a report on the activities of a school club or similar organisation, using the same overall steps as in this section. The report is written by a team of pupils, each describing one aspect of the activities. Each pupil enters his or her section of the report on a word processor, and the co-ordinator copies them all into a single document. This document is then amended by all the team members, and a final version is produced which incorporates all the amendments.

11C Application: Electronic Newspaper Production

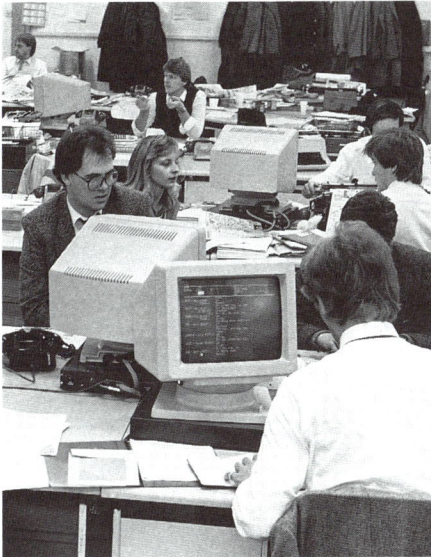

A newsroom with a number of word processors in use by reporters.

For many years, the method of producing newspapers was as follows. Reporters would gather news and write it in their notebooks. They returned to the offices of the newspaper and typed the stories on typewriters. Sub-editors marked up these stories and corrected the errors. The stories were typeset by keying in the text again and producing long strips of the stories, one column wide. The strips were then cut and pasted onto page grids, together with headlines, photographs and advertisements, to form the page masters. These page masters were then photographed to produce the print masters.

This is a slow, inefficient and expensive process. Newspapers are produced to tight schedules, and changes are often made at the last moment. A change in a page often means that the whole page has to be made up again. Because the text is typed twice, it is difficult to correct errors. Large numbers of staff are needed, all of whom are paid high wages.

To overcome these problems, most newspapers in Western Europe and North America are now produced by computerised systems, using word processors to enter and edit text. Some of these systems work in colour, others are restricted to black and white. Newspapers in Great Britain are following this trend. As the leading papers change to the new technology, others are being forced to follow in order to match their efficiency.

The Requirements of the Task

A computerised newspaper production system has the following aims:

- To provide an integrated computer system for entering and editing text, making up pages, incorporating headings, photographs and artwork, and producing page masters ready for printing.
- To be able to cope with changes to articles quickly and easily, and with the minimum repetition of work.
- To provide links between workstations so that material which is entered at one workstation is accessible from any other workstation for editing or viewing.
- To allow articles to be edited to fit into prescribed places on the page.
- To operate efficiently and at minimum cost.

Computer System Design

page description
file

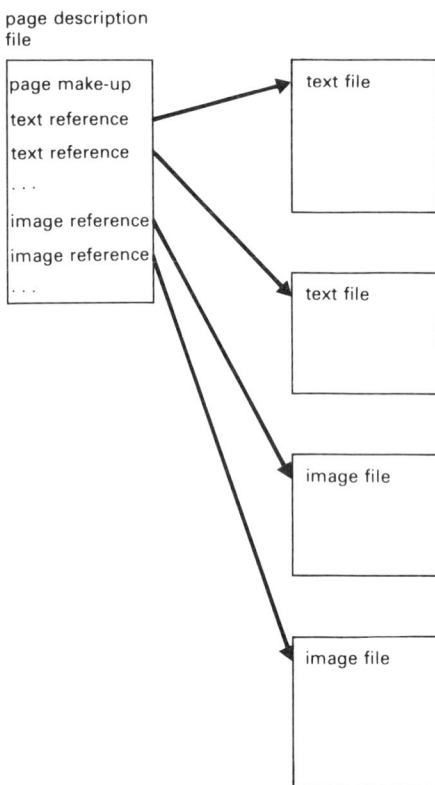

Figure 11.2 Electronic newspaper system:
page description file

A page make-up terminal in use. The
newspaper page is laid out on the screen as
it will appear when printed. Note the quality
of the photograph reproduced on the screen.

System Diagram

Implementation

Outputs

The final output from the system is the image of each complete page, ready for transmission to the printing plant. Intermediate outputs are drafts of articles and proofs of pages for checking.

Inputs

The text of articles is entered on a word processing system. Photographs, advertisements and other artwork are scanned to produce electronic images.

File structure

There is a file for each page, containing a description of the make-up of the page, and references to the text and image files which occupy the blocks in the page. See Figure 11.2.

Each article is stored in a **text file**. This contains the characters of the text, and control characters which determine what size and style of type is used and how the article is set out.

Each photograph and item of artwork is stored as an **image file**. This describes the tone or colour of each dot which makes up the image.

File processing

See the section on the operation of the system, below.

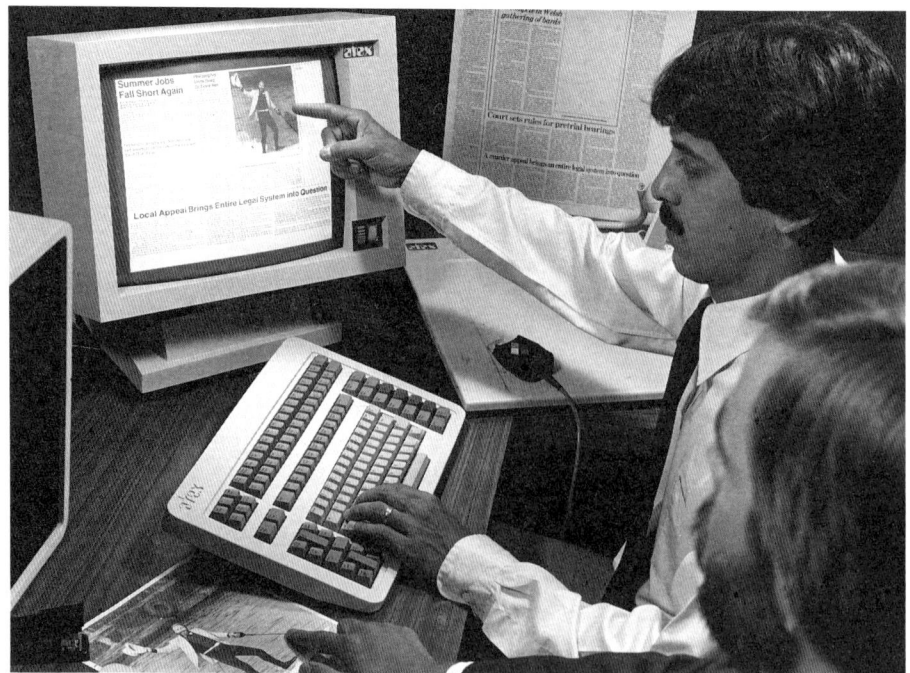

See Figure 11.3.

Hardware

The hardware of an electronic newspaper production system consists of a central computer (a large minicomputer or small mainframe) connected to a number of workstations, as shown in Figure 11.4. The reporters have text entry workstations which operate as ordinary word processors. The page make-up terminals can show the layout of an entire page, or an enlarged portion of a page.

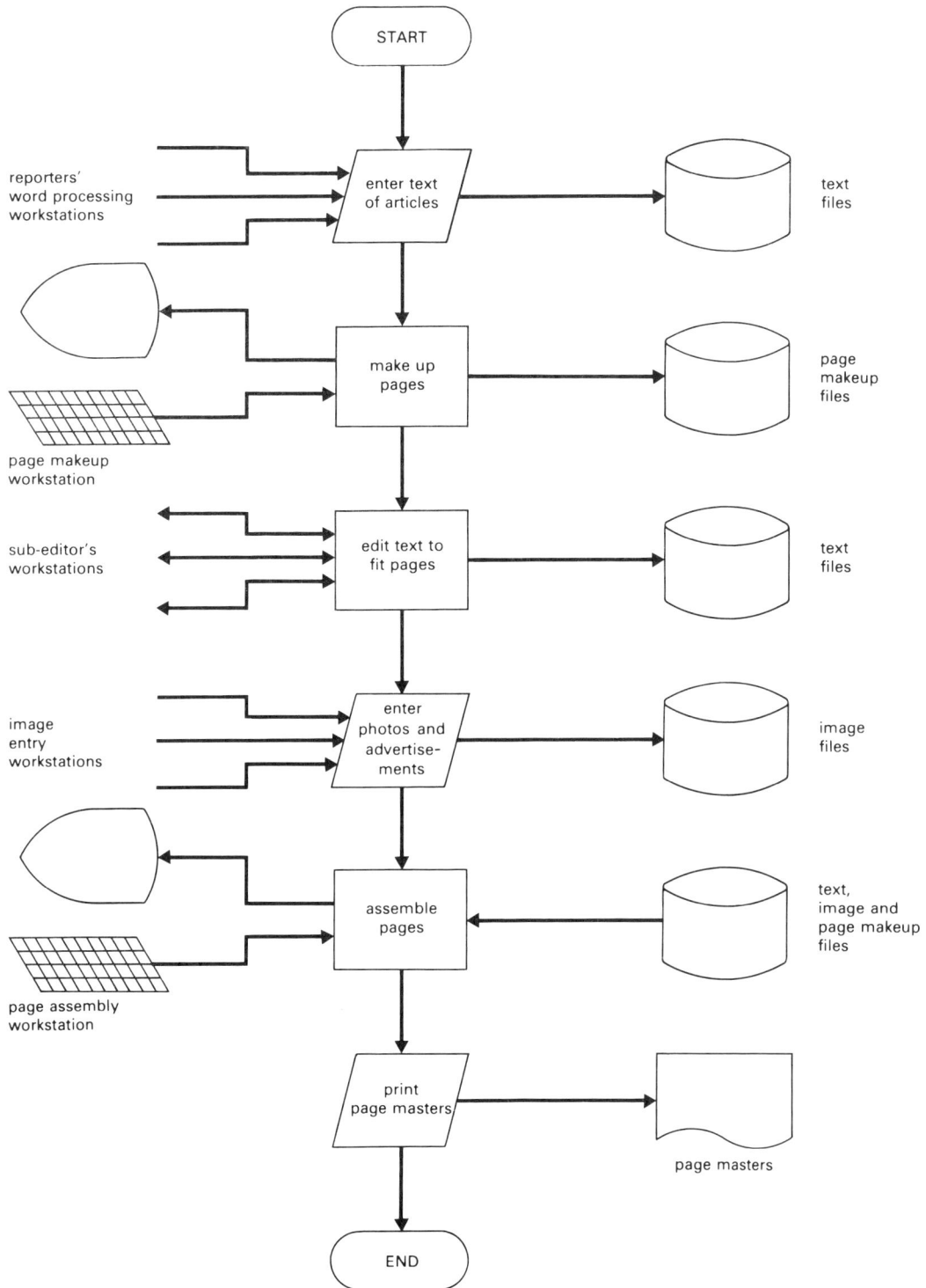

Figure 11.3   Electronic newspaper system: system diagram

The sub-editors have **split-screen** workstations. One half of the screen is for word processing. The other half of the screen shows the part of a page containing the block into which the article fits. The text of the article is shown as a series of lines inside its block. If it is too short, there is blank space at the end of the block; if it is too long, the lines overflow the block.

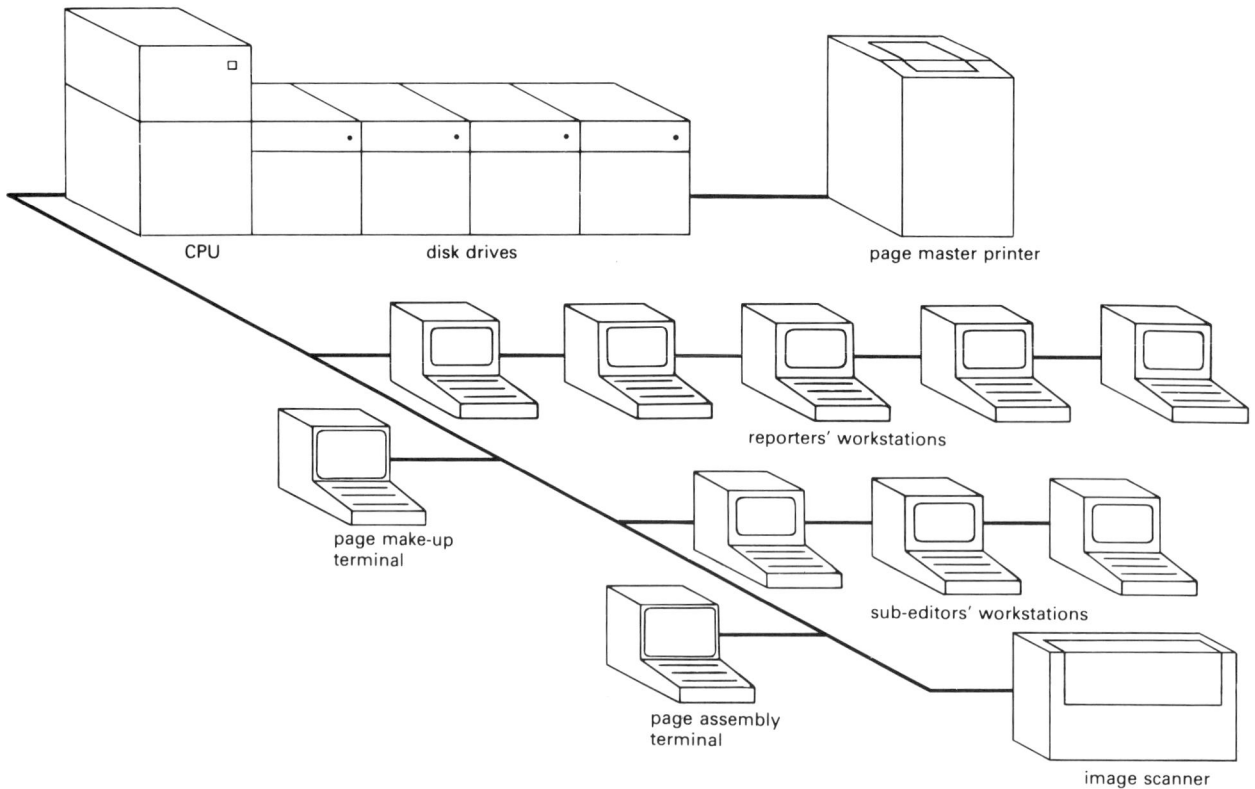

11.4 Electronic newspaper system: hardware

There are scanning stations for the input of photographs and artwork, and image editing stations where they are enlarged, reduced and cropped to fit into their spaces on the page. The image editing stations enable the final image of an entire page to be checked before it is output.

Software

The software for the system is developed by computer companies which specialise in systems of this sort. They supply the software, tailored to the requirements of the particular newspaper, and maintain it.

The software allows simultaneous access to the files in real time. It implements a security mechanism based on passwords. Passwords allow their users to perform certain tasks and have access to certain files only. For example, reporters have access only to articles in their own field—sports, financial news, etc.

Operation of the system

The cycle of events, starting in the middle of the morning and ending in the middle of the night, is as follows:

- The day starts with an editorial conference at which the general layout of the next day's paper is planned. The stories and events to be covered are assigned to reporters.
- The reporters and photographers go out to gather news, interview people, attend events, etc. They also study information sent to the office by news agencies, and monitor radio and television broadcasts.

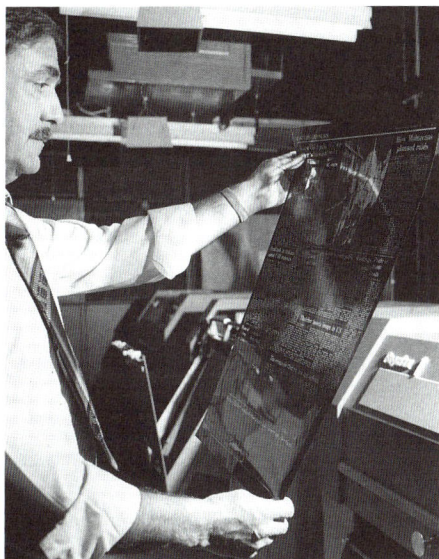

The image of a newspaper page, as it is received on the high-resolution facsimile machine at a printing plant.

- The reporters return to the office and enter their articles on the word processing workstations. The photographers have their films developed. The best photographs are scanned into the system.
- The layouts of each page are entered at the page make-up terminals. The disk reference of each article and photograph is entered into the space it occupies.
- The sub-editors use the split-screen terminals to edit each article, and adjust the length of it so that it fits into the available space.
- Proofs are printed and checked.
- The photographs and artwork are selected and edited to fit the available spaces.
- The image of each complete page is checked carefully.
- The page is printed. It is then read by a high-resolution **facsimile** system and transmitted via a telephone line to the printing plant, where a copy is produced. This is photographed onto the plate used for printing the page.
- When all the pages have been received at the printing plant, the presses are started.

This cycle of operation is seldom as straightforward as the steps above indicate! As late news reaches the office, articles, headings, photographs and page layouts are changed to incorporate it. The advantage of the electronic system is that these changes can be done quickly, and it is easy to adjust existing material to make room for them. Printing a new master copy of a page and sending it to the press takes only a few minutes.

Documentation

The software developers have detailed systems documentation describing the design of the system, the file structures, and the working of the programs which operate on the data.

The newspapers which use the system give their staff training courses in the operation of the equipment. The system is easy enough to operate without user documentation. The computer runs unattended, so no operator documentation is needed.

Questions

1 How is word processing used in the production of a newspaper?
2 (a) How are the page images sent from the editorial offices to the printing plants?
(b) What are the benefits of having a number of printing plants up and down the country, rather than a single, central plant?
3 While a newspaper is being printed, a news item arrives which makes one of the minor stories on the front page more important than the main story. Describe the steps which are taken to change the front page, using a computerised system.
4 Summarise in your own words the main stages of producing a newspaper on a computerised system.

Project starter

1 If your school computer has page make-up software, a group of pupils can put together a class newspaper following the steps of section 11C. Divide the group into reporters, sub-editors, compositors (who design the page layouts) and illustrators to draw the graphics.

Decide what type of news to include in the newspaper: school news, local community news, or your own summaries of national news.

The reporters gather the news and type articles using the word processing program on the school's computer. The compositors design the pages, and the sub-editors edit the articles to fit the pages. The illustrators add drawings and any artwork to improve the appearance of the pages.

The complete pages are checked carefully and then the master copies are printed. Further copies can be photocopied.

11D Issue: Trade Unions and IT

The introduction of information technology into the UK newspaper industry has caused a long and bitter conflict between unions and management. Systems of the type described in the previous section have made large numbers of print workers redundant. A number of crafts have disappeared entirely.

The trade unions representing the workers whose jobs are disappearing have resisted the changes for many years. There have been strikes, lockouts, sudden closures of plants and transfers to new plants, dismissals and redundancies. This has delayed the introduction of new technology, but not prevented it. In the process, the traditional power of unions in newspapers has been severely weakened.

However, all the jobs in newspapers produced by new technology remain unionised, as other unions take over from traditional print unions to represent workers in the new types of job. The reduction in costs brought about by the use of new technology is helping newspapers to stay in business and, in some cases, to expand. This makes the remaining jobs in the industry more secure than they were before the introduction of new technology.

Questions

1 What are the effects on jobs of the introduction of IT in the newspaper industry?
2 In what ways do computers save money in the production of newspapers?
3 In what ways have trade unions responded to the change to new technology in the newspaper industry in the UK?
4 Have computers put an end to the involvement of trade unions in newspaper production?

11E End-of-Chapter Summary

The main points of this chapter are as follows:

- A word processor has facilities for entering and editing text, for saving documents on disk and retrieving them, and for printing documents.
- Word processors are interactive and work in real time.
- Word processing is one of the commonest computer applications. Word processors are used extensively in business, education, the legal profession, and by authors and translators.
- Word processor documents are stored on disk as text files, with no record structure. Each document is identified on disk by a reference.
- During typing and editing, a cursor shows the position of the next character to be typed.
- Word processing is the basis of electronic newspaper production, which is replacing previous methods of producing newspapers.
- Electronic newspaper production has led to the redundancy of large numbers of print workers. There have been bitter disputes between trade unions and newspaper managers over the introduction of information technology in newspapers.

Exercise 11

1   Choose the correct word from the list for each of the following spaces:

edited; keyboard; printed; disk; draft; reference.

The secretary entered a ____ of the document at the ____ of her word processor. She saved the document on disk, giving it a ____. She printed the draft and gave it to her manager to correct. She called up the document from ____ and ____ it. She saved the revised version on disk, and ____ the top copy.

2   Use the word processor on your school's computer to produce any of the following. Follow the steps of section 11A.
(a) an article for a magazine
(b) a poem
(c) a questionnaire to find out pupils' opinions on some topic
(d) a letter of application for a job.

3   Using the word processor on your school's computer, and your letter or another document as a text, do as many of the following as possible:
(a) Move a paragraph from one part of the document to another.
(b) Move a sentence from one part of a paragraph to another. Re-align the paragraph afterwards so that the left and right margins are lined up properly.
(c) Make a copy of a sentence in another place in the document.
(d) Save one section of the text as a separate document with its own disk reference.
(e) Read another document from disk into the one you are working on.
Discuss some of the ways in which these facilities can be used. Comment on the benefits of them.

4   Devise a coding system for the references of word processor documents. For example, you may identify each topic by a set of letters, and number the documents in each category. For example, a set of Biology notes might be identified by the letters BIO; the document BIO12 is the twelfth document in this set.

5   A small business produces wooden toys which it sells to shops. The company buys three identical microcomputers, all with word processing software. Suggest some uses for the word processing facilities. What advantages do they have over the use of typewriters for the same tasks?

Things to find out

1   (a) Find out about some more uses of word processing in addition to those mentioned in the text.
(b) Choose one of the applications and write a report on it. Follow the structure of section 11C in setting out the report.

2   Choose one national newspaper which has changed to computerised production methods recently. Find out:
(a) how many jobs were lost in the process,
(b) what compensation was paid to those who were made redundant,
(c) what negotiations took place between the trade unions representing the workers who lost their jobs and the management of the newspaper, and what the outcome of these negotiations was,
(d) whether other trade unions have taken over the representation of the workers in the new jobs.

Points to discuss

1   Discuss the advantages and disadvantages of the change to new technology at a newspaper from the point of view of:
(a) the managers of a newspaper
(b) the workers who lost their jobs, and their trade unions
(c) the workers who operate the new equipment, and their trade unions
(d) the readers of the newspaper.

Project starter

1   Write a simple user guide for a computer program you often use:
(a) Choose a suitable program, and make sure that you know how to use it. Your user guide does not have to describe every part of the program—it can cover just the parts which you find useful, and which you want others to be able to use.
(b) Write down the main points you want to cover in your user guide: how to start the program, how to operate the features, how to save things on disk and print them, and how to close down.
(c) Type these points into a word processor document, and get someone else to check them. Ask the other person to check whether any important points have been left out, and whether the points are in the right order. They will form the headings of the user guide.
(d) Edit the document to make any changes to the main points.
(e) Now make a first draft of the user guide, using the main points as headings. Use clear English, and keep it as short as possible.
(f) Check the draft carefully, correcting spelling mistakes and other errors.
(g) Print the draft and try out the user guide yourself. Get at least two other people to try it out as well, and make notes of their comments.
(h) Revise the user guide on the basis of your trial and the comments from the other people who have tried it out.
(i) Print a final copy of the user guide.

12 Spreadsheets

A graph being produced from a spreadsheet on an office computer system.

A spreadsheet is a table of numbers on which calculations can be performed. The table is set out in rows and columns; each number occupies a **cell** in the table. A cell may also contain an item of text (a **label**) or a formula. The formula calculates the number in the cell from numbers in other cells. Spreadsheets are interactive: the user enters and edits numbers, labels and formulae, and re-evaluates the formulae whenever required. The current version of the spreadsheet appears on the computer screen.

Spreadsheets are a relatively new computer application. They were first introduced in the late 1970s for use on microcomputers. They are now implemented on every kind of computer and are one of the most popular uses of computers. They are used on home computers for family budgets, in schools and college for setting out calculations and in research for mathematical modelling, but their main area of use is in business. Here, spreadsheets are used for summaries of accounts, analysis of stock levels, and for planning. Their strength is that alternative plans can be tried out easily, and their consequences calculated immediately.

This chapter introduces the use of a spreadsheet to plan the budget for a school visit, and to keep a record of a bank account. It discusses the use of spreadsheets in a company for planning. It puts the general ideas of chapter 9 into practice in a popular type of computer application.

12A Activity: Budget for School Visit

The Requirements of the Task

This activity can be based on an actual school visit which is to take place in the near future, or on an imaginary visit. A suitable journey to plan is a visit to a nearby town, going to a museum in the morning and the theatre in the afternoon.

The aims are:

- To set up a table showing the costs of the visit and the payments made by the pupils going on the visit.
- To work out how much to charge each pupil so that the costs are just covered if a certain number of pupils come on the visit.
- To make a record of the actual amount of money received and spent, and any profit or loss, when the trip has taken place.

Computer System Design

Outputs

Printouts of the budget are made at two stages:

- when the provisional figures are first entered

● when the money has been received and spent, and the final totals are known.

While it is in use, the table is seen on the computer screen.

Inputs

The items in the budget and their costs are entered into the spreadsheet, as well as estimates of the number of pupils on the trip and the fee per pupil. These estimates are replaced by actual numbers when they are known.

Formulae are entered to calculate amounts by multiplying the number of pupils by the cost per pupil, and to add up totals. A formula is needed to subtract the total cost from the total income.

File structure

A spreadsheet is structured as a table of cells, set out in rows and columns. Each cell contains a number, label or formula. The number of rows and columns and the width of each column are specified. The layout of the spreadsheet for the school visit is shown in Figure 12.1.

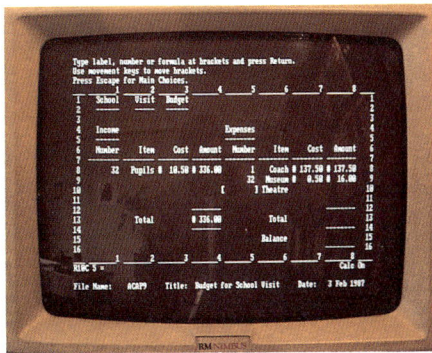

The budget for a school visit as a spreadsheet on a computer screen.

Figure 12.1   Spreadsheet of budget for school visit

File processing

The spreadsheet is set out, and the information is entered as described below. Each time the spreadsheet is recalculated, all the formulae are worked out and the results placed in the appropriate cells.

The spreadsheet may be written to disk or printed at any time. It may be read back from disk and revised whenever required.

System Diagram

Implementation

See Figure 12.2.

Use the spreadsheet program on your school computer. Look at the user guide for the program, and make sure that you understand how to operate it.

Note the way the cells are described. Some spreadsheets refer to cells by their row and column numbers. For example, R3C5 is the cell in the third row, fifth column. A formula to multiply the contents of this cell by the number in R3C6 and place the result in R3C7 is written as:

$$R3C7 = R3C5 * R3C6$$

Note that * is used for multiplication and / for division.

133

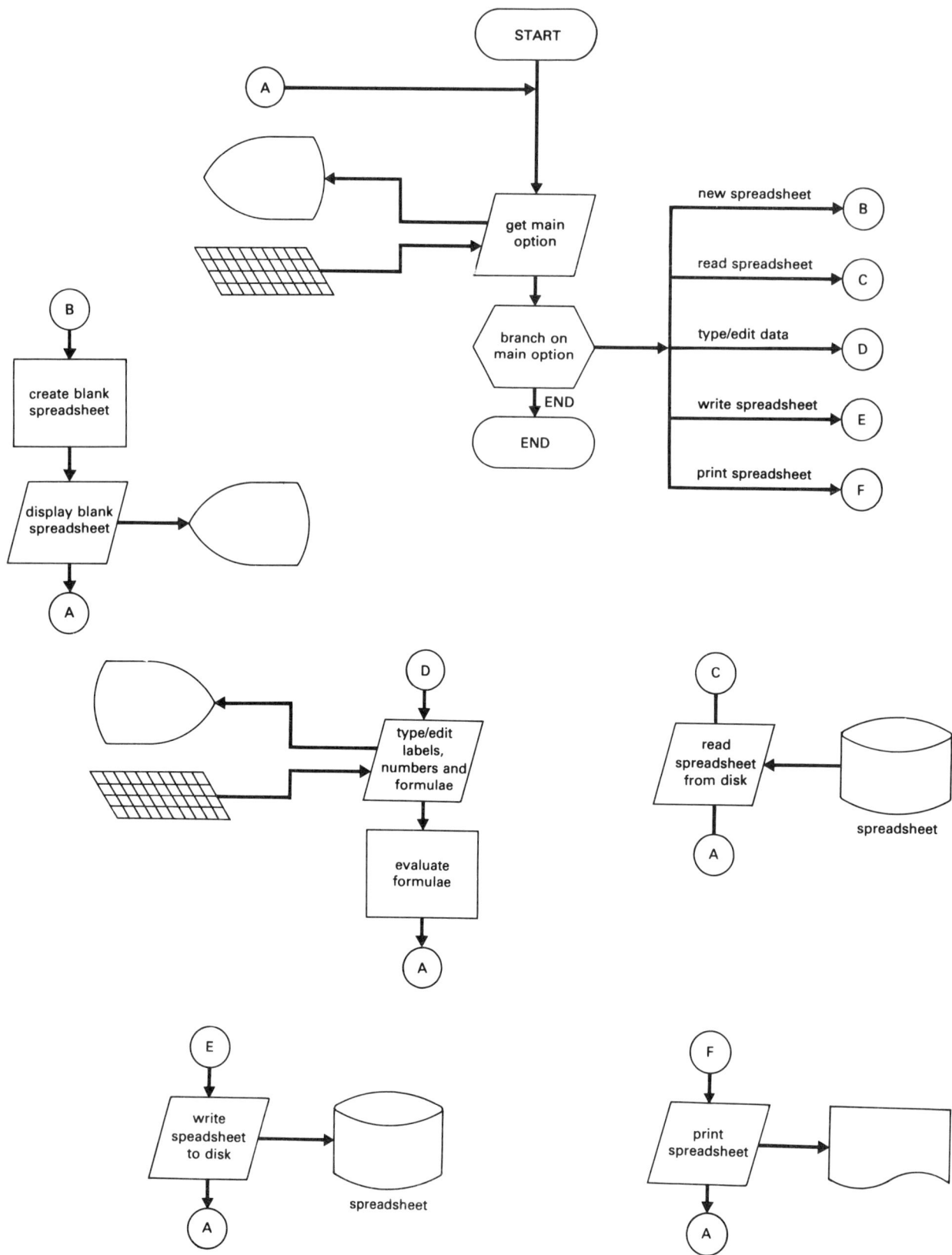

Figure 12.2   Spreadsheet: system diagram

An alternative method of describing cells is with a letter for the column, and a number for the row. Using this notation, the cell in the third row, fifth column is E3, and the above formula is:

$$G3 = F3 * E3$$

Note that the letter for the column occurs in front of the number for the row in the second notation.

- Create a new spreadsheet, and set out the columns as shown in Figure 12.1. Enter the text in the required cells.
- Enter the formulae for the amounts. For example, the amount paid by the pupils is the number of pupils multiplied by the cost per pupil. If the number of pupils is in R8C1 and the cost is in R8C3, the formula for the amount in R8C4 is:

$$R8C4 = R8C1 * R8C3$$

In the alternative notation, this formula is $D8 = A8 * C8$.

Similar formulae are needed for the amounts paid for the coaches, admission to the museum, and for the theatre tickets. It is likely that the cost of the coach is an amount per coach, and not per pupil. This does not affect the formula, but does affect the numbers entered in the cells.

- Enter the formulae for the totals. In most spreadsheets, these are written as the sum of cells from a certain cell to another. For example, the formula for the total expenses in cell R12C8 is:

$$R12C8 = sum(R8C8:R10C8)$$

or $H12 = sum(H8:H10)$.

- Enter the formula for the balance. This is the difference between the total income and the total expenses:

$$R14C8 = R12C4 - R12C8$$

or $H14 = D12 - H12$

- Save the spreadsheet in this form on disk. Give it a suitable disk reference. It has all the text and formulae, and can be used to try out combinations of numbers as often as required.
- Enter a simple set of numbers into the spreadsheet to check that the formulae are being evaluated correctly. When you are satisfied, read the blank spreadsheet back from the disk.
- Enter the cost of entry to the museum, and the price of the theatre tickets. Also enter the cost of hiring a coach.
- Enter a number of pupils which will nearly fill one coach (say 50) in the number column, and a 1 for the number of coaches. Estimate a suitable fee for each pupil to pay, and enter it.
- Switch calculations on, and see how the amounts, the totals and the balance are calculated.
- Change your estimates of the number of pupils and the fee per pupil until the balance comes out right. It should be a small positive number.
- Print the spreadsheet, and save it on disk. Give it a different disk reference from the 'blank' version.
- Make backup copies of the two versions of the spreadsheet.
- If your spreadsheet is for an actual visit, after the money has been

collected and the coaches have been hired, call up the spreadsheet again and make any changes so that the figures represent what was actually collected and paid. Save this version on disk and print it.

Documentation

Write a brief user guide for other pupils who might wish to use the spreadsheet. In your user guide:

- Explain how the spreadsheet is set out, and the purpose of the formulae.
- Provide clear instructions for entering numbers so as to modify the spreadsheet. Also explain how to recalculate the formulae, how to print the spreadsheet, and how to save it on disk.

12B Activity: Bank Account

When money is saved at a bank, it goes into an **account**. An entry is made in the account every time money is paid in and every time money is withdrawn. A **statement** of the account is sent by the bank to the person whose money is in the account. Statements are sent at regular intervals, generally once a month.

It is useful to keep your own record of the money going into and out of a bank account. This enables you to check that the bank statement is correct. It also tells you how much you have in the account after every deposit or withdrawal. You do not have to wait for the next statement to find out. This record can be kept using a spreadsheet.

The Requirements of the Task

The aim of the task is to set up a system which keeps a record of the money in a bank account. The account is updated every time a transaction is made. An up-to-date version of the account is saved on disk, and a printout may be made at any time.

Computer System Design

Outputs

The output is a screen display showing the details for each transaction: date, reference, description, amount, and the **balance** in the account after the transaction. Amounts paid in are shown in one column; amounts withdrawn are shown in another. See Figure 12.3.

```
      _____1_____ _____2_____ _____3_____ _____4_____ _____5_____ _____6
  1  A/C No:                      Month:                      Year:
  2  --------      --------      --------      --------      --------      --------
  3  Date            Ref           Item         Amt In       Amt Out       Balance
  4  --------      --------      --------      --------      --------      --------
  5


      _____1_____ _____2_____ _____3_____ _____4_____ _____5_____ _____6
  1  A/C No:       70101643       Month:        October       Year:         1986
  2  --------      --------      --------      --------      --------      --------
  3  Date            Ref           Item         Amt In       Amt Out       Balance
  4  --------      --------      --------      --------      --------      --------
  5  01/10/86                     Balance                                   £47.32
  6  02/10/86      Ch 189        WH Smith                     £8.95         £38.37
  7  04/10/86      Dep 225       Deposit       £10.00                       £48.37
  8  05/10/86      Ch 190        Cash                         £15.00        £33.37
  9  12/10/86      Ch 191        Next                         £19.95        £13.42
 10
```

Figure 12.3 Spreadsheet for personal bank account. *Top*: Blank account *Bottom*: Account with entries

136

The balance is the amount of money in the account. When money is paid in, it is added to the balance; when money is withdrawn, it is subtracted from the balance.

The display may be printed whenever required.

Inputs
Details of each transaction are typed at the keyboard and displayed on the screen.

File structure
The account is set out as a table, with one row for each entry and columns for each item. The layout is shown in Figure 12.3. A new spreadsheet is started for each month.

File processing
Every time a new transaction is entered, the balance in the account is updated. The new balance is shown on the same line as the entry.

System Diagram

See Figure 12.2.

Implementation

Use the spreadsheet program on your school computer. Set up a spreadsheet as shown in Figure 12.3:

- Enter the first line of labels for the account as a whole: the account number, month and year. Underline these in the cells below, and underline the spaces for the information.
- Enter the column headings as shown. Underline them in the row of cells below.
- Set the columns for Amount In, Amount Out and Balance to show numbers in currency format.
- The first entry in the account shows the balance from the previous month.
- Subsequent entries show one transaction—an amount of money paid in or withdrawn. The Reference is a cheque number, or the number on a deposit slip. The Item states what the money was spent on, or where it came from. Deposits are entered in the Amount In column; withdrawals in the Amount Out column.
- The Balance is calculated by a formula. The new balance is the previous balance plus any amount in, minus any amount out. For the first transaction, in row 6, the formula is:

$$R6C6 = R5C6 + R6C4 - R6C5$$

or $F6 = F5 + D6 - E6$. Enter this formula in the cell R6C6. Enter similar formulae in R7C6 and the cells below it. Allow sufficient lines for a month's entries.
- Save the blank account on disk. Give it a suitable reference.
- To use the spreadsheet for an account, call up the blank account and enter the account number, month and year.
- Enter the initial balance in the account. This can be the balance at the end of a previous month, or the amount with which a new account is opened.
- Enter one or more transactions to bring the account up-to-date.
- Save the up-to-date version of the account on disk, and make a backup copy of it. Give it a disk reference which identifies the account and the month. Do *not* use the same reference as the blank spreadsheet.

The monthly printout of a bank account.

- At a later date, when more transactions have been made, call up the spreadsheet and enter the new transactions. Save the updated version of the account, overwriting the previous version.
- At the end of the month, when all the entries for the month have been made, print the account. Save the final version on disk and make a backup copy of it.
- To start the account for the next month, call up the blank spreadsheet, and head it for the new month. Enter the initial balance, copying it from the final balance at the end of the previous month.

Documentation

Write a user guide so that other people can use the spreadsheet for bank accounts:

- Explain the purpose of the spreadsheet and the way it is set out.
- Describe the steps for starting a new spreadsheet for a new account.
- Describe how to make an entry, and save the updated version of the account.
- Describe how to print and save the account at the end of a month.
- Describe how to start up a spreadsheet for a new month, carrying over the balance.
- Describe how to make backup copies of the spreadsheet.

12C Application: Company Sales Analysis and Forecast

The commonest use of spreadsheets is for analysing figures, putting them into categories, and making plans based on such figures. This section follows an example of the use of a spreadsheet in this way, by a company which produces children's climbing frames. There are two models, the Alpine and the Everest. The Alpine is a small model, for use in gardens. The Everest is a larger model intended for parks.

At the beginning of the year, the marketing manager of the company has the task of estimating the monthly sales of the two models for the coming year. When his estimates have been approved by the other managers, they will form the basis of the production schedule for the year. They will also be used by the accountants to estimate the amount of money the company will receive each month.

The Requirements of the Task

The aim is to produce a table which shows:

- How many of each type of climbing frame were sold during each month of the previous year.
- Estimates of the corresponding sales for the current year.
- The total sales in each month, and of each product.

This table must be able to be updated easily by other managers, as they revise the estimates of the sales.

Computer System Design

Outputs
A screen display of the table is required all the time it is being used. The table may be printed whenever required.

138

Inputs

The sales figures for the previous year and the estimated figures for the current year are entered.

File structure

The file is a table set out in rows and columns. There is a row for each month of the year, and a column for each product and each year. There are totals for the months and the products. See Figure 12.4.

```
          1          2          3          4          5          6          7
   _____
 1 | Product  Classic              Pacer                Total
 2 | --------  --------            --------              --------
 3 |  Month      1987      1988      1987      1988      1987      1988
 4 | --------  --------  --------  --------  --------  --------  --------
 5 | January
 6 | February
 7 |  March
 8 |  April
 9 |   May
10 |  June
11 |  July
12 | August
13 | Septembr
14 | October
15 | November
16 | December
17 | --------  --------  --------  --------  --------  --------  --------
18 |  Total
19 | --------  --------  --------  --------  --------  --------  --------
20 |
```

Figure 12.4   Spreadsheet for company sales analysis

File processing

Whenever a figure is changed, all the totals which include this figure are updated.

System Diagram

See Figure 12.2.

Implementation

Using a spreadsheet program, a table is set up as shown in Figure 12.4.

- The headings for the products, years and months are entered.
- The formulae for the totals are typed in. For example, the total for January 1985 (R5C6) is the sum of the sales for the Alpine model for January 1985 (R5C2) and those for the Everest model (R5C4). The formula is:

$$R5C6 = R5C2 + R5C4$$

or $F5 = B5 + D5$.

The formula for the total Alpine sales in 1985 is:

$$R18C2 = sum(R5C2:R16C2)$$

or $B18 = sum(B2:B16)$.

- The previous year's figures are entered into the 1985 column by the sales department.
- This version of the spreadsheet is saved on disk.
- The marketing manager enters his estimates of the current year's sales figures. He applies his general knowledge of the state of the economy, and takes account of trends which were appearing during the previous year. He also takes into account what he knows of the products launched by other companies which make climbing frames.
- He saves the spreadsheet on disk, prints it, and sends copies to the other managers.

- A week later, the managers have a meeting. The marketing manager has his desktop computer at the meeting, with the spreadsheet program running. He brings up the sales forecast when his colleagues are discussing it.
- The managers suggest various changes to the sales estimates. These are entered into the spreadsheet, and the totals recalculated immediately.
- When all the managers are satisfied, the spreadsheet is saved on disk, backed up and printed. Copies are made for all the managers.

Questions

1 (a) How often is the spreadsheet in the above section printed?
(b) What other output method is used for it?
(c) Comment on the benefits of these methods of output for spreadsheets.
2 (a) Write down the steps of the task of forecasting the sales of the climbing frames if a spreadsheet was not available and the work had to be done on paper with the aid of a calculator.
(b) Comment on the benefits of using a spreadsheet for the task.
3 Why is it important for a company to have a forecast of the sales of its products for a whole year ahead?

Project starter

1 (a) Copy the spreadsheet from this section onto your school's computer.
(b) Enter a simple set of figures to test the formulae, and then a realistic set of figures. Bear in mind seasonal patterns of sales, such as an increase in sales just before Christmas.
(c) Make two more columns, to show the percentage of the annual sales which occur in each month. One column shows the 1985 percentages, the other the 1986 figures. If the column for the 1985 percentages is column 8, the formula for the January percentage is:

$$R5C8 = R5C6/R18C6 * 100$$

Enter the required formulae in each cell in the columns. Also enter formulae for the column totals, as a check. These should add up to 100.

12D Issue: New Jobs for Old in the Office

Spreadsheets are one application of information technology in offices, but are by no means the only one. The introduction of computers, many of which can communicate with each other via networks, is changing the type of work done in offices. Managers can do much more of their work without the need for secretaries, clerks and other assistants. Secretaries are taking over some decision-making functions. Most office work now involves some interaction with a computer system. Much office communication is via computer networks.

The introduction of information technology into offices means that work is done more quickly than before, and there is far less paperwork. Decisions by managers are based on much more information than was previously available. Also, the consequences of these decisions can be measured more precisely. This places a lot of strain on managers who were used to working under less pressure. Those who cannot cope are being passed over for promotion, transferred to jobs with less responsibility, given early retirement or made redundant.

The general changes in the nature of work mean that office staff need to be retrained, both to use the new equipment and to do the new kinds of jobs. Many of the new jobs are more flexible than the old ones and require a different way of thinking. In many companies, the total number of jobs is lower because of the efficiency of the new technology.

Desktop microcomputers and computer terminals in use in an office.

Questions

1 (a) What are the benefits of introducing computers in offices?
  (b) What are the problems which computers are helping to cause in offices?

2 Are large numbers of people being made redundant by office computer systems? Give reasons for your answer.

3 In what ways are office jobs which involve computers different from previous jobs?

12E End-of-Chapter Summary

- A spreadsheet is a table of cells set out in rows and columns. Each cell contains a number, a label or a formula. The formula enables the number in the cell to be calculated from numbers in other cells.
- Spreadsheets are used to perform calculations on tables of numbers. Numbers and formulae are entered and edited, and the formulae are recalculated whenever required.
- Spreadsheets are used for home, educational and business applications. Their main function is for business planning—they enable alternative plans to be entered and their consequences examined.
- Cells in a spreadsheet are referred to by their row and column numbers: the third row, fifth column is R3C5 (or E3 in the alternative notation).

Exercise 12

1 Choose the correct word from the list for each of the following spaces:

model; row; cells; spreadsheet; formulae; column.

The production manager set up a ____ to estimate the production figures at the factory for the next year. He made a column for each ____ made at the factory, and a row for each quarter of the year. He set up rows and columns for the totals: a ____ for the total production of each model, and a ____ for the quarterly totals. He entered ____ for the totals in the ____ where they appeared.

2 The spreadsheet for bank accounts described in section 12B can be extended in a number of ways. Some suggestions are as follows:

(a) Calculate the total amount paid in and the total amount paid out, and show them at the bottom of the account. These are useful as a check.

(b) Set out the amounts of money paid out in several columns. Use one column for each type of spending. Adjust the formulae for the balances to use these columns. The new balance is the previous balance plus any amount paid in, minus each sum paid out.

(c) Calculate the total amount paid out in each category. Also express these totals as a percentage of the overall total spending during the month.

(d) Use the spreadsheet from part (c) as the basis of one for planning the spending in each month. Include a row of spending limits for each category, and another row which calculates by how much the actual total differs from the limit.

3 A small company makes components for computer systems: plugs and sockets, chip sockets, switches, etc. The manager of the company purchases a spreadsheet program for the company's desktop microcomputer.

(a) Suggest some uses for the spreadsheet program.

(b) Choose *one* of these applications, and design a spreadsheet that the company might use.

Things to find out

1 Find out more about the way in which information technology is changing the way work is done in offices. Select a few typical jobs such as secretary, booking clerk in a travel office, and accounts clerk for a gas, water or electricity board. Describe how these jobs were done without computers, and how they are done with them. Discuss the training required to change from the old type of job to the new.

2 A serious problem in office work is the stress experienced by managers. Many work long hours and carry heavy responsibilities, with no one to turn to if they have a problem.

(a) Find out the extent of the problem.

(b) Find out what the symptoms of stress at work are.

(c) Find out how people can cope with the problem.

(d) Find out whether computer systems in the office are making things easier, or making the problem worse.

Project starters

1 Use the steps described in section 12A to design a spreadsheet for one or more of the following tasks. This can form the basis of your GCSE project.

(a) A personal budget planner, showing details of income and spending over a suitable period of time. The spreadsheet may be set out in two sets of columns, one for income and one for spending. See the example in section 12A.

(b) An invoice for use in a shop. An invoice is produced for each sale. It shows details of the items sold: for each item, the quantity, description, price and amount. It also has the total amount, VAT and total plus VAT. There is space for the date, an invoice number and the name and address of the person buying the goods. See Figure 12.5.

Set up the framework for an invoice, which can be copied from disk and details entered for each sale.

(c) A spreadsheet to record details of hire purchase payments. Suggested headings for the columns are as follows:

Item Deposit Payment No Pmts Total Cash Pr Diff

The total hire purchase payment is the deposit, plus the payment multiplied by the number of payments. For the first item, in row 3, the formula is:

$$R3C5 = R3C2 + R3C3 * R3C4$$

or E3 = B3 + C3 * D3.

The last column is the difference between the total hire purchase price and the cash price:

$$R3C7 = R3C5 - R3C6$$

or G3 = E3 - F3.

Visit a local shop which sells goods on hire purchase and write down the details for some of the items. Enter these on your spreadsheet.

```
       _____1 _____2 _____3 _____4 _____5
  1 Invoice:                    Date:
  2 --------  --------          -----  --------
  3
  4 To:
  5
  6
  7   Number                    Item    Price   Amount
  8 --------  --------  --------  --------  --------
  9
 10
 11
 12
 13
 14
 15
 16                                      --------
 17                             Total:
 18                                      --------
 19                             VAT:
 20                                      --------
 21                             Tot+VAT:
 22                                      --------
 23
```

Figure 12.5 Spreadsheet for invoice

142

13 Payroll Systems

Every week or every month, everyone who has a job gets paid. The pay has to be worked out correctly, the right amount of income tax and National Insurance contribution deducted, and the payment must be made on time. Payroll processing can be complicated: some employees are paid weekly, others monthly. Some people's wages are calculated from the number of hours they have worked, with different rates of pay for overtime. Many people are paid allowances and bonuses of various kinds. Calculating income tax is difficult, and tax rates change from year to year. The total amount paid out every pay-day by a large company is millions of pounds.

Computers have been used for many years to process wage payments. They can store the large amounts of information required, and do the repetitive calculations more efficiently than any other method. Many companies have their payroll processing done for them by a **computer bureau** which specialises in this type of work.

Payroll processing is a typical example of batch processing: the

Staff queueing for their weekly pay packets.

input information is prepared and entered, and then the computer works through the employees one at a time, processing each wage in the same way.

This chapter describes the files that are used for payroll processing. It enables you to set up a simple set of payroll files on your school computer. It describes the way in which the files are processed, and the output which is produced. It puts into practice some of the general ideas introduced in chapter 9.

13A Activity: Payroll Master File

The basic information about each employee which is needed to calculate his or her wages is stored in the payroll **master file**. It contains all the details which are carried over from one week or month to the next. When an employee joins an organisation, a record is created in the master file for him or her. The record is updated each time a wage is paid, and deleted when the employee leaves the organisation.

The purpose of this section is to produce a master file of this nature for an organisation which pays monthly salaries at a fixed rate.

The Requirements of the Task

The aim of this task is to produce a payroll master file with up-to-date records of all employees. There must be a simple method of entering, checking (or **validating**) and amending the data.

Computer System Design

Outputs
The output is the payroll details of employees. These may be printed if required, and read from magnetic disk or tape by the payroll processing program.

Inputs
The input information is first written on data entry forms. It is then typed into the computer system. A data entry form for the type of payroll system used in this section is shown in Figure 13.1.

Validation
Validation means checking input data for errors before using it for processing. The payroll data is validated in several ways. All fields are checked for the presence of a data item. Numeric fields are checked to ensure that they contain digits. Currency fields are checked for a decimal point before the last two figures. Alphabetic fields are checked to see that no digits or special characters are entered.

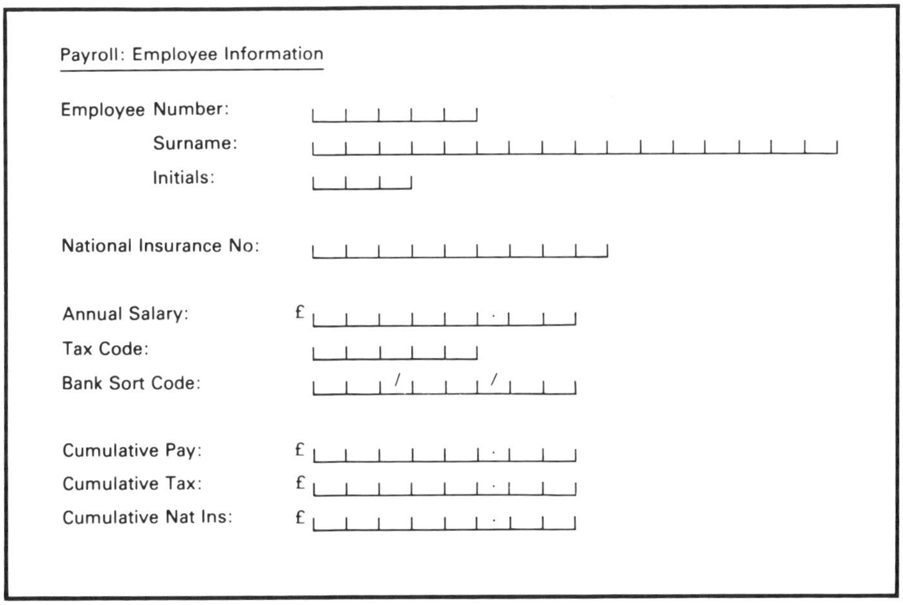

```
Payroll: Employee Information

Employee Number:    |__|__|__|__|__|

        Surname:    |__|__|__|__|__|__|__|__|__|__|__|__|__|__|__|__|

        Initials:   |__|__|__|

National Insurance No:  |__|__|__|__|__|__|__|__|__|

Annual Salary:      £ |__|__|__|__|__|__·__|__|

Tax Code:           |__|__|__|__|__|

Bank Sort Code:     |__|__| / |__|__| / |__|__|

Cumulative Pay:     £ |__|__|__|__|__|__·__|__|

Cumulative Tax:     £ |__|__|__|__|__|__·__|__|

Cumulative Nat Ins: £ |__|__|__|__|__|__·__|__|
```

Figure 13.1 Payroll system: master data entry form

A number of the fields are in **code**. Each code is a particular combination of letters and numbers, as follows:

National Insurance Number: 2 letters, 6 digits, letter A or B
                            Example AB231459B

Tax Code: 4 digits, letter H or L
                            Example 1328L

Bank Sort Code: 2 digits/2 digits/2 digits
                            Example 75/34/91

The bank sort code enables the wage to be paid directly to the branch of the bank where the employee has his or her account.

All the fields in code are given special checks to ensure that they are properly coded.

File structure

There is a record for each employee, containing the same information as shown in the data entry form. The records are stored in order of employee number.

The fields are as follows:

Field	Type	Length	Example
Employee Number	numeric	5	25853
Employee Surname	alpha	16	MacBride
Employee Initials	alpha	3	WJ
National Insurance No	code	9	TM859094B
Annual Salary	numeric	8	14850.00
Tax Code	code	5	2353H
Bank Sort Code	code	6	32/87/51
Bank Account No	numeric	8	50604371
Cumulative Pay	numeric	8	10082.45
Cumulative Tax	numeric	8	2765.78
Cumulative Nat Ins	numeric	8	463.98

File processing

The data for each record is input at the keyboard and saved on backing store in order of employee number. It is validated by a separate program. A report is produced, giving details of all records with errors. Corrections are entered at the keyboard, and the file is again validated.

The file is updated whenever the details of an employee change, for example when there is a pay rise.

The file is read by the main payroll processing program. Some of the fields—the cumulative pay, tax and National Insurance—are updated. A new version of the master file is written to backing store.

System Diagram

Figure 13.2 shows the entry, validation and updating of the payroll master file.

Implementation

Use the information retrieval package on your school microcomputer to set up a file as described above:

- Look at the user guide for the information retrieval system to find out how to carry out each operation.
- Create a data file with the records having fields as described above.
- Make a number of copies of the data input form shown in Figure 13.1. Fill in the information for a set of (about ten) employees in these forms. Design this test data so that the records include correct and incorrect items of information in each field.
- Type the information from the forms, using the input facilities of the information retrieval program. Remember to enter the records in order of employee number. Save the complete file on disk, if this is not done automatically.
- A payroll program validates these records as they are input. Your information retrieval program will probably not have facilities to validate the records—this step will have to be done by hand:

  Check each record on the screen. If it contains an error, make a note of the error. For example:

  Record 6: Bank Sort Code: 32?54/67—wrong character

  This list of errors forms an **error report.**

  (Alternatively, question 2 under 'project starters' in Exercise 13 provides an algorithm for a validation program for employee records. Use this algorithm as the basis for a program to do the validation and produce an error report.)
- Using the error report, work through the records and correct the errors. Check the corrections carefully. Save the corrected file on disk if this is not done automatically.
- Fill in some data input forms with amendments to existing records (three will be sufficient). Call up the payroll master file and enter these amendments. Save the updated file on disk, and validate it again.

entering payroll master records

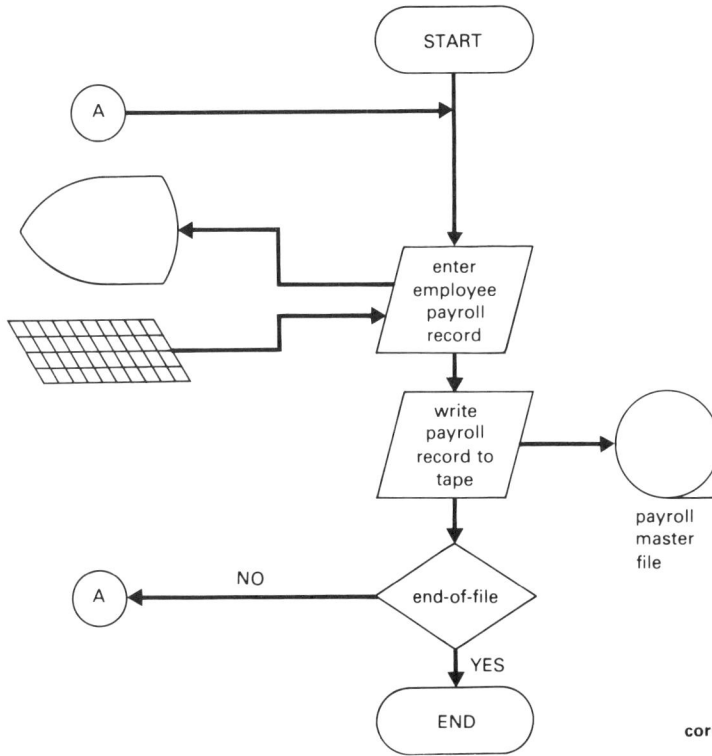

START

A → enter employee payroll record

enter employee payroll record

write payroll record to tape → payroll master file

end-of-file — NO → A

YES

END

validation

START

B → read payroll record ← payroll master file

is record valid? — YES

NO

print error report → error report

end-of-file? — NO → B

YES

END

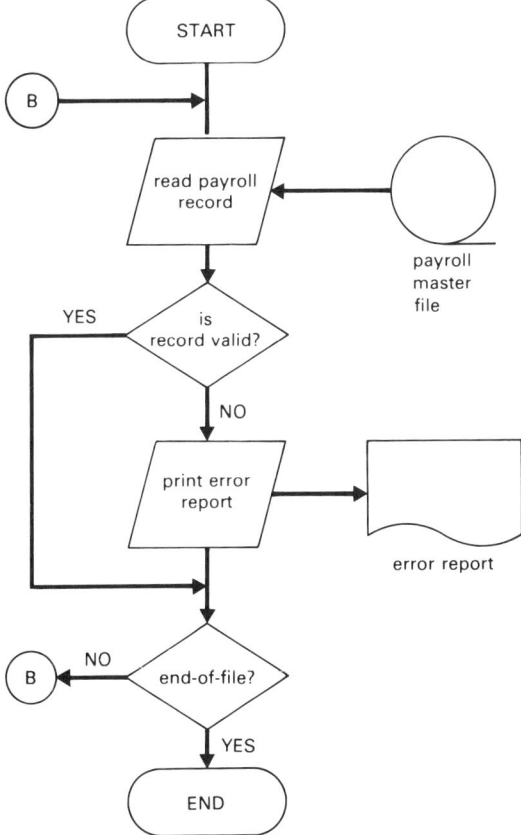

correcting / updating records

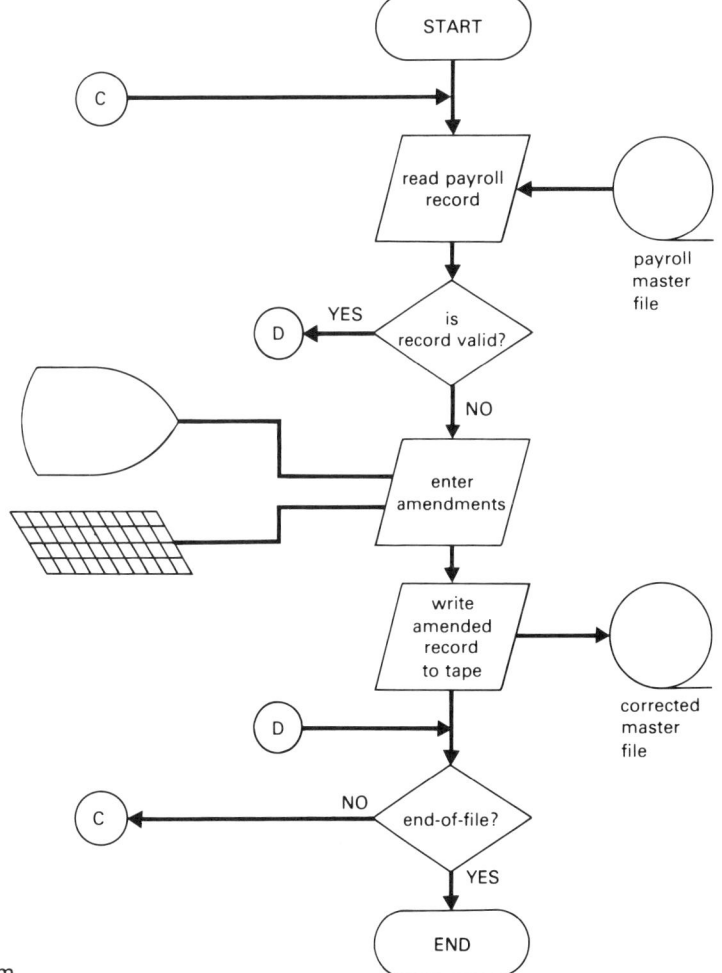

START

C → read payroll record ← payroll master file

is record valid? — YES → D

NO

enter amendments

write amended record to tape → corrected master file

D →

end-of-file? — NO → C

YES

END

Figure 13.2   Payroll system—updating master file: system diagram

147

Documentation

- Write a set of system documentation describing the file structure and the validation procedures. (If you have written a validation program, write algorithms to describe how it works, and include flow diagrams and decision tables where necessary.)
- Write a user guide for others to enter and amend records in the payroll master file. State how to call up the file, how to save it on disk again, and how to print records.

Questions

1 Make two copies of the employee input form show in Figure 13.1. Fill them in for the following employees:

(a) Mrs M G Smith, National Insurance number AD743782AB, employee number 72245, earning an annual salary of £11 445. Her tax code is 1324H, and her salary is paid into account 34258733 at the Midland Bank branch 23/54/51. Mrs Smith is a new employee, and has no cumulative pay, tax or National Insurance.

(b) Mr Alan Davies, employee number 72246, National Insurance number BC54771, earning an annual salary of £10 438. His tax code is 1221L, and his bank account number is 90201743 at branch 98/44/63. His cumulative pay, tax and National Insurance contribution are £8455, £1623.50 and £294.39 respectively.

2 The following is a record from the payroll master file described in section 13A:

Employee Number	7385
Employee Surname	Smethwick
Employee Initials	A P
National Insurance No	CJ843951D
Annual Salary	12546.89
Tax Code	1128M
Bank Sort Code	20–27–19
Bank Account No	9767233
Cumulative Pay	4378
Cumulative Tax	1211.67
Cumulative Nat Ins	309.255

Validate each field using the checks described in section 13A. List all the errors.

13B Activity: Payroll Transaction File

The payroll master file contains the data about each employee which is carried over from month to month. To calculate the weekly or monthly wages, a further set of information is required. This concerns the work done by the employee during the week or month. This data is entered into a **transaction file**.

If workers are paid at an hourly rate and have clock cards which record when they start and finish work, these clock cards provide the transaction data. If workers are paid by the month, the transaction data is the number of days worked and the number of days off sick or on holiday. Any expenses and bonuses to be paid are also entered.

The Requirements of the Task

The aim of this aspect of payroll processing is to produce a valid transaction file, sorted in the same order as the master file, ready for the main payroll program run.

Computer System Design

Outputs
The output is a validated transaction file on backing store, with records in order of employee number.

Inputs
The input data is the number of days worked, off sick and on holiday for each employee, as well as any expenses or bonus payments. This data is written on an input form as shown in Figure 13.3, and then typed into the computer.

Payroll: Monthly Work Record

Employee Number:

Days Worked:

Days Sick:

Days Holiday:

Bonus £

Expenses £

Figure 13.3 Payroll system: payment data entry form

Validation
All the fields in the transaction record are numeric. They are checked to ensure that they contain at least one digit. The fields for the numbers of days must contain numbers no bigger than the number of working days in the current month. Their sum must be the number of working days in this month. The currency fields are checked for a decimal point between the pounds and pence.

File structure
A transaction record is entered for each employee. The records are not input in any particular order. The fields in a record are as follows:

Field	**Type**	**Length**	**Example**
Employee Number	Numeric	5	25853
Days Worked	Numeric	2	18
Days Sick	Numeric	2	1
Days Holiday	Numeric	2	3
Bonus	Numeric	5	58.73
Expenses	Numeric	5	12.54

File processing
The records are entered and validated. After the corrections have been made, a program sorts the transaction file and produces another version of it in order of employee number. This file is ready for use by the payroll processing program.

System Diagram

See Figure 13.4.

Implementation

- Use the steps from section 13A to set up a payroll transaction file and enter a set of test data into it. There must be one transaction record for each master record, but the transaction records are not entered in order of employee number. Include a mixture of correct and incorrect data.
- When the transaction data has been entered and validated, sort the records into order of employee number. Use the sort facility of the information retrieval program. The employee number is the sort **key**—the field which is the basis of the sort.

1 Make two copies of the payroll transaction record form in Figure 13.3 and enter the following transaction data into them for the month of September, with 22 working days:
(a) Mrs M G Smith, employee number 72245, was off sick for 5 days, took 3 days holiday, and worked the remaining days. Her expenses were £39.65, and she had no bonus pay.
(b) Mr Alan Davies, employee number 72246, worked every day of the month. His expenses were £96.87, and his bonus was £25.

2 List all the errors in the following transaction record from the file described in section 13B, for a month of 23 working days:

Employee Number	73167
Days Worked	81
Days Sick	4
Days Holiday	1
Bonus	35
Expenses	43.50

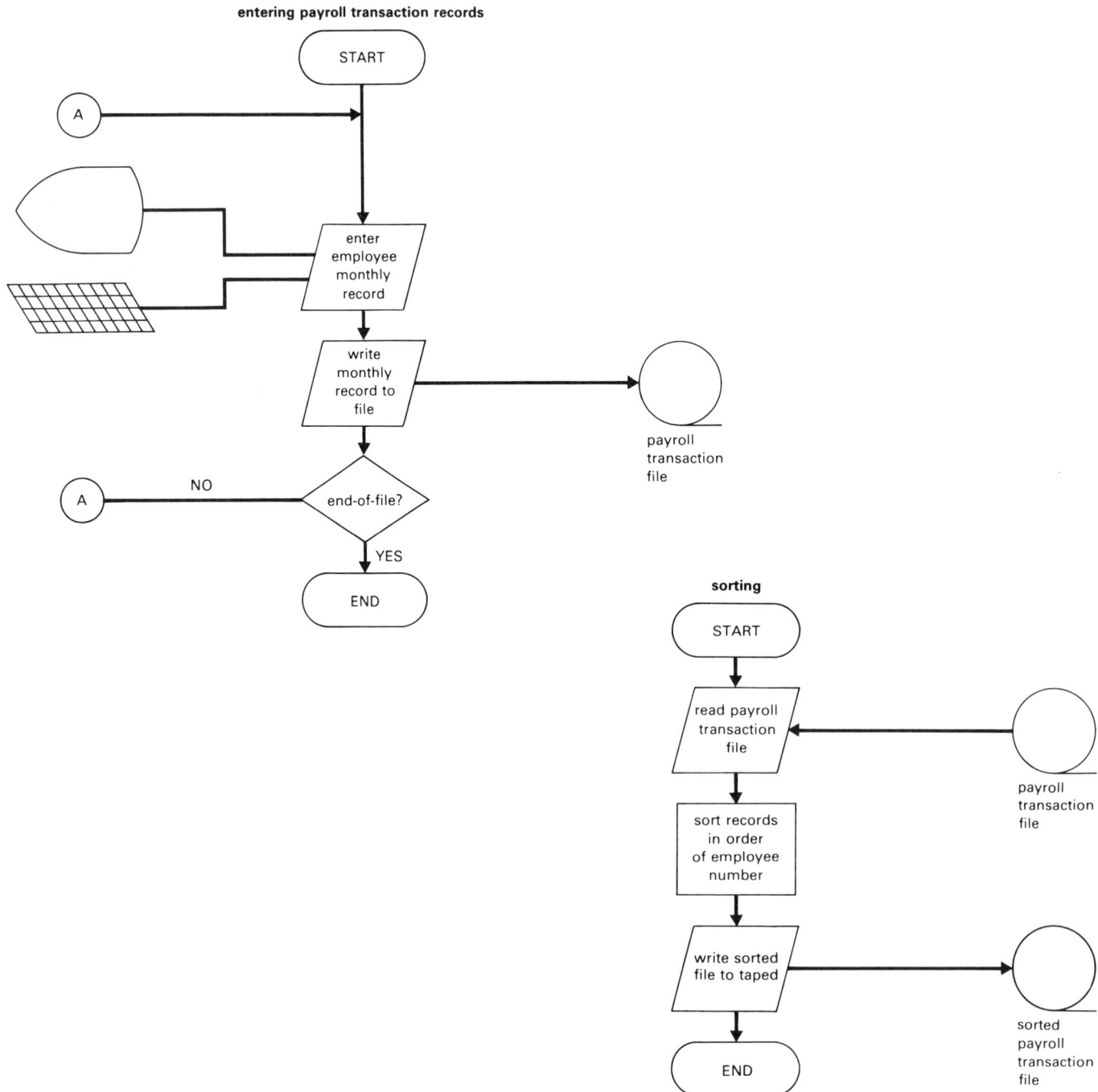

entering payroll transaction records

START

A → enter employee monthly record

write monthly record to file → payroll transaction file

end-of-file? — NO → A

YES → END

sorting

START

read payroll transaction file ← payroll transaction file

sort records in order of employee number

write sorted file to taped → sorted payroll transaction file

END

Figure 13.4   Payroll system—transaction data entry and validation: system diagram

13C Application: Payroll Processing

This section describes how the master and transaction files produced in the previous two sections are processed. You are not expected to do the payroll processing on your school computer.

The Requirements of the Task

The aim is to produce payslips showing monthly gross pay, deductions and net pay. The cumulative pay, National Insurance contributions and tax for the current year are also shown. The net pay is transferred directly into the employees' bank accounts. The payroll master file is updated, and a summary of the payroll figures is produced.

Computer System Design

Outputs
Payslips, similar to those in Figure 13.5, are printed. A listing of the amounts to be transferred into the bank accounts is also produced. A summary is printed of the total pay, tax, National Insurance contributions and net pay for the current month.

W. M. EVANS AND COMPANY	PAY ADVICE		Date 30 JUNE 87
W J MacBride	Employee No 25853	NI No TM859094B	Tax Code 2353H

Payments		Deductions	
Basic Pay:	1237.50	Income Tax:	484.50
Overtime Pay:	350.00	National Insurance:	64.60
Bonus Pay:	27.50		
Total Pay:	1615.00	Total Deductions:	549.10

This year to date:		Bank Sort Code:	Net Pay:
Total Pay:	4827.00	3287-51	£ 1065.90
Total Income Tax:	1403.50		
Total National Insurance:	196.80		

Figure 13.5   Payslip

Inputs
All data for the payroll processing run is already stored in validated files. There are no inputs during the payroll run.

File structures
The payroll master file and transaction file are used, as described in the previous two sections. A file of tax tables is required to work out the income tax.

File processing

A batch processing program works through the employee records one at a time. An algorithm for the main steps of the program is as follows:

Open the payroll master file and transaction file

Create a new version of the payroll master file

151

While the ends of the files have not been reached repeat

Read the next employee's record from each file

Calculate the gross wage, tax, NI contribution and net wage

Add these figures to the previous totals to get the new cumulative figures.

Print the payslip and bank transfer details

Write the updated record to the new version of the master file

Update the totals for the payroll run

Close the payroll files

Print the summary showing the totals for the payroll run

System Diagram

See Figure 13.6.

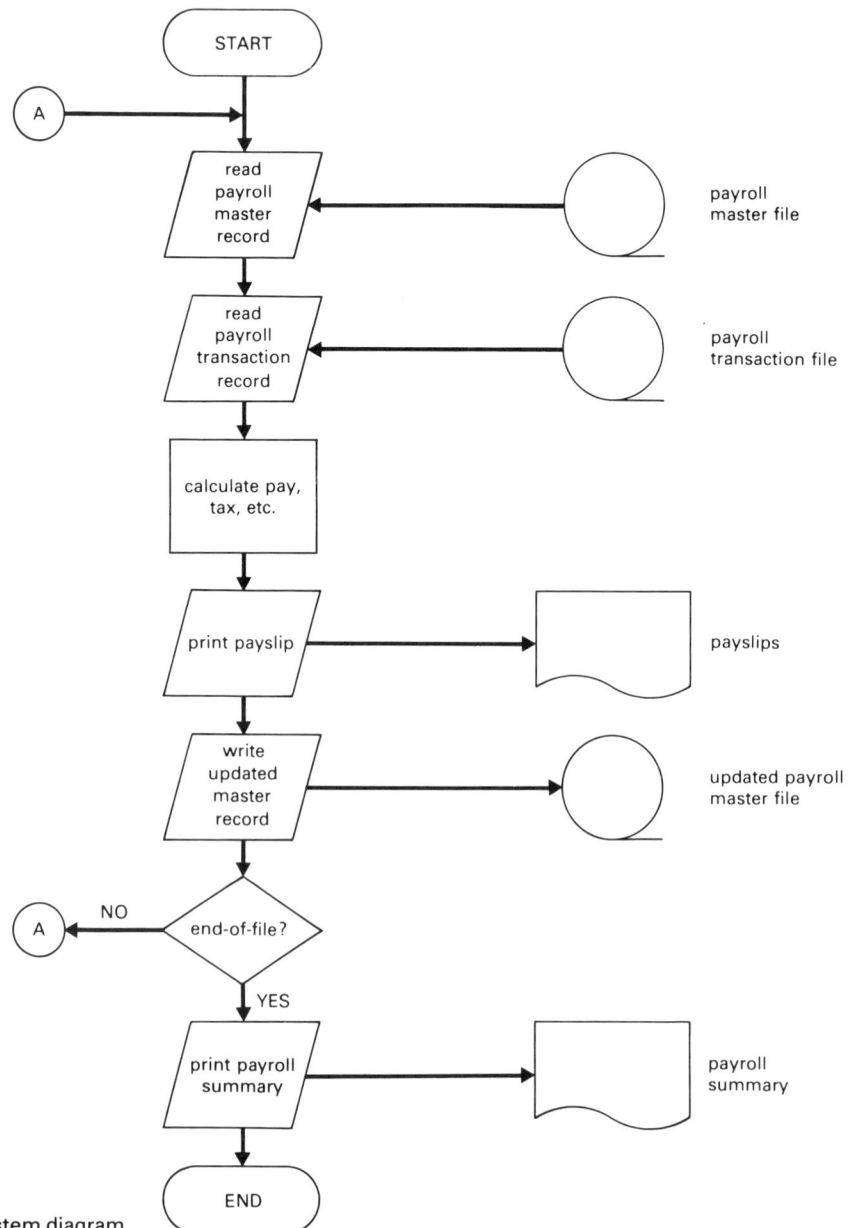

Figure 13.6   Payroll system—pay processing run: system diagram

Implementation

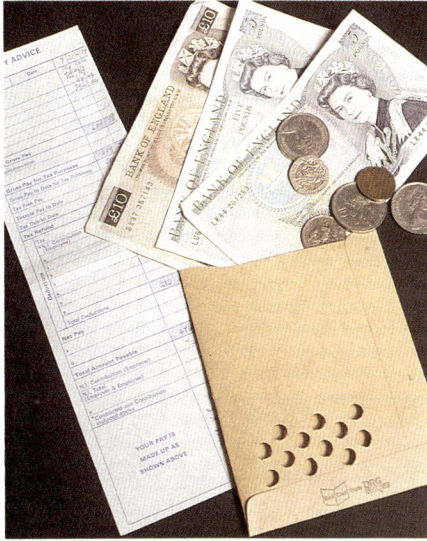

A weekly pay packet. This is likely to disappear soon as companies pay their employees by electronic funds transfer.

The most common way of implementing a payroll processing system is to use one of the standard payroll packages which are available. Very few companies write their own payroll programs. Some companies run the payroll programs on their own computers, others use a computer bureau. The largest payroll bureaus are companies owned by banks. They can do all the bank transfers of the payments themselves, and even lend the money to pay the wages if necessary!

Payroll processing is most commonly done on mini- or mainframe computers. The payslips are printed on line printers, using pre-printed stationery.

Payroll processing is a batch processing operation, using sequential files. Files may be stored on magnetic disk or tape. Whichever medium is used, the grandfather-father-son cycle of updating is followed, as described in chapter 23.

Questions

1 The rates of income tax and amounts of tax-free allowances change every year. What changes are needed to a payroll processing system when this happens?
2 The payroll processing program is an example of batch processing. Explain what batch processing is, using the working of this program as an example.
3 What are the advantages of paying employees' salaries directly into their bank accounts?
4 Payroll processing was one of the first uses of computers in commerce. Suggest some reasons for it being put onto computers in their early years. Remember that early computers were not nearly as powerful as they are today.
5 Suggest some reasons for the fact that few companies write their own payroll processing programs.

13D Issue: Privacy of Personal Information

An employee examining his payslip.

Would you like other people to know how much you earn, and how much tax you pay? Personal information of the sort stored in payroll systems is confidential. So is the personal information stored on computers belonging to banks, insurance companies, hospitals and police forces.

There is a law in Britain—the **Data Protection Act**—which protects the rights of people who have personal information about themselves stored on computers. It gives these people—the **data subjects**—the right to see their own record on these computer systems. If the records are wrong, the data subjects can insist that they are corrected.

The organisations which use the data must register with the **Data Protection Registrar**, who administers the Data Protection Act. They must state what personal data they keep, and the purposes for which it is kept. If the data is used for any other purpose, the organisation can be prosecuted.

Other countries have laws similar to the UK Data Protection Act. These laws also regulate the flow of personal data from one country to another so that the data cannot be used in one country in a way which would be illegal in another country.

Questions

1 (a) What is the purpose of the UK Data Protection Act?
(b) How is this Act administered?
(c) Under what circumstances can an organisation be prosecuted under the Act?

2 A small company has a desktop microcomputer with an information retrieval system. This holds records about the company's customers: their names and addresses, what type of work they do, and a list of the items they have bought from the company.
(a) Should this company register under the UK Data Protection Act?
(b) If so, suggest a list of uses for the data which might be included in the application.

3 (a) Make a list of all the computer systems which you can think of that would hold personal information about a person who has a job, a bank account, a mortgage, a car, a television set, a life insurance policy and who has been to hospital recently.
(b) Write down some possible uses of this personal data which would be contrary to the Data Protection Act. In each case, state what problems these unauthorised uses could cause for the data subject.

13E End-of-Chapter Summary

The main points of this chapter are as follows:

- Producing a payroll is a complex operation involving large amounts of data, complicated calculations and strict deadlines.
- Most payroll processing in industrial countries is done by computer. Many computers use a bureau for their payrolls.
- Payroll processing is a batch operation.
- A payroll program uses a master file and a transaction file of data for the current week or month. It works out the pay for each employee in turn, prints payslips and produces a new version of the master file.
- The information in a payroll system is personal and confidential. In the UK, such information is protected from abuse by the Data Protection Act.

Exercise 13

1 Choose the correct word from the list for each of the following spaces:

transaction; line printer; tapes; version; file; operator.

At the start of a payroll processing run, the computer ____ loads the magnetic ____ with the payroll master ____ and the ____ file. She loads a blank tape for the new ____ of the master file. She places pre-printed stationery in the ____ for the payslips.

2 (a) Which field in the payroll files identifies the records?
(b) What will happen if this field is entered incorrectly in someone's record?
(c) Suggest a change to this field so that it can be validated more thoroughly, and an error in any character can be detected.

Things to find out

1 Obtain a copy of an application form for registration under the Data Protection Act. (These can be obtained from Post Offices.) Read the instructions carefully, and then fill in the form as if you were representing the organisation whose payroll system is described in sections 13A, 13B and 13C.
In filling in the form, describe the data items which are recorded by the system, and the uses of this data.

Project starters

1 Design a payroll master file, and a transaction file to go with it, for a payroll system to produce weekly wages. State the validation for each field. Use the files in sections 13A and 13B as examples.
Employees are paid at an hourly rate, with an overtime rate for extra hours worked each week. The times are recorded on clock cards. These show the employee number, and, for each day, the time of starting work and the time of finishing. They are used as the source documents for the transaction data.

2 An algorithm for the overall operation of the validation program described in section 13A is as follows:

Open payroll master file for reading

While the end of the file has not been reached repeat

Read the next record

For each field repeat

Validate the field

If error found then mark field as incorrect

If any fields marked incorrect then

Print employee number

Print list of incorrect fields

Close payroll master file

Figure 13.7 shows a flow diagram corresponding to this algorithm.

(a) Write detailed algorithms for the checks applied to each field.

(b) Use the overall algorithm above, and the detailed algorithms you have written to write the program.

(c) Test the program with the test data entered as part of section 13A.

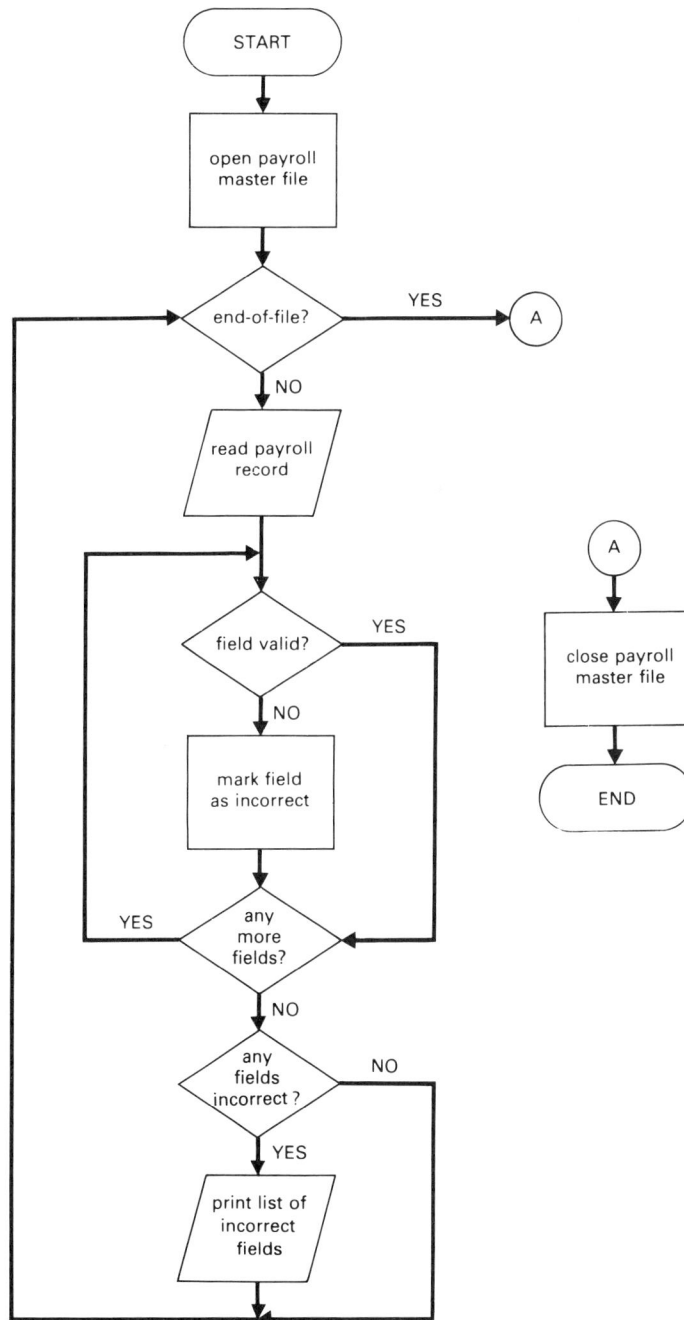

Figure 13.7

155

14 Stock Control

Automated equipment in operation at a warehouse.

Many organisations have to keep supplies of goods. For example, hospitals keep supplies of medical equipment, shops keep stocks of the goods they sell, factories keep supplies of the components they use, and schools keep stocks of books. The value of these stocks can be high: millions of pounds for large shops, factories and hospitals.

It is essential to keep an accurate check on stocks. Items must not be lost, and stock levels need to be controlled carefully. Too high a stock level is a waste of money; too few items means that there is a danger of running out of stock. Some factories operate with only one day's supply of components.

Computers are used to an increasing extent for stock control. They record the movements of stock into and out of a warehouse or shop, keep an up-to-date record of stock levels, and can be programmed to re-order goods automatically if stocks fall below a certain level. Most stock control systems are transaction processing systems: they update stock levels as each stock movement takes place. Some have direct links to robots and other equipment which moves stock into and out of a warehouse automatically.

This chapter describes the files that are used for stock control, and enables you to set up stock control files on your school computer. It outlines the two commonest types of stock control: warehouse systems, and **point-of-sale (POS)** systems using cash terminals in shops. It puts into practice some of the general ideas about computer applications described in chapter 9.

14A Activity: Warehouse Stock Master File

Stock control systems use a **stock master file** to keep the data they need about each item of stock. The stock master file has a record for each stock item. The record is updated each time stock is moved in or out. The purpose of this section is to produce a stock master file for a warehouse which supplies a chain of clothes shops.

The Requirements of the Task

The aim of this task is to produce a file containing the essential information about each item of stock.

Computer System Design

> **minimum stock level** the level of the stock of an item at which more stock is ordered.
> **re-order quantity** the number of items ordered in one consignment.

Outputs
The outputs are the details about each item of stock. These may be printed if required, and are read from disk and updated by the stock control program.

Inputs
The information for each stock item is first filled in on a data entry form, as shown in Figure 14.1. It is then typed into the computer

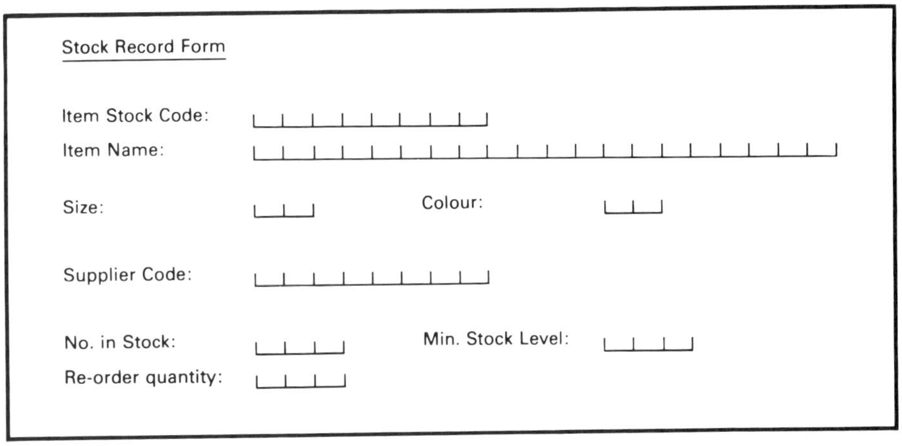
Stock Record Form

Item Stock Code:

Item Name:

Size: Colour:

Supplier Code:

No. in Stock: Min. Stock Level:

Re-order quantity:

Figure 14.1 Stock master file: data input form

system. The minimum stock level is the number below which stock is re-ordered. The re-order quantity is the number of items ordered in one batch. These two numbers are calculated from the rate at which the stock is used up and the time it takes for a new order to be delivered.

Note that the stock file contains the least amount of information needed for stock control. Data such as the name and address of the supplier (which is the same for many stock items) is kept on a separate file.

Validation

The numeric fields are checked (or **validated**) to ensure that they contain numbers. The size and colour codes can only have certain combinations of letters or numbers.

The stock code and supplier code consist of two letters, five digits and a **check digit** (a letter), for example EX63917B. A modified version of the weighted modulo 11 check digit system is used. This is described in question 3 of Exercise 14. More details about check digits are to be found in chapter 23.

File structure

The records are stored in order of item stock code. The fields are as follows:

Field	Type	Length	Example
Item Stock Code	code	8	SE76912G
Item Name	alpha	20	Swingpleat skirt
Size	code	2	14
Colour	code	2	BK
Supplier Code	code	8	PM95087F
No In Stock	numeric	3	327
Minimum Stock Level	numeric	3	100
Re-Order Quantity	numeric	3	250

File processing

The data for each record is input and validated. Any corrections must be made before the record is accepted. When the file is first set up, records are entered in order of item stock code.

Records may be edited, for example to change the minimum stock level or re-order quantity. If a new record is added to the file, it is inserted into its correct place. If a record is deleted, subsequent records are moved up to fill the gap.

The stock master file is used by the stock control system. Records are accessed and updated at random as stock movements are recorded.

System Diagram

The system diagram for entry and validation of records is shown in Figure 14.2.

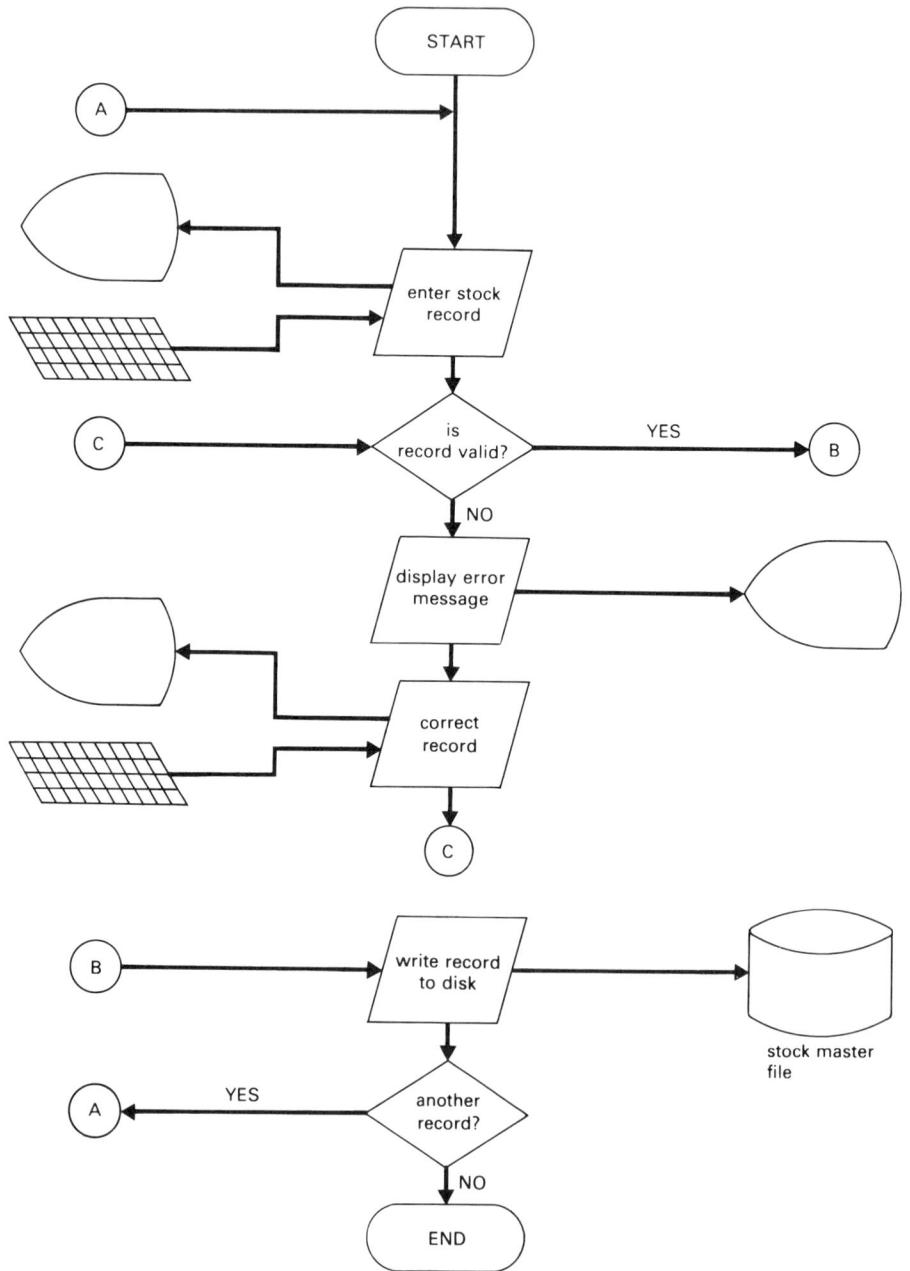

Figure 14.2   Stock master file: data entry system diagram

Implementation

Use an information retrieval package on your school computer, or a stock control package if your school has one, to set up a file as described above.

- Look at the user guide for the program to find out how to carry out each operation.
- Create a data file with records having fields as described above.
- Devise a set of codes for sizes and colours, using two characters for each.
- Work out a sequence of about ten valid item stock codes. For example:

  ED29841J   ED29842L   ED29843N

- Make about ten copies of the data input form in Figure 14.1. Fill these in with a set of test data, using the item stock codes you have worked out. Include correct and incorrect fields.
- Type the data from the forms, using the data entry facilities of the information retrieval or stock control program. Enter the records in order of stock code. Save the complete file on disk, if this is not done automatically.
- It will probably not be possible to validate the records on the computer. Check the records carefully on screen, and note the errors.
- Make the corrections to the records which contain errors. Save the updated version of the file on disk.
- Fill in a set of input forms with amendments to stock records (three will be sufficient). For example, you may wish to change the minimum stock level or the re-order quantity, or allocate a new supplier for the stock.
- Call up the records to be amended, and enter the amendments. Save the amended file on disk.

Documentation

- Write a set of system documentation describing the file structure and the validation procedures.
- Write a user guide for others to enter, edit and insert records in the stock master file. Describe how to call up the file, how to save it on disk again and how to print records.

Questions

1 Make copies of the input forms for the stock master records shown in Figure 14.1. Fill them in for each of the following:
   (a) Item DF35722J: Dress, style Annabel, colour Apricot, size 14, none in stock, minimum stock level 25, re-order quantity 50. The supplier is A B Smith and Company, code SX00134B.
   (b) Item DF35739B: Shoes, style Brogue, colour Tan, size 10, stock level 100, minimum stock 10, re-order quantity 25. The supplier is Alfred Shoes, code SS00872C.

2 Why is it important to keep careful checks on the levels of stock in a shop, factory, warehouse or hospital?

14B Activity: Warehouse Stock Movement Records

Every time an item of stock is moved into or out of the warehouse, a **movement record** is entered into the stock control system. It includes the date, time, stock code and number moved in or out. The movement records are stored, in the order in which they are entered, on a movement file, also known as a **log file**.

A stock control system based on transaction processing updates the stock master file as soon as a movement record is entered. Batch processing systems accumulate a series of movement records over a day, and then update the stock master file in a batch run during the night.

The Requirements of the Task

Computer System Design

The aim of this task is to produce a movement file which is used with the stock master file created in the previous section.

Outputs

The output is a set of movement records. These are stored on disk and may be printed when required.

Inputs

When stock arrives at the warehouse, a **delivery note** is sent by the supplier. An example is shown in Figure 14.3. When stock is to be removed, there is a **stock request slip**, as shown in Figure 14.4.

A movement record is entered for each item, as shown in the file structure on page 161. The movement code, date and time are entered automatically by the computer, the movement code being the next in sequence after that for the previous record. (The last numerical digit of the movement code is increased by 1, and the check digit is calculated for the new number.) The remaining data is entered directly at the keyboard from the delivery note or request slip. The document reference field contains the reference of the delivery note or stock request.

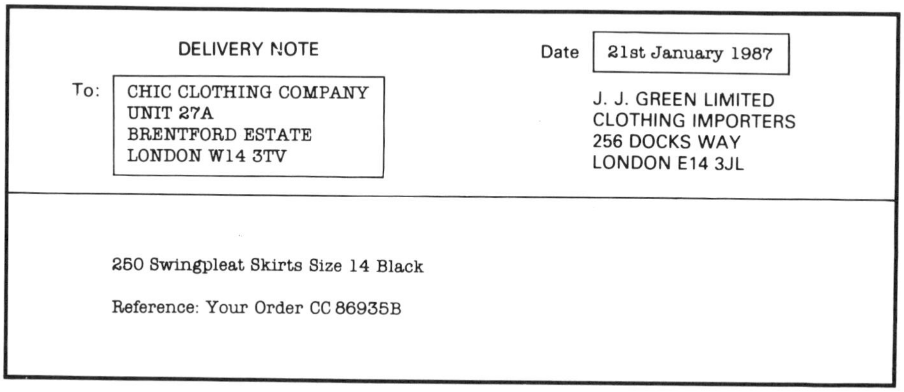

```
            DELIVERY NOTE                    Date   21st January 1987

   To:   CHIC CLOTHING COMPANY                J. J. GREEN LIMITED
         UNIT 27A                              CLOTHING IMPORTERS
         BRENTFORD ESTATE                      256 DOCKS WAY
         LONDON W14 3TV                        LONDON E14 3JL


         250 Swingpleat Skirts Size 14 Black

         Reference: Your Order CC 86935B
```

Figure 14.3   Stock delivery note

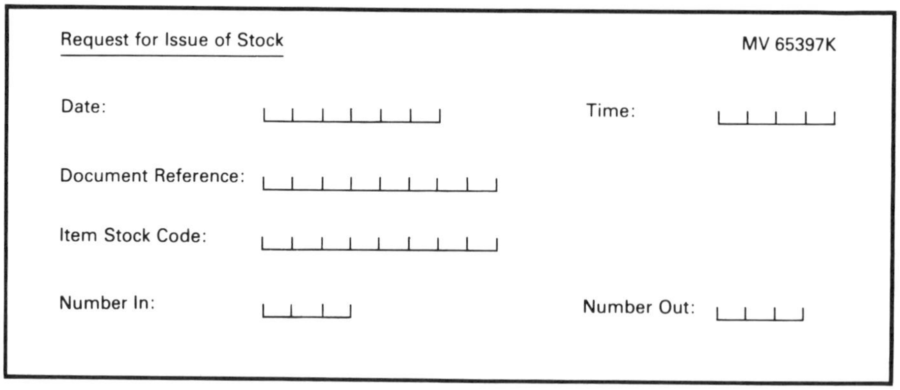

```
   Request for Issue of Stock                                    MV 65397K


      Date:            |_|_|_|_|_|_|        Time:      |_|_|_|_|

      Document Reference:  |_|_|_|_|_|_|_|_|_|

      Item Stock Code:     |_|_|_|_|_|_|_|_|_|

      Number In:       |_|_|_|           Number Out:   |_|_|_|
```

Figure 14.4   Stock request slip

Validation

The item stock code and its validation are described in section 14A. Either the number in or the number out is zero: stock cannot be added and taken out in the same movement.

File structure

Movement records are stored in a log file, in order of movement code. A new file is started each day. The fields are:

Field	Type	Length	Example
Movement Code	code	8	MV65397K
Date	code	6	861203
Time	numeric	4	1342
Document Reference	alpha	8	WXG8653
Item Stock Code	code	8	SE76912G
Number In	numeric	3	64
Number Out	numeric	3	0

File processing

Movement records are entered, validated and written to the stock movement file. The records may be written when required, but may not be edited once the movement has been processed.

System Diagram

Figure 14.5 shows the entry, validation and storage of stock movement records.

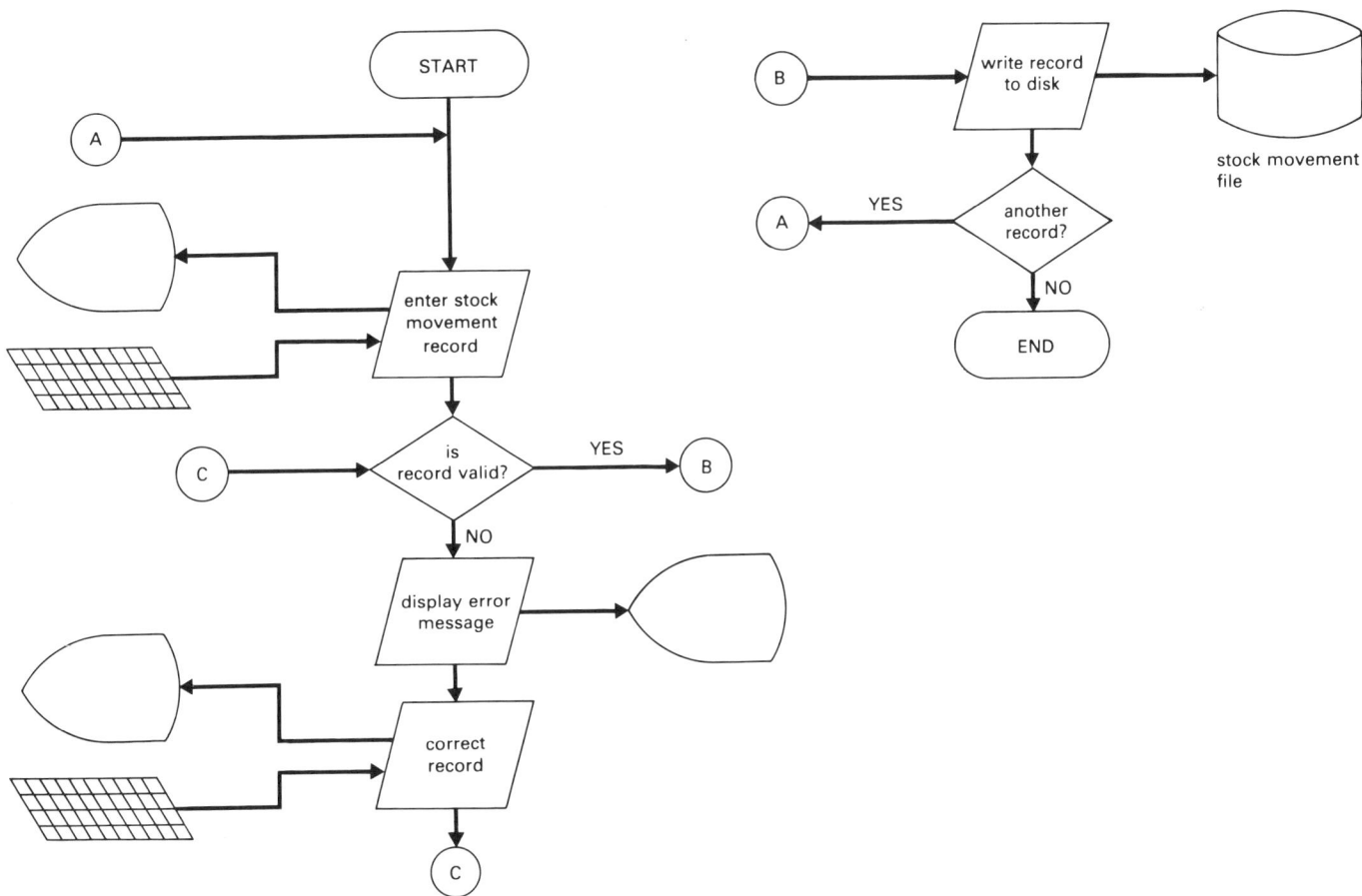

Figure 14.5   Stock movement record: data entry system diagram

161

Implementation

Use the information retrieval program or the stock control program on your school computer to create a file of movement records, as described above.

- Follow the steps of section 14A to set up the file and to enter and validate records. Design a suitable set of test data.
- It is unlikely that your computer system will fill in the movement reference, date and time automatically. Enter these from the keyboard, and validate them with the other data.

14C Application: Warehouse Stock Control System

This section describes how the stock master file and stock movement records are used to keep stock records up-to-date as stock movements take place. If you have a stock control program on your school computer, you will be able to carry out a similar operation yourself. (You are *not* expected to implement this aspect of the stock control system on an information retrieval system.)

The Requirements of the Task

The aim of a warehouse stock control system is to keep stock records up-to-date as movements take place. Stock is re-ordered as soon as levels fall below the re-order level. The levels at which re-orders are placed and the quantities re-ordered are worked out so as to keep stock levels as low as possible without actually running out of stock. This saves large sums of money, as less is spent on stock and insurance and storage costs are lower.

Computer System Design

Outputs
A printed output is not produced for every stock movement. A re-order request is printed if a stock movement results in the stock level falling below the minimum level. A slip is also printed if the stock level is too low for an order to be supplied.

Reports of stock movements and summaries of stock levels can be printed when required. The summaries are used for insurance and stocktaking purposes.

Inputs
The inputs are the stock movement records described in the previous section.

File structures
The stock master file and the movements records are described in sections 14A and 14B.

File processing
When a delivery of an item of stock reaches the warehouse, the sequence of operations is as described in the following algorithm:

Create a stock movement record for the consignment

The movement reference, date and time are entered by the computer

Repeat

Enter the stock item code

Clothes being dispatched from a warehouse.

162

Validate the stock item code

Until the code is correct

Enter the packing note reference and number supplied

Update the record for the item on the stock master file by adding the number supplied to the number in stock

Write the movement record to the log file

When a request is received for stock to be removed from the warehouse, the process is more complicated:

Create a stock movement record for the consignment

The movement reference, date and time are entered by the computer

Repeat

  Enter the stock item code

  Validate the stock item code

Until the code is correct

Enter the request note reference and number to be removed

Look up the record for the item on the stock master file

If there is sufficient stock to meet the request

  then Update the record for the item on the stock master file by subtracting the number removed from the number in stock

  Write the movement record to the log file

  If the number in stock is below the minimum stock level

    then Print a re-order request

  else Print a slip stating that the request cannot be supplied

System Diagram

See Figure 14.6.

Implementation

A stock control system of the type described above is implemented on a mini- or microcomputer, often in the warehouse itself. It is a transaction processing system working in real time and thus requires magnetic disks for data storage.

There are a number of standard stock control software packages available, and they are becoming increasingly popular. The alternative is for a company to develop a stock control system of its own design, either using its own data processing staff or by commissioning a software house.

Security procedures vary depending on the size of the warehouse and the volume of stock movements. A common practice is to make backup copies of the stock master file and movements log file at regular intervals. If the current master file is corrupted, the movements since the last backup are run as a batch against the backup copy of the master file to bring it up-to-date again.

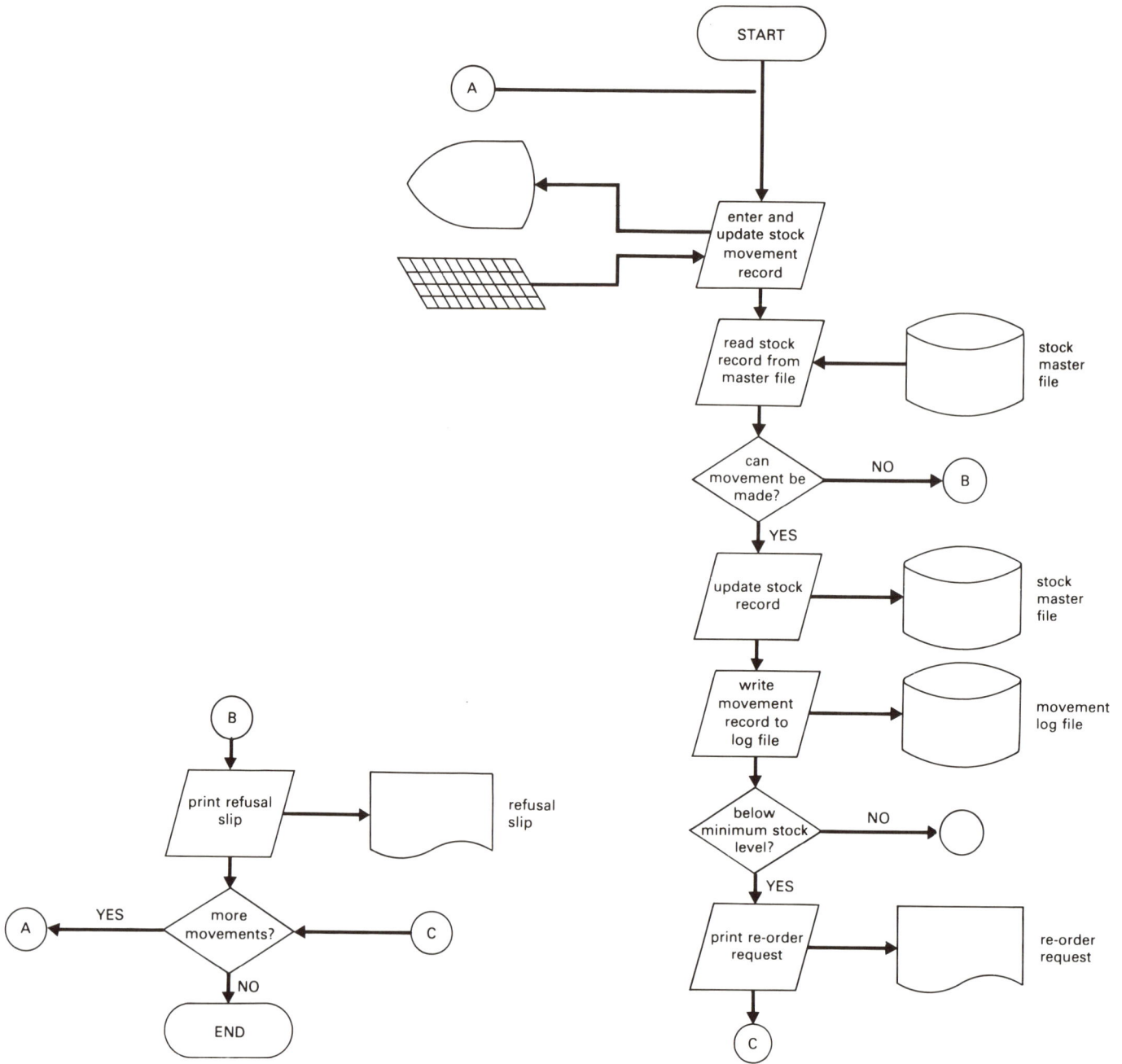

Figure 14.6   Warehouse stock control system: system diagram

164

14D Application: Point-of-sale Stock Control

A point-of-sale terminal in operation.

Stock control is one aspect of the **point-of-sale (POS)** computer systems which are used by many shops in the UK and other industrial countries. Supermarkets are beginning to install similar computer systems. Point-of-sale systems make a precise record of every item sold in the shop at the time it is sold. These records are used for stock control and for accounting purposes. Most POS systems operate in real time: the stock levels are adjusted and the accounts are updated as the sale takes place. Other systems store the records for a day's trading and process them as a batch overnight.

Many shops are in groups (known as **chains** of shops), owned by a single company. The point-of-sale systems in these shops usually operate over a computer network. There is a microcomputer in every shop in the group, linked to the cash terminals. This sends data over a network to the main computer at the company's headquarters. The computers in the warehouses are also connected to this central computer. There are often links to the computers of the companies which supply goods to the shops so that re-orders can be placed automatically. See Figure 14.7.

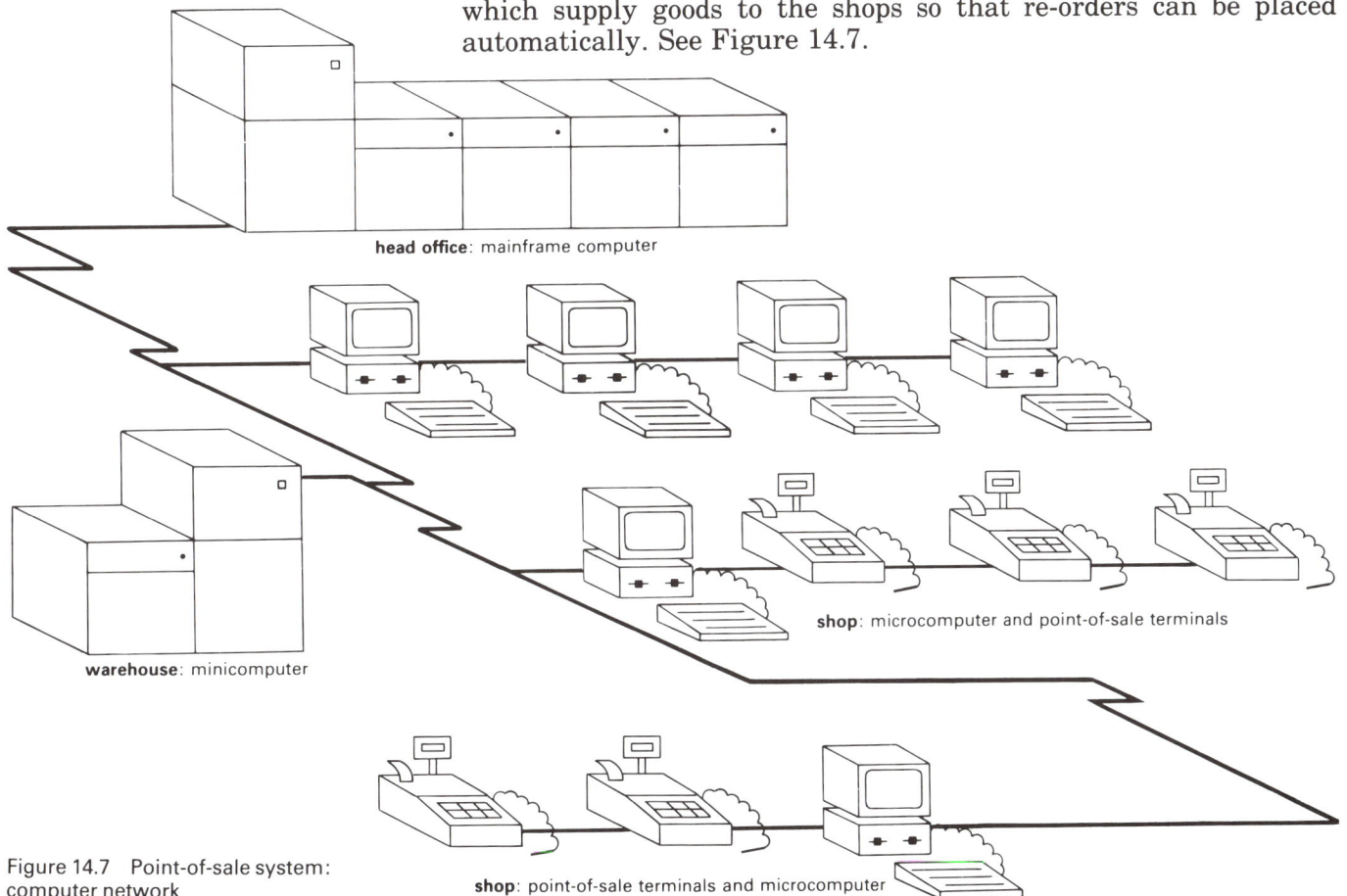

head office: mainframe computer

warehouse: minicomputer

shop: microcomputer and point-of-sale terminals

Figure 14.7   Point-of-sale system: computer network

shop: point-of-sale terminals and microcomputer

The Requirements of the Task

The aims of a point-of-sale computer system are as follows:

- To make a detailed record of each sale as it takes place.
- To keep the records of the stock levels in each shop or supermarket up-to-date all the time.
- To keep a continuous record of the money received from sales.

- To re-order goods from warehouses and suppliers as soon as they are required.
- To produce daily sales summaries. Some shops are given trading targets for each day. The sales summaries are compared with these trading targets by managers.
- To keep stock levels as low as possible in shops and warehouses without running out of stock.
- To respond as rapidly as possible to changes in the demand for goods.

Computer System Design

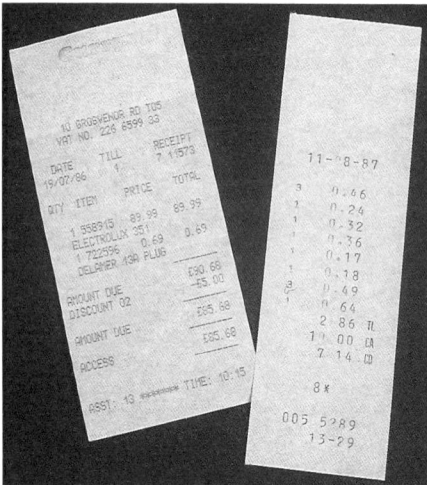

On the right, a slip produced by a conventional till; on the left, a slip produced by a point-of-sale terminal.

Outputs

A till slip is produced for each sale showing the date, time, items sold and their prices, and the total price. Summaries and totals of sales are produced by each cash terminal at the end of each day.

Re-order requests are sent via the communications network to the central computer, or direct to the warehouse.

Reports and summaries of sales are produced on the central computer, which analyses the information reaching it from the microcomputers at the shops and the larger computers at the warehouses.

Inputs

The inputs are the product codes of each item sold. These are read from the bar codes printed on the products, or from the magnetic strips on the item labels. In some systems, the product code is typed by the terminal operator. (In one popular chain of wine shops, staff are expected to memorise the product codes!)

When the goods arrive at a shop, they are recorded on hand-held keypads with bar code or magnetic strip readers attached.

File structures

The files used to record stock levels and stock movements are similar to those described in sections 14A and 14B.

File processing

An algorithm for the operation of a cash terminal is as follows:

Print date and time of sale on till slip

For each item repeat

   Read item from magnetic strip or bar code

   Look up price and description from list stored in cash terminal

   Print and display item description and price

   Add price to sale total

Print and display sale total

Enter method of payment and amount paid

Display and print amount paid

Calculate, display and print amount of change

Send details of items sold and amount received to central computer

A cash terminal with a bar code reader in use at a supermarket.

System Diagram

See Figure 14.8.

A bar code reader and keypad in use for stock checking at a supermarket.

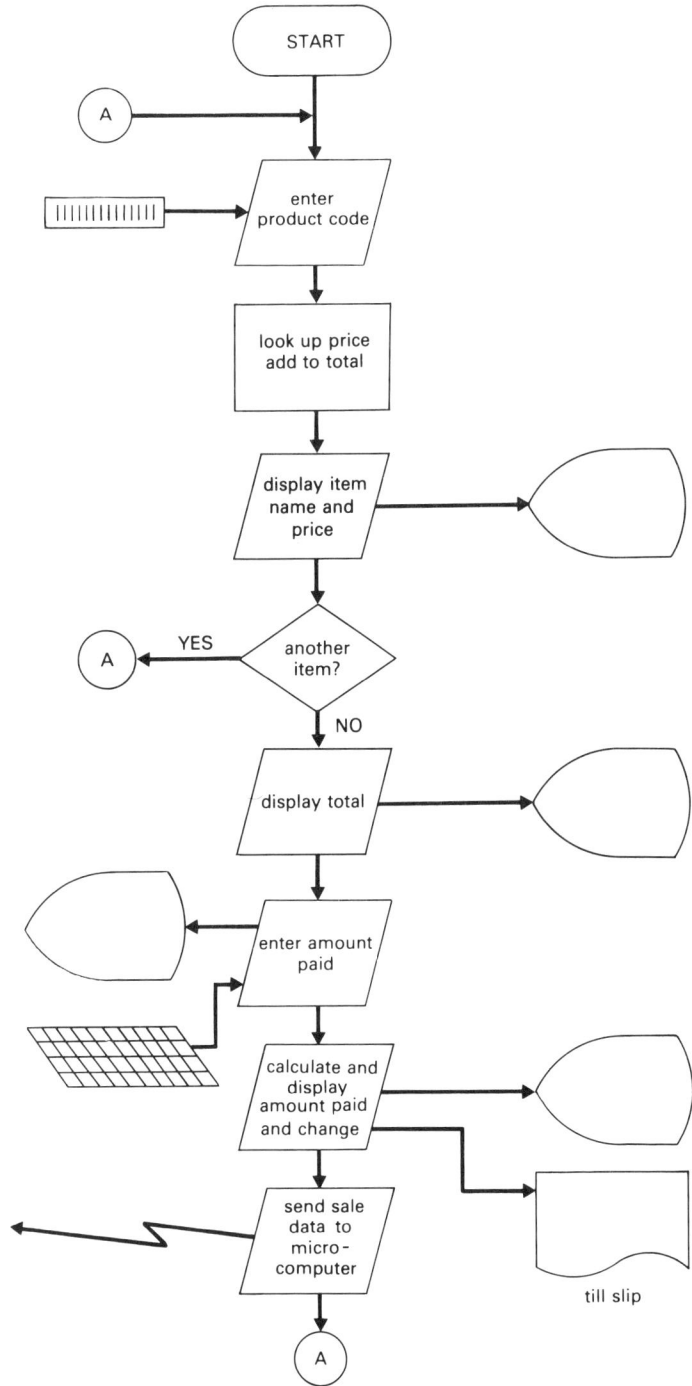

Figure 14.8   Point-of sale system: system diagram

Implementation

A point-of-sale system is an example of **distributed processing**. Some processing is done at the cash terminals: looking up product codes to get descriptions and prices, and calculating sale totals and change. The small computers at each shop collect the data from the terminals and send it to the central computer. In some systems, these computers update the stock records for the shop and issue re-order requests.

The operation of the warehouse computers is similar to that

167

described in section 14C. The central computer at the company's headquarters monitors overall stock levels and the flow of money. It produces summaries and reports of these figures, and allows trends to be observed and acted on by the managers of the company.

Most large chains of shops or supermarkets use software which has been developed specially for them. This is designed to suit their own type of selling and the way processing is distributed amongst the hardware. As most of the systems operate in real time, backup copies of all files are taken at regular intervals. The most common failure in a system of this nature is a fault in a data communications link. Most equipment is designed to continue to operate off-line if this happens, and to store the data until the link is restored. This data is then sent to be processed as a batch.

Questions

1 What is the most common type of fault which occurs in point-of-sale computer systems? How is this fault dealt with?
2 Explain the idea of **distributed processing** using a point-of-sale system as an example.
3 How are goods in a point-of-sale system identified?
4 Why is it important to identify each item as it is sold?
5 For what *two* main purposes is the data gathered by a point-of-sale terminal used?

14E Issue: It's Cheaper by Computer!

We take it for granted in Britain that shops will usually have the goods that we want, and that prices, especially for food items, are reasonable. Perishable goods are fresh and in good supply. This is due to the efficient systems of ordering and distributing goods used by the shops. These systems are relying increasingly on computers, as described in the previous section.

The use of point-of-sale stock control systems saves large sums of money by keeping stock levels low while ensuring that goods are not out-of-stock. Supply is tuned finely to demand and there is very little waste. Consequently, prices can be kept as low as possible.

Competition between groups of shops and supermarkets is intense. Any group which cannot match the others in the quality, freshness or prices of goods is likely to go out of business. The performance of the computer systems operated by each group of shops is a key element in the success of the group.

Questions

1 How widely used are point-of-sale computer systems in the UK?
2 What is likely to happen to a chain of supermarkets which cannot offer goods of as high a standard and low a price as other supermarkets?
3 State the advantages of the introduction of point-of-sale computer systems in shops for:
(a) the people who own the chains of shops
(b) the managers of the shops
(c) the staff of the shops and warehouses
(d) the customers.
List any disadvantages of these systems that you can think of.

14F End-of-Chapter Summary

The main points of this chapter are as follows:

- Computers are used to keep records of goods stored in shops and warehouses, and to record the movement of items in and out.

Goods can be re-ordered automatically.

- Most stock control systems aim to keep stock levels as low as possible without running out of stock.
- There is a stock master file which records the permanent details of each item in stock, as well as the current stock level. A set of movement records describes the movement of stock into or out of the warehouse.
- Most stock control systems are transaction processing systems, updating stock levels as each movement takes place.
- Point-of-sale (POS) systems in shops and supermarkets record details of the sale of each item as it takes place. This data is used to update stock files and keep records of the money received.
- Benefits of computerised stock control systems include lower prices, fresher goods and goods less likely to be out-of-stock.

Exercise 14

1 Choose the correct word from the list for each of the following spaces:

record; written; code; updated; master; movement; valid.

When stock is received at the warehouse, the storeman enters a ____ record for the goods. He types the stock ____, and re-enters it if it is not ____. The ____ for the goods is read from the ____ file. The number in stock is ____ and the record is ____ back to disk.

2 Figure 14.9 shows a delivery note for a consignment of goods, and Figure 14.10 a request slip for the issue of goods. Write down the movement records to be entered into the stock control system from section 14B relating to these movements.

```
┌─────────────────────────────────────────────────────────────────┐
│           DELIVERY NOTE                    Date │ 27th June 1988  │
│                                                 └───────────────  │
│    To: ┌──────────────────────────┐        J. J. GREEN LIMITED    │
│        │ CHIC CLOTHING COMPANY     │        CLOTHING IMPORTERS     │
│        │ UNIT 27A                  │        256 DOCKS WAY          │
│        │ BRENTFORD ESTATE          │        LONDON E14 3JL         │
│        │ LONDON W14 3TV            │                              │
│        └──────────────────────────┘                              │
│                                                                   │
│        75 Cocktail Dresses    Colour: Red    Size 16             │
│                                                                   │
│        Reference: Your Order JKS 88417                           │
└─────────────────────────────────────────────────────────────────┘
```

Figure 14.9   Stock delivery note

```
┌─────────────────────────────────────────────────────────────────┐
│    Request for Issue of Stock                        MV 65397K    │
│                                                                   │
│    Date:          8 8 0 6 2 7          Time:    |_|_|_|_|         │
│                                                                   │
│    Document Reference:  W X 7 9 3 1 7                             │
│                                                                   │
│    Item Stock Code:   S E 7 6 9 1 2 G                            │
│                                                                   │
│    Number In:     |_|_|_|_|          Number Out:  2 7            │
└─────────────────────────────────────────────────────────────────┘
```

Figure 14.10   Stock request slip

169

3 The check digit system for the item stock code, supplier code and movement code used in sections 14A and 14B works as follows:

Multiply each character in the code by its **weighting factor**. Letters are counted according to their place in the alphabet. For example:

$$
\begin{array}{ccccccc}
E & D & 2 & 9 & 8 & 4 & 1 \\
\times\,1 & \times\,3 & \times\,5 & \times\,7 & \times\,9 & \times\,11 & \times\,13 \\
\hline
5 & +12 & +10 & +63 & +72 & +44 & +13 \\
\end{array}
\;=219
$$

weighting factors

(E counts as 5, D as 4)

Things to find out

1 Select a small number of local shops and supermarkets, and note whether or not they use point-of-sale systems and, if so, how they operate.
(a) Write a brief report on the system used by each type of shop, describing the method used to enter the product

Project starters

1 The stock control system described in sections 14A and 14B uses a separate file of suppliers when re-ordering goods.
(a) Design a suitable record structure for this file.
(b) Design a suitable form, to be filled in by the computer, for the re-ordering of goods. Indicate which fields are printed in which positions in the form.
2 A small, independent hardware shop installs a point-of-sale computer system. It consists of a cash terminal connected to a microcomputer. The shop deals directly with suppliers, and all goods received are put straight into the shelves—it has no storeroom at the back.

Divide the sum of the products by 11, and take the remainder:

$219/11 = 19$ remainder 10

The remainder is the place in the alphabet of the letter used as the check digit. If the remainder is zero, the letter Z is used. In the example, it is the tenth letter, J. The complete item code is ED29841J.
(a) Work out the check digits for the following codes: AC83217, CA83217, AC81237 and AC13287.
(b) Which is the correct version of each of the following pairs of item codes:
BG23167D or BG21367D
FD99713H or DF99713H?

codes, and whether the terminals are on-line to a remote mainframe computer or to a smaller computer in the shop.
(b) Discuss the similarities and differences in the systems you observe. Try to work out why each type of shop has implemented its particular type of POS system.

Use the information from this chapter to design the stock control system for this shop. Use a system of stock codes for the goods, and assume that these are typed at the terminal when the goods are sold.
(a) Design an input form for the stock master file.
(b) Design a till slip to be printed with each sale.
(c) Set out the record structures for the stock master file and movement file.
(d) Describe how the files are updated.
(e) Draw a system flow diagram.
(f) Suggest the most suitable way of implementing the software for the system.

15 Analysing Scientific Data

When electronic computers were first developed, immediately after the Second World War, their main use was to analyse the results of scientific experiments. The speed at which they could do complex calculations and the large amounts of data they could process soon made them indispensable for this type of work.

Since then, many new uses for computers have been found. Nevertheless, analysing experimental results is still one of the most important applications of computers. The measurements for many experiments are taken by electronic sensors which are connected directly to computers. In some cases, measurements are taken many times a second. Most of these experiments could not be performed if this equipment were not available. Many advances in physics, chemistry, biology, medicine and engineering are due to the experimental work which is analysed on computers, some of which are the most powerful in existence.

This chapter describes two simple experiments which can be performed in the classroom and the results analysed on a school computer. It then outlines an important type of experiment: the monitoring and analysis of pollution levels in a river. It makes use of the general ideas about putting computers to work, as discussed in chapter 9.

> **monitor** to monitor something such as a person's heartbeat is to measure it continuously, or at frequent intervals.
> **analyse** to analyse a set of data is to work out averages and other statistics, in order to find patterns in the data.

15A Activity: Handspan, Foot Size and Height

Is there a relationship between a person's height, and the size of their hands and feet? Do people with large hands also have large feet? This section describes a scientific way of finding answers to these questions.

The Requirements of the Task

The aim of this activity is to investigate the relationships between:

- a person's height and the span of their hand
- a person's height and the length of their foot
- the span of a person's hand and the length of their foot.

(The span of your hand is the width of your hand when your fingers are spread out as widely as possible.)

The method is to measure the height, handspan and foot length of a number of pupils, and plot scatter graphs of the above combinations of them. Any pattern in the points on the graph indicates a relationship between the quantities.

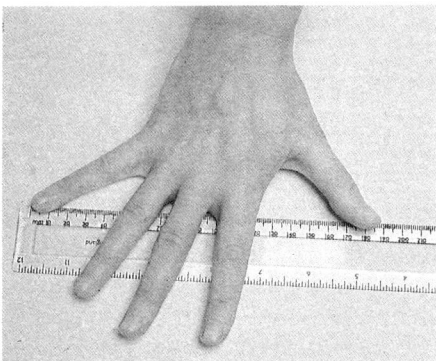
Measuring handspan.

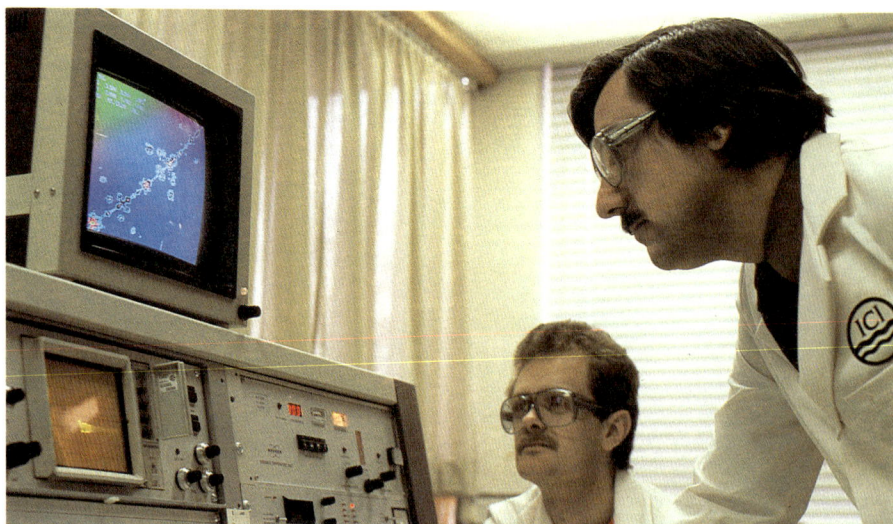

Scientists using computers to investigate the structure of molecules.

Computer System Design

Outputs
The outputs are scatter graphs of:

- handspan against height,
- foot length against height, and
- handspan against foot length.

These graphs are displayed on the computer screen and printed.

Inputs
A set of measurements of height, handspan and foot length are collected and input for as many pupils as possible.

File structure
The data is set out as a table, with three columns headed as follows:

Height mm	Handspan mm	Foot Length mm

If the group includes boys and girls, and there are sufficient of each, the results for the boys and those for the girls can be analysed separately.

File processing
Scatter graphs are plotted of the three combinations of these measurements. If possible, straight lines are fitted to the sets of points. The graphs are then examined to see how closely the points lie to the lines.

System Diagram

See Figure 15.1.

Implementation

For this activity you will need a metre stick or a tape measure marked in millimetres, and some rulers marked in millimetres.

- Set up a metre stick against the wall of the classroom to measure heights. Place the bottom end of the stick one metre above the floor, and remember to add one metre to the heights measured.
- Let a group of pupils measure their height, the length of a foot and the span of a hand. For consistency, decide whether to use left or

right hands and feet. Take all measurements in millimetres, correct to the nearest millimetre.

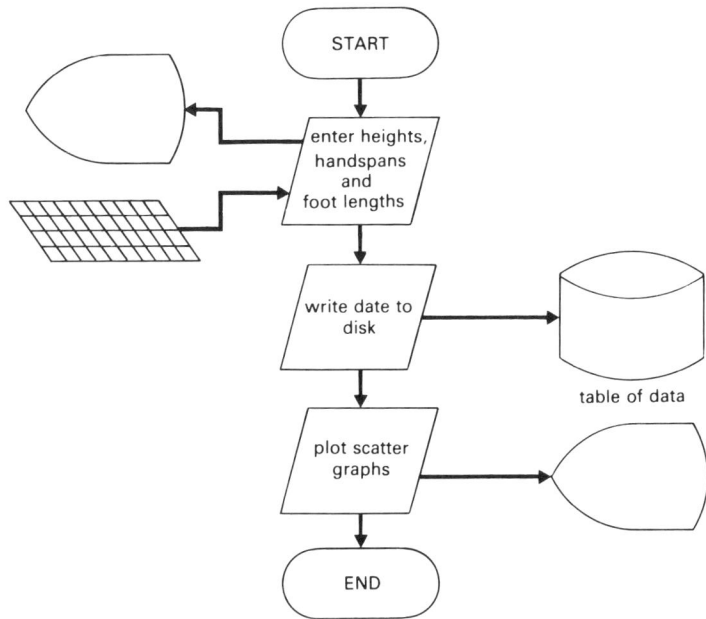

Figure 15.1   Height, handspan and foot length experiment: system diagram

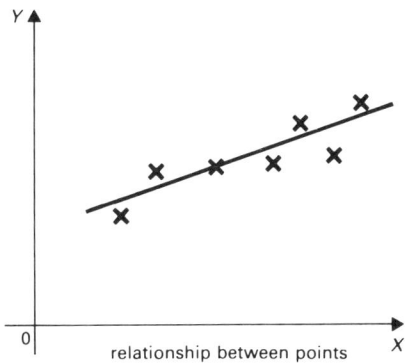

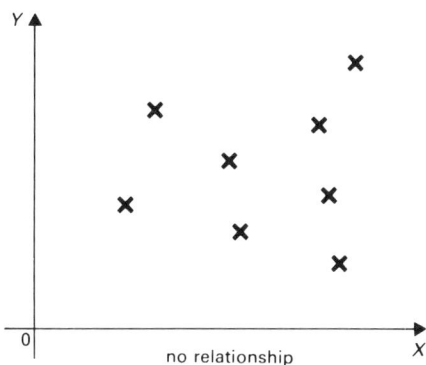

Figure 15.2   Straight lines fitted to scatter graphs

Use the program on your school computer which stores and analyses tables of numbers. Look at the user guide for the program to find out how to perform the various operations below.

- Open up a new table and head the first three columns as shown in the section on file structure, above.
- Enter the measurements for each pupil. Each pupil's height, handspan and foot length forms one row of the table.
- When all the numbers have been typed and checked, save the table on disk.
- Call up the graphs section of the program, and choose the line graphs option.
- Plot a graph of height on the x-axis against foot length on the y-axis. If possible, fit a straight line to this set of points. Print the graph, if you are able to do so.
- Look carefully at the pattern of points on the graph and see how closely they lie to the line fitted to them. Describe the relationship you can see between foot length and height.

If the points all lie fairly close to the line, then there is a simple relationship between foot length and height: taller people have longer feet. If there is some other pattern, then the relationship is more complicated. If the points are scattered at random, there is no relationship. See Figure 15.2.

Repeat the above two steps for the relationship between handspan and height, and that between foot length and handspan.

173

Documentation

- Write a brief user guide for this activity, in terms of the computer program you are using. Explain how to set up a table for the measurements, how to enter the data, and how to call up the graphs. Describe how to save the information on disk, and how to make backup copies of the disk.

15B Activity: Heat Loss Experiment

In a cold country such as Britain, it is very important to conserve heat. We wear thick clothes to keep warm in winter, and put insulating material in buildings and around hot water tanks to keep the heat in. Saving energy saves money: coal, gas and electricity are expensive. It also reduces pollution.

This section investigates how heat is lost from a warm object in colder surroundings. It also investigates the effects of various types of insulating materials.

The Requirements of the Task

The aims of this activity are:

- To investigate the relationship between the loss of heat from a warm object and the difference in temperature between the object and its surroundings.
- To investigate the effects of insulating materials on this loss of heat.

The method is to fill a container with hot water, and take the temperature of the water at regular intervals until it cools to room temperature. The temperatures are entered into a computer system and analysed.

The process is repeated with the container enclosed in various insulating materials: paper, cloth, fibreglass, etc.

Computer System Design

Outputs
The outputs are tables and graphs of heat loss against temperature for different insulating materials.

Inputs
Sets of temperatures of the object are recorded at regular intervals as it cools. These are entered as input data.

File structure
Each set of times and temperatures is entered into a table. The columns are headed as shown below. The first two columns are for the times and temperatures as they are recorded. The third column is for the difference between the temperature of the water and that of the room. The fourth column is for the drop in temperature during each time interval. This is a measure of the loss of heat. The numbers in the third and fourth columns are calculated by the computer.

Time	Temp	RelTemp	TmpDrop
Sec	Deg C	Deg C	Deg C

The snow covering these houses acts as an insulating layer.

There is one table for the uninsulated object, and others for the object enclosed by insulating materials.

File processing

The relative temperatures are calculated by subtracting the room temperature from the temperature of the object.

The drop in temperature during each time interval is calculated by subtracting the previous temperature from the current one.

The table is saved on disk, and a graph plotted of the drop in temperature against the relative temperature.

System Diagram

See Figure 15.3.

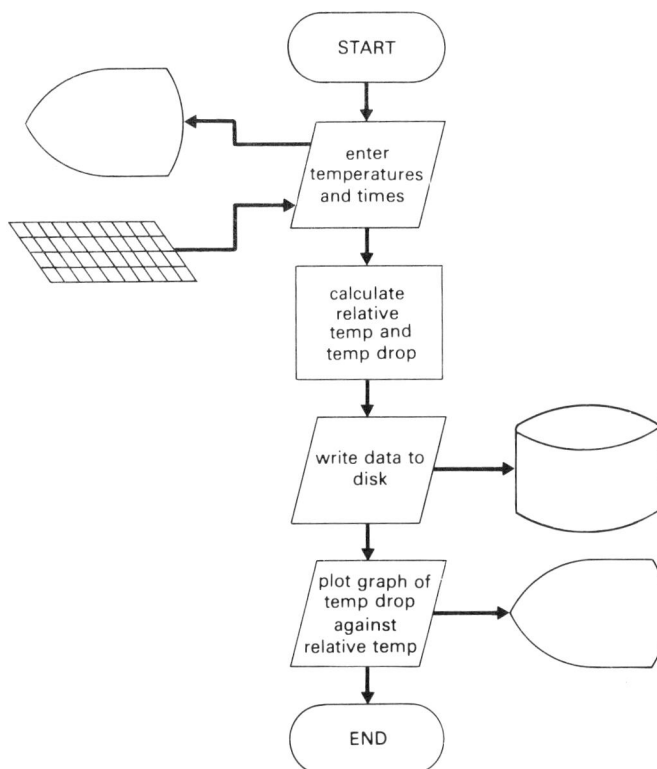

Figure 15.3 Temperature experiment: system diagram

Implementation

You will need the following equipment:

- A container which will hold at least a litre of water. A laboratory flask or a glass jar with a screw top is suitable.
- A thermometer which will measure temperatures from room temperature to boiling point.
- A watch which can show time in seconds.
- Some sheets of paper, fibreglass and cloth, large enough to wrap around the container.
- A source of hot water (a hot tap or kettle).

The steps are as follows:

- Make a hole in the lid of the jar large enough for the thermometer to be inserted. If you are using a flask, push the thermometer through the hole in a rubber stopper which fits the flask.

175

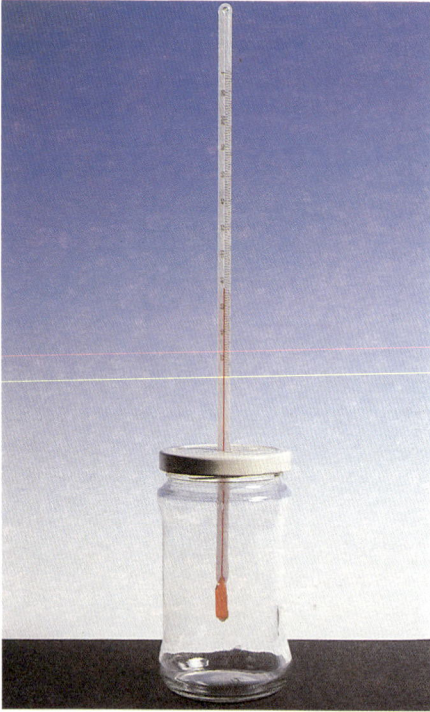

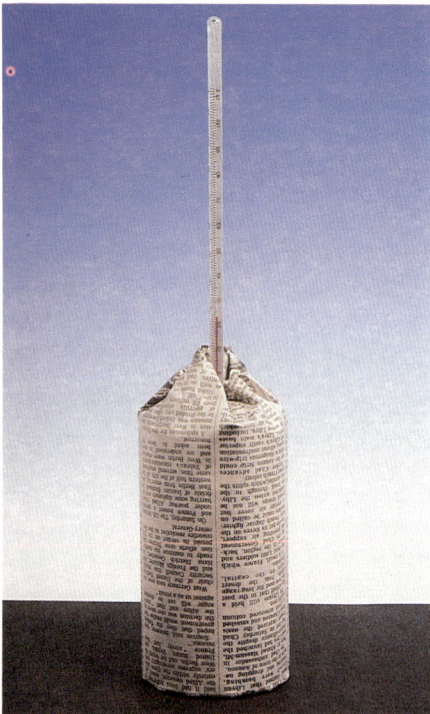

Top: Measuring the temperature of water in a glass jar. *Bottom:* Insulating the glass jar with newspaper.

Documentation

- Measure the temperature of the room.
- Fill the container with hot (but not boiling) water. (If you are not using a laboratory flask, warm the container gradually so that it does not crack.) Close the container, and position the thermometer so that it reaches into the water.
- At regular intervals (twenty seconds is suitable) write down the time and temperature. Continue to take measurements until the temperature is within five degrees of room temperature.

Use the program on your school computer which stores and analyses tables of numbers. Look at the user guide for the program to find out how to carry out the steps below.

- Create a new blank table, and head the first four columns as shown in the section on file structure on page 174.
- Enter the times and temperatures in the first two columns.
- Enter a formula which calculates the relative temperatures. If the program you are using accepts the column headings in formulae, and the room temperature is 16°C, then the formula is:

$$\text{RelTemp} = \text{Temp} - 16$$

- Also enter a formula to calculate the drop in temperature over each time period, as follows:

$$\text{TmpDrop} = \text{diff(Temp)}$$

Note that this formula gives negative results, as each temperature is lower than the previous one.

- Instruct the computer to evaluate the formulae, if it does not do so as soon as you have entered them.
- Plot a scatter graph of the relative temperature (on the *x*-axis) against the temperature drop (*y*-axis). Fit a straight line to the points, and note how closely they lie to this line.
- Save the table of results on disk and, if possible, print the graph.
- The drop in temperature is a measure of the amount of heat which is lost by the object during a certain period of time. Study the graph carefully and explain the relationship between this loss of heat and the difference in temperature between the object and its surroundings.

Repeat the process from the beginning, this time wrapping the container in one of the insulating materials. Put the same volume of water into the container as before, and start at the same temperature. Measure temperatures at the same time intervals. Compare the graph you get this time with the one which was produced when there was no insulation. Describe the effect of the insulating material on the rate of heat loss.

Carry out the experiment a number of times, each time using a different insulating material, or more layers of a material you have already used. In each case, comment on the effect of the insulating material on the rate of heat loss.

- Write a version of the above instructions in terms of the steps required for the computer program you are using. State how to open up a table for the results, how to enter data, how to enter and evaluate formulae, and how to produce graphs.

15C Application: Monitoring River Pollution

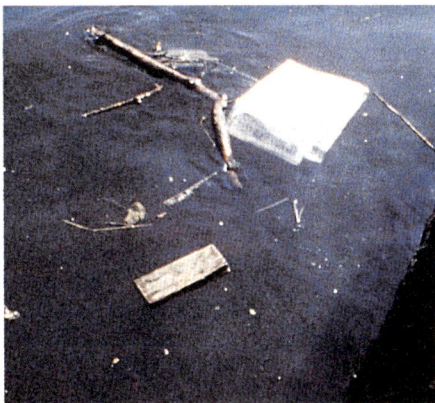

Polluted water in a river.

Rivers provide a number of important services. They are a source of water for drinking and for industrial processes. They carry away waste. They support many different life forms, such as fish, plants and insects, and are an essential part of the environment.

Over the years, many rivers have become heavily polluted. The waste from cities, factories and farms has poisoned them. Some rivers are no longer able to support any form of life. The more polluted the river, the more difficult and expensive it is to purify the water for drinking purposes.

In an effort to reduce or eliminate pollution in rivers, most countries have laws which state what waste products can be discharged into them. These laws have been very successful in reducing the level of pollution. In order to check that the pollution laws are being obeyed, it is necessary to **monitor** the levels of pollution in rivers. This monitoring is done by the water boards which have overall responsibility for the rivers in their areas.

The Requirements of the Task

Samples of river water being analysed at a Water Board laboratory.

The task of a water board is to keep a continuous check on the levels of certain chemicals in rivers. More specifically, the aims are:

- To monitor the level of oxygen, acidity (pH) and concentration of certain pollutants in a stretch of river.
- To produce a warning if any of the measurements goes above or below the safe limits.
- To transfer the measurements to a computer at regular intervals for analysis.

The measurements are taken by **probes** placed in the river at a suitable point. These are connected to automatic data logging equipment in a monitoring station on the river bank. At regular intervals, the data is transferred to the computer via a telephone link.

The probes measure the data in **analogue form**, and the data logging equipment changes it to **digital form**. See section 6D for more information about these terms.

Computer System Design

Outputs
Tables and graphs are plotted of the way pollution varies with time. An alarm signal is sent immediately if one of the levels goes outside the safe limits.

Inputs
Measurements are taken by the sensors of the various levels.

File structure
The data is stored in tables, one for each set of data transmitted by the logging equipment. A typical table is headed as follows:

Time	Oxygen	Acidity	Nitrate	Mercury	Lead
Min	%	pH	mg/cu m	mg/cu m	mg/cu m

File processing

The measurements are input directly from the data loggers via the communications link. The computer calculates averages and other statistics, and plots graphs of the measurements against time. The data is saved on disk.

System Diagram

See Figure 15.4.

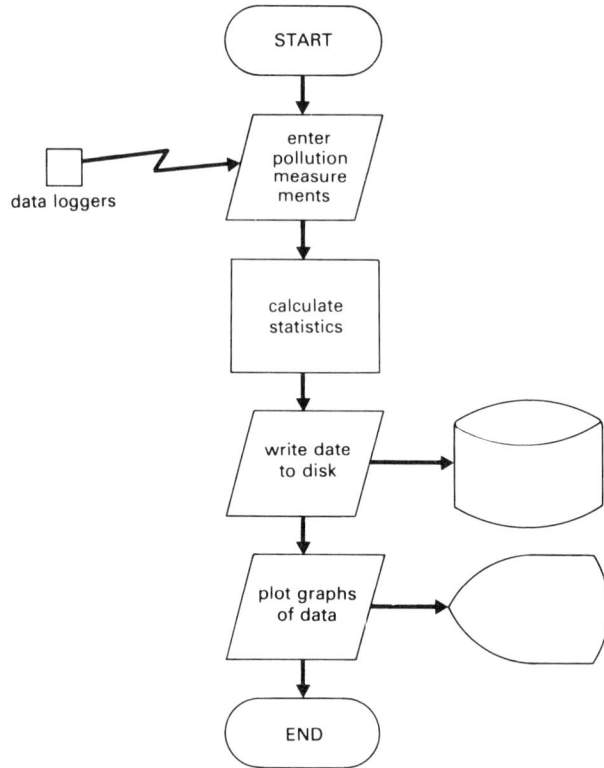

Figure 15.4   River pollution monitoring system: system diagram

Implementation

A monitoring system of this sort is implemented on a large minicomputer or a mainframe computer using software developed by the data processing department of the water board. The routine logging, transmission and processing of the data is done in batch mode. If any special processing is required, it is done interactively.

The alarm system which is triggered if a reading goes outside safe limits operates in real time. It interrupts any other work being done by the computer.

Testing

The data logging, transmission and processing aspects of a system like this are first tested separately. When each is working satisfactorily using large batches of test data, the system as a whole is tested. Two types of tests are carried out: one type uses sets of test data where the averages and other statistics are already known. This enables the results to be checked. The other type of test uses actual measurements, which are repeated using manual equipment. The results from the manual measurements and those produced by the computer system are then compared.

Questions

1 Explain the ideas of analogue and digital data, using the river pollution monitoring system as an example.
2 How are interrupts used in the river pollution monitoring system?
3 What are the benefits of keeping a continuous check on pollution levels in a river?
4 Why is it essential to compare the results from the computer system with ones calculated manually?

15D End-of-Chapter Summary

The main points of this chapter are as follows:

- Analysing scientific data is one of the oldest applications of computers. It is still one of the most important.
- Computers are ideal for the analysis of scientific data because they can perform complex calculations very quickly, and store large quantities of data.

Exercise 15

1 Choose the correct word from the list for each of the following spaces:

analogue; probes; input; logging; digital; apparatus; data; link.

The laboratory assistant set up the ____. She linked the ____ at the points where ____ was to be measured. She connected the probes to the data ____ module, which stores the data and changes it from ____ to ____ form. She plugged in the data ____ between the data logger and the ____ port of the computer.

2 The activity described in section 15A can be extended in a number of ways. Here are some suggestions:
(a) Measure the lengths of left and right feet, and the spans of both hands. Have separate columns for these four measurements, and investigate any relationships which may exist between them. For example, is there a stronger relationship between the size of the right hand and left foot than that between the right hand and right foot?
(b) The **correlation coefficient** measures how closely related two sets of figures are. If there is a precise relationship, so that the points on a graph of the two sets of figures lie on a straight line, then the correlation coefficient has the value 1.0000 (or − 1.0000 if the line slopes

downwards). A value of 0.8000 indicates some relationship, but not an exact one. A correlation coefficient of 0.0000 indicates no relationship; the points are scattered at random on the graph.

If your computer program can calculate correlation coefficients, calculate the correlation coefficient of foot length and height, that of handspan and height, and that of foot length and handspan. Comment on the values as they compare with your observations from the graphs.
3 The activity described in section 15B can be automated if a temperature probe and data logger such as the **Vela** are available. The temperature probe replaces the thermometer and is connected to the data logger. This is set to record temperatures at regular intervals. When the experiment is complete, the data logger is connected to the computer. The temperatures are transferred to the computer to be analysed as before.

An alternative is to connect the temperature probe directly to the analogue input port of the computer. A program is required to read the temperatures at regular intervals, convert the analogue readings to degrees centigrade, and store the data in a form which can be analysed.

Points to discuss

1 (a) Make a list of a number of serious problems which have not been solved by our present state of scientific knowledge. An example is finding the cause of, and a cure for, cancer.
(b) For each problem in your list, discuss the ways in

which information technology could be used to help find a solution to the problem. In each case, decide which capabilities of IT systems are of particular benefit.

Project starters

1 The methods used in sections 15A and 15B can be applied to any of the following activities. One of these can form the basis of a GCSE project.

(a) Measuring the speed and acceleration of a runner or cyclist. The times to cover a set of distances are measured and entered into the computer program which analyses data. If distance and time are both measured from the start, then:

$$\text{speed} = \text{diff(distance)/diff(time)}$$
$$\text{acceleration} = \text{diff(speed)/diff(time)}$$

where diff is the difference between one measurement and the previous one.

(b) Enter a set of world record times for running various distances. For each distance, calculate the average speed. Plot a graph of average speed against distance. Compare current world records with those standing, say, ten years ago.

(c) Enter a set of weather data: temperatures, hours of sunshine, pressure, relative humidity, etc. for each day over a period of time. Plot graphs of the data against time, and scatter graphs of the sets of data against each other. See if there are any relationships between the data; for example, is there a relationship between maximum temperature and the number of hours of sunshine?

2 There are two scientific concepts which are often confused:

accuracy is how close a measurement is to its 'true' value, for example, how close is the length of a metre stick to an exact metre?

precision is the amount of variation in a particular method of measurement, for example if two people time a runner during a race using identical stop-watches, how close are the two times?

An interesting demonstration of these two concepts is the variation in the times shown on people's watches. The method of section 15A can be used to analyse a set of times for accuracy and precision, as follows:

- Decide on a standard for the 'correct' time. A radio time signal on the hour, or the time on the speaking clock will do.
- Get all the pupils in a group who have watches to look at them as a precisely known time approaches.
- One member of the group calls out at exactly the known time, and all the others note the time on their watches.
- Convert all the times into seconds before or after the precise time. For example, if the precise time was 11:00:00, then a watch which showed 10:58:32 is 88 seconds slow.
- Enter these times into the computer program which analyses results. Open up a new table, and enter all the results into one column. The times fast are entered as positive numbers and the times slow as negative numbers.
- Calculate the **mean** (average) of the numbers, and the **standard deviation** of them. The standard deviation is a measure of the spread of the results: approximately two thirds of them lie within one standard deviation of the mean.

  The mean is a measure of the accuracy of the set of watches: it measures how close they are, on average, to the correct time. The standard deviation measures the precision: the smaller it it, the less variation there is in the times.
- Comment on the results obtained from your group.

Reservation Systems

Making airline reservations at a travel agent.

flight record the record of the passengers on an air flight.

Booking people into hotels, to see plays or to travel on aircraft is a simple task. There are a fixed number of places available, and each place is either booked or not booked. Tickets can be printed in advance, one per place, and given out when a booking is made. Manual systems for making reservations have worked efficiently for many years.

However, when an airline operates hundreds of flights per day, each flight carrying hundreds of passengers, and bookings for any flight can be made at thousands of booking offices and travel agents all over the world and seats paid for in dozens of different currencies, then a computerised booking system is essential. Airline reservation systems were the first large-scale computer application to operate in real time: each seat is booked on the central computer as the reservation is entered at a terminal. The number of seats booked on any flight is kept up-to-date all the time. The computers for airline seat reservations are linked to a worldwide data communications network.

The computer systems used for airline reservations have proved so efficient that simpler versions of the systems have been developed for holiday companies, hotels and theatres. This chapter describes computerised reservations of this sort. It puts into practice some of the general ideas about computer applications introduced in chapter 9.

16A Activity: School Play Booking System

It is possible to set up a simple computer system for bookings for a school play. The software required is either a reservations package or a spreadsheet program (chapter 12) which is large enough to take a booking plan. Tickets can be printed using a word processor document (chapter 11).

This activity can be based on an actual play which is to be performed at the school, or one at a local youth club or drama group. If no such performances are coming up, then the reservation system can be set up ready for the next one!

The Requirements of the Task

The aim of the task is to set up a reservation system for a school play which can be used to:

- make bookings
- provide booking reports: the number of tickets sold and the amount of money received for each performance
- print tickets.

A school play in progress.

Computer System Design

Outputs

The outputs are an up-to-date booking plan and the tickets, after each booking is made.

Inputs

The date of the performance and the number of seats required are input.

File structure

A spreadsheet is set up for each performance, with rows and columns arranged to match the rows and seats for the performance. Each cell represents one seat: it contains a 0 if the seat is vacant, and a 1 if the seat is booked. An additional column is used for the total number of seats booked in each row. Cells are set up to contain the total number of seats booked in each price block and the money received from these bookings. See Figure 16.1.

A word processor document is set up containing all the constant information on a ticket. When a booking is made, this document is called up, and the particular information for each ticket—date and seat number—is entered. The ticket is then printed.

```
       _1 _2 _3 _4 _5 _6 _7 _8 _9 _10 _11 _12 _13 _____14 _____15
 1                                                       8pm Saturday 24/01/87
 2                                                       --- -------- --------
 3  Seat  1  2  3  4  5  6  7  8  9  10  11  12      Total   Income
 4  Row  --- --- --- --- --- --- --- --- --- --- --- ---  -------- --------
 5  A     0  0  1  1  1  1  1  1  1   0   0   0          7
 6  B     0  0  0  1  1  1  1  1  1   1   0   0          7
 7  C     1  1  0  0  1  1  0  1  1   0   0   0          6
 8  D     0  0  0  1  1  1  0  0  0   0   1   1          5
 9  E     0  0  0  0  1  1  1  0  0   0   0   0          3
10  F     0  0  0  0  0  0  0  1  0   0   0   1          2
11  G     0  0  0  0  0  0  0  0  0   0   0   0          0
12  H     1  0  0  0  0  0  0  0  0   0   0   0          1
13                                                       --------
14  £5                                                         31  £155.00
15                                                       --------
16  I     1  1  1  1  1  1  1  1  1   1   1   1         12
17  J     0  1  1  1  1  1  1  1  0   1   1   1         10
18  K     0  0  1  1  1  1  1  1  0   0   0   0          7
19  L     0  0  0  1  1  1  1  0  0   0   0   0          4
20  M     0  0  0  0  0  1  1  0  0   0   0   0          2
21                                                       --------
22  £3                                                         35  £105.00
23                                                       -------- --------
24                                                           Total  £260.00
25                                                       -------- --------
26
```

Figure 16.1 Spreadsheet for school play booking system

File processing

An empty spreadsheet is first set up and saved on disk for each performance. A blank ticket is created and saved on disk using a word processor. When a booking is made, an algorithm for the process is as follows:

Call up the spreadsheet for the required performance

If there are seats available

then For each seat to be booked repeat

Change the cell for the seat from 0 to 1

Collect the money and give change if necessary

Re-calculate the total seats booked and amount of money received

Save the updated spreadsheet on disk

For each seat to be booked repeat

Call up the ticket blank on the word processing program

Enter the ticket details

Print the ticket

System Diagram

See Figure 16.2.

Implementation

Use a spreadsheet program or a reservation system on your school computer. Look at the user guide for the program to find out how to carry out each step. The steps below assume that a spreadsheet program is used—a reservation program is simpler.

- Set up a spreadsheet for the reservations like the one in Figure 16.1. Adjust it to suit the arrangement of seats in your school hall.
- Using the cells in a suitable column, enter a formula for the total seats reserved in each row. For example, if there are twenty seats in each row, in columns 2 to 21 of the spreadsheet, then a formula in the 22nd column for the total in the row is:

$$R4C22 = sum(R4C2:R4C21)$$

or $V4 = sum(B4:U4)$. You will need a formula like this in each row.
- If all the tickets cost the same, choose a suitable cell and enter a formula for the total number of seats booked, by adding up the total from each row. If blocks of seats have different prices, enter a formula for the total number booked in each block.
- Enter a formula for the total amount of money received from each block of seats. This is the price of a ticket multiplied by the total number of seats booked in each block. If necessary choose an appropriate cell and enter a formula for the overall total amount of money received.
- Check all the formulae carefully, and fill the cells for the seats with zeros. Test the spreadsheet by booking a few seats and seeing if the totals and amounts of money are correct.
- When you are satisfied that the spreadsheet is correct, change all the seat cells back to zero, and save a copy of the spreadsheet on

disk for each performance. Also save a spare copy of the blank spreadsheet for use in future productions.

- Call up each copy of the spreadsheet and enter the date of the performance into it. Save these versions of the spreadsheet.
- Using the word processing program, enter a document containing the constant information for a ticket. Check the document carefully and save it on disk.

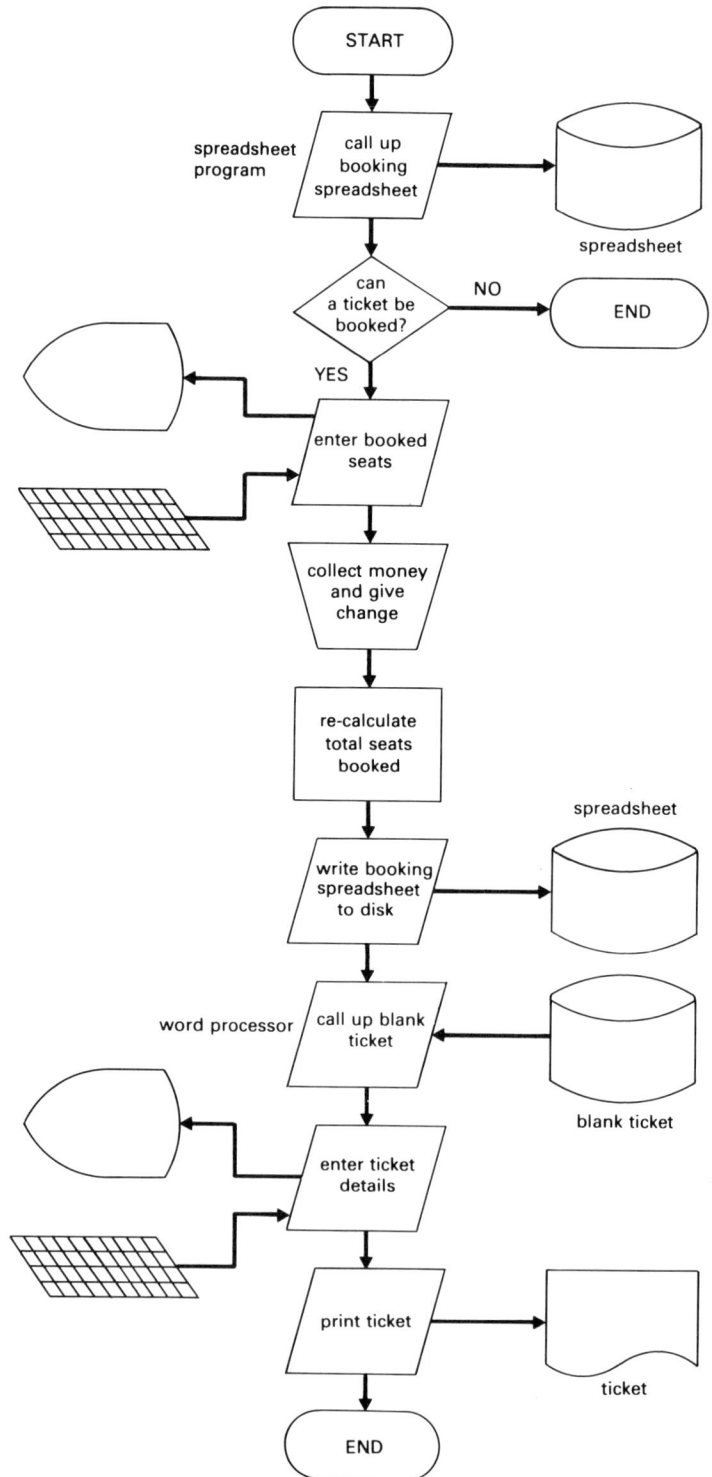

Figure 16.2   School play booking system: system diagram

- For each booking, follow the procedure in the above algorithm to reserve the seats and print the tickets.
- From time to time, call up the spreadsheet for each performance and check the total amount of money against the money which has been received.

Documentation

- Write a set of system documentation describing the structure of the spreadsheet. Explain how it can be modified if the arrangement of seats is changed or the prices are altered.
- Write a set of instructions for someone to take bookings using the reservation system you have implemented. Explain the steps needed to carry out each operation, and how to save the updated spreadsheets on disk.

16B Application: Hotel Booking System

Computer systems for hotel reservations and keeping the accounts of guests are becoming increasingly popular. They are proving to be more efficient than paper-based systems, and save the time of hotel staff.

The Requirements of the Task

The aims of a reservation system for a hotel are:

- To reserve rooms for guests when bookings are made.
- To produce an account for each guest showing all charges during the stay.
- To generate reports on room occupancy and money received.

Computer System Design

Outputs
The outputs are a record for each night, showing the number of each type of room reserved and the number still available. These records may be viewed on screen and printed when required.

An account for each guest, itemising all charges, is also output. These are printed when the guest checks out.

Reports of room occupancy rates and amounts of money received are produced from time to time.

Inputs
The main input is requests for reservations. If a reservation can be made, an account is opened for the guest containing the name and address of the guest, the type(s) of room(s) required, and the length of the stay.

During the stay, each item to be charged to the guest's account is entered.

File structure
A room occupancy file has a record for each night. It has the following structure:

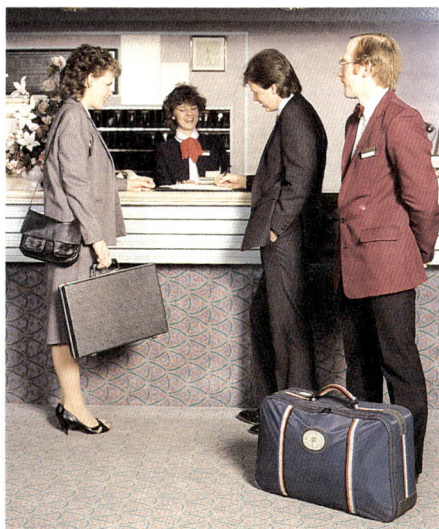

Guests checking out at a hotel. Their account has been produced by the hotel's computer.

Field				Example		
Date:	Date Code			12/12/86		
Suites:	Total	No Reserved	No Free	13	5	8
Double Rooms:	Total	No Reserved	No Free	85	67	18
Single Rooms:	Total	No Reserved	No Free	73	51	22

The account for each guest has the following structure:

Field	Type	Length	Example
Account Reference	code	8	GX7534TY
Name	alpha	20	Ms K Macintosh
Address 1	alpha	20	33 Hill Rise
Address 2	alpha	20	Diss
Address 3	alpha	20	Norfolk
Postcode	alpha	8	NR27 6GT
Room Type	code	1	S
Room No	numeric	4	1409
Arrival Date	code	8	12/12/86
Checkout Date	code	8	13/12/86
For each charge:			
Date	code	8	13/12/86
Item	alpha	20	Single Room
Cost	numeric	6	47.50
....			
Total Cost	numeric	6	47.50

File processing

When making a reservation, the room occupancy records for the required dates are called up and viewed on screen. If a room is available, an account is opened for the guest. It is given a reference by the reservations system, and the name, address, room type and dates of stay are entered. The room occupancy records are updated. The account file and updated room files are saved on disk.

When the guest arrives at the hotel, a room is allocated and entered into the account file. During the stay, charges for the room, meals, telephone calls and drinks at the bar are entered into the account.

When the guest checks out, the total charge is calculated and the account printed. The payment details are entered.

System Diagram See Figure 16.3.

Implementation Most hotel reservation systems are based on standard software packages running on small computers in the hotel. Chains of hotels have larger computers at their headquarters which receive daily reports from the hotel computers, and analyse them.

Questions
1 Briefly describe, in your own words, the process of reserving a room at a hotel using a computerised system.
2 What information does a hotel booking system supply for managers to use?
3 (a) What type of software do most hotel reservation systems use?
  (b) Why is this software usually chosen?

16C Application: Airline Seat Reservations

One of the largest and most complex real-time computer systems in operation is the international network used for airline reservations. Each airline has its own mainframe computers which make the reservations in real time. These are connected via a worldwide data

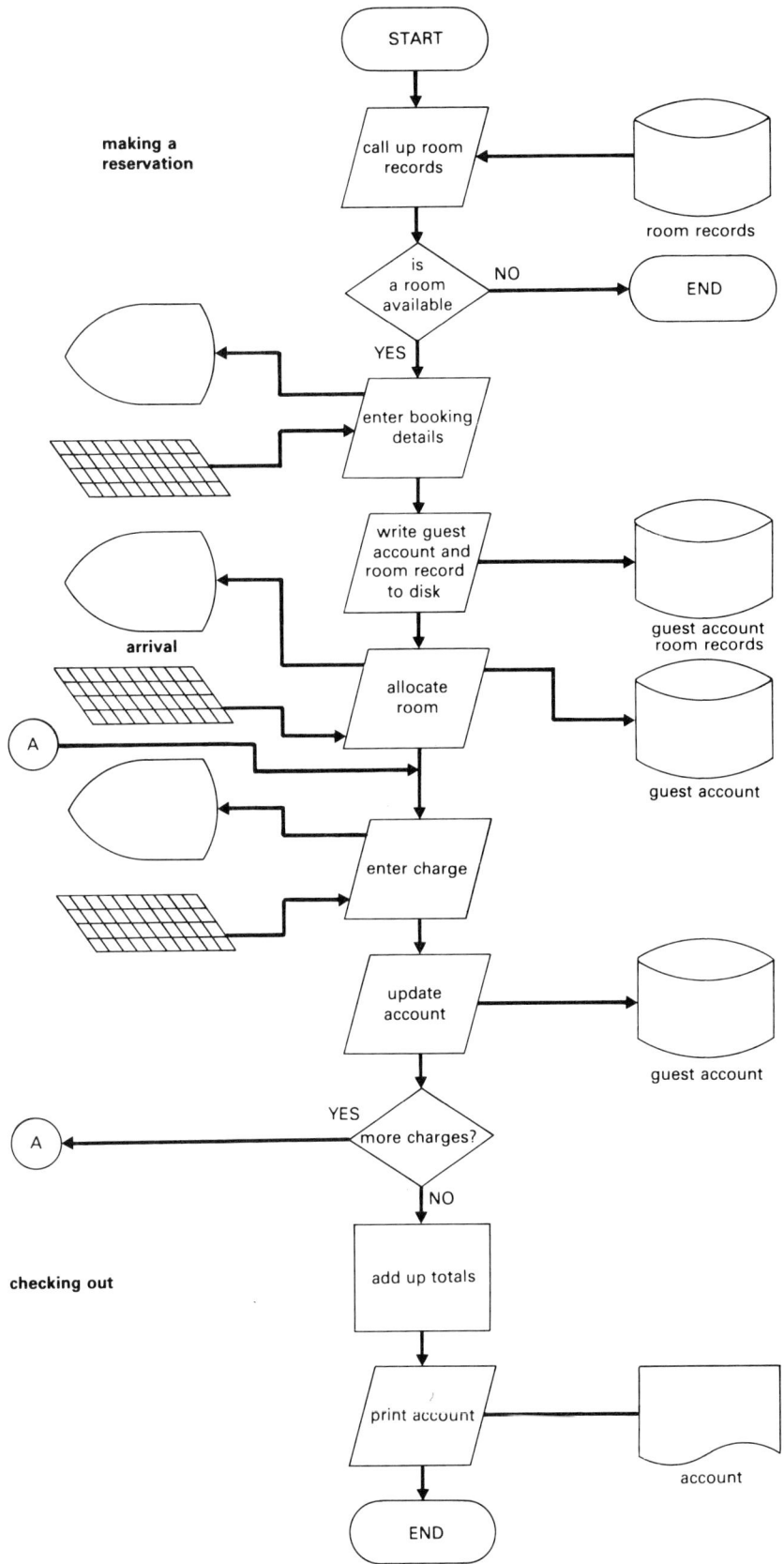

Figure 16.3   Hotel reservations system:
system diagram

communications network called **Sita** to airline offices and travel agents around the world. See Figure 16.4.

The computers run under transaction processing operating systems. Each reservation is made, and the flight records updated, as the reservation is entered at the terminal. A large number of reservations can be in progress simultaneously.

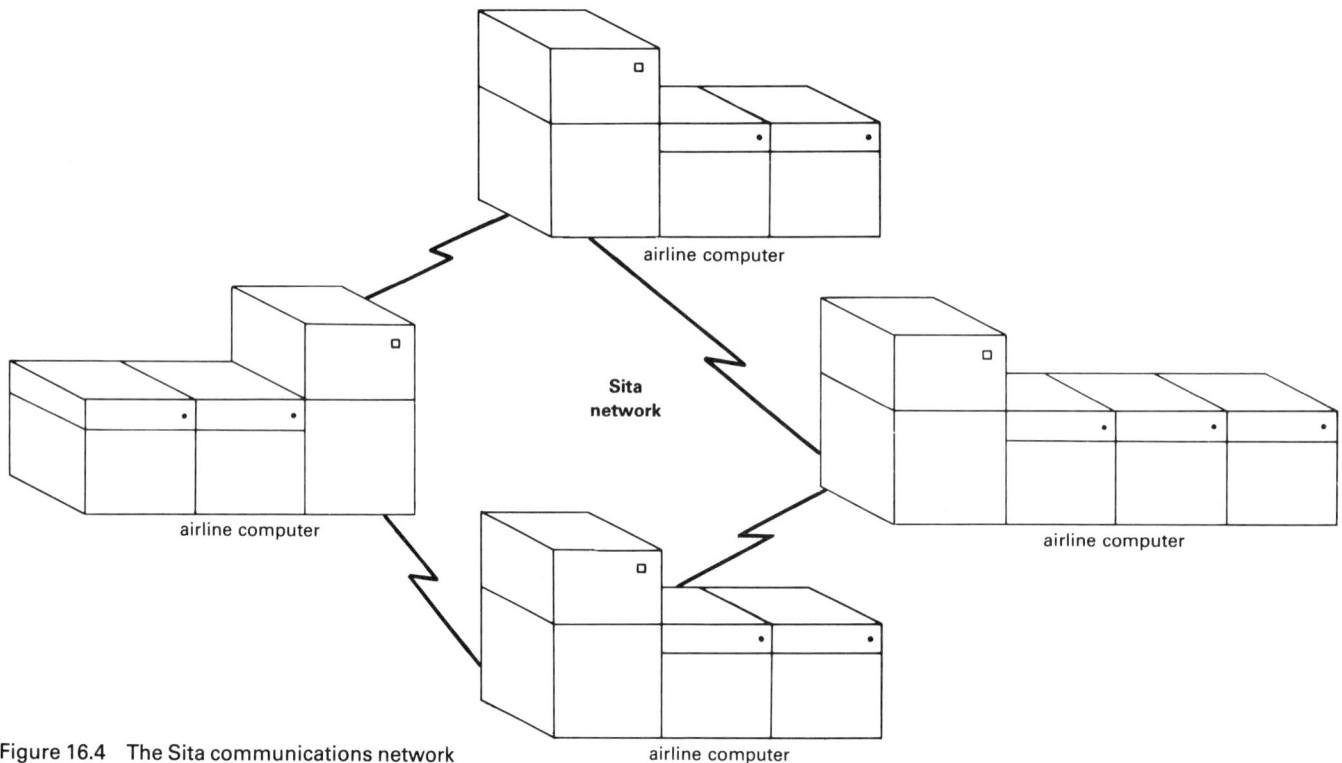

Figure 16.4   The Sita communications network

The Requirements of the Task

The aim of the system is to enable reservations to be made for flights from terminals anywhere in the world. The system must be able to cope with hundreds of flights, each carrying hundreds of passengers, every day. Flight records must be kept up-to-date in real time, and the system must be able to cope with peak rates of hundreds of reservations per second. Although the reservation system for each individual airline is slightly different from those of the others, they all have the same interface to the data communications network.

Computer System Design

Outputs
The final output from the system is passenger lists for each flight. Some systems print tickets, in others the tickets are written out by hand.

Inputs
Requests for reservations: the date and flight number of each flight are entered. If a seat can be booked on the flight, the name of the passenger and the ticket reference are entered.

File structure
The actual file structure is complicated, with multiple indexes in order to locate the record for each flight as quickly as possible. (See chapter 23 for details about file indexes.) The record for each flight includes the flight number, date and a list of the names and ticket

Aircraft queueing to take off at a busy international airport.

references of the passengers. It also has the total seats in each class, the number booked and the number available.

File processing

When a reservation is made, the person making the booking calls up the computer of the airline from the terminal, if it is not permanently on-line. The date and number of the required flight are entered, and the flight record is accessed on the disk.

If a reservation can be made, the passenger details and ticket reference are entered. While this is happening, the flight record is **locked** so that another terminal cannot make a booking at the same time. As soon as the booking is complete, the updated flight record is written to disk and made available to other terminals.

The ticket is either printed or written by hand.

System Diagram

See Figure 16.5.

Implementation

Most airlines are now using their second or third computer system for reservations. Making a reservation is simple: the problem is handling the large volumes of reservations quickly, and managing the worldwide data links to ensure that there are no communications bottlenecks.

Airline reservations systems use large mainframe computers with processors and other units duplicated. This means that the units can work in parallel, and that the system as a whole can continue to function if an item of equipment breaks down. The computers and communications networks are designed for continuous operation— 24 hours a day, 7 days a week, 365 days a year—even while maintenance work is in progress.

The software has been developed and enhanced by the data processing departments of the airlines over the years. The detailed operation varies from one airline to another, but the general

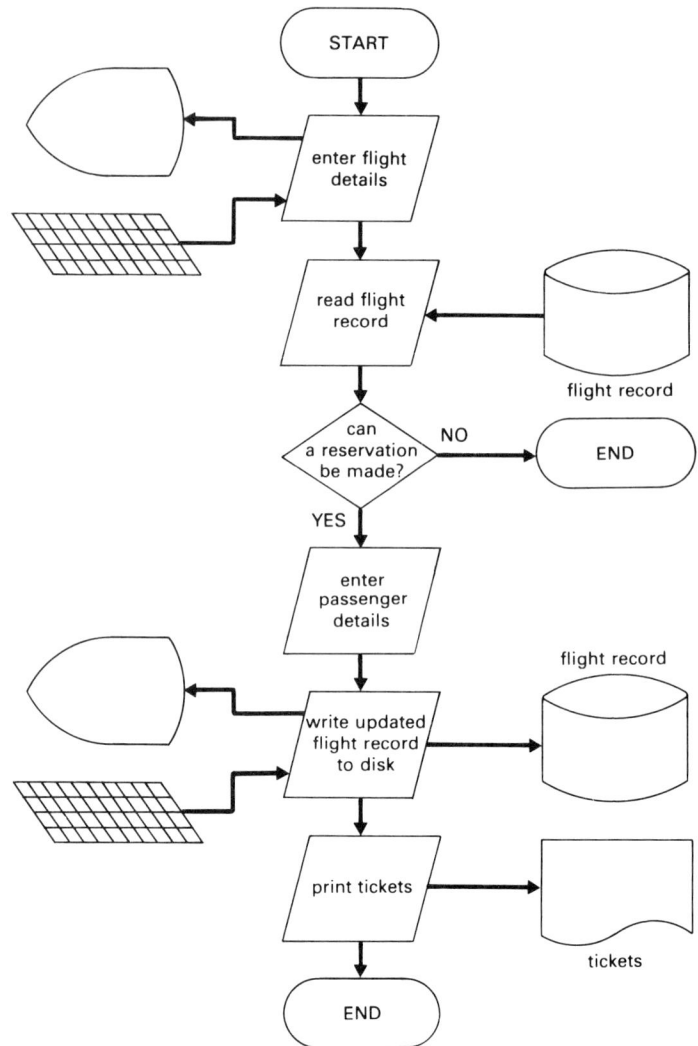

Figure 16.5   Airline bookings: system diagram

operation is as described above. The data communications aspect of the software has standard interfaces so that terminals can access any computer and information can be exchanged between the computers of different airlines.

Most airline reservation systems keep backup copies of data files updated every few minutes; a few duplicate all data as it is saved. Copies are kept of all reservation messages so that a file can be re-created quickly if one is corrupted.

Questions

1 What are the main problems to be overcome in the design of a reservation system for an airline?
2 Why must a flight record be locked to other terminals while a reservation is being made?
3 Why is it necessary for the reservation computers of different airlines to be able to communicate with each other?
4 Why is it necessary for airline reservation computers to operate around the clock?
5 Explain what is meant by the term **real-time system**, using an airline reservation system as an example.

16D Issue: Keep Ahead with IT!

Some travel brochures showing the variety of holidays that are available. The travel company with the best computer system has an advantage over the others in attracting customers.

Hotels, travel companies and airlines operate in an intensely competitive environment. Each tries to provide a better service at lower cost than its competitors. Information is a critical factor in the operation of these companies. Within each company, it is essential for managers to have an up-to-date picture of the levels of bookings. This enables them to vary prices, arrange extra flights or holiday places and plan special promotions as the need arises. Each company also needs to provide up-to-date information for customers. It is not good enough just to offer an excellent service: people must know about it and be able to book for it easily.

The quality of the IT systems for reservations, communications and reporting are critical for these purposes. To some extent, the success of a travel company depends on the efficiency of its computers and data communications. The companies with the best IT systems prosper, those with obsolete equipment do not.

The people who benefit from this competition are the customers: cheaper flights and holidays, better information about what is available and a more efficient service.

Questions

1 In what ways is information important in the running of a travel company?
2 Why can a travel company not afford to allow its reservation system to get out-of-date?
3 Who benefits from the competition between holiday companies to provide the most efficient service?

16E End-of-Chapter Summary

The main points of this chapter are as follows:

- Computers and data communications networks are used by airlines, travel companies and hotels for reservations. They are transaction processing systems, completing each reservation as it is entered at a terminal.
- Airline reservation systems are interconnected via a worldwide data communications network. They are some of the largest and most complex real-time computer applications in operation.
- Airlines, hotels and travel companies operate in a competitive environment. Their success or failure depends to a large extent on the quality of their IT systems.

Exercise 16

1 Choose the correct word from the list for each of the following spaces:

network; disk; updated; number; printed; mainframe; reference; index; record; terminal; clerk; written.

When a flight reservation is to be made, the travel ____ enters the flight ____ and date at her ____. This information is sent via the international data communications ____ to the ____ computer at the airline offices. The computer reads the ____ for the flight from ____. It uses the ____ to the file to locate the record as quickly as possible. If a reservation can be made, the name of the passenger and the ticket ____ are entered. The flight record is ____ and ____ back to the disk. The ticket is ____.

2 Modify the reservation system developed in section 16A so that it can be used to book the stalls at a school fête or a local fair. Change the booking plan to match the layout of the stalls. For each stall, include a cell which holds a code for the organisation which has booked the stall. Produce a list on a word processor document with the codes and the names of the organisations.

Things to find out

1 Obtain two or more brochures from different travel companies for similar types of holiday at the same resorts. Select about five holidays which are offered by both companies. Set out the details of the holidays in a table, as follows:

Resort	No of Days	Price per Person	
		Company A	Company B
e.g. Majorca	14	137	149

For *each* of the five holidays, decide which company you would prefer to travel with. Give the reasons for your choice in each case. Use this information to discuss:
(a) How a travel company can make its holidays more attractive to customers.
(b) How a travel company can operate profitably if the prices of its holidays are determined by the prices charged by other companies, and not by its own costs.

Points to discuss

1 Discuss the benefits of using computers and data communications for reservations from the point of view of:
(a) a holiday company, airline or hotel
(b) the travellers.

2 Discuss the effect that the introduction of computers in the travel industry is having on the number of people employed in the industry.

Project starters

1 Use the steps of section 16A and the information in section 16B to design a reservation system for a small holiday company which rents apartments at resorts in Europe. There are three types of apartment, with one rate for each type. The apartments are rented for one or two weeks, and guests make their own travel arrangements. This can form the basis of a GCSE project.

17 Computer-aided Design

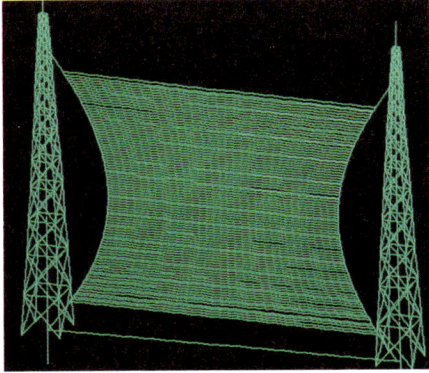

A radio transmitter designed on a CAD system.

What do new buildings, roads, cars, aircraft, door handles and microchips have in common? Answer: they are just a few of the things which are designed these days with the aid of computers. **Computer-aided design** (CAD) is replacing the use of drawing-boards in the offices of architects, advertising agencies and engineers. Animated films and film advertisements are also being produced by CAD systems.

Computers used for design purposes are much more versatile than drawing-boards, and enable designs to be produced more quickly. CAD systems are interactive and work in real time. Designs are entered on high-resolution graphics screens. An image can be enlarged or reduced, and, on CAD systems which work in three dimensions, rotated and shown in different perspectives. Portions of a drawing can be 'cut out' and 'pasted in' at another position. A design library of standard images can be built up, and images can be called up from the library into a drawing whenever required. Designs can be printed on digital plotters or laser printers whenever required.

This chapter describes some of the ways that CAD systems are used, both in and out of the classroom. It puts into practice some of the general ideas of computer applications introduced in chapter 9.

Two views of a bicycle saddle on a CAD system, and the final product. Note the resolution of the picture of the saddle on the screen.

Right: A classroom computer network—in the foreground is a CAD program operation.

17A Activity: Design a Computer Laboratory

In this section you will use the CAD system on your school computer to design a computer laboratory for the school. If there already is one, your design can be for a different one, possibly with more up-to-date equipment. If your school does not have a computer laboratory, the photograph gives an idea of what they look like.

The Requirements of the Task

A computer laboratory is designed to be used by teachers of various subjects, and their classes. Sometimes the class will be working together as a group; at other times pupils will be working independently. The laboratory must fit into an existing classroom and accommodate the computers and other equipment. If the computers are arranged in a network, the layout of the network and its cabling are important. Fileservers and network printers must be in the most convenient positions. It is also important to consider power supplies to the computer, lighting and lines of sight: for example, can all the pupils see the overhead projector screen if necessary?

Think about these requirements and how they apply to your school. Draw up a **design brief** for the project, stating the requirements of the laboratory: intended ways of use, number of pupils, number of computer workstations, number of power points, overall dimensions, etc.

Computer System Design

> **design brief** the instructions given to an architect or designer at the start of a project.
> **elevation** a view of a building from one side.
> **perspective** the line of sight used when showing a three-dimensional object in a two-dimensional drawing.
> **plan** a view of a building from above.

Outputs
The outputs are a **plan** of the laboratory (as viewed from above) and **elevations** of the walls (as viewed from the side). Detailed plans can be made of benches and other fittings if necessary. These designs are displayed on the computer screen and printed.

Inputs
The designs are drawn on the screen using a light pen, mouse or digitising pad (see section 4B). Design elements such as windows may be stored in a library on disk and copied into a plan when required.

File structure
Each plan is stored as a separate file on disk. The way in which designs are represented varies from one CAD system to another; the details are beyond the scope of this course.

File processing
The designs are entered and edited using the light pen, mouse or digitising pad. They are saved on disk and retrieved when required. Final versions are printed.

System Diagram
See Figure 17.1.

Implementation

Use the CAD system on your school computer:

- Look at the user guide for the CAD program and make sure that you know how to carry out each operation.
- Start a new drawing for the plan of the laboratory. Draw the

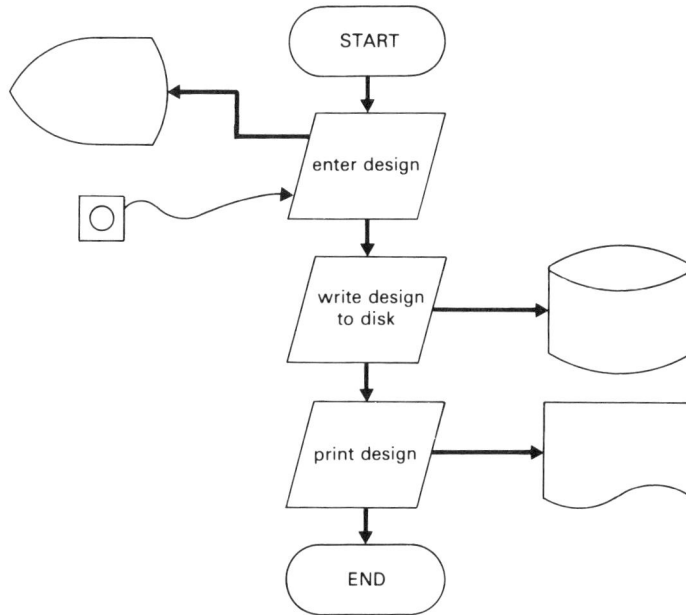

Figure 17.1 Computer laboratory design with CAD: system diagram

outline of the room and mark doors, windows and any other fixtures. Save this outline on disk for later use if your design goes wrong!

- Draw the benches and chairs and the outlines of the computers. Avoid too much detail. The quickest way is to make a separate drawing of each object and save it on disk. Call up a copy of the drawing and place it in position on the plan as required.
- Using different colours if possible, draw the cables which supply power to the computers and the network cables which connect the computers together. Also mark the sockets for the mains plugs. If this makes the plan too messy, make copies of the overall outline and draw one set of cables on each copy.
- Save the plans on disk and print them.
- Using the plan as a basis, draw elevations of each wall. First sketch the outline and any doors and windows. Then add the elevations of any benches which are built against the wall and sketch the computers on them. Once again, do not put in too much detail.
- Save each elevation on disk and print it.
- Make a backup copy of the disk with your design on it.

17B* Activity: Design a Computer Trolley

If the CAD system on your school computer can work in three dimensions, follow the steps of section 17A to design a computer trolley. First decide what the trolley must carry—in addition to the computer, you might want to include a printer, manuals, coil of mains cable, etc. Also check the narrowest space that the trolley must be able to pass through. Write a design brief with these requirements in mind.

Working in three dimensions means that you have more flexibility, but it is easier to get confused! A possible sequence of steps is as follows:

- Draw the frame of the trolley, as viewed from the front.
- Use a copy of this front view as the basis of the rear frame.
- Rotate to a plan view, and place the front and back frames in their required positions. Draw in the top shelf.
- Working in sections of the image, draw in the lower shelves.
- Rotate the design to suitable perspectives which show the features of the trolley as clearly as possible. Print these perspective views.

17C Application: Design a Building

Most firms of architects are installing CAD equipment for their designs. This section describes how such a system is used to design a typical large building. The design process takes anything from six months to two years.

The Requirements of the Task

The aim is to design a building to suit the needs of the client: its intended use, size, internal layout, heating requirements, etc. The appearance and style of the building must match its surroundings and meet planning regulations. The cost of the project must be within the client's budget.

The design is developed in a number of stages, with more details added at each stage. From time to time working drawings are submitted to the client for approval and amended if necessary.

Computer System Design

Outputs
The outputs are initial sketches and then plans and elevations of the building, with more detail added as the design progresses. These are printed whenever required.

Inputs
Plans and elevations are drawn on the screen using a digitising pad. Design elements such as windows are stored in a library and copied from it into drawings when required.

File structure
The CAD system has a file for each drawing. Details of the structure of these files are beyond the scope of this course.

File processing
A file is created as each drawing is first entered. The file is updated every time the drawing is amended.

System Diagram

See Figure 17.2.

Implementation

The CAD systems used by architects are developed by specialist computer companies. They are sometimes modified by the architects to meet their particular needs. Most are based on graphics terminals connected to a large minicomputer or small mainframe. The drawings are held in a common database which can be accessed from any terminal.

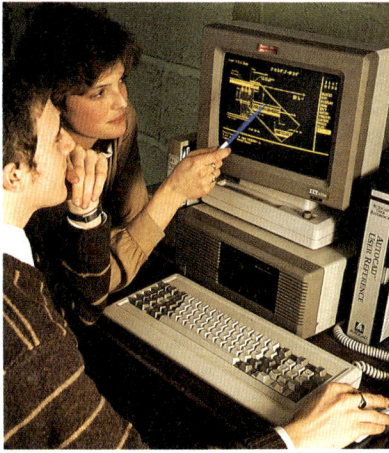
Architects discussing a design produced using a CAD program.

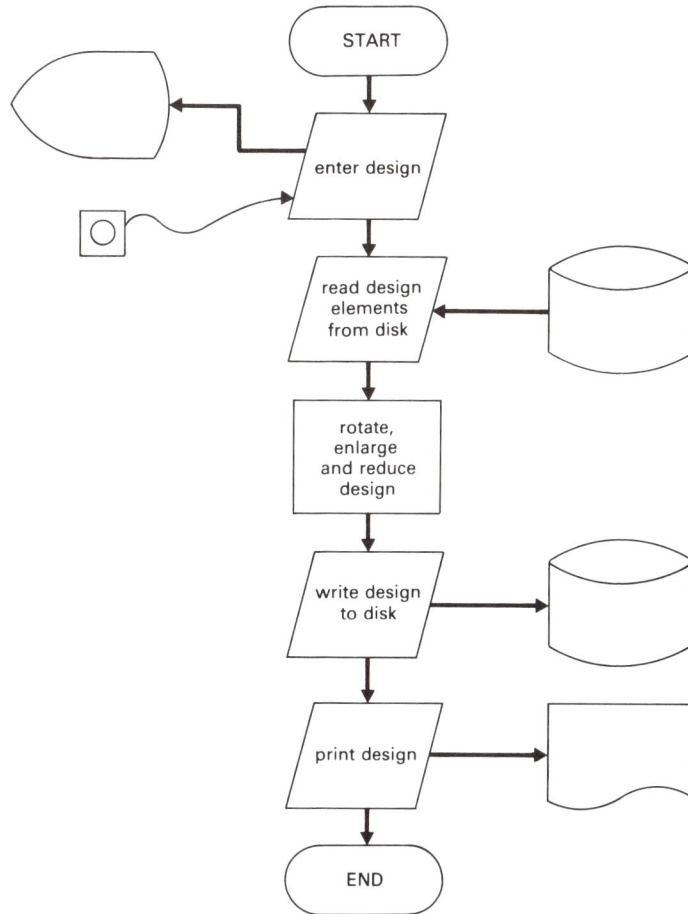

Figure 17.2   Building design with CAD: system diagram

Part of the new Lloyd's Insurance building in London. The building was designed using a CAD system.

At the start of the project, the design brief is agreed between the architect and the client. Initial sketches of the proposed design are made and entered into the CAD system. These are given to the client for approval. The sketches are amended after discussion with the client.

When the design outlines have been approved, the architects set to work on the main drawings. Aspects of the work are assigned to members of a team of architects who decide how to organise the files of the drawings on backing store. In most cases the overall structure of the building is drawn in three dimensions, with details shown in plans and elevations based on this design.

When the main drawings are complete, they are checked very carefully by the architects and printed. The printouts are given to the client for approval. It is unlikely that they are approved as they stand: there is generally a period of discussion, with modifications being suggested and implemented if they are agreed.

When this round of modifications has been made, the final details are added to the drawings. These show the **services**: the heating or air conditioning, plumbing, wiring, ducts for telephone and data communications cabling, security systems, etc. For a large building, more than a thousand drawings are eventually produced. However, when a CAD system is used, most of these are projections from a smaller number of three-dimensional drawings.

197

There is a further round of checking and modifications from the client before the detailed drawings are accepted and construction of the building commences.

Questions

1 In what ways does a CAD system speed up the process of designing a building and reduce costs?

2 List the uses of a design library in the process of designing a building.

3 What facilities does a CAD system offer which are not possible with a conventional system based on drawing-boards?

4 Give a brief summary, in your own words, of the stages of designing a large building using a CAD system.

17D Application: Microchip Design

Microchips are the most complex objects ever manufactured. VLSI chips have hundreds of thousands, or even millions, of separate elements. Their small size makes this complexity even more difficult to manage. Producing chips of this complexity would be impossible without some of the most sophisticated CAD systems in existence.

The Requirements of the Task

The aim is to produce very large-scale integrated circuits which must carry out precisely specified Boolean operations. The timing of each operation is critical and all the electronic circuits must fit into a limited area, generally about 5 mm square. The number of layers in the chips should be kept to a minimum in order to reduce costs. At present, the limit imposed by the methods of chip fabrication is about ten layers. The cost of designing and producing a chip must be within a given budget. Furthermore, the design process must be completed within a short time, generally a few months.

Computer System Design

Outputs

There are two stages in the design process, each with its own output. The first stage leads to a **logic diagram** for the chip using logic circuits such as those introduced in section 2E. The output from the second stage is the design of each layer of the chip itself. This shows the position of each element on the chip and the interconnections between them. This **artwork** is in the form of large drawings which are photographically reduced to make the masks used in chip fabrication.

Inputs

The operations required of the chip are input using truth tables or some other means. The logic circuits are built up on the screen of a CAD workstation by calling up standard elements (AND, OR and NOT gates, and combinations of these) from a library, and positioning them as required. The connections between the gates are drawn in using a light pen or digitising pad.

The layers of the chip are drawn in a similar way, using a library of standard elements corresponding to logic gates. Newer CAD systems for chip design produce at least some of the artwork automatically from the logic diagram.

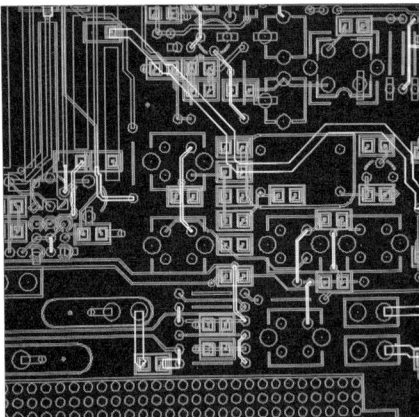

Part of the artwork of a microchip, produced on a CAD system.

File structures

There is a file for the logic diagram, and one for each layer of the artwork. The structure of these files is complex, as the computer stores information about the nature and position of each element and also about its operation.

File processing

When the logic diagram is complete, the CAD system simulates the functioning of the design and checks it against the required operation of the chip. If it does not perform correctly, the chip designer modifies the logic diagram until all errors have been put right. CAD systems are often able to transform the logic circuits automatically so as to reduce the number of gates, while still doing the same tasks.

Some CAD systems generate part of the artwork automatically from the logic diagram. In the future this is likely to be increasingly automated. Most CAD systems can check that the artwork corresponds to the logic diagram. Some are able to re-arrange elements automatically so as to reduce the length of the internal connections within the chip. The length of these connections determines the speed at which the chip operates.

System Diagram

See Figure 17.3 for the logic diagram aspect of chip CAD.

Implementation

Most chip manufacturers use CAD systems which they have designed themselves. They have a number of design workstations connected to a powerful mainframe computer. Each workstation has a large, high-resolution graphics screen, a smaller control screen and a light pen or digitising pad for input. The detailed workings of these systems are kept secret so that rival chip manufacturers cannot benefit from them.

The CAD systems are operated by highly skilled electronics engineers. Although the CAD systems give a great deal of assistance in the design of a chip, it is the expertise of these engineers which is ultimately responsible for the correct operation of the chip.

Documentation

Because most CAD systems for chip design are developed by the chip manufacturers, and often by the people who use them, there is no clear distinction between systems documentation and user guides. Most of the engineers who use CAD equipment have a thorough understanding of how it works, and its capabilities and limitations. The documentation tends to be at a very technical level, describing the complex details of the file structures and operations of the system.

The CAD systems for chip design are enhanced more or less continuously, and the documentation is amended to reflect the new features as they are incorporated.

Questions

1. Would it be possible to design VLSI chips without a CAD system? Give reasons for your answer.
2. What are the *two* outputs from a CAD system used for microchip design?
3. What automatic features do most chip design systems incorporate?
4. How long does it take to design a microchip?
5. Most microchips only cost a few pence to buy, but their design costs are very high. Explain how this happens, and discuss the problems it causes for microchip producers.
6. Summarise, in your own words, the main stages of the design of a microchip.

A CAD workstation for microchip design.

logic diagram

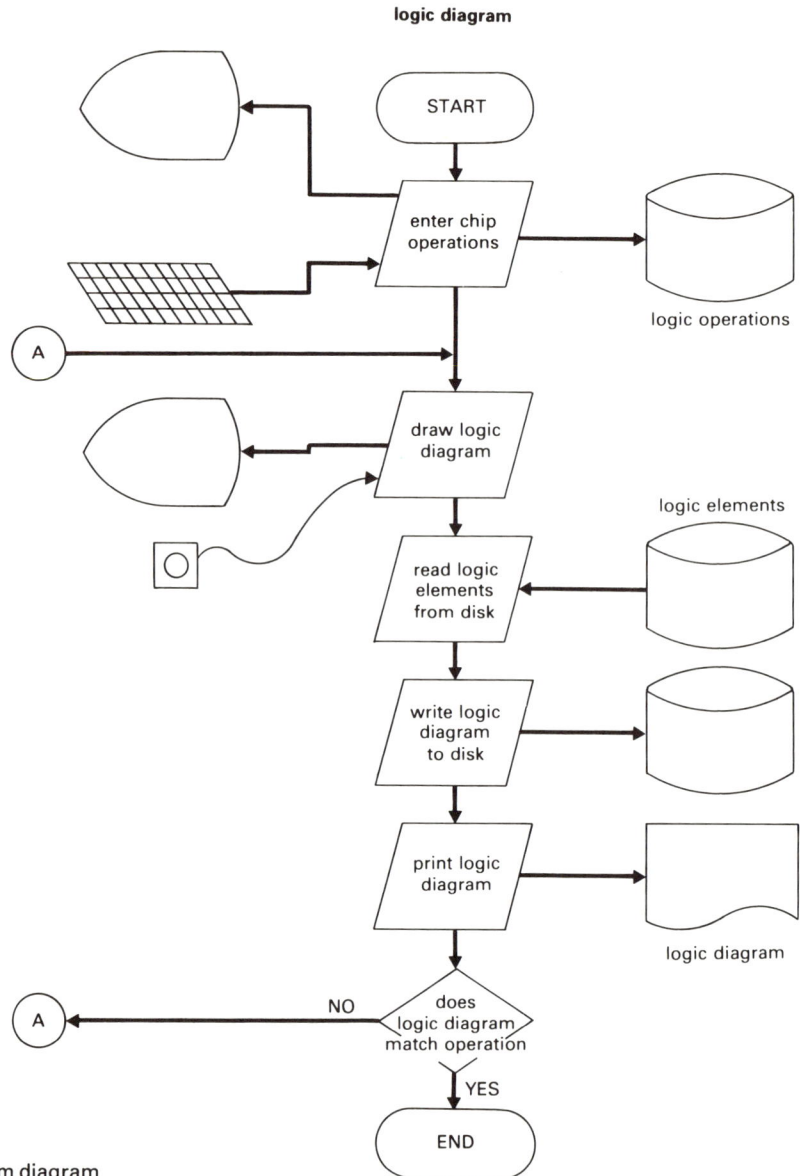

START

enter chip operations

logic operations

A

draw logic diagram

read logic elements from disk

logic elements

write logic diagram to disk

print logic diagram

logic diagram

NO — does logic diagram match operation

A

YES

END

Figure 17.3   Microchip design with CAD: system diagram

17E   Issue: Retraining Staff

Professional staff such as architects and engineers have many years of training and experience. Their skills are valuable to their companies. But when new tools such as CAD systems are introduced, they need to be retrained to use them. Retraining is expensive and time-consuming, and many older people find CAD systems difficult to use. A company which has bought an expensive CAD system and is investing heavily in retraining expects the people who have been retrained to put their new skills to productive use for some time.

Because CAD systems are so efficient, they sometimes lead to a reduced need for professional staff, and hence redundancies or early retirement. A major problem is whom to make redundant: it is often older staff, with fewer years left before retirement, who are chosen.

It is often difficult for middle-aged people who have been made redundant to find new jobs.

This can cause great distress. Experienced professional staff, who are expecting promotion to positions which reflect their seniority, are instead offered early retirement or redundancy.

Questions

1 Why is it often older staff who are made redundant when new technology is introduced at architects' and engineers' offices?
2 Why is it difficult for some older people to learn to use new technology in their jobs?
3 What are some of the effects of making older people redundant instead of promoting them?

17F End-of-Chapter Summary

The main points of this chapter are as follows:

- Computer-aided design is replacing the use of drawing-boards for many design applications: architecture, vehicle and aircraft design, engineering, microchip design, graphic design and animated films.
- A CAD system consists of a number of workstations linked to a central computer. Each workstation includes a high-resolution graphics screen, and a mouse, light pen or digitising pad for input.
- A CAD system enables designs to be drawn on screen, stored on disk and printed when required. Libraries of design elements can be built up, and elements called up from the library into drawings when required.

- CAD systems enable drawings to be enlarged and reduced, and portions 'cut out' and 'pasted in' elsewhere. Three-dimensional systems enable designs to be rotated and shown in different perspectives.
- Benefits of CAD include the more rapid development of designs, easy modification, the elimination of repetitive printing and the automatic checking of designs.

Exercise 17

1 Choose the correct word from the list for each of the following spaces:

gate; simulation; pad; circuit; workstation; diagram; disk; engineer; plotter.

The electronics _____ used the digitising _____ at his CAD _____ to move a logic _____ from one position in the logic _____ to another. He saved the revised logic _____ on _____ and printed it on the digital _____. He then ran the _____ program to check that the revised design was functioning properly.

Things to find out

1 Find some photographs of new buildings designed with the aid of CAD systems, and some which are not. In your opinion, has the use of CAD systems resulted in better designs? Give reasons for your opinion, and find out what other people's thoughts are on this issue.
2 Find out about the way in which CAD is used in areas other than those described in the text. Examples include the design of roads and road junctions, the design of motor vehicles and aircraft and the design of the printed circuit boards used in computers. For each application area you choose, write an account following the steps of sections 17C or 17D.

Points to discuss

1 Discuss the problems of retraining older professional staff described in section 17E. State the arguments for making people such as these redundant, and the arguments

Project starters

1 The CAD system on a school computer can be used for a variety of simple designs. Some suggestions are:
   a house
   a road junction
   a simple rail network or station
   a car, aircraft, train or boat.

2 The computer network designed in section 17A can be extended throughout the school if workstations are located in different classrooms instead of (or in addition to) a central laboratory.

Follow the steps of section 17A to enter a plan of the area of the school to be served by the network, and show the layout of the network cables. Work out a layout for the cables which keeps them as short as possible. Do not put too much detail into the design.

3 Many CAD systems have other capabilities in addition to their design function. For example, the chip design system has facilities to simulate the operation of the chip being designed, and to transform the design to reduce the number of logic gates. Find out about additional facilities such as these in other CAD systems. For example, some building design systems have facilities to estimate the quantities of materials required. Engineering CAD systems can sometimes do stress calculations on the designs. Some design systems have direct links to manufacturing processes: **CAD/CAM** (computer-aided design/computer-aided manufacture).

Write brief accounts of your findings, using the steps of sections 17C or 17D.

against. Give your suggestions for making sure that problems of this nature do not arise in the future.

Choose one of these, or another design project within the capabilities of your CAD system, and follow the steps of section 17A to develop the design. Do not include too much detail; it is more important to get the basic design right than to overload it (and the computer) with detail. One of these can form the basis of a GCSE project.

18

Simulations

A **simulation** is when something is tried out rather than happening 'for real'. For example, flight simulators allow pilots to try their skills at flying a plane. If they crash on the simulator, no actual damage is done. A military exercise is a simulation, as is a rehearsal for a play.

Computers are ideal for running simulations. A **model** of a system can be built up on a computer and then allowed to run under various conditions. The behaviour of the system can be studied in this way. Simulations can be made of nuclear reactors, transport networks, ecological systems and of the spread of diseases, to name just a few examples. Simulations save time and money, and also reduce risks: if the design of a nuclear reactor is faulty, it is better to find out from the simulation than when the real thing fails.

This chapter describes a simulation which you can run using the spreadsheet program on your school computer. It also describes an actual simulation, of fish stocks in a fishing ground. It shows how the general ideas introduced in chapter 9 can be put into practice in a particular way. It contains more mathematics than most other chapters of the book.

18A Activity: Simulate a Bus Journey

If bus companies changed their routes and operating practices every few weeks, no one would know which bus to catch! Nevertheless it is important for bus routes and bus operations to change with changing patterns of travel. One of the best ways of planning changes in bus operations is to simulate them, and try out the new ways of operating in the simulation. Only those changes which work in the simulation are actually put into practice.

The Requirements of the Task

The aim of this task is to simulate the operation of a bus for a journey covering a number of stops. The time it takes to load passengers and the travel time between stops are investigated in order to calculate the total time for the journey. The key relationship is between the time it takes to load a passenger and the total journey time. If the bus has a conductor, the loading time is how long it takes a person to climb aboard. If fares are collected by the driver, the loading time is the time it takes to pay the fare. This can be reduced by simple fare schemes, and encouraging people to buy bus passes.

The simulation makes use of **random numbers**. These are numbers selected at random by the computer, in a given range. They are used to simulate the numbers of people waiting at the bus stops. They are also used to simulate the times taken to travel between the stops.

Computer System Design

Passengers boarding a bus. We can simulate the number of passengers by means of a spreadsheet.

System Diagram

Implementation

Outputs

The output is a table showing the information about the journey: the time taken to load the passengers and the time taken to travel from the previous stop. The total time since the start of the journey is also shown. This table is shown on the computer screen and printed when required.

Inputs

The average time taken for one passenger to board the bus, and the formulae for generating the numbers of passengers and the travel times are input. A simple way of simulating the number of passengers boarding the bus at each stop is to enter the maximum number for the stop, and select a random number between 0 and this maximum. The maximum number of passengers depends on the position of the stop, whether it is near a shopping centre, railway station, etc. The travel times can be a random number between a minimum and a maximum time.

File structure

The file is a table set out as shown in the implementation below.

File processing

For each run of the simulation, a boarding time is entered, and the formulae are evaluated. The total travel time for this boarding time is recorded. The simulation needs to be repeated a number of times for each boarding time, to take account of the random variations.

See Figure 18.1.

Use the spreadsheet on your school computer. Look at the user guide for the program, and make sure that you can carry out each operation.

- Set up a table as shown below. The cell references (R1C3 etc.) refer to formulae, as described below the table.

	1	2	3	4	5
1	Boarding	time:	0.1	minutes	
2					
3	Stop No	Max Pass	Ldg Time	Tr Time	Tot Time
4					
5	1	12	R5C3	0	R5C5
6	2	20	R6C3	R6C4	R6C5
7	3	...			

The boarding time for one passenger, and the maximum number of passengers at each stop, are entered as input. It is best to work in minutes: a loading time of 6 seconds is entered as 0.1 minutes. These times may be updated for each run of the simulation as required.

The cell references in Row-Column format contain formulae:

The loading times, in cells R5C3 and R6C3, are the number of passengers multiplied by the boarding time. The number of passengers is a random number between 0 and the maximum number of passengers. On most spreadsheets, the formula is as follows:

$$R5C3 = int(rnd(R5C2)) * R1C3$$

The **rnd** function selects random numbers, and the **int** function rounds down to whole numbers. The symbol * is used for multiplication. Similarly, the formula for the second loading time is:

$$R6C3 = int(rnd(R6C2)) * R1C3$$

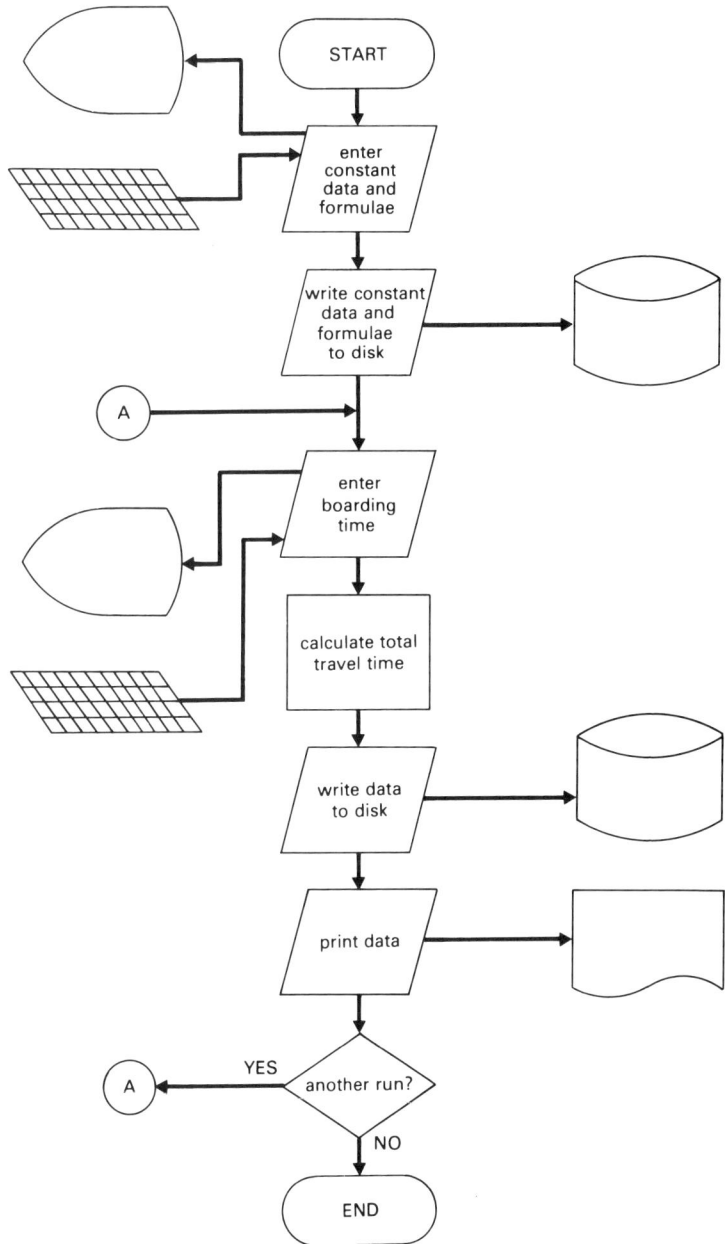

Figure 18.1   Bus journey simulation: system diagram

The travel time is the minimum time plus a random number between 0 and the difference between the minimum and maximum times. For example if the minimum and maximum times between stop 1 and stop 2 are 5 and 8 minutes (a difference of 3 minutes), the formula for R6C4 is:

$$R6C4 = 5 + rnd(3)$$

The total times are the times when the bus sets off from each stop, measured from the start of the journey. The first one, in R5C5, is the loading time at the first stop:

$$R5C5 = R5C3$$

The second and subsequent total times are the previous total time plus the loading time and the travel time from the previous stop:

$$R6C5 = R5C5 + R6C3 + R6C4$$

- With calculation switched off, enter formulae as described above, and continue the table for, say, ten stops.
- Enter a suitable maximum number of passengers at each stop, and a boarding time. Experience indicates that passengers take about three seconds to board when there is a conductor, and between ten and fifteen seconds when they have to pay the driver.
- Switch calculation on, and evaluate the formulae. Note the total travelling time and the boarding time. Re-evaluate the formulae several times, each time noting the total travel time.
- Save the spreadsheet on disk, and print it.
- Change the boarding time, and run the simulation again. Make a number of runs with the new boarding time, and note the total travel time.
- Make a table of total travel times against boarding times, and draw a graph of them. Describe any relationship that can be deduced from the graph.

Documentation

- Write a set of system documentation, describing the structure of the table you have set up, and the operation of the formulae. Explain what assumptions have been made in setting up the simulation.
- Write a user guide to enable someone else to operate the simulation. Summarise the aims of the simulation. Explain how to call the spreadsheet up from disk, how to enter numbers, and how to evaluate the formulae.

18B Application: Fish Stocks Simulation

Fish are one of our best sources of food. The stocks of fish in an area such as the North Sea are of great value to all the countries which adjoin it. Experience has shown that large numbers of fish can be caught without depleting the stocks. But there is a limit to the number which can be caught. Above this limit, the numbers of various kinds of fish are permanently reduced, and some species may disappear from the area altogether.

The best way of studying the effects of fishing policies in an area like the North Sea is to set up a simulation. The simulation models the natural growth of the fish populations, the reduction of these populations by predators such as larger fish, and the catching of fish by trawlers. Other factors such as ocean currents, pollution and the migration of shoals of fish are also taken into account.

A simulation of the sort described in this section is run by the **Fisheries Research Laboratories** in Lowestoft, Suffolk. It is a complex model, needing a large computer to run it.

The Requirements of the Task

The aim is to study the effects of various fishing policies on the fish stocks in the area. Fishing policies specify, amongst other things:

- the numbers of the various types of fish which can be caught
- the areas which are fished
- the times of the year when fishing is permitted
- the minimum size of the fish caught. (Using nets with wider gaps between the cords means that only larger fish are caught.)

The simulation studies the effects of these policies on the fish stocks. In particular, it allows limits to be set which will ensure that stocks do not decline until they are exhausted.

Computer System Design

Outputs
The outputs are tables and graphs of fish stocks over a number of years under various fishing policies.

Inputs
There are two sets of input data. The first is the figures which describe the current state of the fish stocks: estimates of current fish populations, natural growth rates, etc. The second set is for particular fishing policies: maximum numbers caught, minimum size of fish, times and locations of fishing, etc.

File structure
The output file is a table set out in rows and columns. A number of input and working files are created, containing tables or lists of numbers.

Processing
The mathematical equations which describe the behaviour of the fish stocks are applied to the input data in order to produce the tables of output. Most of the equations calculate changes in the fish stocks over small periods of time. They are evaluated repeatedly to run the simulation over an extended period of time.

System Diagram

See Figure 18.2.

Implementation

The software of the fish stock simulation has been developed by the scientists at the research laboratories. It runs in batch mode, with each run taking up to an hour of computer time. Input data is entered at a terminal and stored as a file on disk. The output is written to another file, and printed after the run is complete.

The simulation software is modified frequently in the light of experience and changing circumstances. From time to time it is run with current fishing policies as data to check that it produces results which match what is actually happening to fish stocks.

Documentation

The functional specification for a simulation as large as this runs into hundreds of pages. The mathematical formulae are very complicated, and much of the documentation is taken up describing how they work, and the assumptions behind them.

Most of the time, the simulation is run by the scientists who designed it and wrote the software, so no user guides are necessary. A brief set of operator documentation is produced so that the person operating the computer knows what files to load and how to run the program.

A catch of mackerel being landed at Newlyn.

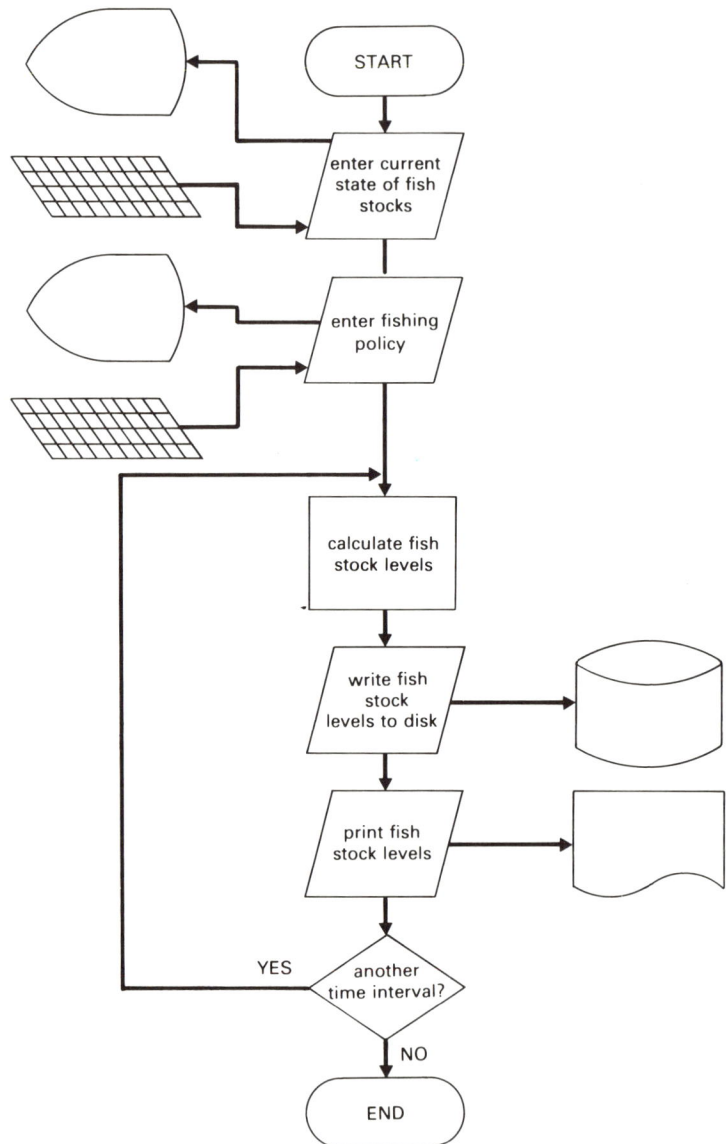

Figure 18.2 Fish stocks simulation: system diagram

18C End-of Chapter Summary

The main points of this chapter are as follows:

- A simulation of a system is a simplified version of the system which is run on a computer or some other device.
- Computer simulations save time and money, and enable dangerous situations to be tested in safety.
- Simulations are used for a variety of situations: aircraft and spacecraft flight simulators, computer simulations of nuclear reactors, transport networks and ecological systems.

Exercise 18

1   Choose the correct word from the list for each of the following spaces:

program; model; equations; aim; network; simulation.

In order to study the way the water supply system for a large town works, a ＿＿ was set up. Engineers at the water board worked out a mathematical ＿＿ of the way the water flowed from the reservoirs through the ＿＿ of pipes. The ＿＿ for the simulation used a set of ＿＿ to calculate the flow of water at various points in the network. The ＿＿ was to find out how much more water could be supplied with the existing network of pipes.

2* The simulation set up in section 18A can be extended in a number of ways. For example, set up a column for the number of passengers on the bus, and one for the number getting off at each stop. Formulae are required to generate a random number of passengers getting off, and to calculate the number on the bus. The number boarding can be restricted so that the capacity of the bus is not exceeded.

Things to find out

1   Find out how an aircraft flight simulator works. Either visit a library and look in back issues of flight magazines, or contact a local airline office. Write a description of the workings of a flight simulator, using the steps in section 18B as a guide.

2   The UK Budget is presented by the Chancellor of the Exchequer every March. It sets out the amount of income the government expects to raise through taxes, and the amounts of money it intends to spend, over the next financial year (from April to the next March). It takes account of such factors as inflation and world oil prices, which are outside the control of the government. The Budget is prepared with the aid of a simulation model of the UK economy. Find out how this simulation model works, and how it is used in the preparation of the budget. Comment on your findings.

Project starters

1   The mathematical model used in the fish stocks simulation is based on the following ideas:

The increase in the population of a particular species of fish over a period of time is proportional to the size of the population at the start of that time interval. As a formula:

$$D = K * P \text{ (* means multiplication)}$$

where D: change in population
K: growth factor
P: population at start of time interval

The growth factor K is made up of two parts. There is a natural rate of increase, G, at which the population would grow in an ideal environment. This is reduced by a term which is proportional to the current population to take into account the limited supplies of food etc. In other words:

$$K = G - E * P$$

When the population reaches a limiting size, L, the growth is zero. In other words:

$$0 = G - E * L$$

from which it follows that:

$$E = G/L$$

and from the equation above:

$$K = G * (1 - P/L)$$

Putting this value for K into the original equation gives:

$$D = G * (1 - P/L) * P$$

This is the change in population during one time period, taking into account the natural growth G and the limiting population L. The value of D is added to the population P to get the population at the start of the next time period.

Set up a spreadsheet based on this formula, to calculate the change in a population of fish over a period of time. Use time intervals of one year. Try various values of the natural growth G, the limiting population L and starting population P. Note that G is normally a fraction: a value of 0.1 means that a population grows by 0.1 (10%) of its size during a time interval.

Then introduce a factor for the number of fish caught. The equation becomes:

$$D = G * (1 - P/L) * P - F$$

where F is the number of fish caught during the period.

Try various values of F, and see how many fish can be caught while keeping the population at a steady level. Also see how quickly stocks are depleted if there is over-fishing, and how quickly they recover if fewer are fished.

6 The technique described in section 18A can be used for a number of similar simulations. Three suggestions are as follows:

(a) Simulate a queue, with a random number arriving in the queue and being served during each time period. See the effects on the length of the queue of different patterns of arrival and being served. For example, try a fixed number being served during each period (up to the number in the queue). Also try different ranges of random numbers for those arriving and being served. Keep a record of the total length of the queue after each time interval.

(b) Extend the queue simulation to one of a set of supermarket checkouts. Generate a random number of people arriving at the checkouts at each time period. Try different ways of allocating these people to the queues: shared evenly among the queues, all going to the shortest queue, etc. Keep a record of the length of each queue after each time interval.

(c)* Simulate the operation of a telephone switchboard. The switchboard has a number of outside lines (between two and five) connected to a number of extensions (between five and 100). Calls start at random from outside lines or extensions, and are connected to other extensions or outside lines at random. The length of the calls is also random.

The aim of the simulation is to see how busy the switchboard is under different patterns of use of the telephones: the length of the calls, and the time between them. Both of these are random but vary between limits, like the numbers of people waiting for a bus. If more extensions require outside lines than the number available, then some calls cannot get through.

19 Viewdata

dividend the profits of a company are divided among the shareholders: each shareholder gets his or her dividend.
portfolio the set of shares in a number of companies, owned by one person.
shareholder a person who owns shares in a company.

Computers can store large quantities of data. Television sets can display data, and are found in almost every household. Telephones can carry data signals, and almost every household has one. Combining the three technologies—computers, the telephone network and television—gives rise to **viewdata**.

A viewdata network has one or more central computers which store large numbers of **pages** of useful information. A page is one screenful of data, in large characters and with simple graphics, suitable for display on a television set. Users connect their special television sets (or microcomputers used as viewdata terminals) to the viewdata computer via their telephone lines, and call up pages which are displayed on their screens. Viewdata is interactive: users enter instructions, and the pages are displayed immediately. Figure 19.1 shows a viewdata network.

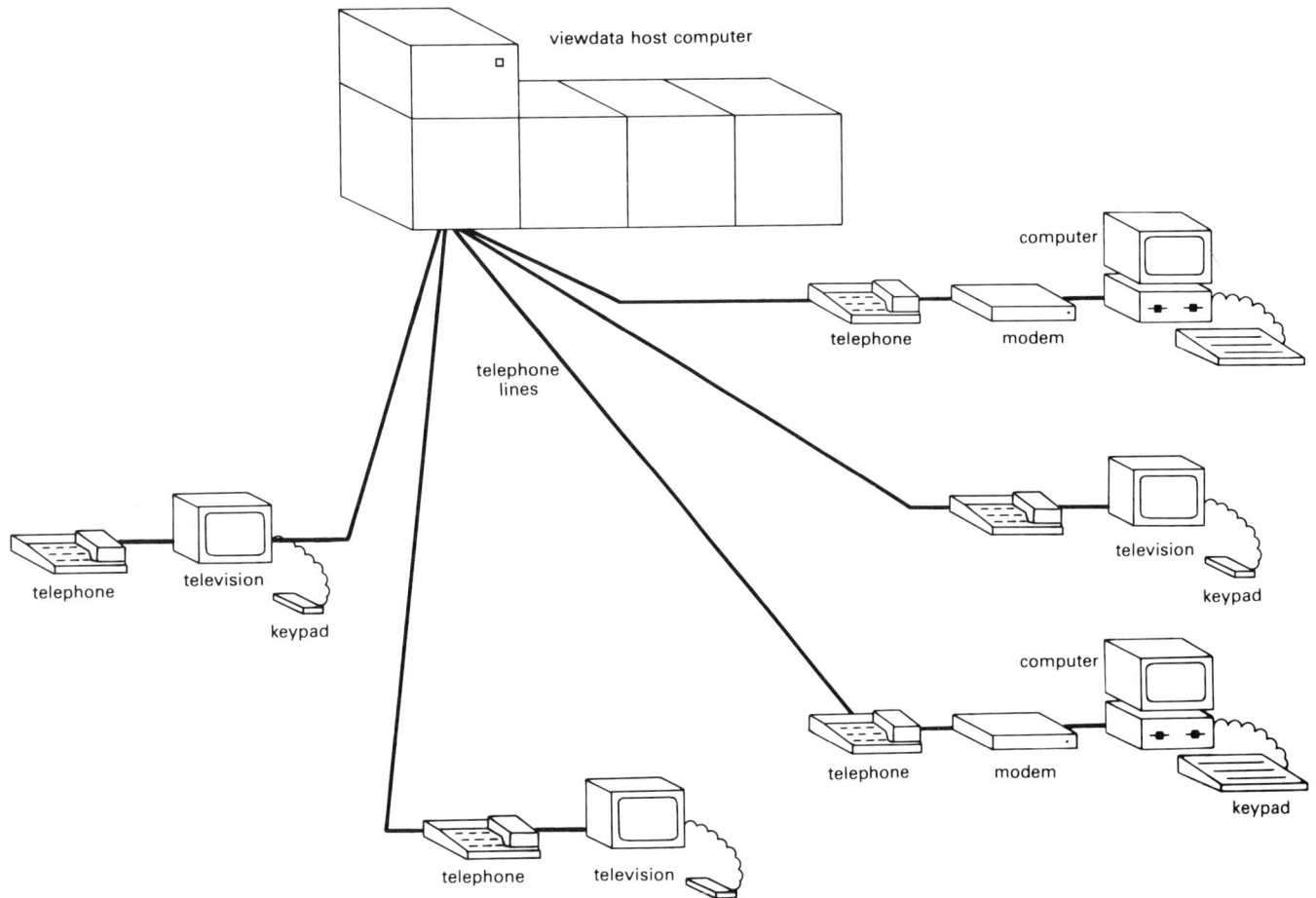

Figure 19.1 Viewdata network

Each page in a viewdata information base is numbered. A page can be called up directly if its number is known. The pages are also linked to each other by subject in a tree structure, as shown in Figure 19.2. When a user calls up the viewdata network, the page at the 'top' of the tree appears. This is the header page for the whole system. It contains a set of choices for the pages at the next level. Each of these in turn has choices for pages at the level below it, and so on. The choices are entered by typing a number on the viewdata keypad. In this way a user can scan the pages in a systematic way without having to know the number of each individual page.

The nationwide viewdata network in the United Kingdom is the **Prestel** system provided by British Telecom. The Prestel network provides home users with news and information on a wide range of topics: weather, sport, travel, local events, car hire and insurance, to name just a few. The information is supplied and kept up-to-date by **information providers**. In addition, users may order goods, book travel and theatre tickets, make bank transactions and even place bets via the viewdata network. Users also have a **mailbox** to which other users can send messages. Users of home computers have their own viewdata network, which they can use to exchange programs.

Prestel is becoming increasingly popular with certain types of businesses. Travel agents have a set of travel information which is not accessible to general viewdata users. Insurance companies and other financial organisations use viewdata to check prices and foreign currency rates. Many farmers use the agricultural database. Educational users have their own set of pages, and can load software and data files from the Prestel computers.

This chapter provides some activities which make use of viewdata, and describes a typical use of viewdata in business. It puts into practice some of the general ideas of computer applications introduced in chapter 9.

Operators entering data at the Viatel computer centre. Viatel is the Australian equivalent of the UK Prestel service.

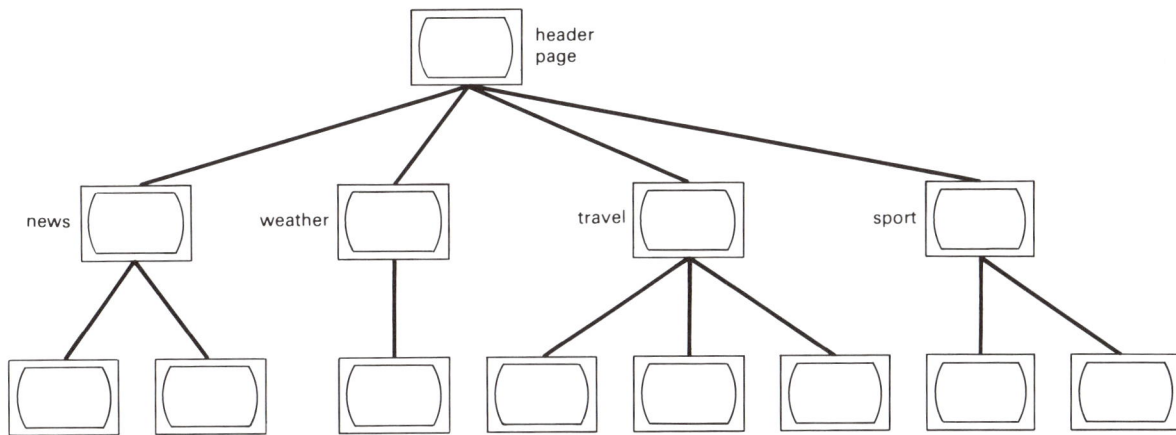

Figure 19.2   Viewdata pages: tree structure

19A Activity: Plan an Overseas School Visit

Prestel contains all the information needed to plan an overseas trip: package tours, flights, hotels, foreign currency conversion rates, insurance, etc. This information can be used to plan a (real or imaginary) school trip to a foreign country, possibly a skiing trip or a cultural visit.

The Requirements of the Task

The aim is to produce an itinerary and a budget for a visit by a party of pupils to a foreign country. The itinerary includes the travel schedules, the places where the party will be staying, and the planned activities for each day. The budget shows details of the costs: fares, accommodation, entry charges to museums, hire of equipment, insurance costs and spending money. It also shows the amount to be paid by each pupil for the visit, and the balance. The information for the itinerary and budget is to be obtained from a viewdata system, either Prestel or a local viewdata network.

Computer System Design

This is essentially a manual task, done with the aid of a viewdata system to supply the information. If possible, the budget should be prepared on a spreadsheet (as in section 12A) and the itinerary produced using a word processor (section 11A).

Outputs
The outputs are a table of the travel arrangements and one showing the figures for the budget.

Inputs
The possible travel dates, the number of pupils in the party, the maximum amount that pupils should have to pay, and the type of visit are input.

The alternative travel and accommodation possibilities are displayed on a viewdata system.

File structure
The viewdata page structure is shown in Figure 19.2. The travel pages are grouped together in their own 'tree'. The structure of an

213

individual viewdata page is an internationally agreed standard. This means that viewdata pages can be passed from one computer to another without any changes to their internal structure.

File processing
The viewdata system is used to look up the information, as described in the previous section.

Implementation

A school party on a trip to France.

First of all, decide on the type of trip, the approximate number of pupils in the party, and the maximum cost of the journey including spending money. Make a short list of the countries which are suitable for the type of trip you have chosen.

- Look at the user guide for the viewdata system your school uses. Find out how to operate the system.
- If your school uses Prestel or another system which is accessed by telephone, remember that it can be expensive to use! If possible, copy the pages you might need onto a local viewdata system on your school's computer. Then close down the telephone link, and use the local system.
- Call up the travel section on the viewdata system. Look at the pages which give details of possible destinations. Look at packages which include travel and accommodation, and places where the accommodation and travel must be arranged separately. Make a note of the page numbers of the most promising ones.
- Draw up a short list of possible places to go to. For each one, make notes of the dates, travel arrangements, places visited and costs. Check whether discounts are given for school parties.
- Discuss these places with other pupils and members of staff. Note the advantages and disadvantages of each place. Select the arrangement which is most suitable in the light of these discussions.
- Call up the viewdata pages which have the details of the tour which you have selected. Either print these pages or write down the information you need from the screen.
- Set up a spreadsheet or draw up a table and enter the costs for travel, accommodation, and insurance. Use Figure 19.3 and section 12A as examples.

	1	2	3	4	5	6	7	8
1	Income				Spending			
2	Number	Item	Price	Amount	Number	Item	Price	Amount
3	--------	--------	--------	--------		--------	--------	--------
4	25	Pupils	£145.00	£3625.00	1	Coach	£53.50	£53.50
5					25	Air Fare	£67.35	£1683.75
6					25	Hotel	£49.50	£1237.50
7					25	Insurnce	£3.85	£96.25
8					25	Pkt Mony	£20.00	£500.00
9					1	Extras	£50.00	£50.00
10								--------
11								£3621.00
12						Balance		4.00
13				--------				--------
14				£3625.00				£3625.00
15				--------				--------
16								

Figure 19.3 Spreadsheet for overseas school tour

- Decide on a suitable amount of spending money for each pupil to take. Use the foreign currency pages of the viewdata system to convert it into the local currency of the country you are visiting. Enter this amount into the table for your budget.

214

- Include any extra items, such as a coach to the airport, in the budget, and work out the price per pupil for the visit. Enter this in your budget. Check the entire budget carefully and print it (or make a neat copy).
- Finally, write an itinerary for the visit, either on paper or on a word processor document. Set out the travel and accommodation arrangements, and the activities for each day. Include all departure and arrival times, as well as checking-in times at airports. Take into account any difference in time between the UK and the country you are visiting.

19B Activity: Optional School Subjects

Schools offer pupils choices of subjects to be taken at GCSE level, and again at A level. The choice of these subjects is important for pupils' future careers. It is essential to have as much information as possible available for pupils and their parents when they are making their choices of optional subjects. A **local viewdata system** is one way of providing some of this information. A local viewdata system works in the same way as a system such as Prestel, but all the information is held on the computer or network from which it is accessed. Telephone links are not required.

The Requirements of the Task

The aim is to set up a local viewdata system of optional subjects to be taken at GCSE or A level. Each subject has one or more pages, which give brief details of the subject. The system should work in the same way as a conventional viewdata system such as Prestel. It is intended for use by pupils, and possibly by parents at parents' evenings.

Computer System Design

Outputs
The output is a set of viewdata pages of optional subjects. If possible, these should be structured to reflect the way the options are set against each other. For example, if subjects are grouped so that one subject must be chosen from each group, then the viewdata pages should be grouped in the same way. See Figure 19.4.

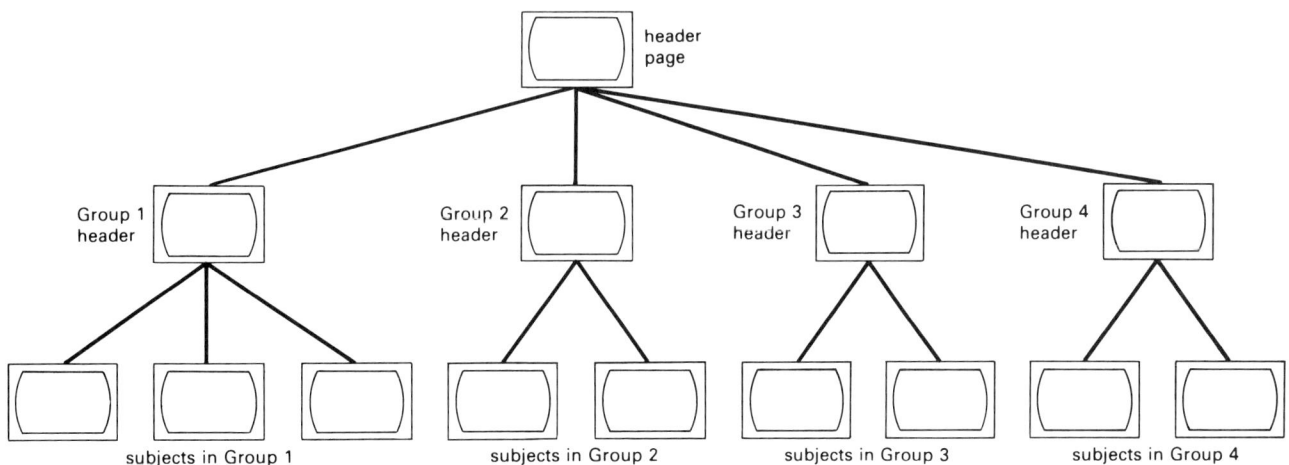

Figure 19.4   Optional subjects viewdata pages: tree structure

Pupils at a lesson in an optional school subject.

Inputs

The information about each subject is entered into the pages. This needs to be set out on the viewdata pages in a clear, concise way, with a similar layout for each subject.

File structure

The standard viewdata page structure is used.

File processing

The pages are entered and edited using a viewdata editing program. The connections between the pages are set up so that they form the required tree structure.

When the viewdata pages have been set up, the system is used in the normal way.

System Diagram

See Figure 19.5

Implementation

Use the viewdata program on your school microcomputer. Look at the user guide and find out how to enter and edit pages, and how to save them on disk. Also find out how to link pages together.

- Collect the information about the optional subjects. Read it carefully and decide how to set it out on the viewdata pages. Remember that the pages can only hold a limited amount of information, and are difficult to read if the information is not set out well. Also decide what colours to use: a few well-chosen colours look very attractive, but too many colours makes a page look confusing.
- Decide how many pages to use for each subject, and how to link the pages together. Draw a sketch of the tree structure you require.
- Type the pages for one or two subjects. Print them if possible. Check them carefully, either on the screen or on the printouts. Make any corrections and changes to improve the appearance of the pages.
- Now type the information for the other optional subjects. Check each page carefully and correct any errors.

216

setting up viewdata pages

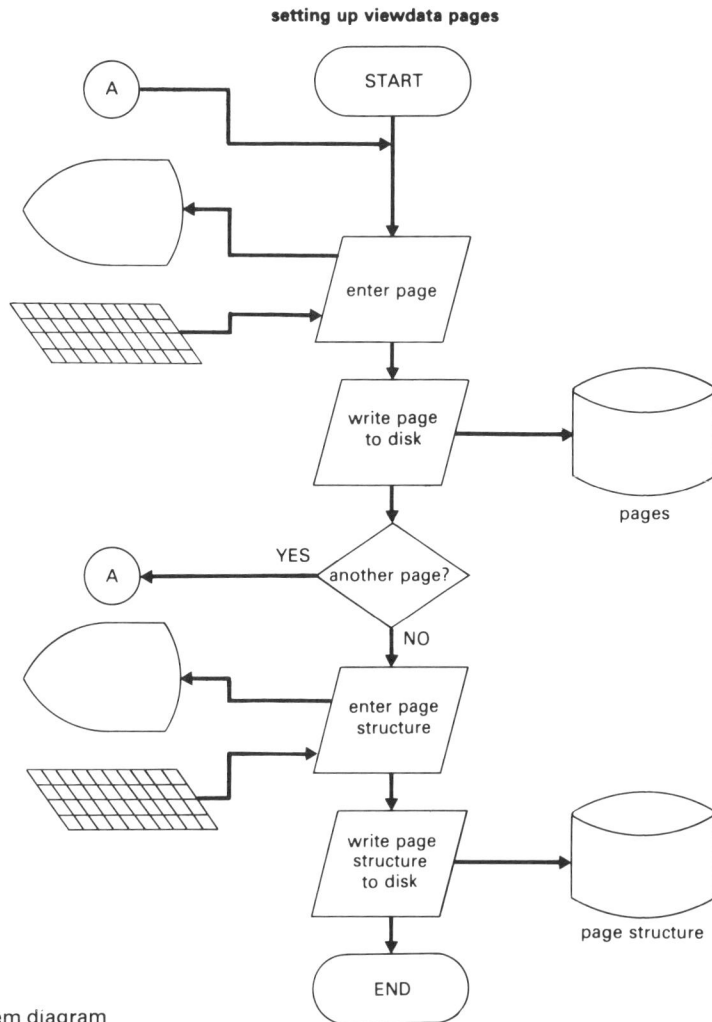

Figure 19.5   Optional subjects viewdata system: system diagram

- Create a header page for the viewdata system, and header pages for each subject group. Enter clear instructions for users to call up the subject pages from the header pages.
- Set up the connections between the pages so that they can be called from each other in the required tree structure.

Testing

- Get other pupils to test the viewdata system. Ask them to check that the pages are correctly linked, and that the instructions and information in the pages are clearly set out.
- Using the comments you get from these tests, make any changes which are required to the viewdata system.

Documentation

- Write a set of system documentation, explaining the way the pages of the optional subject viewdata system are set up, and how information is entered and edited. Include a diagram of the tree structure of the pages. This documentation is for anyone who wants to extend or alter the information in the viewdata system.
- Write a brief user guide for people who want to look at the pages. Explain how to start the program running, and how to go from one page to another. Also explain how to print pages, if this facility is available.

One of the major uses of the Prestel network is for travel agents to see information about holidays. The travel agents have a private section of the network which is not accessible to other users. The viewdata network also provides **gateways** to the computers of travel companies. Working through these gateways, travel agents can make bookings from their Prestel terminals.

The Requirements of the Task

The viewdata part of the system must provide up-to-date information of available holidays from a number of travel companies. This information is kept up-to-date by the information providers—the travel companies.

The reservations system enables bookings to be made for holidays from the viewdata terminal. It stores details of each booking, and prints tickets and confirmation slips.

Computer System Design

Outputs
While looking at alternatives for holidays, the system shows viewdata pages. When a holiday has been selected, the gateway links the travel agent to the travel company's computer. This produces tickets, invoices and confirmation slips of the holidays which have been booked. These are either printed at the travel agent, or (more commonly) at the central computer of the holiday company, and posted to the travel agent.

Inputs
Initially, the inputs are the type of holiday required by the client, and the dates and approximate prices. Once a holiday has been selected, precise details are required: name and address, names of others in the party, dates of travel and any special requirements. These are entered at the keyboard, and displayed on the screen.

File structure
The information pages follow the normal viewdata page structure. The reservation files are similar to those described in sections 16B and 16C.

File processing
The viewdata system is operated in the normal way to look at alternative holidays. If one is selected by the client, a response is entered at the viewdata keyboard. This automatically calls up the travel company's computer to make the booking. The booking is made by filling in a form on the screen. A record is created for the booking, and the required documents are printed.

System Diagram

See Figure 19.6.

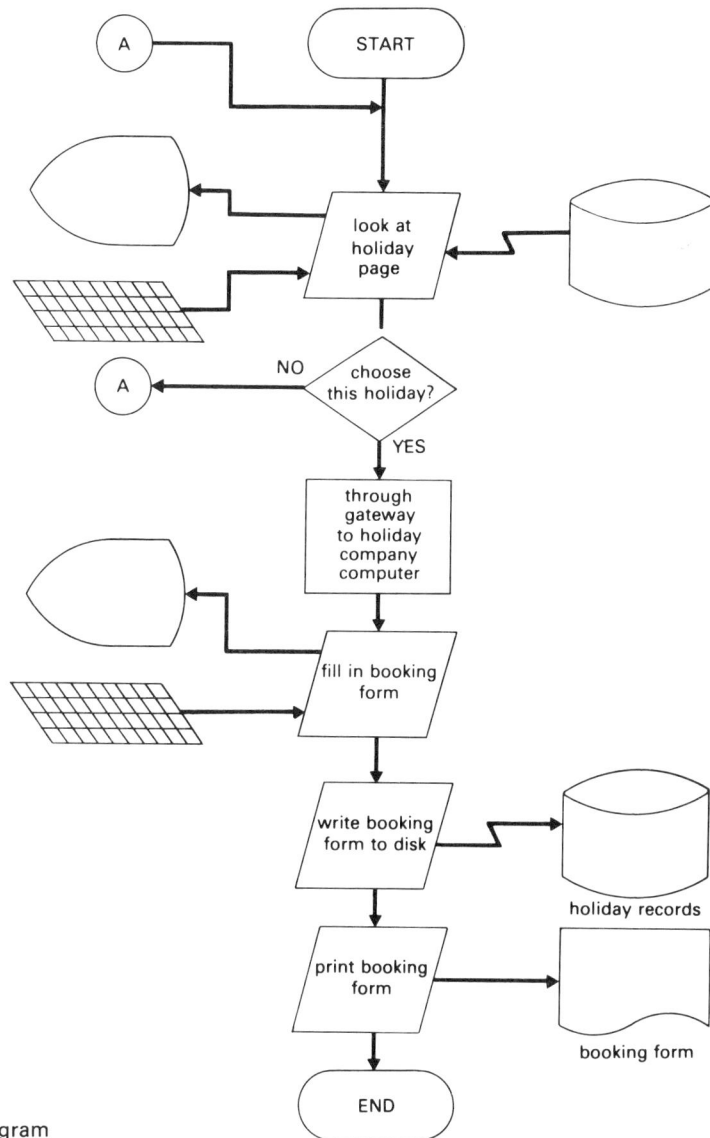

Figure 19.6   Travel agent viewdata system: system diagram

Implementation

The travel agents' reservation system is implemented on the Prestel network, which has the gateways to the computers of the travel companies. The Prestel network is based on a number of minicomputers at centres throughout Britain which have been chosen to minimise the distance over which telephone calls are made. Most users are able to access the computers via local calls.

The travel companies have a variety of computers, mostly large minicomputers or mainframes. They can deal with large numbers of enquiries in short periods of time, and do all the bookings in real time. They use complex transaction processing software to make the bookings.

1 Explain the idea of a **gateway**, using the travel agents' reservation system as an example.
2 What are the benefits of viewdata and gateways to reservation computers for:
   (a) travel agents
   (b) people going on holiday?
3 What is the main cost to a travel agent of using a viewdata system? How does the travel agent justify spending this money?
4 Why is the Prestel network based on a number of regional computers rather than a single central site?

19D End-of-Chapter Summary

The main points of this chapter are as follows:

- Viewdata combines the technologies of computers, telephones and television. It provides pages of information from a central computer on adapted television sets, viewdata terminals or microcomputers running viewdata software.
- A viewdata page is one screenful of information. It is displayed in large letters and simple graphics, in colour. The pages are linked together in a tree structure.
- Prestel is the national viewdata network in the UK. It is run by British Telecom on behalf of a large number of information providers who supply the information and keep it up-to-date.
- Prestel serves home and business users. It is popular with travel agents, farmers, insurance companies and schools and colleges. Users have mailboxes to exchange messages, and may order goods or request further information by filling in forms on the screen.
- Some Prestel users (such as travel agents) have their own sets of pages which are not accessible to all users. They also have gateways from Prestel pages to gain access to other computers, for example to make travel reservations.

Exercise 19

1 Choose the correct word from the list for each of the following spaces:

gateway; pages; screen; key; real; posted; computer; terminal.

Mr and Mrs Jones visited their local travel agent to enquire about a holiday. They told him what type of holiday they wanted, and how much they could afford. The travel agent used his viewdata ____ to call up ____ of information on possible holidays. He pressed a ____ to move from one page to the next. When they found a holiday they liked, the agent pressed another key which connected his terminal through a ____ to the ____ of the particular holiday company. He filled in a booking form on the ____, with details provided by Mr and Mrs Jones. The computer made the booking in ____ time, and printed a confirmation form and invoice later that day. It was ____ to the travel agent, who forwarded it to Mr and Mrs Jones.

Things to find out

1 Prestel is a viewdata system. It sends pages of information from a central computer via telephone lines to television sets or microcomputers. Similar systems, but much more limited in scope, are the **teletext** systems operated by television companies.
(a) Find out what teletext services are provided by the television companies in the UK.
(b) Find out how teletext information is structured, how it is stored, and how it is sent to the user.
(c) Make a list of the similarities and one of the differences between teletext and viewdata.

(d) Comment on the usefulness of teletext compared with that of viewdata.

2　The Bank of Scotland and the Nottingham Building Society offer home banking services via Prestel. Customers can look at the balances in their accounts, transfer money between accounts, pay bills and enquire about interest rates—all from their home Prestel terminals.

Project starters

1　Look at the estate agent's information retrieval system described in section 10B. Design a similar, but simpler, system for the same purpose, based on a local viewdata system instead of an information retrieval system. Comment on the advantages and disadvantages of the two systems.

2　Follow the steps of section 19A to use a viewdata system to gather information on the following topics. In each case, write a report (using a word processing system if possible) or set up a table of the information (using a spreadsheet or statistical program if possible).

(a) The **exchange rate** is the amount of one currency that can be bought with one unit of another. For example, if $1.45 could be bought for £1.00, then the exchange rate for dollars is 1.45. These exchange rates fluctuate from day to day, and patterns can sometimes be seen in the way they rise and fall over a period of time.

Use a viewdata system to look at the exchange rates each day between a set of suitable currencies (for example the pound against the US dollar, German mark and Japanese yen). Draw up a table of these exchange rates, and draw a graph of the way they change over a period of time. Also look at the news during the same time, and try to explain the fluctuations. (They are not always obvious!)

(b) The money to run many companies comes from **shares** in the companies. These are sold by the companies to investors, including members of the public. The **shareholders** own part of the company. They are paid a **dividend** once or twice a year, the amount depending on the profits made by the company. They may also sell their shares to other people, and buy other shares. The prices of shares change every day, sometimes by quite large amounts. The changes depend on the performance of the

Find out more about these home banking services. Write a report which discusses the advantages and disadvantages of them compared with the services provided by other banks and building societies.

company and of its competitors, whether the company is likely to be taken over by another company, and the state of the economy in general.

Use a viewdata system to watch the changes in price of a selection of shares. The best way is to start with a certain sum of money (say £1000.00) and spend it on a **portfolio** of shares. Set up a table showing the numbers of shares bought, and the prices of these shares at intervals of one week. Also calculate the value of the portfolio for each set of prices. See Figure 19.7.

Draw a graph showing the change in price of each share in the portfolio, and of the value of the portfolio as a whole, over the period of time. Look at the news pages on the viewdata system during the same time, and try to explain the changes in the share prices. (Like the fluctuations in currency, these changes are not easy to explain!)

3　Set up a local viewdata system, using the steps in section 19B, for one or more of the following:

(a) A local tourist guide, with details of places of interest, shops, theatres, cinemas, art galleries, discos, etc. Collect the information from local newspapers and libraries, as well as the places themselves. Include opening times and admission prices wherever possible.

(b) A guide to the facilities offered by your school library or resource centre. Include information about the types of books and equipment available, how to use the indexes, and how to borrow items.

(c) A brief history of the kings and queens of England and Britain. Allocate one page for each monarch, and connect the pages to reflect the order of succession. Include a brief summary of the reign of each monarch, with dates and names of husband, wife (or wives) and children.

	1	2	3	4	5	6
1			Week 1		Week 2	
2	Number	Share	Price	Value	Price	Value
3	--------	--------	--------	--------	--------	--------
4	100	Br T'com	216	£216.00		
5	200	Br Gas	59	£118.00		
6	50	Pilk'ton	670	£335.00		
7	200	Horizon	150	£300.00		
8						
9						
10						
11						
12				--------		--------
13	Total	Value		£969.00		
14				--------		--------
15						

Figure 19.7　Share portfolio table

20 Electronic Mail and Electronic Funds Transfer

Operators at a computer used for electronic funds transfer.

Most companies use word processors for correspondence. When a letter is sent from one such company to another, the letter is typed and corrected on the word processor screen and then printed. The printed copy goes into the company's internal post system and is then posted, in many cases the day after it was written. A day or so later, or a week later for international mail, the letter is received at the other company. It is distributed via this company's internal mail system (which may take another day), after which it finally arrives on the desk of the person to whom it is addressed. This person then dictates a reply to be entered at a word processor...

If the companies are connected to an **electronic mail** network, several days are saved in this process. The letter, once it has been corrected, is sent from one company as a computer message, via the telephone network, to the **mailbox** of the receiving company. The process takes only a few seconds, even for a long letter sent to the other side of the world. The person to whom the letter is addressed looks at the mailbox at least once each day and copies any letters in it to his or her own computer where they may be viewed on the screen or printed. Electronic mail is not only quicker than the post, it is also cheaper. Once the computer links have been paid for, the cost per message is much less than sending it by post.

There are a number of electronic mail networks in operation at present. They have one or more central computers, connected to each other and to users via telephone lines. The lines may be carried by fibre optics cable, microwave radio or satellite links. The central computers switch incoming messages to their destinations. They may select the best route for the message, if several are available, and may store the message if the receiving computer is not ready for it. Each user has a mailbox for incoming messages, and may send messages to the mailbox of any other user. See Figure 20.1. The messages may be computer files of any type. The commonest are word processor documents, spreadsheets and the data files for information retrieval systems.

The most popular electronic mail service in the UK is the **Telecom Gold (BTG)** system operated by British Telecom. Some UK schools use **The Times Network for Schools (TTNS)**. A problem with electronic mail is that different networks are not always interlinked. TTNS and BTG are an exception to this, and can pass messages to each other.

Electronic funds transfer (EFT) is a special type of message service between the computers of banks and other financial institutions. The messages are all to do with financial transactions, mainly transferring sums of money from one account to another. Banks in the UK use the **Chaps** system, those in the USA have the **Chips**

system, and the International **Swift** network links banks in most countries via a central computer in Belgium.

This chapter describes a use for electronic mail between schools, and the international electronic funds transfer system. It puts into practice some of the ideas about computer applications introduced in chapter 9.

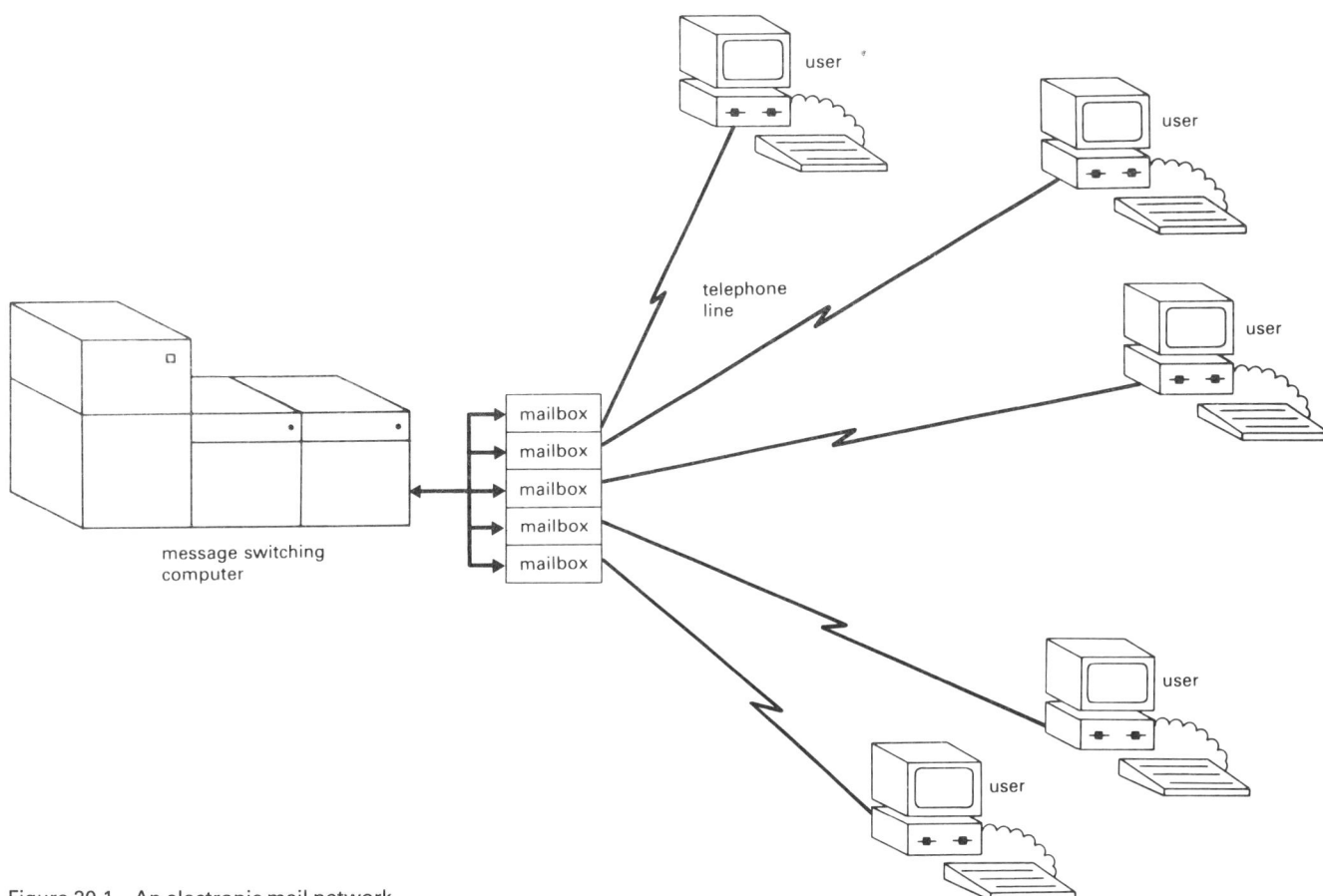

Figure 20.1   An electronic mail network

20A Activity: Joint Local History Project

The best way of using an electronic mail link between two or more schools is to share information about a common project. This section is based on a joint local history project. It could equally well be based on joint projects to do with local employment, amenities, land use or wildlife in rural areas, or a network of foreign correspondents for school newspapers. Other possible projects of this nature are outlined in Exercise 20.

The Requirements of the Task

The aim of the project is to set up local history projects in at least two schools, and to share the information between the schools using electronic mail. The reports can be based on the information coming from all the schools in the project. A number of local history topics are possible, depending on the area. One of the simplest is to select a period of fairly recent history, such as the time from the turn of the century to the start of the First World War, and try to build up a picture of what life was like for local people in the period. Many buildings from the period are still standing, and there are parish records, old newspapers, paintings, old books and even a few old photographs from the period to be found.

Other more ambitious topics can be selected. These include emigration from an area in the UK and the corresponding immigration to a country in the New World. There is the Norman Conquest, with information from the areas in Normandy from which the invaders came, and information from areas in Britain where they settled in significant numbers.

Computer System Design

Outputs
The outputs include text, maps, diagrams, tables and database records on matters of local history, in accordance with the selected topic. Some of these are printed by computer; other material is drawn by hand.

Inputs
Information is researched by pupils at each participating school. This is gathered as notes on paper and then entered into the appropriate software package: word processor, information retrieval program, etc. It is then sent to the other schools in the project via the electronic mail network.

File structure
The file structures are those of the software used for word processing, information retrieval, etc. See chapters 10, 11, 12, 15 and 17. The electronic mail system has a mailbox for each school, which holds these files.

File processing
The files of information are entered, edited and printed in the usual way. Once a file has been received by electronic mail from another school, it may be used as if it had been entered on the receiving computer in the first place. (This is provided that the same software packages are used by all the schools in the project.)

System Diagram

See Figure 20.2.

Implementation

First of all make contact with one or more schools on the same electronic mail network. They may be nearby, or in distant countries. Suggest and discuss possible joint projects, such as the local history one described above. The initial discussions can take place via letters exchanged on the electronic mail network. Decide on the type of joint project which will be undertaken.

- Agree on an outline of the project. This sets out the aims of the project and the subject matter to be covered. It also states what research will be done by the pupils at each school, and how it will be exchanged.
- Decide which software package is to be used for each type of information. For example, all the schools must use the same word processing package. In a few rare cases, different software packages can exchange data files, but do not believe this until you have tested it!

Pupils collecting information for a local survey.

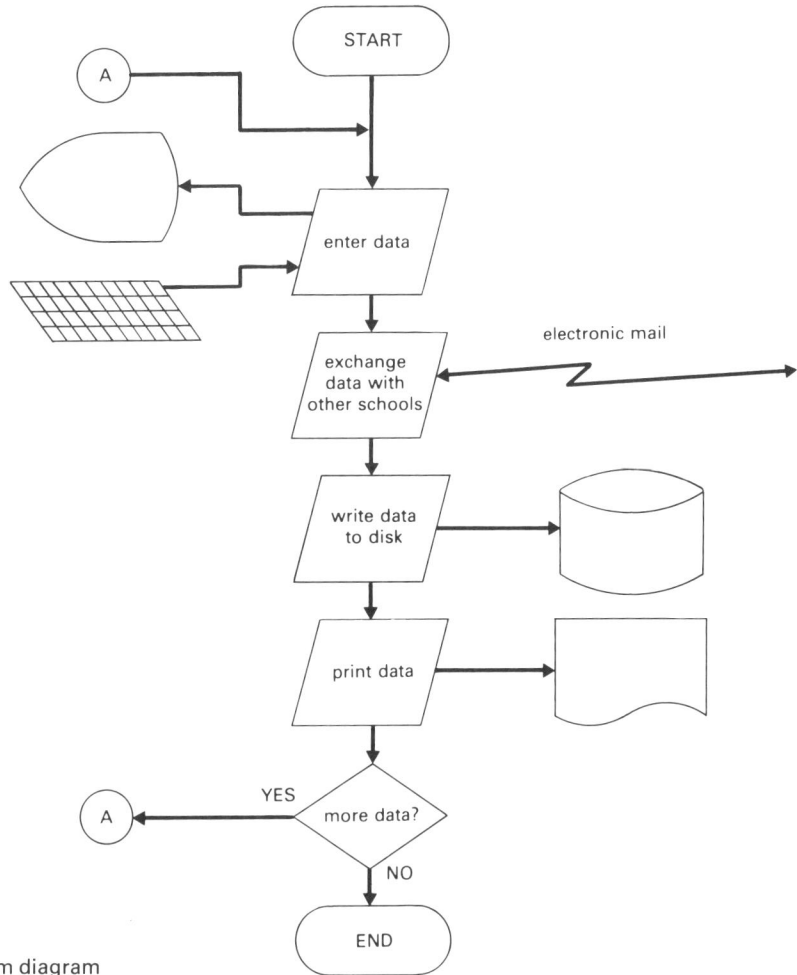

Figure 20.2   School joint local history project: system diagram

- Set up the record structures you need on any information retrieval software which is going to be used. In a similar way, create blank spreadsheets and set up the headings in statistical data files.
- Transfer test files of data between the schools, using each software package in turn. Make sure that what is written by one school can be read by the other schools.
- Share research tasks among pupils or groups of pupils. Make sure that each pupil or group is clear about his or her tasks, and in what form their findings should be recorded.
- Carry out the research: look at the old documents, maps, paintings, buildings and other sources of information, and record the required information.
- Enter the findings at the computer using the appropriate software. Use the record structures and blank spreadsheets which have already been set up.
- Send the data files to the other schools. It is best to collect them together and send them in batches. This reduces the telephone times and therefore the charges, especially if files are being sent to another country.
- Look at the school's mailbox at regular intervals, and copy incoming data files to the school's computer.
- Share the tasks of writing the reports and producing the final illustrations amongst the pupils.

- Each pupil uses the data files relating to the topic for his or her report. Some of these originate from the pupil's own school and some from other schools in the project. The reports should summarise the main points which emerge from the information, and compare local conditions with those in the other areas surveyed.
- Enter the reports on word processors and print them. Send copies via electronic mail to other schools in the project.
- Print or draw maps, diagrams and tables to go with the reports in order to present the information as clearly and attractively as possible.

Documentation

- Write brief user guides for the programs used in the project. Describe the structures of the files which are set up for the information. Also describe how to send files to the other schools, and how to copy incoming files from the school's mailbox to the computer.

20B Application: Electronic Funds Transfer

Banks and other financial organisations in the UK handle hundreds of millions of pounds every day, as do their counterparts in other countries. Many of the transactions involve the movement of money over long distances. In the past, money has been transferred as physical objects: notes and coins, cheques, and banker's drafts. This is far too slow, cumbersome and expensive for modern banking. Most large financial transactions are now done by messages sent between the banks' computers: **electronic funds transfer (EFT)**. The use of cash terminals involves EFT—a message is sent from the cash terminal to the bank computer giving details of the amount of cash withdrawn from a particular account. EFT is likely to become even more widespread in the next few years, with direct transfers of money from banks to shops to pay for purchases.

The Requirements of the Task

The aim of EFT is to provide a real-time system for the transfer of money from one bank account to another. The money is transferred as a message which gives details of the account from which the money is coming, the account into which it is to be paid, and the amount of money. A method of establishing direct links between the computers of the banks is required.

The EFT system must handle large volumes of transactions, be available at all times, and be secure against unauthorised access.

Computer System Design

Outputs
For each transaction, there is an entry in the source account showing the sum of money withdrawn. There is an entry in the destination account showing the same amount of money paid in.

Inputs
The details of the transaction are entered at a terminal connected to the computer of the bank from which the money is being sent. These details include the source and destination account numbers, a code which identifies the destination bank, and the amount to be transferred.

Message structure

The message is sent as a **packet** from one bank computer to the other. The packet is of a fixed structure, and is sent as one unit. It includes the account numbers, bank branch codes and amount, as described above.

Processing

When an EFT request is entered at a terminal, the computer checks that the account exists and that there is enough money in it for the transaction to take place. If so, a message is sent to the computer of the bank into which the money is being transferred.

This message travels along high-speed telephone links via one or more **packet switching computers** which act as exchanges in the EFT network. These route incoming messages to their destinations. They may store messages if they cannot go forward immediately, and take account of the differences in transmission speeds of the telecommunications links. The EFT network is similar to an electronic mail network—see Figure 20.3.

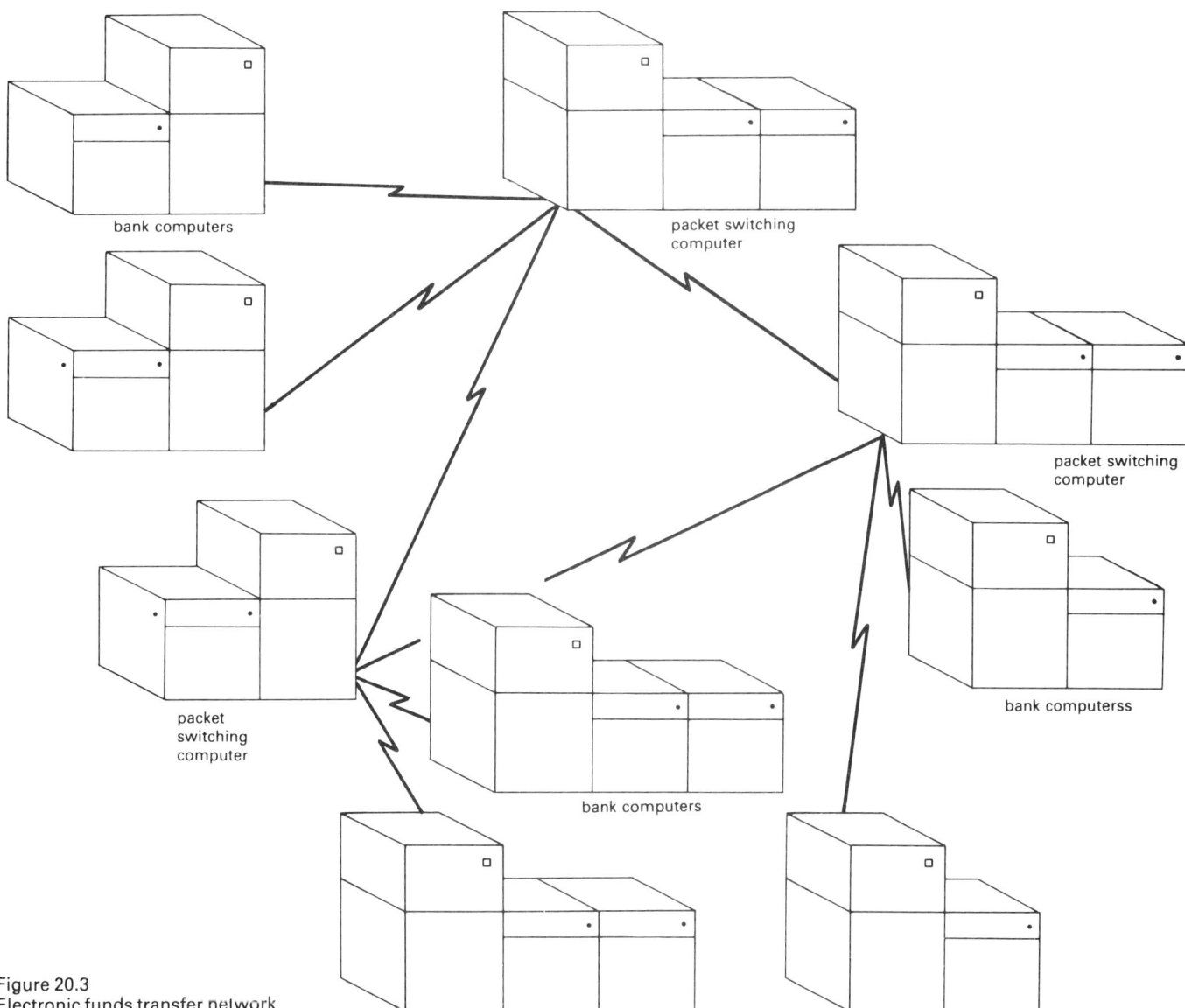

Figure 20.3
Electronic funds transfer network

When the message arrives at the destination bank, the money is transferred into the required account and a confirmation message is sent back to the bank from which the money was sent. If necessary, the money is converted from one currency to another during the transaction.

System Diagram

See Figure 20.4.

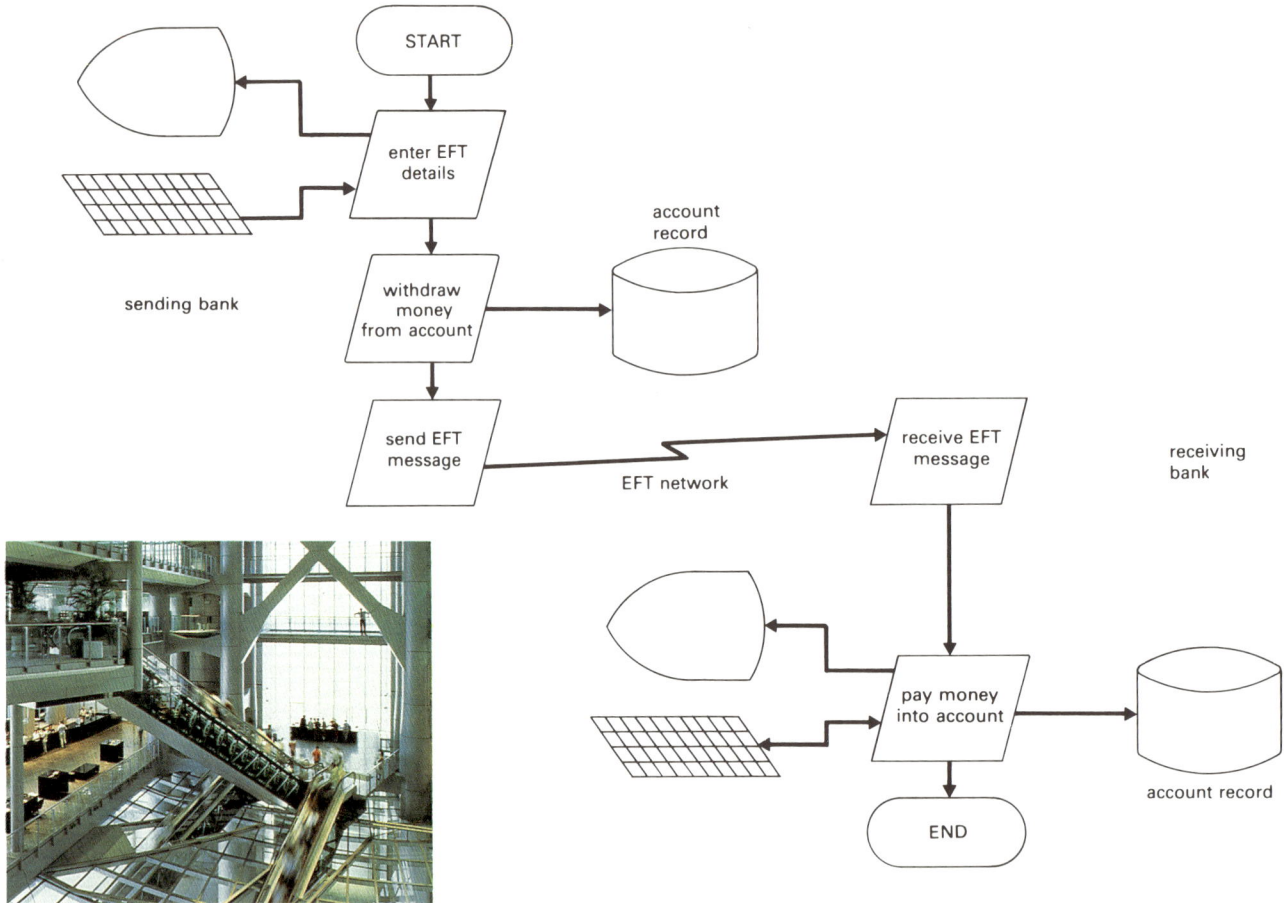

Part of the interior of the Hong Kong and Shanghai Bank headquarters, in Hong Kong. All the bank's work is done with the aid of computers.

Figure 20.4   Electronic funds transfer: system diagram

Implementation

Banks throughout the world have large mainframe computers which deal with their accounts. Software for EFT has been written for these computers. It is transaction processing software, running in real time, and capable of large numbers of transactions per second. The international nature of banking, with banks in every time zone, means that EFT systems run 24 hours a day.

The message switching computers are also provided with custom-designed software to handle the large volumes of messages passing through them. It is essential that these message switching systems are reliable: they must be operational all the time without interruptions for any reason. Some of these computers have all their processing facilities duplicated so that they can continue to operate even if one unit has broken down.

Security

All the messages on an EFT system concern money, and many authorise the transfer of large sums. It is therefore essential to protect the EFT system against unauthorised interference. A number of security methods are used. These include restricting access to the terminals from which EFT transactions can be sent, and requiring all those who are authorised to use these terminals to have passwords. Messages are sent in scrambled form so that they cannot be intercepted in transit and other people cannot enter spurious messages into the EFT system.

Documentation

The banks in the same EFT network (such as Chips, Chaps or Swift) use the same type of EFT software, although it is implemented on different computers. The system documentation is in two parts: the part describing the common features, and the part describing how the system is implemented on the bank's own computer system. This documentation is confidential and only available to the small number of software engineers who maintain the system.

The bank clerks who operate the EFT terminals are given short training courses in their use and provided with brief user guides. Entering EFT transactions is a simple process, and the user guides are not required unless an unusual transaction is required. Some banks, such as the Hong Kong and Shanghai Bank, are installing EFT terminals in their banking halls for customers to operate themselves for certain types of transaction.

Questions

1 A company in Britain, RSJ Electronics, makes a payment to one of its component suppliers, Kwee Components, in the Philippines. Write down the stages of making the payment if it is done:
   (a) by cheque
   (b) by electronic funds transfer.
   Estimate the time taken for the transaction in each case.

2 Assume that an EFT message has the following structure:

source bank branch code	source account number	destination bank branch code	destination account number	amount

For example, a transfer of £100.00 from account 80201643 at branch 20–33–98 to account 78564791 at branch 31–22–78 would be as follows:

20–33–98	802016432	31–22–78	78564791	100.00

Assume also that three companies have accounts as follows:

J J Smith and Company	Account 54983762 at Branch 34–88–09
DRX Electronics	Account 32086733 at Branch 21–66–73
Owen Edwards PLC	Account 18439756 at Branch 30–05–83

Write the EFT messages for each of the following transactions:
(a) £50 000.00 paid by J J Smith to DRX Electronics

(b) a payment to Owen Edwards by DRX Electronics of £357.54
(c) a payment of £2378.43 from Owen Edwards to J J Smith.

3* Assuming an EFT message structure as shown in question 2, write down a set of validation rules for each field.

4 Why must EFT systems be available for use 24 hours a day?

5 Why is the hardware of the EFT switching computers duplicated?

229

20C Issue: Computer Fraud

The slow methods of traditional banking generated their own checks. Documents had to be signed and authorised, and large transactions required authorisation at higher levels. Because the paperwork took some time to clear, a telephone call could often halt a dubious transaction before it had been completed. In spite of these checks, a certain amount of fraud was committed. Forged cheques and other documents were sometimes processed without being detected.

The speed and convenience of EFT is making it more and more difficult to safeguard against fraud. Large amounts of money are moved halfway across the world in seconds, with no written record of the movement being produced. There are many opportunities for fraud open to clever and determined people, particularly those with inside knowledge. The size of the problem is unknown: some cases are widely publicised, but there is suspicion that many more are being kept secret by banks in order to avoid bad publicity and reveal weaknesses in security.

Questions

1 (a) List some of the safeguards of traditional banking procedures.
(b) For each measure, state whether or not it is still effective when EFT is used.
(c) What security measures are taken to protect EFT transactions?
(d) What is the main weakness in the security measures which protect EFT transactions?
2 How widespread is computer fraud?
3 Why are some cases of computer fraud possibly being kept secret by the banks?

20D End-of-Chapter Summary

The main points of this chapter are as follows:

- Electronic mail allows users to send data files from their computers to those of other users.
- Many companies are being connected to electronic mail networks. Word processor documents are most commonly sent, as well as spreadsheets and data files for information retrieval packages.
- An electronic mail network consists of one or more central message switching computers. Each user has a mailbox for incoming messages.
- Electronic funds transfer is the use of computer messages for financial transactions between banks.
- The advantages of electronic mail and EFT are the speed with which messages are sent, and the low cost compared with postal services.
- Electronic banking is creating new opportunities for fraud. Strict security measures are in force to try to prevent dishonest transactions, but there is evidence that fraud is taking place.

Exercise 20

1 Choose the correct word from the list for each of the following spaces:

balance; EFT; amount; account; code; personal identification number; terminal; number.

When Mrs Brown arrived at her bank, she found that an electronic funds transfer ___ had been installed. She sat at the terminal and typed her ___ . She wanted to pay her gas bill. She first looked at the ___ in her account. She then entered the details of the transaction: the bank branch ___ and account ___ of the gas company, and the ___ to be transferred. The computer sent a message to the terminal to say that the ___ transaction had been completed. Mrs Brown again looked at the balance in her ___ and saw it was now less by the amount paid to the gas company.

2 A company manufactures a range of medicines which it sells to hospitals and chemists all over the world. It has a head office in Europe, and branch offices in a number of countries on every continent. It has a single research laboratory near its head office, and three production plants: one in Europe, one in North America and one in Singapore.
(a) Make a list of all the uses you can think of for electronic communications systems by this company.
(b) For each item in your list, write down the advantages of electronic communication over traditional methods.

Things to find out

1 Investigate some of the following computer applications which involve electronic mail, EFT or a similar system. Write a report on the application(s), following the steps of section 20B.
(a) Magazine articles sent by electronic mail from foreign correspondents to their magazines.
(b) The master copies of newspapers and magazines sent from news offices to printing plants.
(c) Contracts sent between companies or solicitors by electronic mail.
(d) New banking services made possible with EFT.

2 In the near future, shops in Britain are planning to introduce computer systems where goods are paid for, as they are purchased, by electronic funds transfer from the customer's bank account to that of the shop. The system is known as **electronic funds transfer at point-of-sale (EFTPOS)**.
(a) Find out how the proposed EFTPOS system will work.
(b) List the advantages it might have for:
   the shops
   the banks
   the customers.

(c) List any disadvantages of EFTPOS you can think of.
(d) In your opinion, will EFTPOS prove to be popular when it is introduced? Give reasons for your answer.

3 An electronic communications system which can be used for text and documents is the **facsimile (fax)** system. It is becoming quite popular in offices.
(a) Find out how the facsimile system works.
(b) Find out how it is being used.
(c) Make a list of the advantages and disadvantages of facsimile systems over electronic mail.

4 Look in the press for articles about computer fraud. For each case you find:
(a) Describe the type of crime that was committed.
(b) Write down the amount of money involved in the crime.
(c) State whether or not the criminals were caught.
(d) If anyone was convicted of the crime, write down the sentence which they received.
(e) Give your comments on the case.

Points to discuss

1 Make a list of the advantages and disadvantages of electronic funds transfer. Include those mentioned in the text, and others you have thought of. State, with reasons, whether you think that the advantages outweigh the disadvantages.

Project starters

1 Use the steps of section 20A for one or more of the following activities:
(a) The exchange of news items for a class newspaper.
(b) A chess tournament by electronic mail. Each school is represented by a team of pupils. A chessboard for each match is set up at each school. Each move is sent as one electronic mail message, and the board at each school is updated accordingly.
(c) A combined pollution survey by a number of schools, covering air pollution, pollution damage to buildings, acid rain, river pollution or sea pollution. A survey of river pollution by a number of schools at different positions on the river is particularly useful.

21

Process Control and Robots

Computers are replacing paper-based systems in offices; electronic control systems and robots are replacing manual (or manually-controlled) processes in factories. The reasons for the change are the same in both cases: IT systems are faster, more flexible and produce a higher standard of work than previous methods. Electronic control systems are interactive, and work in real time. Electronic control systems and robots are expensive to install, but their running costs are much lower than those for the manual processes. The cost of each item produced by the new technology is lower than before.

Electronic control systems and robots are used extensively in motor vehicle assembly plants throughout the world. Robots are used in many other assembly plants, including some which make computers. Electronic control systems are used in steelworks, power

Computer-controlled trolleys moving jet engine components at the Rolls-Royce Aims production plant. In the background is some of the equipment which works on the components. Most of this equipment is controlled by computer.

stations (particularly nuclear power stations) and in glass production, to name just a few. Space rockets and satellites are controlled almost entirely by computer. Modern weapons such as missiles and torpedoes include electronic guidance systems.

This chapter describes some control activities that can be tried out if an electronics kit is available in the classroom. It illustrates the two main kinds of control system: **hard-wired control** (using logic circuits) and **programmable control**. It describes an application of robots, a process control system and an integrated manufacturing system using computer-controlled machines and robots. It puts into practice some of the ideas of Boolean logic introduced in chapter 2, the general ideas of control systems from chapter 6, and those of computer applications from chapter 9.

21A Activity: Burglar Alarm

It is unfortunately necessary to protect property against intruders. One way of doing this is an alarm system which is triggered by the presence of a person or by something the person does. The most effective alarms are triggered in several different ways.

The Requirements of the Task

The aim is to design a burglar alarm system which can be triggered if a person:

> breaks a light beam, or
> approaches a heat sensor, or
> breaks an electric circuit by breaking a window.

The alarm system has a switch which turns it on and off.

Computer System Design

The control centre at a company which operates burglar alarms. All alarms going off are reported here.

Outputs
A buzzer sounds when the alarm is triggered.

Inputs
A light sensor, a heat sensor, a switch to simulate the circuit in the window glass, and an on/off switch. The light sensor sends out a signal when light is shining on it. The heat sensor sends out a signal when a warm object is near it. The switches allow a current to pass (which is the same as sending a signal) when they are closed.

Processing
The states of the inputs and output can be written as 0 if they are OFF (no signal), or 1 if they are ON (sending a signal). The logic of the alarm system is as follows:

Buzzer ON (State 1) if

  on/off switch ON (State 1) AND

  (light sensor OFF (State 0)   OR
     heat sensor ON (State 1)   OR
     window circuit OFF (State 0)   )

This can be drawn as a logic circuit (section 2E), as shown in Figure 21.1. An operation table for the circuit is shown thus:

On/off Switch	Light Sensor	Heat Sensor	Window Circuit	Buzzer Output
0	0	0	0	0 switched off
0	0	0	1	0
0	0	1	0	0
0	0	1	1	0
0	1	0	0	0
0	1	0	1	0
0	1	1	0	0
0	1	1	1	0
1	0	0	0	1 alarm on
1	0	0	1	1
1	0	1	0	1
1	0	1	1	1
1	1	0	0	1
1	1	0	1	0 all clear
1	1	1	0	1
1	1	1	1	1

For the first eight lines of the table the burglar alarm is switched off. When it is switched on, the third line from the bottom shows it in the 'all clear' state. This means that the light beam is unbroken, the window circuit intact and no-one is near the heat sensor. The other seven lines in the bottom half of the table show the alarm sounding.

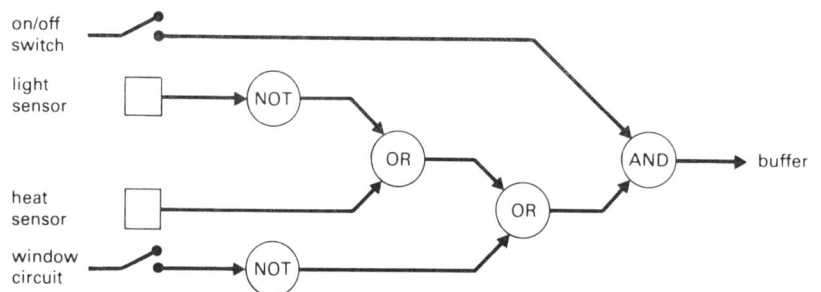

Figure 21.1   Logic circuit for burglar alarm

Implementation

The burglar alarm is a **hard-wired** control system. It is implemented by connecting a set of sensors, switches and gates, and a buzzer to a logic circuit, as shown in Figure 21.1.

Use the logic circuit elements in your school's electronics kit to make the burglar alarm:

- Connect the sensors and switches to an AND gate, two NOT gates and two OR gates as shown in Figure 21.1. Connect the output to a buzzer.
- Switch the on/off switch to the OFF (open) position. Check that the buzzer does not sound no matter what the state of the other inputs.
- Close the switch which simulates the window circuit, and switch the on/off switch ON. The alarm is now active, but 'all clear'.
- Now try out the triggers, one by one:

    — place your finger over the light sensor to block off the light

— place your hand near the heat sensor to provide a source of heat

— open the switch which simulates the window circuit.

In each case, the buzzer should sound.
Also check that it sounds if two or more of the triggers are activated at the same time.

- If the alarm does not work properly, check that all the connections are making proper contact. Also check that the logic circuit has been wired up correctly.

Documentation

- Write a brief description of the way the equipment from your school's electronics kit is put together to make the burglar alarm circuit. Include a wiring diagram if necessary.

21B Activity: Stage Lights

The stage lighting equipment in a modern theatre is powerful and versatile. Many different effects can be created, and the lights can be changed rapidly from one setting to another. Controlling the hundreds of lights in a large theatre is a complex task, and all theatres use some form of electronic control. Some of them, such as the National Theatre in London, use a computer for lighting control. This activity simulates a stage lighting system controlled by computer.

The Requirements of the Task

The aim of a lighting control system is to make it possible for the lights in a theatre to be operated in real time, as a play progresses. It is impossible for the lighting technician to control each light individually. The control system allows the light settings for each scene to be set up beforehand. When a particular setting is required, a single switch for that setting is pressed, and the lights for that setting are all turned on automatically. Most lighting control systems can also control the gradual dimming and brightening of lights automatically, but this facility is not simulated here.

Computer System Design

Outputs
For each setting, the signals to control the brightness of each light are output.

Inputs
When the lighting system is being set up for a play, the required level of each light for each setting is entered. While the play is running, there is a switch for each setting. Every time a particular setting is required, the switch for that setting is pressed by the lighting technician.

Processing
An algorithm for the operation of the lighting control system is as follows:

Repeat

Wait until a setting switch is pressed

If setting

    1   then Set lights for setting 1

    2   then Set lights for setting 2

    3   then Set lights for setting 3

    . . .

Until end of play

Note that this algorithm means that settings do not have to follow each other in any particular order, and that settings can be used as often as required. Each setting algorithm ('Set lights for setting 1') is written in more detail in another algorithm.

System Diagram

See Figure 21.2.

Implementation

Some of the lighting effects for the play *Starlight Express* in London.

In order to simulate the action of a stage lighting control system on your school computer, you need a set of output channels (eight will be enough) for the lights, and a set of input channels (again eight is sufficient) for the switches. A simple control programming language is also required.

- Look at the user guide for the electronics kit, and the one for the control programming language, and make sure that you understand how they work.
- Connect up the input and output channels. Connect a set of hand switches to the input channels, and a set of small lights to the output channels.
- Design your lighting control program as a module which implements the overall control algorithm above, and a set of modules called from it (one for each setting of the lights).
- Some control systems output a binary number, with a bit for each output channel. If a bit is 0, there is no signal on the channel and the light connected to it is off; if the bit is 1, there is a signal and the light is on. For example, the output

$$0\ 0\ 0\ 0\ 1\ 0\ 0\ 1$$

means that the lights on the first and fourth channels (reading from the right) are on; the others are off.

The program module for a particular setting may simply switch on certain lights. For example:

Setting 1 is

    Output 0 0 0 0 1 0 0 1

Alternatively, a setting might involve a sequence of outputs. For example, an algorithm for a setting which starts with a blackout, and then brings up lights in a sequence is as follows:

Setting 2 is

    Output 0 0 0 0 0 0 0 0

    Pause 1 second

    Output 0 0 0 0 0 0 0 1

Pause 5 seconds

Output 0 0 0 0 0 1 0 1

Pause 10 seconds

Output 0 0 0 1 0 1 0 1

- Decide on the effects you require for each setting. Write algorithms for them if necessary.
- Change the algorithms into program modules in the control programming language of your computer. Enter the program carefully, and check it for typing errors.
- Run the program, and test it by pressing each input switch in turn. Correct any errors which you find.

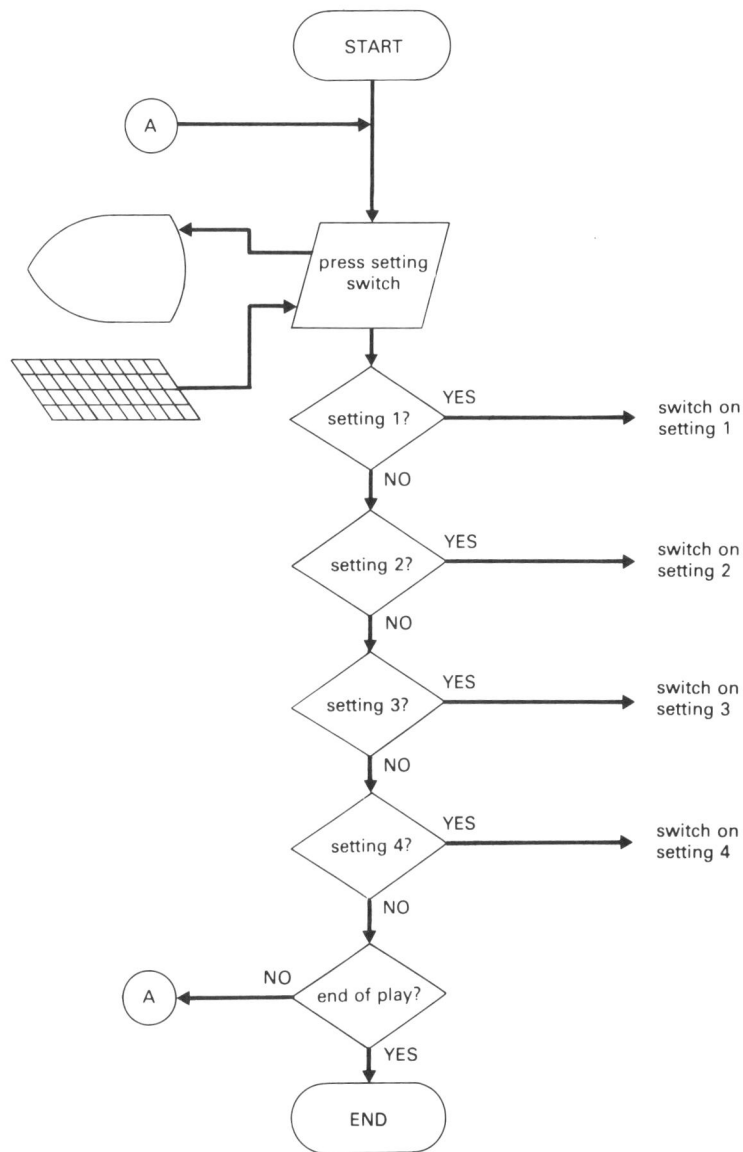

Figure 21.2   Stage lighting controls: system diagram

Documentation

- Write a set of program documentation, describing the algorithms the program uses and how it is written from them. This is so that someone else can modify the program or write another one for a different play.
- Write a user guide for someone who is operating the system while a play is in progress.

21C Activity: Buggy Fetching Boxes

Many tasks in factories and warehouses involve fetching and carrying things, and most of these tasks are routine. They follow a fixed sequence of movements which is repeated for each object to be fetched. Increasingly, such operations are automated, as described in the next section. This section simulates the operation of a mobile robot which fetches things.

The floor layout of an imaginary warehouse is shown in Figure 21.3. Boxes of identical size are laid out one behind the other by delivery lorries. The task of the robot is to fetch a set of such boxes and bring them to the point shown in the diagram. The robot has a contact switch on the front which tells it if it has bumped into something.

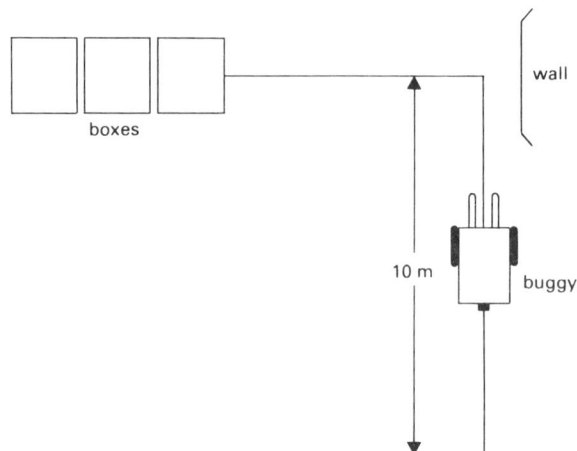

Figure 21.3   Warehouse floor layout

The Requirements of the Task

The aim of the task is to design a control system for a classroom buggy which simulates the operation of the robot described above. The minimum requirement for the buggy is that it can move forwards and backwards and turn under program control, and that it has a contact switch on the front. If it has a lifting mechanism, then so much the better.

Computer System Design

Outputs
A sequence of control instructions is sent to the buggy so that it performs the task described above.

Inputs
A signal is received from the contact switch when the buggy bumps into something.

A buggy which can be controlled by a school computer.

Processing

The buggy follows a fixed control cycle, with an algorithm as follows:

Repeat

Forward 10 m

Left 90 degrees

While no contact on switch repeat

Forward 1 box-length

Pick up box

Left 180 degrees

While no contact on switch repeat

Forward 1 box-length

Right 90 degrees

Forward 10 m

Put down box

Left 180 degrees

Note that this algorithm drives the buggy back along the line of boxes until it bumps into the wall shown in the diagram.

System Diagram

See Figure 21.4.

Implementation

Use your school's computer-controlled buggy, and a control programming language such as control Logo or control Basic.

- Look at the programming manuals to find out how to write the specific commands that are needed for the above algorithm.
- Write a program to implement the above algorithm as closely as possible. Choose the size of the box to match some boxes that you have, or can construct.
- Check the program carefully, and enter it into the computer.
- Place a large sheet of paper on the floor or on a suitable table, and make a one-tenth scale copy of Figure 21.3 on it.
- Put some boxes on the paper in the required positions.
- Place a suitable object to act as the wall where the buggy turns on its return journey.
- Connect the buggy to the computer, and place it at the starting position on the paper.
- Run the program, and check that the buggy follows the required path.
- If the buggy cannot lift the boxes, remove one by hand each time the buggy reaches it. Check that it travels to the next box in the row on its next visit.
- Make any corrections to the program that are required, and test the revised version.

Documentation

- Write a set of program documentation to describe the workings of the program. If it does not implement the above algorithm closely, include the algorithm that you used to design the program.
- Also write a set of user documentation to enable others to run the program.

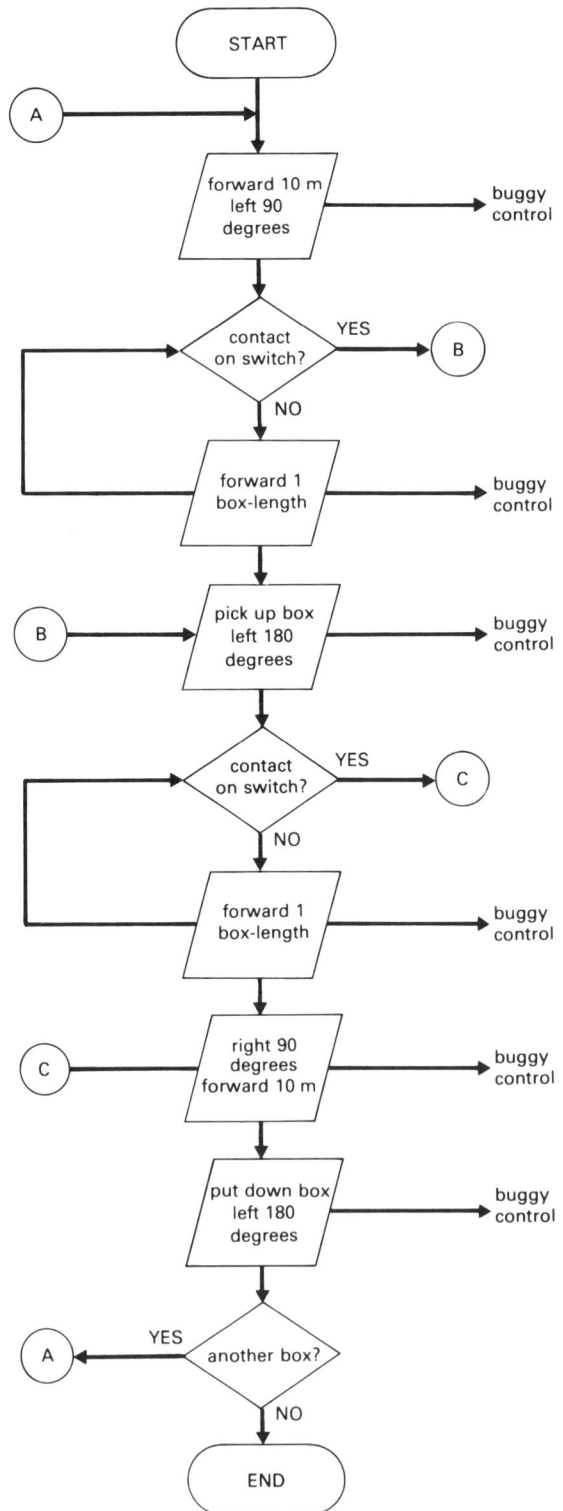

Figure 21.4   Buggy controls: system diagram

21D Application: Robots to Supply Newspaper Presses

A fetching and carrying task, very like the one simulated in the previous section, is the job of carrying rolls of newsprint to newspaper presses. Each roll weighs about a tonne, and is placed on the printroom floor when the delivery lorries are unloaded. The rolls are laid out in rows in known positions. When the presses are running, these rolls must be supplied to them as soon as they are needed. A typical layout of a pressroom floor is shown in Figure 21.5.

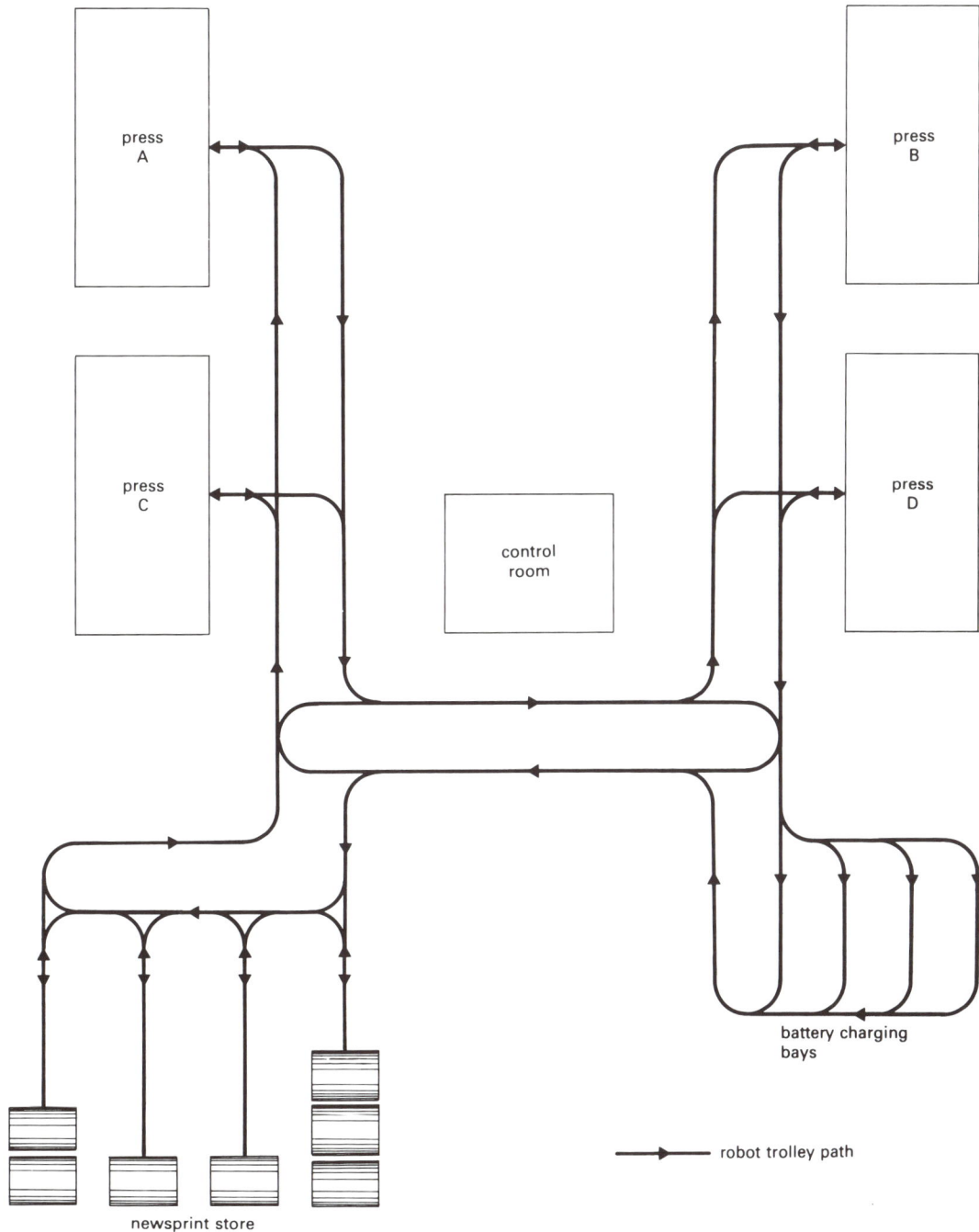

Figure 21.5 Newspaper pressroom floor layout

The Requirements of the Task

The aim of the task is to design the control system for a set of robot trolleys which carry the rolls of newsprint to the presses when they are needed. The presses issue requests for paper automatically, and the robots need to respond automatically: find a roll of paper, pick it up and take it to the press. Robots must not collide with each other, nor with people.

The robots follow paths on the floor which they detect from cables buried in the concrete. They have on-board microprocessors which deal with the details of each instruction: turning, lifting a roll of paper, etc. These microcomputers also stop the robot when a heat sensor detects that it is near a person, or a pressure switch indicates that it has bumped into something.

Computer System Design

Outputs
A sequence of control instructions to robots. These are sent by short-range radio from the computer to the robots. Each instruction starts with the number of the robot to which it is addressed. The instructions tell the robots to start, stop, reverse, pick up or put down a roll, and which way to turn at a junction.

Inputs
Before a print run starts, the initial positions of the rolls of newsprint are entered into the control system.

During a print run, the most important inputs are requests from presses for paper. The robots send a signal each time they reach a junction in their tracks and each time they have completed a task.

Processing
The computer keeps a list of requests for rolls of paper which have not been fulfilled. Each request is broken down into a set of instructions to a robot. An instruction is issued whenever a robot is free to accept one or when a robot signals that it needs information, such as which way to turn at a junction.

System Diagram

See Figure 21.6.

Implementation

The robot trolley control system uses a central computer, and local processors in each robot. The software is supplied with the robots and the computer in a complete package.

The control system works by **interrupts**. The requests from the presses take priority over all other signals, and are dealt with straight away by calling up a sequence of instructions to be issued one at a time to a robot. Incoming signals from robots also generate interrupts, but at a lower priority. At times, robots wait until the instruction they require is sent to them.

Testing

The robot control system is tested by its suppliers when it is first installed. Special test software is used to put each robot through all the operations it can do. Then the robots are tested together to make sure that the system as a whole works properly. Finally, the first few runs of the presses are supervised by engineers from the suppliers to ensure that nothing goes wrong. After any modifications have been made, the system is handed over to the newspaper staff.

Documentation

The system documentation is written and updated by the development engineers at the company which supplies the robots and the

A robot trolley carrying a roll of newsprint at the Manchester press of the *Daily Telegraph*.

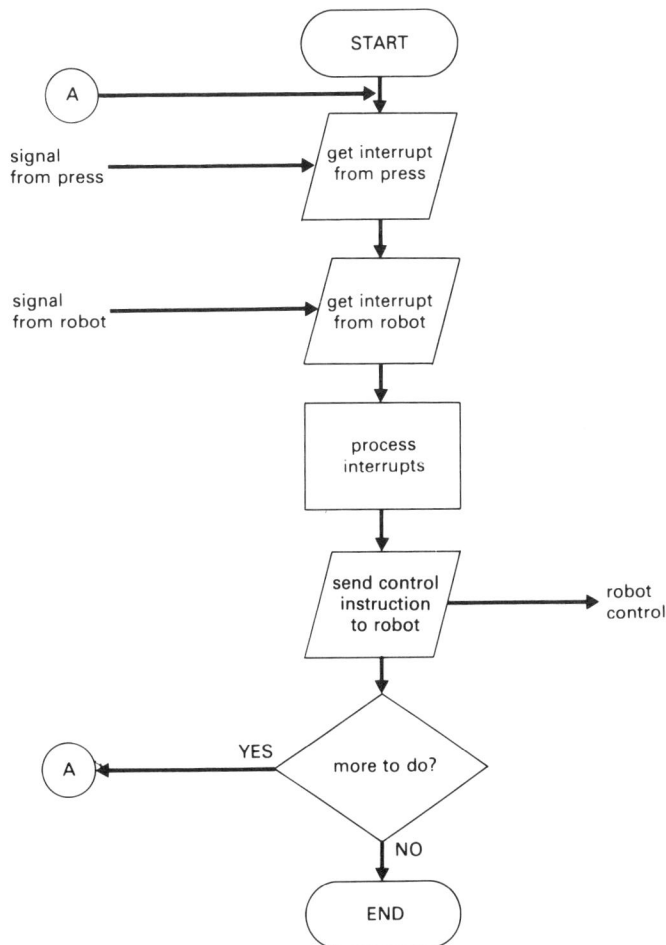

Figure 21.6   Pressroom robot control: system diagram

control computer. It contains the detailed control algorithms used, and describes the data structures used by the computer while it is running.

A set of operator documentation is supplied with the system. The robots are set up for each print run by the production manager at the newspaper. The positions of the rolls of newsprint are entered, together with such details as the number of available robots. The operator documentation describes how this is done. Once the system starts running, it operates entirely automatically.

Questions

1   What *two* safety precautions do the robots have against bumping into someone?
2   (a) In what ways do the robots save money for the newspaper company?
    (b) Do they have any other benefits, apart from cost savings?
3   Explain how **interrupts** work, using the robot control system as an example.
4   A press comes to the end of a roll of paper and issues a request for another one. Summarise the steps taken by the computer which controls the robots, and one of the robots, in dealing with the request.

At the end of the float glass process, the ribbon of glass is cut into large sheets. Here, the ribbon is running over rollers towards the cutter.

Making flat sheets of glass is an industrial process which has been practised for many centuries. A number of different techniques have been used, each able to produce larger sheets with smoother surfaces than the ones before it.

The most recent technique is the **float** process. It uses a pool of heated tin several hundred metres long. The ingredients for the glass (mostly a special type of sand) are mixed and heated in a furnace, and poured out on one end of the pool. The glass floats on the surface of the tin (hence the name of the process), and is made to flow towards the other end of the pool. By controlling the temperature at various points along the pool, the rate at which the glass flows, and the pressure on the rollers, the thickness of the glass can be controlled very precisely. As it passes over the last stages of the float run, the glass sets. It is cut into large sheets as it comes off the end of the run. A simplified diagram of the float glass production process is shown in Figure 21.7.

The float process operates around the clock. Once it has been started up, it runs non-stop for months before being halted for maintenance. The equipment represents an investment of millions of pounds by the glass manufacturer, and takes several years to construct and install. It is controlled by a computer system.

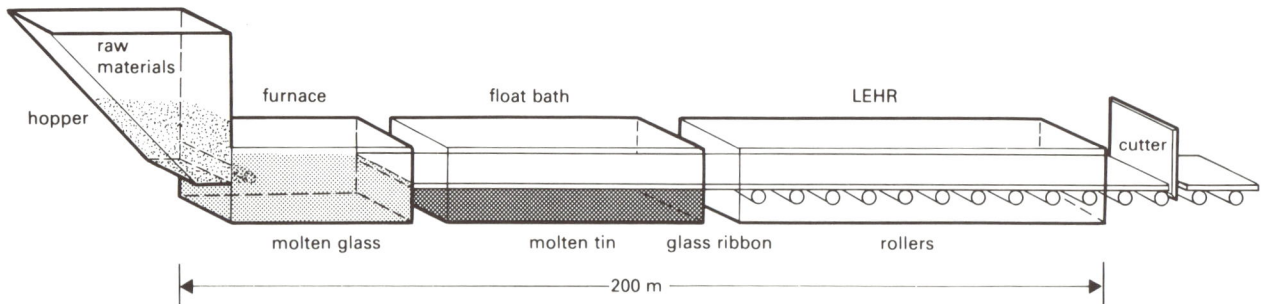

Figure 21.7 Float glass production process

The Requirements of the Task

The aim is to develop a real-time control system for the float glass production process. The system must control every aspect of the float run, and ensure that it operates non-stop. This includes the composition of the raw materials, the temperatures at all points of the run, the speed at which the glass travels, the thickness of the glass, and the cutting equipment at the end of the run.

The control system must also satisfy a number of longer-term aims:

- Production must be matched precisely to orders. The production scheduling must keep ahead of the operation of the plant, as the plant cannot stop and wait for schedules to be completed.
- The amount of wasted glass must be kept to a minimum. In particular, the width of the glass at the end of the run must be precisely controlled, as well as the size into which the sheets are cut.

- Costs need to be kept to a minimum. The main cost of production is energy: heating the glass and the large volumes of tin use large amounts of energy.

The glass itself must be of a high standard: the surfaces must be as smooth and flat as possible, the thickness even, and the composition regular.

Computer System Design

Outputs
Control instructions are sent at regular intervals to the equipment at each stage of the float run. This includes the heaters, rollers, equipment which feeds raw materials, and cutters at the end of the run.

Inputs
The immediate inputs are the sensor signals at each stage of the float run. In particular the measurement of the width and thickness of the glass at the end of the run is critical.

The longer-term inputs are types and quantities of glass required.

Processing
There are two aspects of the processing: production scheduling and real-time control. The production scheduling system analyses the requirements of each order, and works out the best sequence in which to produce the glass for them.

The control system works on a fixed cycle, as shown in the following algorithm:

Repeat indefinitely

Receive signals from sensors

Decide what control instructions are needed

Issue control instructions to heaters, cutters and rollers

This cycle is repeated every few seconds. There are a few dozen sensors, and a similar number of control elements: the computer has to send and receive hundreds of messages per second.

System Diagram

See Figure 21.8.

Implementation

The float glass control system has been developed by Pilkingtons, the glass manufacturers, who have also designed the production equipment itself. The software is custom-designed for the process, running on a central mainframe computer, with microprocessors at some of the control stations. The main problem to overcome in the design of the system is the need to run for months on end without interruption. The float glass system is operated under licence by a number of glass manufacturers in Europe and the USA.

Testing

The control system is first tested on a **simulation** of the production process. It is put through a number of test sequences, starting with simple tests and building up to more complex ones. When the control software works correctly on the simulated production process, it is tested on the newly installed equipment. The only way to test the production system as a whole is during full productive running. This is expensive, and errors in the control system could be dangerous. This is why the control software is thoroughly tested on the simulated process before being tried out 'for real'.

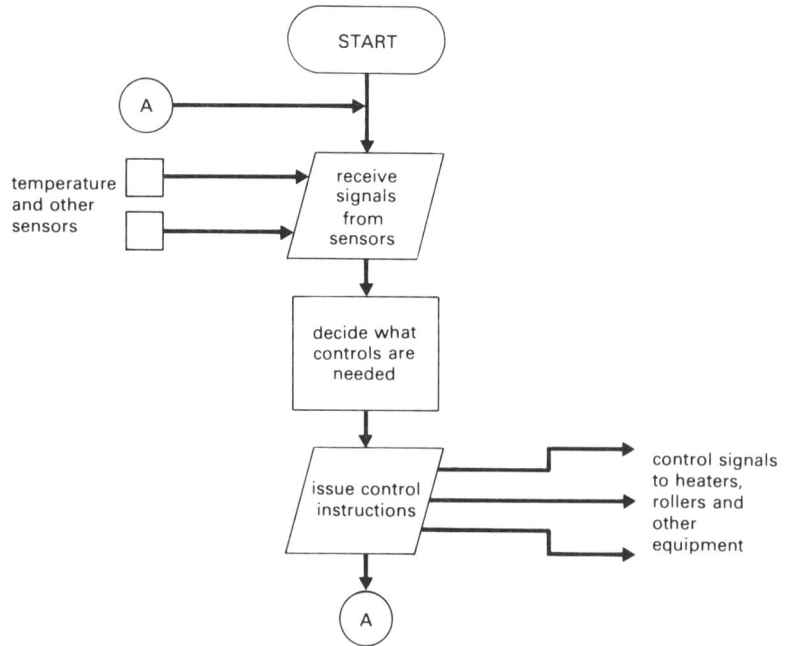

Figure 21.8 Float glass control: system diagram

Documentation

Detailed system documentation is written by the development engineers at the glass manufacturers, describing the workings of the float production equipment and the control software. This includes all the engineering drawings for the equipment, and the decision tables and operating algorithms for the control software.

Operator documentation is provided for the technicians who supervise the production process. Although the process is fully automated, it is a large and complex installation and needs constant checking. The supervisors are highly trained, and have access to detailed documentation describing each aspect of the workings of the equipment.

Questions

1 Explain the meaning of the term **real time**, using the float glass control system as an example.

2 How is the thickness of the glass controlled in a float system?

3 Why must a float glass production system operate for long periods without interruption?

4 Why must the control program be checked especially carefully before it is put into operation?

5 What are the benefits of using a computer system to control a production process such as the float system?

21F Application: Rolls Royce Aims System

A jet engine consists of a central shaft on which are mounted a number of discs, each supporting a set of turbine blades. See Figure 21.9. When the engine is running, the shaft rotates at high speed, and the gases which flow through the engine reach high temperatures and pressures. The engines must propel aircraft safely for thousands of kilometres between checks, and for millions of kilometres during their working lives. Fuel consumption, air pollution and noise must be kept to a minimum.

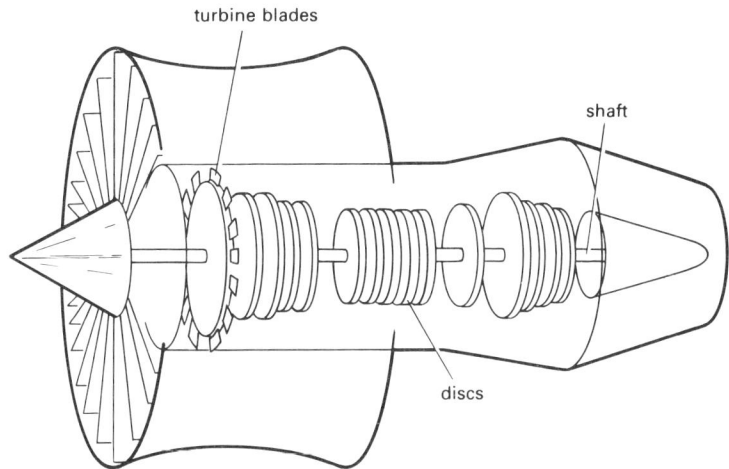

Figure 21.9 Discs and turbine blades of jet engine

In order to meet all these stringent requirements, jet engines are manufactured to the highest possible standards. Components are made from metal alloys with no cracks or impurities, and are machined to shape to fine tolerances. Thorough tests, including X-ray photographs, are made at every stage of manufacture.

Making jet engines is a highly competitive business, with manufacturers in the UK, Europe and the USA constantly trying to produce better engines at more attractive prices. Rolls Royce is the only manufacturer of jet engines in Britain, and has a substantial share of the world market. In order to maintain its share of the market, Rolls Royce has introduced a number of automated manufacturing systems over the last few years.

Several years ago, it became apparent that the way Rolls Royce was building jet engines was not very efficient. Components were machined on complex tools controlled by skilled machine operators. These were set up to make a batch of identical parts, and then readjusted to make a different batch. The readjustment process was slow, and the need to make parts in batches led to inefficient production scheduling. Each jet engine was taking more than six months to build.

Accordingly, it was decided to automate as many aspects of the production of a jet engine as possible, and bring the operation under a computerised scheduling system. Introducing computer-controlled equipment to make the turbine blades was fairly straightforward: there are hundreds of identical blades in each engine. The most complex part to automate was the fabrication of the discs on which the blades are mounted. Each engine has about sixteen discs, all of different sizes and all subject to different temperatures and pressures. The discs are very expensive: even the forged blank from which a disc is machined costs thousands of pounds.

The Requirements of the Task

The task was to replace the existing manually co-ordinated production system with an integrated set of computer-controlled equipment, with the following aims:

- To simplify the design of discs and the manufacturing operations done on them so that they can all be made by a small number of standard processes.

247

One of the workstations at the Rolls-Royce Aims production plant. The operator uses the terminal on the right, but the detailed control of the work is by computer.

- To schedule the machining stages of each component so that all the components of one engine are completed together, and the engine can be assembled as soon as possible.
- To reduce the time needed to change a machine from working on one type of component to another.
- By these means, to reduce the production time of an engine from six months to six weeks, and reduce the stocks of discs at intermediate stages of machining.
- To ensure that existing quality requirements are met or exceeded.

System Design

The only way of achieving these requirements was to introduce an **advanced integrated manufacturing system (Aims)**. The designs of the discs were simplified and standardised using CAD equipment. The forged blanks from which the discs are machined were re-designed, so that less metal needs to be cut away. (This saves money as well as time, as the cost of the disc blanks is reduced.) The general principle is the **batch of one**: each disc is worked on individually and follows the best production schedule for the engine as a whole.

Aims consists of a central computer system which co-ordinates a number of machines. Some of the machines were already in use, others are new. These carry out the various milling and turning operations on the discs. A set of robot trolleys moves the discs from one machine to another, or to an automated storage rack where they are held between operations if necessary. See Figure 21.10.

A Boeing 747 aircraft fitted with Rolls-Royce jet engines.

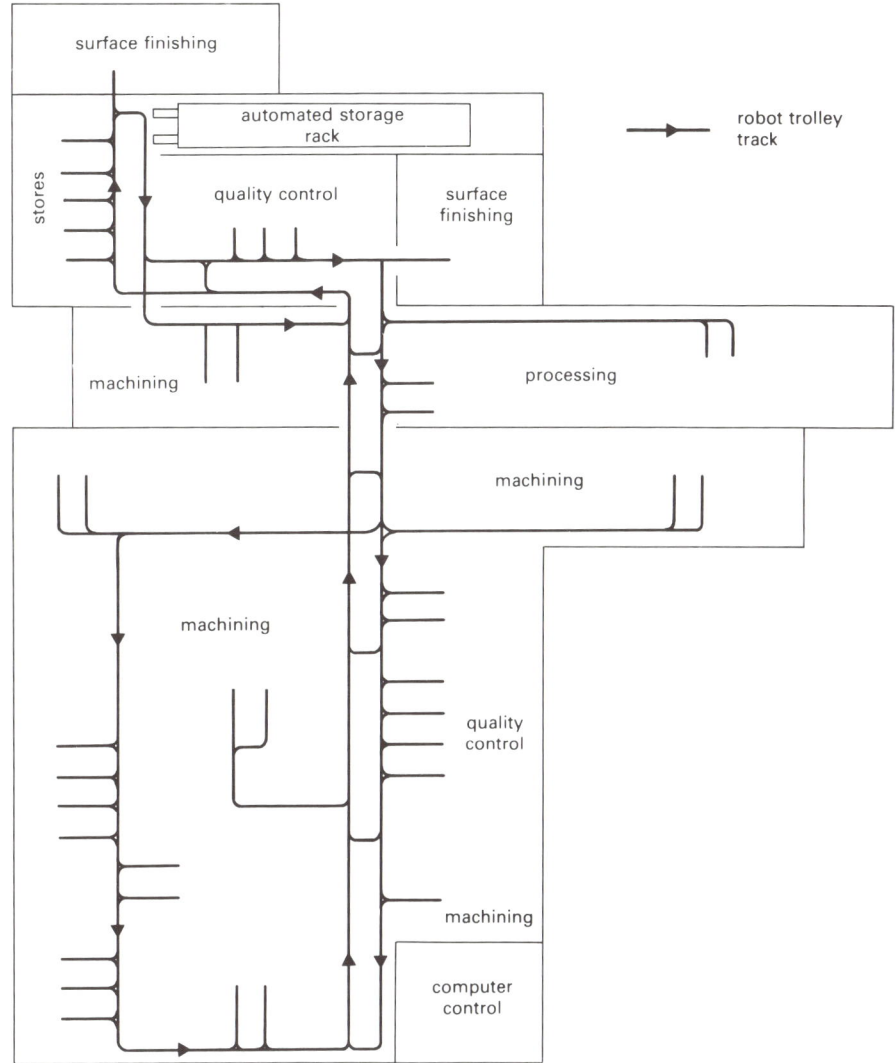
Figure 21.10   Aims production system: overall layout

Outputs

The central computer system controls some of the machines which work on the discs; others are operated manually. The computer system schedules all aspects of production and controls the stages followed by each disc. It controls the movements of the robot trolleys and the automated storage rack.

The computer system produces up-to-the minute reports on the state of manufacturing, and the progress of any component can be checked.

Inputs

The composition of each type of engine and the relevant design details of each disc are input. Also input are the production requirements: how many of each type of engine are needed on what dates. Incoming disc blanks are logged into the system.

Sensors on the robot trolleys and machines and on the automated rack store report the work done. Each disc is measured and checked after every operation; these results are input. If a disc fails a test, it may require further machining or, in rare cases, it may have to be discarded and replaced.

Processing

Aims operates in real time, around the clock. The scheduling computer system plans the stages of production of each component, according to the order schedules. Once a sequence of operations has been decided on, instructions are sent to the machines and robots to carry out this sequence. The detailed operation of some of the machines is controlled by the computer system. The computer checks constantly that production is on schedule. If something goes wrong, schedules are adjusted to compensate.

System Diagram

See Figure 21.11.

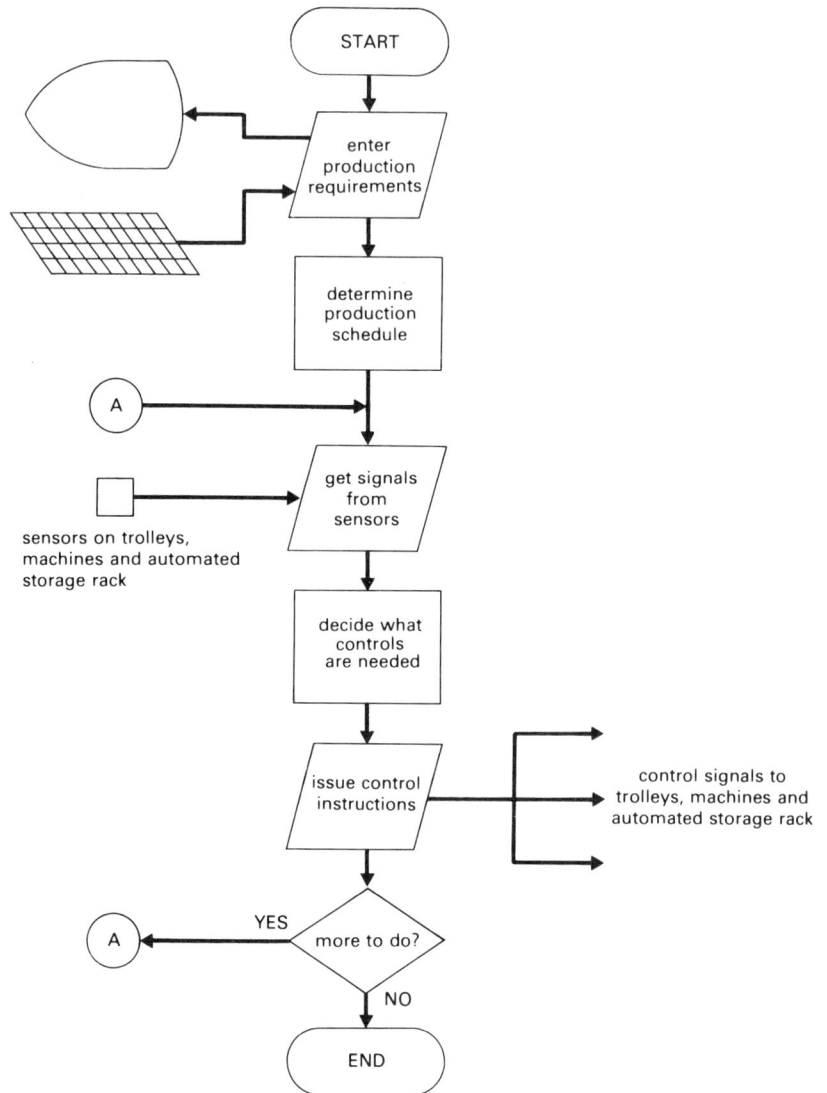

Figure 21.11   Aims system diagram

Implementation

Aims was built in an existing production area using a mixture of old and new equipment. It is the final stage of a revision of production techniques which has been going on for several years. The installation of the computers, robot trolleys and new machines was done without disrupting production. The system consists of a mainframe computer for central control, two minicomputers for workflow and handling, and a number of data collection terminals and local microcomputers for detailed movement control. It has links to the main Rolls Royce computer system.

There are eight battery-powered robot trolleys, with 45 docking stations. These are controlled via the local microcomputers, and report automatically to a battery charging area when necessary. Twelve of the 38 machine tools are computer-controlled, and there are a further 27 processing cells. Other equipment includes measuring machines, chemical facilities, electron beam welding apparatus and a variety of test equipment.

Aims paid back its design and development costs within the first year of its operation. It was installed without requiring any redundancies, and with full agreement of all the trade unions involved.

Questions

1 Why is such strict quality control necessary in the production of jet engines?
2 In what ways does the Aims system speed up the production of an engine?
3 (a) Are all the machines in the Aims system controlled by the computer?
   (b) What aspects of the system are completely computer-controlled?
4 (a) What are the benefits of the installation of the Aims system?
   (b) How long did it take to pay off its development cost?
   (c) What effects did Aims have on employment at Rolls Royce?
5 Summarise the main stages of the operation of the Aims system from the time an order is placed for an engine to the time the engine is complete.

21G Issue: Robots In, Workers Out!

Staff leaving a factory at the end of a shift.

Robots and automated process control are more reliable, cheaper and able to operate under harsher environments than manually operated equipment. Processes such as float glass manufacture could not be carried out under manual control. Automated production enables short runs of items to be manufactured for specific orders as cheaply as mass-produced goods.

One consequence of factory automation is redundancies, in large numbers in some industries such as motor manufacturing. Automated equipment needs far fewer staff than previous production methods. One of the major advantages of the new technology is lower running costs, because fewer employees have to be paid. However, the staff who are needed to supervise the new equipment are often more highly skilled than those they replace and sometimes require extensive training.

Automated production systems produce higher quality goods at lower prices, and match production to demand. They have enabled a number of companies, notably vehicle manufacturers, to reduce the huge losses they were making with previous techniques. In a number of cases, the company has been faced with the choice between changing to new production methods, or going out of business. Modern production methods enable companies to compete successfully on world markets. They lead to greater job security and higher wages for workers who remain, and contribute to the economic growth of the country.

Trade union responses to the introduction of new technology have varied from outright hostility to guarded acceptance. The first round of changes in the motor trade in Britain were bitterly resented, with

251

strikes and other forms of disruption. Recently, as companies have learned more about the process of introducing new production systems, and have consulted their workers at all stages, the opposition of trade unions to the introduction of new technology has lessened. Unions still insist on agreed working practices and reasonable wages for those who operate the new equipment, and adequate redundancy terms for those who leave. But they would not want a company to close down because it was impossible to change to new work practices. In recent years it is beginning to appear that short-sighted managements are more of an obstacle to the introduction of new technology than obstructive unions.

Questions

1 In what ways does the introduction of computers, robots and electronic control systems cause job losses?
2 What has sometimes been the alternative to the introduction of new technology?
3 What effects does the introduction of new technology have on workers who are *not* made redundant?

4 (a) Are all trade unions opposed to the introduction of new technology?
(b) Give some examples of situations where unions have opposed new technology completely, some where there has been opposition to aspects of the new systems and some where there has been agreement to introduce new technology.

21H End-of-Chapter Summary

The main points of this chapter are as follows:

- Robots and electronic control systems are being installed extensively in factories. They are used particularly in motor vehicle assembly plants, steelworks, chemical plants, oil refineries, glass manufacturing plants and other assembly plants.
- There are two types of electronic control systems: hard-wired control using logic circuits, and programmable control where a control program is run on a computer or dedicated microprocessor.
- Robots and electronic control systems have led to large numbers of redundancies. On the other hand, they have helped a number of companies to stay in business and led to higher quality goods at lower prices.

Exercise 21

1 Choose the correct word from the list for each of the following spaces:

computer; real; flow; sensors; dedicated; control; signals.

At a chemical plant, the temperature and pressure in the reactor vessels are measured by ____. These send ____ to the control ____ which processes them, and decides what ____ signals to send to the heating elements and to the valves which control the ____ of chemicals to and from the vessel. The control computer has a number of ____ microprocessors which run fast enough for the control system to operate in ____ time.

2 Modify the burglar alarm circuit in section 21A so that there are two independent light beams. The alarm is triggered if either beam is broken by someone passing through it. Draw a circuit diagram showing the modification.

3   Figure 21.12 shows the two doors used at the entrance to a high-security building. The space between the doors is only large enough for one person. The first door may be opened only if a valid pass is placed in the slot, the correct password is entered at the keypad for that pass, and the second door is closed. The second door may be opened only if the first door is closed, there is only one person in the space

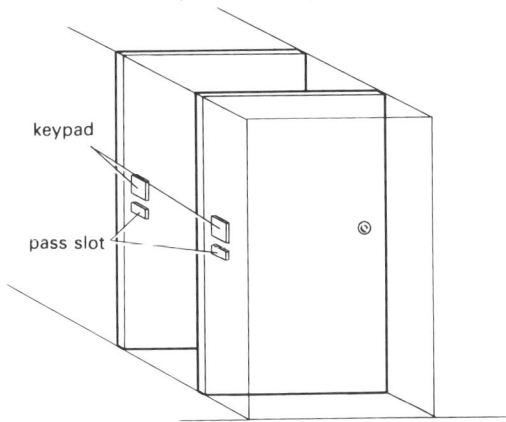

Figure 21.12   Double door entrance to high-security building

between the doors, and the pass is placed in the slot and the correct password is again entered at the keypad.

Using suitable sensors for the inputs, design logic circuits to control the operation of the two doors.

4   The stage light control system described in section 21B can be modified to control a set of disco lights. As before, a number of preset effects can be selected by the person operating the lights. Each effect can include a sequence of instructions which is repeated until a control key is pressed. It may also be possible to synchronise the lights with the music by waiting at certain points until a particular sound is detected. This requires the use of sensors which can detect high or low notes, or distinctive sounds such as cymbals.

5   The control program for a classroom buggy described in section 21C can be modified in a number of ways. Some suggestions are as follows:
(a) Wait for a control signal before the buggy fetches another box.
(b) Have several rows of boxes rather than a single one. Enter the row number of each box to be fetched before the buggy fetches it.
(c) Do not bump into the wall on the way back. (You will need to record how far the buggy has travelled to the box before it turns and comes back.)

Things to find out

1   Find out how sheets of glass were produced before the float process was introduced. (Several techniques have been used over the centuries.) Discuss the advantages and any disadvantages of the float system over previous techniques.
2   Follow the steps of sections 21D, 21E or 21F to investigate some of the applications of robots and electronic control systems listed below:
    (a) robots in motor vehicle manufacturing
    (b) robots in underwater exploration
    (c) robots in space
    (d) flexible manufacturing systems.
3* The rate at which computers and electronic control systems have been introduced in factories has been much

slower than the rate of introduction of IT in certain aspects of commerce, notably banking.
(a) Find out which types of industry have been particularly slow in the introduction of IT.
(b) Find out some of the reasons for this, and suggest some reasons of your own.
(c) Find out the consequences of this slow rate of change to IT, in particular the effect it is having on imports and exports of the type of goods concerned.
(d) Give your opinion, with reasons, of the rate at which IT is likely to be introduced into this industry in the future.

Project starters

1   A control program similar to the one in section 21C can be written for a buggy which works in a model warehouse.

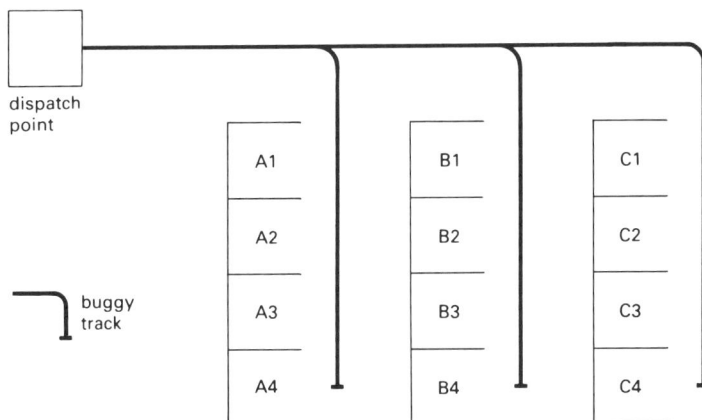

Figure 21.13   Warehouse floor layout

The storage spaces are marked out in rows, as shown in Figure 21.13. Each storage space in the warehouse is allocated a code. The buggy fetches and carries goods from a dispatch point to the storage spaces. Each time it returns to the dispatch point, it is given the code of the next storage space to visit. It then uses the module of the control program for that storage space to guide it there and then back to the dispatch point.

2   Follow the steps of section 21A, 21B or 21C to design a control system to simulate the operation of any of the following:
(a) a door which opens automatically when someone approaches
(b) a set of traffic lights
(c) a railway level crossing
(d) an automatic signalling system on a model railway
(e) a lift.

22

Artificial Intelligence, Expert Systems and Fifth Generation Computers

Over the past forty years, developments in computing have been aimed at producing smaller, faster and cheaper information processing machines. Very recently, the direction of research in computing has changed. Now the aim is to produce computers which are more intelligent. Fifth Generation computers, as they are being called, will be much more powerful than any computers in use today, and will have greater reasoning powers.

This chapter introduces three background topics of Fifth Generation computers—artificial intelligence, knowledge representation and expert systems—and then discusses the idea of a Fifth Generation computer, and some of the projects at present under way to develop them. If the projects are successful, Fifth Generation computers will come into use during the 1990s.

22A Artificial Intelligence

An Inmos transputer chip. It contains input, output, processing memory circuits. It can be used to build up a computer used for artificial intelligence applications.

The extent to which machines, and computers in particular, can behave in a manner which we would judge as intelligent has been a source of fascination for many years. Scientists, engineers, writers of both fiction and non-fiction, philosophers, poets, musicians and film-makers have explored the possibilities of machine intelligence in their own ways. Unfortunately, most of the success has been in fiction—films such as *2001: A Space Odyssey* are masterpieces of art, but not of computer design. Nevertheless, some progress towards artificial intelligence has been made, in the areas discussed below.

One of the most serious problems connected with artificial intelligence is that there is no simple, agreed definition of human intelligence to act as a reference point. We agree that some people are more intelligent than others, and that a word processor is more intelligent than a typewriter, but the precise notion of intelligence is not clear. We have only a limited knowledge of how the brain and nervous system works, and even less knowledge of the workings of the subconscious mind. We do know that intelligence has to do with recognising patterns, making reasoned decisions and using and understanding language, but it is more than all these. It contains an elusive 'spark' which enables us to evolve new ideas and gain new insights.

Another problem with artificial intelligence is knowledge representation, a topic discussed in section 22B.

The Turing Test for Artificial Intelligence

Alan Turing (1912 to 1954).

The only accepted definition of artificial intelligence was proposed by the mathematician Alan Turing in 1950. It gets around the problem of our lack of an accepted definition of human intelligence in a very simple way.

The Turing test requires two identical computer terminals in a room. One is connected to a computer in an adjacent room, and the other is connected to another terminal, also in an adjacent room, operated by a person. See Figure 22.1. If anyone using the two identical terminals cannot tell which is connected to the computer and which is connected to the person, then the computer passes the test of having artificial intelligence.

In practice the Turing test is extremely difficult and no computer has come anywhere near to passing it. As made clear in chapters 1 to 3, computers are information processing machines which can make complex yes/no decisions but have no powers of understanding. Nevertheless, some progress has been made towards the goal of the Turing test, as described in the next few sections.

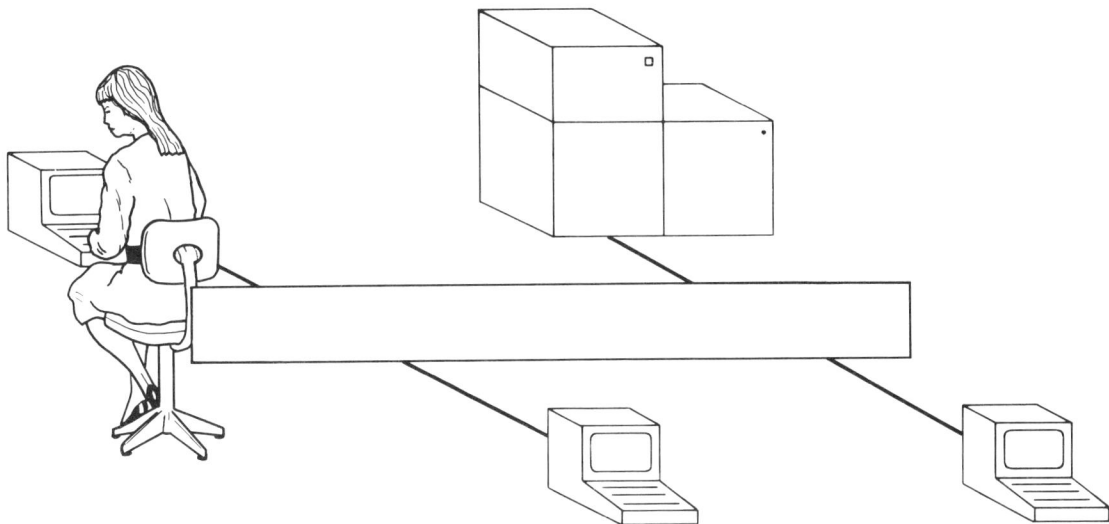

Figure 22.1   Turing test for artificial intelligence

Developments in Artificial Intelligence

Intensive work by a small group of dedicated researchers has led to progress in four areas of artificial intelligence: game playing programs, reasoning programs, natural language recognition and expert systems. The first three are discussed here; the fourth in section 22C.

Game playing programs have recently been developed to an extent which few people would have thought possible ten years ago. For example, chess playing programs were very crude until quite recently, whereas the best ones are now approaching grandmaster level and a good game can be played by many microcomputers. At present the world backgammon champion is a computer program. Progress has been due partly to a better understanding of the strategies and tactics behind various games, and partly to the increased power of modern computers. Some simple games (such as noughts and crosses, but not chess) can be won by the computer trying every possible combination of moves at each stage and choosing the best one.

Reasoning programs have been the subject of intensive research, with significant progress in several areas. The programming language **Lisp** used for most reasoning programs is beginning to achieve widespread popularity. Two other languages which have evolved from Lisp, **Logo** and **Prolog**, are even more promising. Logo is being used to teach programming to very young children and lies behind the idea of turtle graphics, a very powerful teaching tool. Prolog is used for programs which draw conclusions from large stores of structured information—see section 22B. It is being used in a number of Fifth Generation projects. (Prolog is also being taught in some schools.)

The most significant achievement of reasoning programs came in 1977 when a computer was used to assist with the proof of the famous **Four Colour Theorem**. This theorem states that only four colours are needed to shade a map of any degree of complexity without any adjacent areas having the same colour. See Figure 22.2. The Four Colour Theorem has been known for centuries, but was not proved until a computer was used to generate and test the large number of basic configurations that a map can have.

It is now known that languages can be classified according to their complexity. Natural languages such as English are the most complex, and computer programming languages are in the next category. It follows that computers in their present form are not capable of understanding long passages of text in a natural language. However, they can come fairly close to an understanding in certain specialised areas. For example, there are some military systems in existence which can interpret the various commands needed to steer a ship or submarine. At frequent intervals, applications are announced which can cope with a larger vocabulary than before, but the general problem of natural language interpretation remains unsolved.

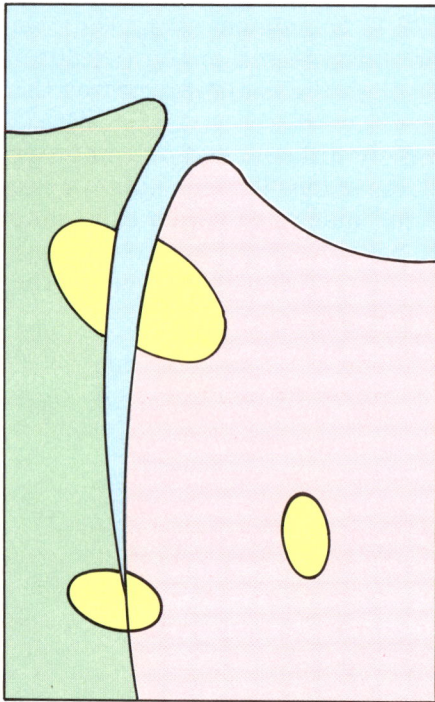

Figure 22.2 Map shaded in four colours

Questions

1 What are the main difficulties facing people working in artificial intelligence?
2 What approach does a computer take when playing a game?
3 What is the difficulty in developing a computer system which can cope with a natural language?
4 (a) If it were possible to construct a robot which could see, hear and walk like a person, discuss the problem of programming the robot to cross a road safely.
(b) Use this discussion to draw some conclusions about the limits to human intelligence, and the extent to which it can be transferred to a computer.

22B Knowledge Representation

Computers as we use them today process information. Methods of representing information as data for use by a computer are discussed in chapter 2. Intelligent computer systems process knowledge—items of information and relationships between the items. Figure 22.3 shows a simple set of knowledge: the family tree of Queen Elizabeth II. It contains a number of items of information, and a relationship 'child-of'.

The relationships in a diagram such as Figure 22.3 can be written down as follows:

Charles child-of Elizabeth
William child-of Charles   etc.

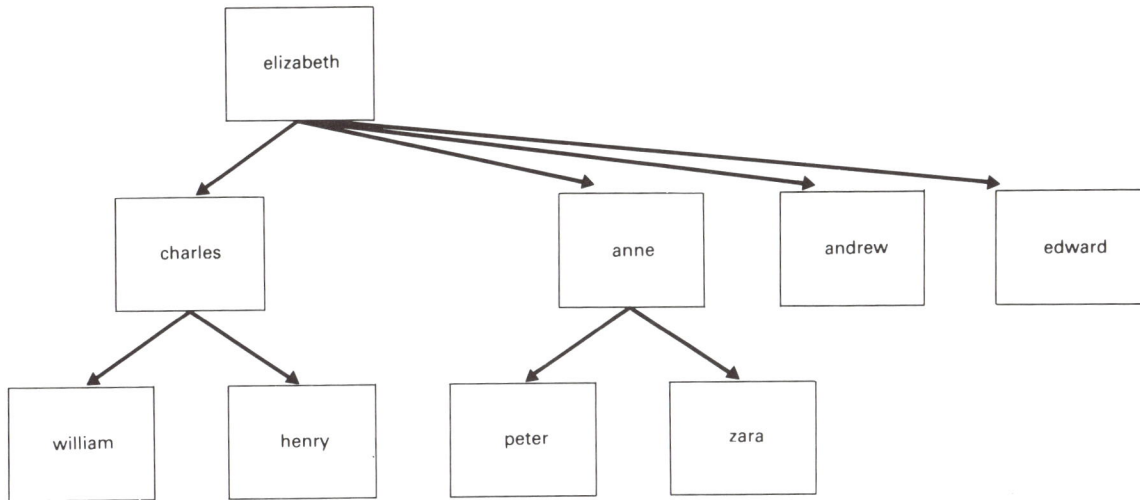

Figure 22.3   Family tree of Queen Elizabeth II

Rules can be added which provide additional knowledge. For example, a new relationship 'parent-of' can be defined as the opposite of the 'child-of' relationship:

x parent-of *y* if *y* child-of *x*

Relationships and rules in this form can be entered into a computer using a programming language such as Prolog. Questions can then be asked of the computer, which uses the knowledge base to answer them. For example if the relationships from Figure 22.3 and the above rule were on a computer, it could be asked:

Which *x*: *x* child-of Elizabeth?

to which the answers are:

Charles   Anne   Andrew   Edward

If asked the question:

which *y*: *y* parent-of William?

the answer is:

Charles

Questions

1 Using Figure 22.3, and the 'parent-of' rule, write the answers to the following questions:
  (a) Which *y*: *y* child-of Anne?
  (b) Which *x*: Charles parent-of *x*?
  (c) Which *y*: *y* child-of Edward?

2 Relationships can be written which concern only one item of information. For example, the relationships which divide the royal family into male and female members are:

Charles is-male
Elizabeth is-female   etc.

A rule can be based on two relationships joined by AND. For example:

x father-of *y* if *x* parent-of *y* AND *x* is-male

  (a) Write the remaining 'is-male' and 'is-female' relationships for the royal family.

  (b) Which *x*: *x* father-of William?
  (c) Which *y*: Charles father-of *y*?
  (d) Which *z*: *z* father-of Anne?
  (e) Write a rule for the relationship 'mother-of'.
  (f) Which *x*: *x* mother-of Zara?
  (g) Which *z*: Elizabeth mother-of *z*?

3 Write a rule for 'grandparent-of'. Use the rule to answer the following questions:
  (a) Which *x*: *x* grandparent-of Peter?
  (b) Which *y*: Elizabeth grandparent-of *y*?

4 Draw a diagram of your own family tree, starting from one of your grandparents.
  (a) Write the 'child-of' relationships for your family tree.
  (b) Write a set of questions using the 'parent-of', 'mother-of', 'father-of' and 'grandparent-of' relationships for your family tree. Write the answers to these questions that a

257

computer would produce.

5* Other relationships such as 'married-to', and the additional family members they involve, can be added to the royal family tree or your own family tree. Relationships such as 'brother-of' are a little complicated:

x brother-of y if x child-of z AND y child-of z AND x is-male

(a) Add the husbands and wives of the members of the royal family to a copy of Figure 22.3, and write down the 'married-to' relationship.

(b) Define a 'sister-of' rule like the 'brother-of' rule above.

(c) Use the brother, sister and child rules to define *two* rules for 'cousin-of'.

22C Expert Systems

The aspect of artificial intelligence in which the most progress has been made, and which is likely to be the main application of Fifth Generation computers, is **expert systems**. An expert system is a computer program which will give reasoned advice on a particular topic, drawing on a large store of information about the topic. Some expert systems are even able to learn from their mistakes.

An expert system is built up by 'picking the brains' of a human expert—a surgeon, geologist, lawyer or social security administrator, for example. An information store is built up of all the facts known to the expert, as well as the 'rules of thumb' used in the interpretation of these facts. In many cases, these rules are incomplete or contradictory, and various measures have to be adopted to resolve these inconsistencies.

The first widely used expert system is one which assists in oil exploration. It accepts as input various geological evidence, and outputs sites which are relatively favourable for drilling wells. It is by no means perfect, but with the huge costs of oil exploration, even a small improvement in the success rate of wells brings about great savings. The cost of the expert system is negligible compared with the other costs involved.

Several types of expert systems are now under development. The one with most potential is medical diagnosis. Diagnosis is a very difficult process, relying on a combination of scientific knowledge, experience and insight. Expert systems for the diagnosis of certain types of ailments, such as kidney diseases, are already in operation. If a general practitioner's diagnosis system proves to be feasible, then it will have wide applications, particularly in Third World countries. There is already some evidence that patients will answer questions more thoroughly and honestly at a computer terminal than when asked directly by a doctor.

Questions

1 What is an expert system? Explain the term in your own words, giving some examples.

2 What do expert systems do which other (present-day) computer systems cannot do?

3 Would you rather be interviewed by a doctor, or use a computer terminal to enter the symptoms of a medical problem? Give reasons for your opinion.

4 List some potential applications of expert systems. In each case, comment on the benefits of the application.

22D Fifth Generation Computers

The idea of a Fifth Generation computer was publicly launched in Japan in October 1981. The Japanese **Ministry of International Trade and Industry (MITI)** announced that it was setting up a project to bring Fifth Generation computers into existence, and invited other countries to join an international programme based on this project. For various reasons, the other leading information technology countries (the USA, Britain and the other EEC nations) have decided not to join the Japanese initiative. Instead, each has started a Fifth Generation research programme of its own. Accordingly, the race is on to produce the first Fifth Generation computer, and the prize is big—leadership in the world computing industry for the winner, if there is one.

What is a Fifth Generation Computer?

A Fifth Generation computer is one which is able to draw reasoned conclusions from a body of knowledge. The knowledge is structured as explained in section 22B. For example, a Fifth Generation computer used by an airline might be able to advise the airline managers on the routes to plan for its services and the prices to charge for its tickets. A Fifth Generation computer might be able to work out the best arrangement of components on a chip, or the layout of the heating system in a large building.

Figure 22.4 shows the essential components of a Fifth Generation computer. It consists of a **knowledge base**, an **inference processor** and an **intelligent user interface**. The knowledge base stores not only very large quantities of information, but also relationships between the information and rules defining other relationships. A knowledge base has a much more complicated structure than the largest databases in use at present, and requires sophisticated accessing mechanisms.

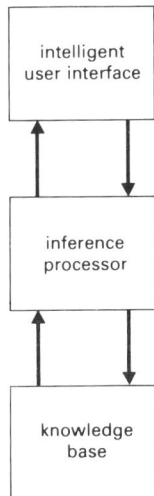

Figure 22.4   The components of a Fifth Generation computer

An inference processor is able to draw reasoned conclusions from the knowledge and rules in the knowledge base. It consists of a large number of processing elements working in parallel. It needs to be able to resolve inconsistencies in the knowledge base, make 'educated' guesses, and demonstrate its line of reasoning if required.

The intelligent user interface is intended to enable people to use Fifth Generation computers very easily, even if they are not computer specialists. Input/output techniques such as image processing, voice recognition and speech synthesis will almost certainly be used. However, the main difference between intelligent user interfaces and those in use today is that they will be much more closely matched to the requirements of the people using the computer rather than to the requirements of the computer.

Fifth Generation computers require much greater processing speeds and data storage capacities than the best available at present. Furthermore, the software controlling them will be far more complex than anything written for present-day computers. There are several research projects at present in progress to bring about the technological advances necessary for Fifth Generation computers to be produced. They are described in the next few sections.

Japan: The Icot Programme

Fifth Generation computer development in Japan is centred at the **Institute for New Generation Computer Technology (Icot)**. Icot was set up in 1982 with a ten-year, three-phase programme. The first phase (now complete) is to carry out feasibility studies and develop the hardware and software tools needed for further research. The second phase is to develop and test knowledge bases and inference processors, and to develop parallel computer architectures. The final phase, starting in 1989, is to build a prototype Fifth Generation computer. Icot is staffed by scientists and engineers from Japanese universities and IT companies.

The USA: Darpa and the MCC

The USA has no national Fifth Generation computer project, but there are two advanced research programmes in this field. One is a series of military projects sponsored by the **Defense Advanced Research Project Agency (Darpa)**. These include work on voice recognition, speech synthesis, natural language analysis, relational databases, image processing and advanced semiconductor design.

The other project, the **Microelectronic and Computer Technology Corporation (MCC)** is a consortium of leading American information technology companies. Emphasis is on computer-aided design techniques for chip fabrication, image processing and expert systems. IBM is not a member of the MCC, but with a research and development budget of $1 billion per year, it is no doubt doing some Fifth Generation research of its own.

The EEC: Esprit

The **European Strategic Research Programme in Information Technology (Esprit)** was set up in 1982 to co-ordinate the European Fifth Generation work. It is a ten-year programme, providing EEC funds for projects carried out by European IT companies and universities covering various aspects of advanced information technology. In addition to work on expert systems and intelligent user interfaces, the programme covers such topics as office automation. Esprit encourages projects which involve collaboration between universities and companies. A number of projects are already under way, several being carried out by British companies.

Britain: The Alvey Programme

The British Fifth Generation programme was set in motion by a committee chaired by John Alvey, Technology Director of British Telecom. The committee heard evidence from all sectors of the UK information technology industry and produced a report outlining what should be done. The **Alvey Report** was published in October 1982 and adopted in April 1983. It outlined a five-year national programme for advanced information technology, concentrating on four key enabling technologies. These are **software engineering**, **VLSI chips**, **intelligent user interfaces** and **intelligent knowledge-based systems (IKBS)**. (An intelligent knowledge-based system is the term used in the Alvey Report to describe an inference processor operating on a knowledge base, as described above.) A fifth line of development, parallel computer architectures, has also been followed.

A directorate was set up to administer government grants to companies and university departments undertaking projects in the four key areas. Up to 50% of the research and development costs of each project can be funded. Contacts are maintained with the Esprit programme to ensure that there is no duplication of effort. All the Alvey funds have now been allocated to projects, and the programme is in its final stages.

Questions

1 What are the parts of a Fifth Generation computer?
2 In what ways does a Fifth Generation computer differ from previous types of computer?
3 Why is it necessary for a Fifth Generation computer to have an intelligent user interface?
4 (a) In what ways does the Icot programme differ from the other Fifth Generation projects?
   (b) What are the three stages of the Icot programme?
5 What work is IBM doing towards Fifth Generation computers?

22E End-of-Chapter Summary

The Fifth Generation projects are giving a strong sense of direction and purpose to the computing industry throughout the world, and providing a means of injecting large sums of state funds into IT research. Even if the ultimate aim of an intelligent computer is not achieved, there is no doubt that a lot will be learned along the way.

The main points of this chapter are as follows:

- Artificial intelligence is the idea that a computer can be made to behave in a way which people would judge as intelligent.
- The Turing test for artificial intelligence is based on a computer being compared with the actions of a person, both working through identical terminals.
- Significant progress has been made in four aspects of artificial intelligence: game playing programs, reasoning programs, natural language recognition and expert systems.
- An expert system is a computer program which gives reasoned advice, based on a store of information, on a particular topic.
- A Fifth Generation computer is able to draw reasoned conclusions from a knowledge base. It consists of a knowledge base, an inference processor and an intelligent user interface.
- Fifth Generation computer development projects are at present under way in Japan (Icot), the USA (Darpa and the MCC), Europe (Esprit) and Britain (the Alvey programme).

Exercise 22

1 Choose the correct word from the list for each of the following spaces:

inference; network; single; results; logical; processors; data; memory; parallel.

A computer based on ___ architecture contains a number of ___ connected to a segmented ___ by a high-speed parallel ___. Each processor operates independently, taking the instructions and ___ it needs from memory and returning the ___ to memory. This computer could be used as an ___ processor in a Fifth Generation system. It can make ___ inferences far more quickly than a conventional computer based on a ___ processor.

2 The following relationships and rules describe the optional subjects taken by a group of school pupils:

John takes History	John takes French
Susan takes Physics	Susan takes Biology
Paul takes French	Paul takes History
Alice takes Physics	Alice takes French
Samantha takes French	Samantha takes Biology

x classmate-of y if x takes z AND y takes z

(a) Draw a diagram like Figure 22.3 to show the above relationships.
(b) Which x: Susan takes x?
(c) Which y: y takes Physics?
(d) Which z: z classmate-of Susan?
(e) Which x: x classmate-of John?

3 Assuming that Fifth Generation computers are produced, which of the following applications will they be capable of:
(a) long-range weather forecasts
(b) medical diagnosis
(c) assistance with making social security claims
(d) making laws
(e) advising lawyers about cases
(f) replacing most of the work of a teacher
(g) replacing most of the work of a factory manager
(h) advising a factory manager in his or her work?

Points to discuss

1 In your opinion, what benefits will be gained from Fifth Generation research, even if intelligent knowledge-based computers are not produced as a result? What disadvantages are there in starting a research programme when the end result may prove impossible to achieve?

2 Based on your knowledge of the capabilities and limitations of present-day computers, how close do you think we will come to producing Fifth Generation computers? Give reasons for your opinion.

23 Applications Review

This chapter covers a number of general points which arise from the previous thirteen chapters on types of computer application. It discusses a way of classifying computer applications, the elementary data processing operations, and the structure of data files. The material is more technical than that in the previous application chapters.

23A Types of Computer Application

Computer applications can be classified according to the way the information is processed, and how a person using the computer system interacts with it. The classes are similar to the types of operating system described in section 8F, and an application can belong to more than one class.

Batch Processing

A major batch processing application—cheques are being sorted and the data on them being input at the Bankers Automated Clearing System.

Batch processing systems process large collections of similar sets of data. Each set of data refers to one transaction, such as the cashing of a cheque. The sets of data are processed one at a time, each going through the same input–process–output cycle. The batch processing system works through a large number of such sets of data in one operation.

The commonest example is payroll processing: a set of data is input for each person on the payroll. It is processed in the same way, and the output—a payslip—is the same for each person. The entire payroll is processed in one run of the program.

Batch processing systems have no external interaction while they are running. The input data is prepared beforehand and stored on magnetic disk or tape. This **transaction data** is used to update one or more files of **master data**. New versions of the master files are produced. The output is printed or stored on tape or disk. See Figure 23.1. Batch processing systems can take a long time to run: several minutes, a few hours or even running overnight are common.

Interactive Processing

Interactive computer systems operate by means of a **dialogue** between the user and the computer system. The person using the computer enters data and instructions, generally from a keyboard or mouse, and the computer responds immediately. The most highly interactive computer application is word processing: the word processor responds to each keystroke, displaying the character on the screen, lining up the text, moving to a new page, etc.

Real-time Processing

A real-time computer system must keep pace with some external process. The computer system responds to inputs quickly enough for the outputs to be acted upon by the external process. **Process**

control systems which monitor and control equipment are all in this category. An example is the on-board guidance system of a missile. It monitors the path of the missile and the movements of the target, processes this data very quickly, and sends control signals to the rockets.

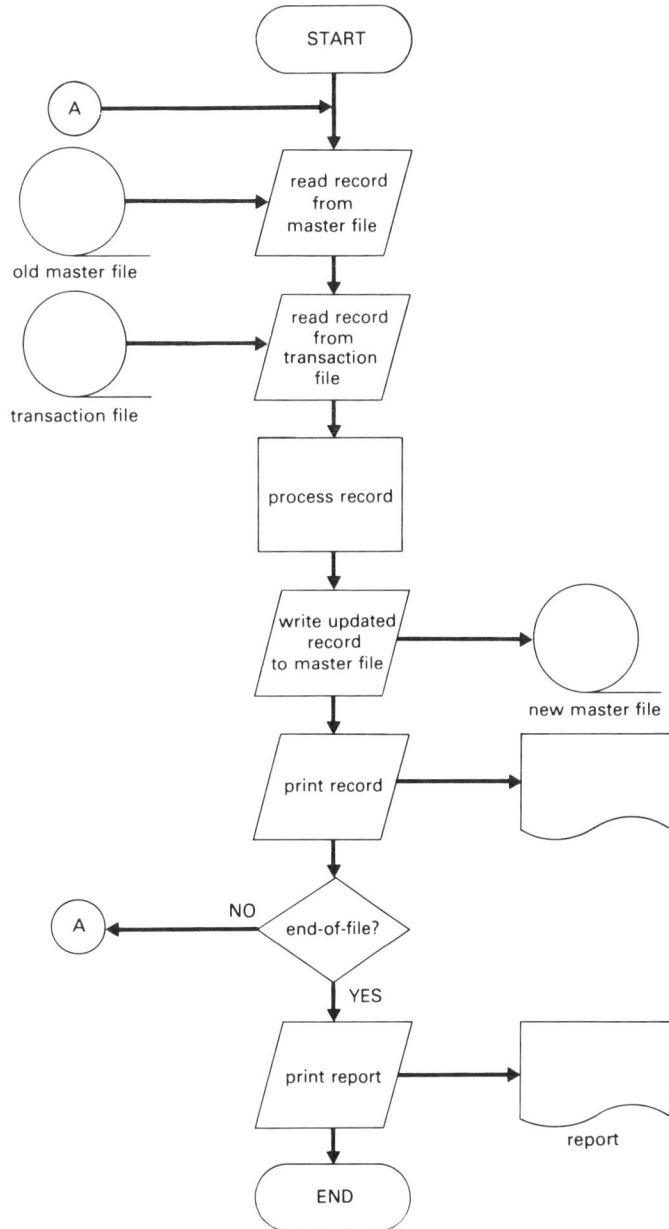

Telephone bookings being entered into the British Caledonian flight reservation computer.

Figure 23.1   Batch processing system: system diagram

Transaction Processing

Transaction processing systems carry out a complete input–process–output cycle on a set of data in real time. The set of data concerns one transaction. An example is airline reservation systems. The information for a reservation is input, the reservation is made and the tickets are printed straight away. The files containing the reservation information are updated on disk during the process. If the transaction cannot be completed, for example because no seat is available on the required flight, the files are 'rolled back' to their state before the transaction was started.

263

Database Systems

A database system has a large, central store of data which is used by all the computer applications in an organisation. Many businesses use database systems for stock control, order processing, accounting and planning. The benefit of a database system is that information is not duplicated. For example, there is only one file of customer addresses. If a customer moves to a new address, this is entered once and is then available to all the applications.

Multi-access and Distributed Systems

Multi-access computer systems have networks of terminals linked to a central computer. The terminals may be in the same building as the processor, or may be linked to it from other sites by telephone. Many transaction processing systems are also multi-access systems. These require simultaneous access to the central data files from any terminal. Some systems like this have to handle high data through-put rates: a few airline reservation systems can cope with hundreds of transactions per second.

Distributed systems have the processing shared by a number of computers. These can be at the same site or linked remotely by high-speed data channels. In most cases, different computers on the network do different tasks. For example, the head office of a company may have a computer for planning and recording reports of production, and computers at a number of processing plants which control the machines and do order processing and stock control.

Questions

1 Choose the correct word from the list for each of the following spaces:

database; multi-access; distributed system; transaction processing; terminals; applications; batch processing.

In the past, the stock control system at a warehouse recorded stock movements every night in a single ____ operation. At present a ____ system is used, where each stock movement is recorded as it takes place. The company is planning to integrate stock control with other computer ____ in a single ____ system. The planned system will be ____, with a number of ____ linked to a central computer.

2 Can a computer application be both:
   (a) batch processing and interactive?
   (b) real-time and interactive?
   (c) real-time and transaction processing?
   (d) batch processing and part of a database system?
   (e) batch processing and process control?
   (f) multi-access and transaction processing?
   (g) batch processing and a distributed system?

   Give an example in each case where the answer is 'yes'.

3 Classify each of the following applications as batch processing, interactive, real-time, process control, transaction processing, distributed processing or database system (or more than one of these):
   (a) a weekly payroll system
   (b) a word processing system
   (c) a control system for a gas pipeline
   (d) a system which records experimental results, and analyses them when the experiment is finished
   (e) a cash terminal system at a bank
   (f) a stock control system which records stock movements as they take place, and updates the stock levels every night.

4 (a) What is the main benefit of database systems?
   (b) Write down any disadvantages of database systems you can think of.

23B Data Processing Operations

Most computer systems are based on a set of standard operations. The details of these vary from one system to another, but the principles are the same in all cases. These standard operations have been mentioned in some of the applications chapters. Their general features are described here.

Data Capture and Input

Computer systems need to **capture** data from external sources. Various methods of data capture have been developed to allow the data to be transferred as quickly as possible to the computer with the minimum of errors. As described in section 4C, techniques of data capture include reading from sensors, bar code readers and magnetic strip readers. Optical character readers (OCR) read data which is printed in a special typeface; magnetic ink character recognition (MICR) equipment recognises the characters printed in magnetic ink on cheques. In this way data is read directly from **source documents** without having to be retyped. This reduces errors during input.

In many data processing systems, the output from one process is the input for the next. The commonest examples are gas, water, electricity and telephone accounting systems. The accounts which are printed and sent to customers include payslips. The payslips are the input documents for the system which records payments. These **turnaround documents** have OCR figures which are printed by the first process and read back by the second. This saves a lot of time because, for routine payments, no additional input data needs to be entered. Errors are also less likely.

If it is not possible to capture data directly from source, the commonest method of input is to type data at a keyboard. This input data is first written on specially designed **input forms**. These are set out as clearly as possible, with any data codes explained carefully. The forms are designed to be easy to fill in and easy to read when typing the data. The aim is to reduce errors during data entry. Figure 23.2 shows a data input form for the club membership system from chapter 9.

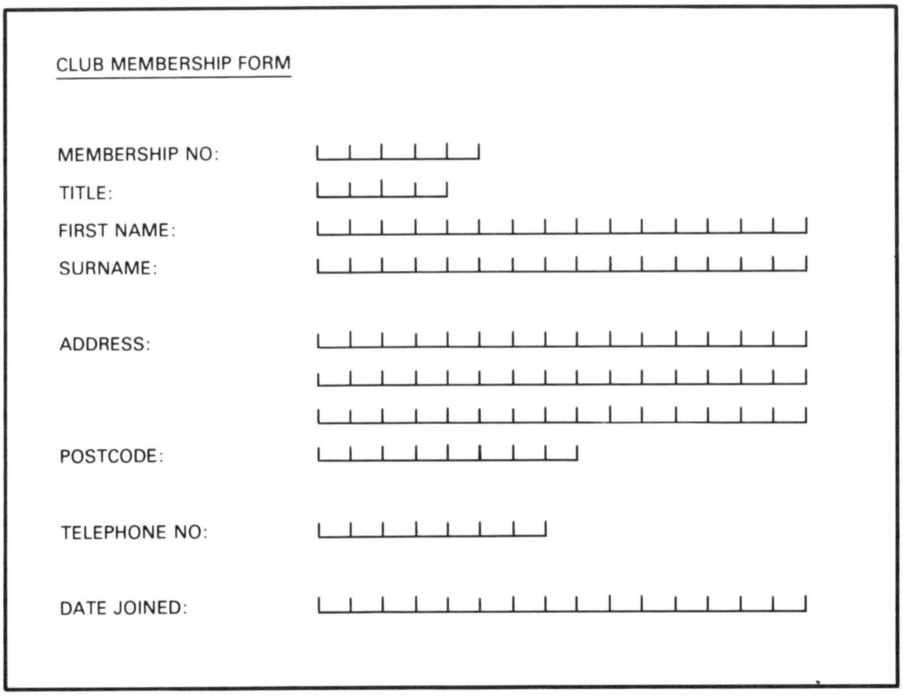

Figure 23.2 Club membership system: data entry form

Managers at a meeting—a large amount of information is needed for a meeting of this nature, which must be presented as clearly as possible.

Verification

In the days of punched cards, data was punched by one operator and then verified by another operator. The second operator entered the same data and the card punch checked to see whether what was being punched was the same as the data already on the card.

This practice is still used today on a few data entry systems. The data is entered twice at a terminal, the second time as a check against what was entered the first time. In most systems, operators check the data on the screen against what they are entering and correct any errors which they see.

Validation

Input data is **validated** (checked) in a number of ways, to eliminate errors as far as possible before they cause problems in processing. Automatic checks are carried out by bar code readers, magnetic strip readers and OCR and MICR equipment on each item of data as it is read. Most indicate by a light or sound that the data has been read successfully.

Data entered at the keyboard is tested according to its nature. Transaction processing systems check each item as it is entered, and reject an item if a check fails. Some batch processing systems work in this way; others check all the data in one operation and produce an **error report** listing the errors. See Figure 23.3.

```
Payroll Validation Run          Error Report        26/01/87

Data File: Transaction Data - January 1987

Record      Employee No     Error(s)
  17        J1783M          Missing No of Days Worked
  29        M4379P          Bonus out of range
  74        P3127J          No of Days Worked out of range
 172        R9123F          Missing No of Days Worked
 183        R9721G          Alphabetic character in Bonus
 201        T4342P          Alphabetic character in Days Worked
```

Figure 23.3 Batch processing system: error report

Presence checks

The first check is to see that there is a data item there at all! Many data items, particularly account numbers, credit card numbers and other identification, cannot be blank—if no item is entered, this is regarded as an error.

Type checks

Many data items are of a particular type: numbers, dates, sums of money, etc. For such items, each character can be checked as it is typed, and incorrect keystrokes can be rejected. For example, each character of a whole number must be a decimal digit. In other cases, the data item as a whole is checked, and rejected if it is of the wrong type.

Range checks

Numbers must almost always be within a certain range. For example, a rate of pay must be a positive number below a certain limit. Once a number has been entered, it is compared with the upper and lower limits. If it is outside the range, it is rejected.

Control totals

If a series of numbers is entered, the total of the numbers can be calculated and entered as well. The computer recalculates this **control total** (also known as a **batch total**) and compares it with the one entered. If the totals are not equal, then one of the numbers could have been entered wrongly.

Check digits

Data items such as credit card numbers are used to identify records in a computer system. An error in such a number has serious consequences—a transaction could be entered in the wrong account. To reduce the chances of entering numbers like this wrongly, they have **check digits** added to them. A check digit is a digit whose value can be calculated from the other digits in the number. The check digit is recalculated after the number has been entered, and compared with the one entered. If they are not the same, there has been an error in entry.

A number of algorithms are used to calculate check digits. Some produce more than one digit and enable the position of the wrong digit to be determined. A common algorithm for check digits is introduced in question 6 in section 23B.

Special checks

Dates and data items in code can only have certain values. For example, the Subs Paid field in the club membership file can only have the values Y or N. Special checks are carried out on data items of this sort to ensure that they are within the set of permitted values. It is one of the benefits of using codes for data that strict validation procedures can be used.

Sorting

All batch processing systems, and many other types of data processing system, need to sort the records in their files. Records are sorted in order of one or more **key** fields. For example, the membership records of a club can be sorted in order of the members' surnames as the **primary key**, and their first names as the **secondary key**:

Primary Key	Secondary Key
Adams	Andrew
Adams	Stephen
Atkins	Anne
Atkins	Barry
Atkins	Susan

Sorting can be a slow process if the file is too large for the memory of the computer.

Selecting

It is common to select certain records of a file for processing. Selection is done by **conditions** on one or more fields in the records. For example, in the club membership system from chapter 9, all the members whose subscriptions are due are selected by the condition:

Subs Paid = N

Conditions may be combined using AND or OR. For example, the members with membership numbers in the range 85100 to 85199 are selected by the conditions

Membership No >= 85100 AND Membership No <= 85199

Selected records may be printed, copied to another file, processed in some way, or in some cases deleted.

Searching

The first stage of many data processing operations is to search for the record required for processing. As in the case of sorting, one or more **key** fields are used for the search. For example, in the club membership system, when a member changes address, a search is made for his or her record. The Surname and First Name fields are used as search keys.

Merging

Two files with the same record structure and both in order of the same keys may be merged to form a single file. The single file is in order of the same keys as the original files. See Figure 23.4. If the club whose membership records have been described were to combine with another club with membership records kept in the same way, then the two sets of records could be merged to produce a single set.

Merging is an important data processing operation in its own right, but it is also part of the process of sorting files which are too large for the computer memory.

Updating

Records in files are brought up-to-date during processing. The entries in certain fields are replaced by new data items. For example, every time a payroll system is run, the accumulated pay and income tax of each employee is brought up-to-date by adding the current pay and income tax. When a club member changes his or her address, his or her membership record is updated.

During the updating of a file, new records may be inserted and redundant ones deleted. Depending on the way the data is organised on the file, this may require shifting subsequent records backwards or forwards to make space. Such movement of records is normally confined to the sector on disk in which the deletion or insertion took place.

In a batch processing system, each run of the program creates an updated version of the master files. These are stored on a different magnetic tape or disk from that holding the previous version. See Figure 23.1.

A security door at a computer installation, and the magnetic card needed to unlock the door.

A fire-resistant safe being tested in a furnace.

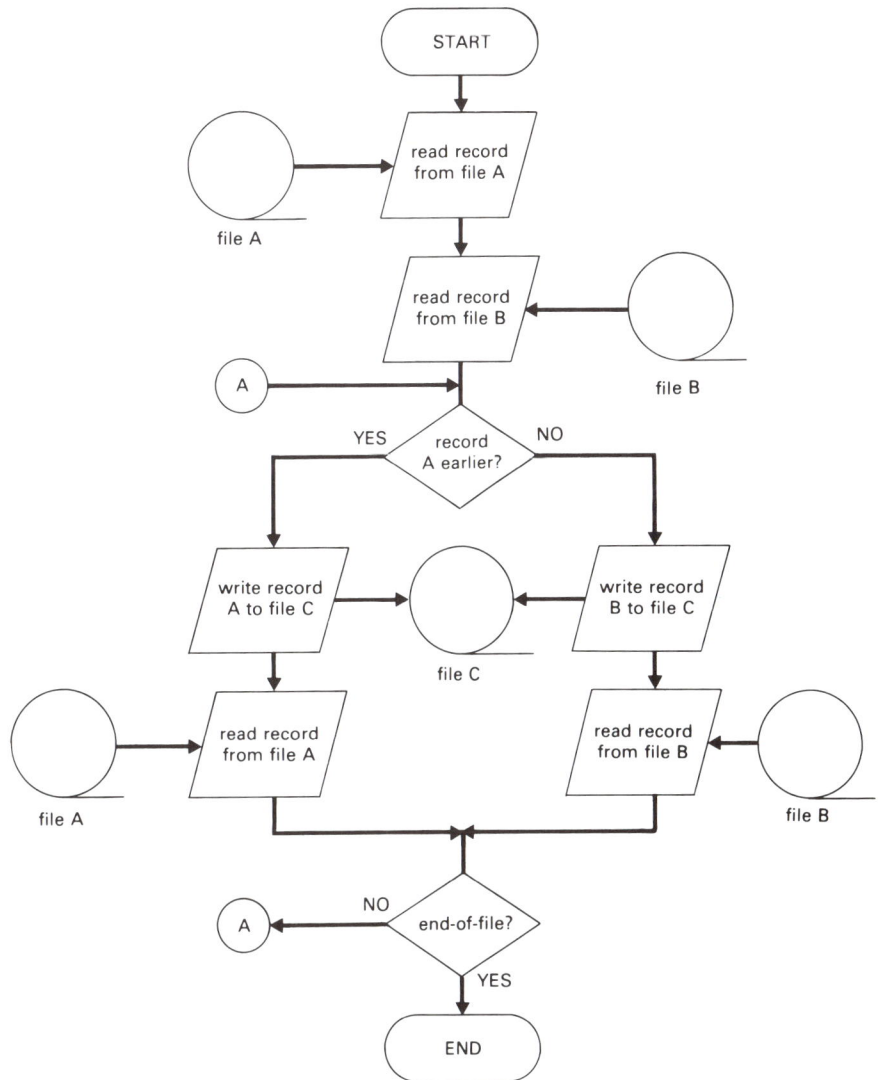
Figure 23.4   Merging two sequential files

Backup

Although computer systems are generally very reliable, problems do occur from time to time which result in the loss of data. See sections 4H and 4I for some of the things which can go wrong with magnetic tapes and disks.

To safeguard against a loss of data, **backup** copies of operational files are made from time to time. In transaction processing systems, **dumps** of files are made at regular intervals (ranging from once an hour to once a day depending on the application). A copy is made of all transaction data since the last backup. If the current data is lost for some reason, the up-to-date file is re-created by running this transaction data as a batch against the backup file.

Many software packages automatically create a backup of a file whenever it is updated. The backup holds the version of the file before the update began. This means that if there is a consistent error in the update, or the file is corrupted in the process, the previous version can be recovered.

Batch processing applications use the **grandfather-father-son** technique of keeping backup files. Each run of the program creates a new **generation** of the file. Three generations of the files are kept: the current one (the son), the previous one (the father), and the one before that (the grandfather). The transaction data used to produce these generations is also retained. Whenever the file is updated, the new version overwrites the oldest one, in a cyclic process. See Figure 23.5. The worst possible problem is a failure which corrupts both the father and the son during an update. In this case, the files are re-created from the grandfather, using the appropriate transaction data.

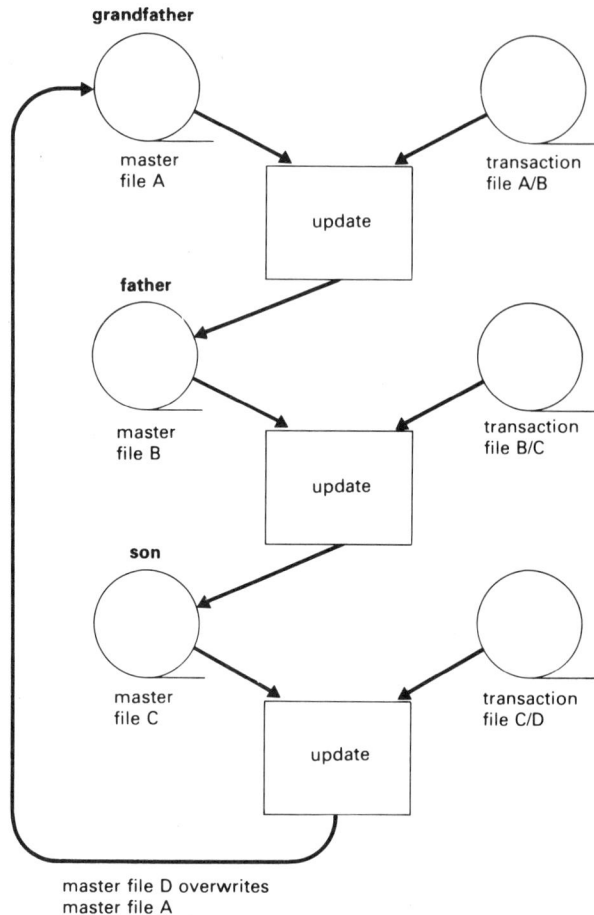

Figure 23.5   The grandfather-father-son updating cycle

Security Procedures

Backup procedures guard against accidental loss or corruption of data. Security measures are also needed to prevent deliberate corruption or copying of sensitive data. For example, fraud can be committed by altering computer records of bank accounts.

The aim of most security measures is to restrict access to data files to a small number of authorised people. Computers are kept in secure rooms to which access is severely limited. Magnetic tapes and disks are kept in fireproof safes. Staff are only allowed to use the computer for their own jobs: programmers and operators may not enter data, programmers may not operate the computer, and operators may not write programs.

In many installations, each person using the system has a **password** for identification. These give different levels of access: at the lowest level, only certain files or records may be read and no data may be written. Higher levels of security clearance give access to more data, and permit data to be written to files as well as read from them. In most cases the highest level of security clearance is required to be able to run programs and delete data.

Sensitive data is **encrypted** by storing it in a secret code. This requires encoding and decoding algorithms as part of the computer system. Encryption is also used when data is sent from one computer to another, or from a terminal to a computer.

The effectiveness of these security measures, and some of the consequences of their use, are discussed in chapter 25.

Questions

1 Choose the correct word from the list for each of the following spaces:

range check; grandfather-father-son; data capture; key; updating; turnaround documents; generations; validated; check digit.

A gas board sends out bills every three months. The bills have a tear-off slip which customers return with their payments. These ____ are used for ____ in the batch processing run for recording payments. They are read by optical character recognition, and each field is ____: the account number has a ____, the amount paid has a ____. The account number is used as the ____ to sort the payment records before ____ the master account files. The account files are updated according to the ____ principle, using three ____ of the disk.

The turnaround document at the foot of a gas bill.

2 (a) What are the benefits of capturing input data directly from source documents?
(b) List some uses of turnaround documents.
(c) Describe the advantages and disadvantages of turnaround documents.

3 (a) Why is it important to validate data on input?
(b) Which methods of data capture include automatic checks?
(c) Why is it easy to check for errors if data is entered in a code?

4 A particular application requires dates to be entered in the form 29/09/86. There are two digits each for the day, month and year, with the / character in between. The day and month are given range checks.
(a) Identify the error in each of the following dates: 1/12/87 23/22/85 15?09/88 31/09/83.
(b) In each of the above cases, state the rule which was broken to cause the error.
(c) Why is a date entered in this form not suitable as a key field for sorting records in order of date?
(d) Suggest an alternative format for a date which makes it suitable as a sort key.

5* Write a set of rules for validating UK postcodes.

6 A common method of calculating check digits is the **weighted modulo 11** method. Each digit of the number is multiplied by a **weighting factor**, which depends on its position in the number. The products are added up, and the total is divided by 11. The remainder is the check digit. If the remainder is 10, the check digit X is used. For example:

Number:	4	9	3	7	5	
Weighting factors:	$\times 9$	$\times 7$	$\times 5$	$\times 3$	$\times 1$	$= 140$
Products:	36	$+63$	$+15$	$+21$	$+5$	

Divide sum of products by 11: $140/11 = 12$ remainder 8.

Check digit: 8

Use this method to calculate the check digits on each of the following numbers:
(a) 28714 31879 90748 41268
(b) 37259 32759 35279 35729
Comment on the effects of transposing digits of a number on the value of the check digit.
(c) Find out how check digits are calculated for international standard book numbers (ISBN) and credit card numbers.

271

7 Using the club membership record given in section 9B, write a condition to select each of the following categories of member:
(a) the women
(b) all members whose subscriptions are due in September
(c) all members with membership numbers in the range 86001 to 86050
(d) all members with surnames starting with the letters A to E.

8 Two branches of a business keep lists of their clients in order of surname and first name. If the files of the client lists are merged, write down the portion of the merged file resulting from the following separate portions:

Branch A		Branch B	
Allen	Albert	Adamson	John
Allen	Emily	Allen	Brian
Ashton	Anne	Atherton	Jean
Atkins	Hugh	Atkins	Herbert
....		....	

9 A transaction processing system has backup copies of the files taken every hour on the hour. A batch file is accumulated of all transactions since the last backup. The average rate of processing is 25 transactions per minute.
(a) If a file is corrupted at 0923, state the steps taken to recover the file.
(b) Approximately how many transactions will be processed again?
(c) Can any more transactions be processed in real time while the recovery operation is under way? Give reasons for your answer.

10 A computer operator starts his shift to find six tapes for a batch processing system left for him by the previous operator. They are:

Master Files:	Generation 91
	Generation 92
	Generation 93

Transaction Files:	Generation 91/92
	Generation 92/93
	Labelled in pencil 'today'

His instructions are to run the batch system using today's transaction file.
(a) How should he label the transaction file marked 'today'?
(b) Which generation of the master file should he use?
(c) Which generation of the master file should be overwritten by the new master file? How should the new master file be labelled?
(d) During the update, the computer displays a message to say that it cannot read the master file. The operator halts the batch run. Which master and transaction tapes should be run to re-create the corrupt tape?
(e) When the batch run has finally been completed, which transaction file is no longer required?

11 A transaction processing system is based on a central mainframe computer accessed from a number of terminals. Some terminals are used for data entry, others are used by managers to look at reports on the data. The levels of access granted by the security system are:

> read data only
> enter transaction data
> run programs
> delete files

Each level of access includes the previous levels.
Suggest which level of access should be given to each of the following personnel:
(a) junior computer operator
(b) senior operator
(c) data entry staff
(d) sales manager
(e) managing director.

23C File Structure

A **file** is a collection of related data organised in a precisely defined structure. For example, all the information in the club membership system is kept in a file. Most data processing systems are based on a number of files.

Most files have a **header** which gives certain information about the file: its length, the format of a record, and information relating to the way the file is arranged on backing store. The file header is usually set up by the operating system, and is not a part of the application program.

Records, Fields and Keys

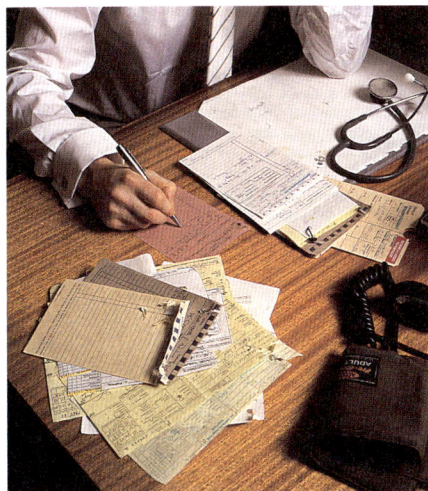

A manual filing system—a patient's records being used by a doctor.

A file consists of a set of **records**. The records either have an identical structure, or all have a very similar structure. Each record holds a set of data concerning one person, one transaction or one event. There is often a special record marking the end of a file. As with a file header, the **end-of-file record** may be set up automatically by the operating system. In a few cases, it is filled with suitable dummy items of data by the application program so that tests can be made for the end of the file.

Each record consists of a set of **fields**. A field holds one item of data. See section 9B for an example of a set of fields in a record.

Fields may be of fixed or variable length. Fixed length fields mean that a record stays the same size every time it is updated. This makes storage of the file easier, and is essential for random access files (see below). Variable length fields save space on backing store.

Fields are of a particular **type**. Data items may be numeric or alphabetic, in a special format for items like dates or sums of money, or in code. These types are illustrated in the example in section 9B. A **key** field may be used to identify the record, or as the basis for searching a file or sorting the records in order. If a sort is based on more than one field, the **primary key** determines the overall ordering. Records with identical primary keys are sorted in order of **secondary keys**. See section 23B for an example. Most files have one field in each record which is unique to the record—no two records have the same values of these fields. Examples are bank account numbers and credit card numbers. Such fields can always be used as the key when searching for a record.

An Index to a File

Searching for a record in a large file can be a slow process. To speed it up, many files have an **index** which relates one or more keys to the position of the records on backing store. The index is sorted in order of the keys. For example, an index to the club membership file might relate Surname and First Name to Membership No, as follows:

Surname	First Name	Membership No.
Allen	Andrew	85079
Allen	Anne	83175
Atkinson	Estelle	86225

When a new record is added to a file with an index, the record can be added to the end of the file, and the new entry sorted into the index. This is much quicker than sorting the new record into the file and moving all the records back on disk or tape. When searching for a record, the index is searched rather than the whole file. When the required entry is found, it is used to look up the record.

Types of File

The simplest type of file is one in which there is no particular ordering of records. **Serial files** of this sort are used in batch processing systems to hold the transaction data before it is sorted.

A **sequential file** is one which is in order of one or more keys. The club membership file is an example of a sequential file: it is in order of membership number. If an index is provided to such a file, it becomes an **indexed sequential file**. The keys used in the index are not necessarily the same as those used to sort the records, as shown in the above example. A sequential file may have more than one index.

A **random file** has its records scattered in random positions on backing store. However, there is an algorithm for obtaining the

The British Telecom computerised directory enquiries system. Names, addresses and telephone numbers are kept on large computer files.

location of a record from one or more keys. Random files are particularly useful in transaction processing systems where a number of terminals have access to the same file. If two terminals need to use the same portion of the file at the same time, one has to wait until the other has finished. The chances of two terminals needing to use the same portion of the file at the same time are reduced by scattering the records at random.

An **inverted file** is one in which each record contains fields taken from a number of records in another file. For example, a file might be set up containing the names of the club members whose subscriptions are due each month. There is a record for each month, set out as shown below:

Field	Type	Length	Example
Subs Month	alphabetic	3 characters	Jan
Surname 1	alphabetic	20 characters	Atkins
First Name 1	alphabetic	20 characters	Eileen
Surname 2	alphabetic	20 characters	Jackson
First Name 2	alphabetic	20 characters	Edward

This is an example of a file with variable length records: the length of each record depends on the number of members whose subscriptions are due that month.

Random and Serial Access

A computer filing system—rows of reels of magnetic tape.

Computer systems vary in the way in which they allow access to files. **Serial access** systems only allow records to be read from or written to a file in the order in which they are placed on backing store. To find a particular record, the file has to be read from the start until the record is located. If one record is updated, the whole file is read, the one record changed, and a new version of the file is written to backing store.

Serial access is suitable for batch processing, where files are processed in the order in which the records appear on backing store. It is the only method of file access possible with magnetic tape. It is also used by small microcomputers with simple operating systems.

Random access systems allow any record of a file to be read or written at any time. Random access is essential to make proper use of indexed sequential or random files. Transaction processing applications rely on random access to files. Random access filing systems require fixed length fields and records, or a fixed upper limit to the size of a record. The club membership system discussed in this chapter requires a random access filing system, as records may be accessed and updated in any order.

Logical and Physical File Structures

The **logical** structure of a file is its composition in terms of records and fields, as discussed above. Its **physical** structure is the way the data is arranged on backing store. This is in terms of blocks and sectors, as discussed in sections 4H and 4I.

A file extends over a number of blocks. Each block holds one or more complete records, as shown in Figure 23.6. A portion of space at the end of each block is empty. In some applications, space is left in each block for additional records. In this way, the file can grow without having to move large numbers of records each time one is added.

In a random access filing system, when a particular record is required the sector containing the record is read from backing store and the record is located in the sector. The record is updated and the entire sector written to backing store, overwriting the previous version. In multi-access computer systems, the sector is **locked** during the process so that two users cannot update the same sector simultaneously.

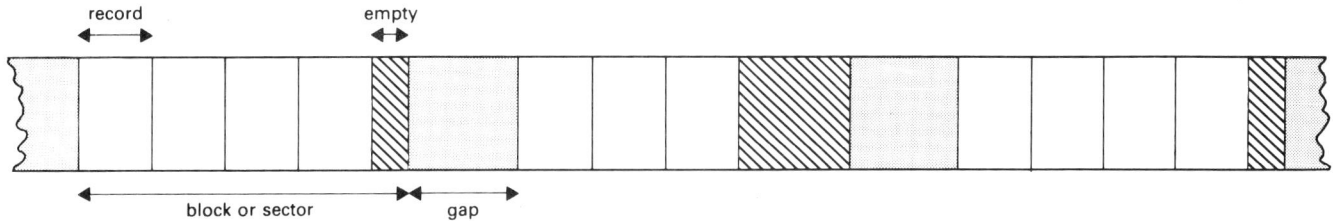

Figure 23.6   Records of a file on blocks of a backing store medium

Questions

1 What are the differences between:
   (a) serial, sequential and random files?
   (b) serial access and random access files?
2 For what purposes is the key field in a record used?
3 Suggest a suitable field type, number of characters and any validation for each of the following data items. Use codes wherever possible.
   (a) the price of an item in a clothes shop
   (b) the type of weather on a particular day
   (c) the number of hours worked in a week
   (d) an optional subject chosen by a pupil
   (e) a person's date of birth
   (f) a person's opinion on the state of the economy.
4 A fashion designer keeps a file of the companies which purchase the clothes he designs. The record for each company includes the name and address of the company, and the name and telephone number of the person who he deals with at the company. It also includes the type of clothes which the company is interested in.
   (a) Draw up a record structure for this file. State the type of each field, the number of characters, and any validation.
   (b) What is the most suitable type of file for these records?
   (c) Suggest *two* indexes which could be used to locate records quickly.
   (d) In what way could the fashion designer make use of an inverted file?
5 For each of the applications in question 3 in section 23A, state whether serial access or random access is most suitable.
6 In a particular computer system, a disk sector holds 1K bytes. The records of a file are of fixed size, each occupying 220 bytes.
   (a) How many records will fit into one sector?
   (b) What percentage of the sector is not used?
   (c) When the file is first written to disk, space is left for one additional record in each sector. Why is this? What percentage of the capacity of the sector is initially used?

23D End-of-Chapter Summary

The main points of this chapter are as follows:

- Batch processing systems process large collections of similar sets of data. Each set of data goes through the same input–process–output cycle.
- Interactive systems operate by means of a dialogue between the user and the computer system.
- A real-time computer system keeps pace with an external process.
- A transaction processing system carries out a complete input–processing–output cycle on a set of data in real time.
- A database system has a central store of data which is used by all the applications in the organisation.
- Standard data processing operations include data capture and input, validation (checking), sorting, selecting, merging, updating, backup and security procedures.
- A file consists of a set of records, all having the same structure. A record contains a set of fields, each containing one data item.

- A key field identifies a record, and is used in sorting and searching.
- An index uses key fields to locate records.
- A serial file has records in any order.
- A sequential file has records in order of one or more keys. It may also have an index.
- A random file has the records in random order with an algorithm for locating a record from its key.
- An inverted file has records each containing fields taken from a number of records in another file.
- A serial access filing system can read or write files only in the order in which the records are arranged on backing store.
- A random access filing system allows any record of a file to be read or written at any time.
- A file occupies a number of physical blocks or sectors on backing store. Each block contains one or more complete records.

Exercise 23

1 Choose the correct word from the list for each of the following spaces:

secondary; sequential; primary; random; fields; index; code; record; key.

A solicitor's secretary is setting up a file of the solicitor's clients. She enters a ____ for each client, with ____ for the name, address, and case references. She also gives each client a ____ number based on the date of first introduction. She decides to use a ____ file, with clients in order of code number. She also creates an ____ to the file, using the client's surname as the ____, and including the code number. This index is sorted with the surname as ____ key and first name as ____ key.

2 Over the years, many companies have progressed from manual systems, to batch processing, interactive and then database systems using computers.
(a) Briefly define each of the above types of computer system.
(b) State the main advantages that each type of system has over the previous one.
(c) What is the next general type of computer system likely to be? What advantages will it have over the present type?

3 Summarise the steps involved in sorting the records in a file which is too large to be held in the memory of the computer doing the sort.

4 The central computer system of a large bank occupies a self-contained site. The staff include programmers, data entry staff and operations staff. Data is entered at terminals, and processed in a batch processing run: the computer system is not interactive, and is not accessed from external terminals.
(a) What security precautions would you expect to be operating at the site?
(b) If the computer is linked to a number of cash terminals running a transaction processing program, what additional precautions would you expect?

5 Twenty years ago, most computers used punched cards for input and magnetic tapes for backing store.
(a) What type of computer application is best suited to these media? Give reasons for your answer.
(b) What types of data file are best suited to magnetic tape? Give reasons for your answer.
(c) What system of file access must be used with magnetic tape?

Working with IT

An advertisement for jobs in IT.

The stage will soon be reached when most people in industrial countries use information technology, directly or indirectly, in their work. The rapid spread of IT is helping to cause major changes in working practices. When computers were first introduced, companies set up data processing departments with specialist staff to program and run the computers. Now many users work on computers directly: desktop microcomputers or terminals linked to central processors. The wide access to information technology is changing the types of work done. New jobs are being created, and jobs which depended on older technologies are disappearing.

IT helps people to be more efficient and more productive. With this efficiency and productivity comes pressure: deadlines have to be met, and standards of work must be maintained. Although the IT industry is growing, its growth is not steady. A number of IT companies have prospered for a while, and then gone out of business or been taken over by other companies. The compensation for the pressure, uncertainty and constant change is high salaries for the people who design, program and operate computers.

Trading workstations at the Hong Kong Stock Exchange. Each workstation has a computer terminal and a telephone.

24A IT Component Manufacture

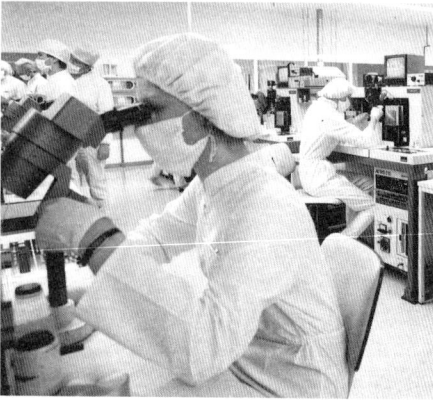

Microchips being tested electronically and examined under microscopes during fabrication.

Computers, digital telephone exchanges, robots and other items of IT equipment are made from the same types of components. The most important components are **microchips**. Microchips, disk drives, display screens and other components are made by companies known as **original equipment manufacturers (OEMs)**.

OEMs employ highly skilled **electronics engineers** and **physicists** to carry out the research and development of microchips. They use computer-aided design (CAD) equipment to design the chips and test their workings. Microchips are made in fabrication plants from which all dirt and dust is excluded. The people who work in the clean areas wear special clothes so that no dirt gets into the chips. The work is highly skilled, as the tolerances involved are very fine.

OEMs also employ marketing and sales staff. Their job is to find out what types of chip and other components are in demand, and to sell as many of their company's products as possible. The world market for chips tends to fluctuate from shortages to over-supply, and the prices of chips reflect this. Chips are expensive when there is a shortage, and cheap when there is a surplus. There is intense competition between the two major production areas: Japan and the USA.

24B IT Systems Manufacture

Some of the largest companies in the world are involved in the production of IT systems: computers, digital telephone exchanges, robots, etc. Most prominent is IBM, which sells more than three quarters of the world's computers. These companies together employ millions of people in plants all over the world.

Computers are designed by **computer architects**, who are usually trained as electronics engineers. Even a large company requires only a small number of computer architects: Cray Research, for example, is named after its computer architect Seymour Cray. Teams of electronics engineers work with the computer architects in order to bring designs into production. Computers are made from standard components mounted on printed circuit boards. Assembling a computer is a fairly straightforward task, taking only a few minutes for a microcomputer. Most computer companies employ large numbers of assembly workers, although in a few cases assembly is done by robots.

One of the most skilled jobs in a computer company is developing and maintaining the systems software which controls the computers. The **systems programmers** who do this work are responsible for some of the most complex software in existence (and are generally extremely well paid).

Computer manufacturers have large teams of people responsible for **marketing** and **sales**. The marketing departments find out what types of computers are needed, and ensure that new computers are designed to meet the needs of customers. The sales staff have the task of selling as many computers as possible. Selling a large computer system involves long negotiations with customers. It is a highly competitive process: in most cases a customer will invite a number of companies to negotiate for the sale of a computer system, and then choose the best system which is offered in terms of price, performance, maintenance, etc.

Most IT equipment manufacturers maintain their equipment while it is in use. They have **field engineers** who supervise the installation of the computers and ensure that they are running properly before they are handed over. The field engineers visit the installations for regular maintenance and whenever something goes wrong. Field engineers must be prepared to be called out at any time of the day or night.

Engineers assembling the units of minicomputers.

24C Software Houses

Software houses develop software packages and are commissioned by users to develop software to meet their requirements. Most of the people working for software houses are **software engineers**. They are involved in all stages of the design, development, testing and maintenance of software. There are seldom any rigid distinctions between jobs. The software engineers work in teams under a **team leader**, who is a senior software engineer. Teams are formed for a particular project, which may last for a few months or a few years, and then disbanded. The software engineers then join other teams.

If a software house develops software packages, there is a marketing and sales team to handle the distribution of the software.

Questions These questions cover sections 24A, 24B and 24C.

1 What are the consequences of the changes in the IT components market from over-supply to shortages of microchips?
2 Which are the two leading countries in microchip production?
3 What is the job title of a person who:
   (a) designs microchips
   (b) designs computers
   (c) develops operating systems
   (d) develops software packages
   (e) decides whether there is a demand for a new IT product
   (f) maintains computers at user sites?
4 What are the benefits of a flexible team structure in a software house?
5 What do the marketing staff do in companies which produce computer components, computers and software?

24D Data Processing Departments

Most companies which use a mini- or mainframe computer have a **data processing (DP) department** to manage the computer installation. The DP staff have two roles: developing applications software (if it is not done by a software house), and running the computer. The job structure of a typical DP department is shown in Figure 24.1.

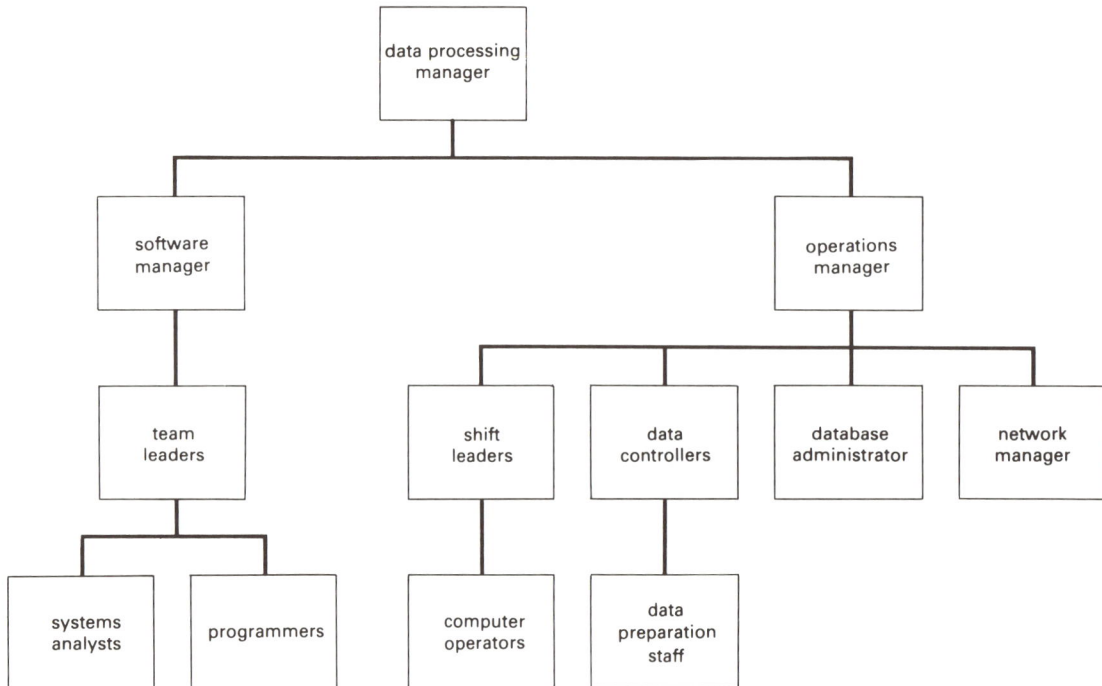

Figure 24.1   Staff of a data processing department

A computer operator loading a magnetic tape at a mainframe computer installation. In the foreground are rows of magnetic disk drives.

The **data processing manager (DPM)** is in overall charge. Software development is done by teams managed by **team leaders**. Some companies have **systems analysts** who work with users to design the computer systems, and **programmers** who design, write, test and maintain the software. In other companies, these jobs are combined as **analyst/programmer**. The detailed work of designing and developing a software system is described in chapter 9.

There is usually an **operations manager** in overall charge of the running of the computer. If the computer operates around the clock (as is generally the case for a large computer), the **computer operators** work in shifts to keep the computer running. There are **shift leaders** in charge of each shift. If staff are required for data entry, they are supervised by **data controllers**. If the computer system includes a network, there is a **network administrator** responsible for its running. If the applications are centred on a database, there is a **database administrator (DBA)** to co-ordinate the way the database is used.

24E Computer Bureaus

Some companies which use computers do not have a computer system of their own. Instead they make use of a **computer bureau** for their data processing. Computer bureaus develop software and run programs for other companies. They are particularly useful for such routine tasks as payroll preparation. The staff structure of a computer bureau is similar to that of a DP department.

Computer bureaus are now less popular than they used to be. This is because computers are much cheaper than they were years ago. Most companies can now afford a computer system of their own. An in-house computer system is more flexible than an outside bureau.

A payslip produced by a computer bureau which specialises in payroll processing.

24F IT Users

An increasing number of people work directly with computers or other items of IT equipment. In some companies, the central computer system has been replaced by a network of microcomputers running software packages. In the process, the DP department has been disbanded.

Desktop microcomputers and terminals in use in an office.

In offices, desktop microcomputers are being used by secretaries, clerical workers, managers and directors. A number of companies are getting close to being **paperless offices**: all letters are prepared on word processors, internal memos are sent on the computer network, electronic mail is used for much of the external communications, and invoices and orders are sent via computer links with clients and suppliers. Many changes are taking place in the job definitions in such offices. There is seldom a need for a typing pool. Some people can work at home, at least for some of the time, and link their home computer with the office network by telephone. Working hours can be more flexible, and secretaries can spend less time on routine typing and more time helping with management tasks.

In factories, manual tasks are being taken over by robots and automatic machines. The people who work at these factories program and service these machines. Managers are able to use computers to help them plan production and keep costs under control.

In the armed forces, electronic equipment is becoming the norm. Ships, aircraft, submarines, tanks and many weapons systems are controlled with the aid of computers. Military personnel require skills in electronics and computing in order to make the best use of this equipment.

Questions

These questions cover sections 24D, 24E and 24F.

1 What is the job title of a person who:
   (a) decides how a computer application will work
   (b) writes programs
   (c) co-ordinates the use of a database
   (d) co-ordinates the use of a computer network
   (e) supervises the operation of a computer system
   (f) supervises a team of computer operators?
2 A small company decides to replace its minicomputer with a network of desktop microcomputers, using standard software packages.
   (a) What changes of staff will this involve?
   (b) Discuss the other consequences of this change.
3 What are the advantages and disadvantages of using a computer bureau for data processing, as against doing the work on in-house computers?

24G End-of-Chapter Summary

The main points of this chapter are as follows:

- Large numbers of people work directly or indirectly with information technology. IT helps people to be more efficient and productive. It brings with it new working practices which demand high standards, meeting deadlines and keeping costs under control.
- The manufacture of IT components requires the skills of electronics engineers and physicists, and fabrication staff who work in clean rooms.
- Producing computers and other IT systems requires computer architects, electronics engineers, systems programmers and assembly workers. Field engineers look after IT systems once they leave the factory.
- OEMs and IT systems manufacturers have marketing and sales staff who work in an intensely competitive environment in order to sell IT products.
- Software houses are staffed by software engineers who design, develop and maintain programs.

- Data processing departments develop applications software and operate the computer systems of user organisations.
- Applications software is developed by teams of programmers and systems analysts.
- The running of a computer installation is supervised by an operations manager, to whom report shift leaders, operators, data controllers, database administrators and network managers.
- The services provided by a computer bureau are similar to those of a DP department. The staff structure at a computer bureau resembles that of a DP department.

Exercise 24

1 Choose the correct word from the list for each of the following spaces:

database administrator; modules; team leader; programmers; operations manager; data entry staff; computer operator; data processing manager; systems analysts.

The managers of a company decide to develop a new computer system. The ____ sets up a software development team. He nominates a ____, two systems analysts and four ____. The software will use the company's database, so the ____ is included in the team.

The ____ work with the users of the system to draft a functional specification. When the programmers have completed the first versions of the program ____, the ____ schedules computer time for them to be run. The ____ on duty runs the programs, and some of the ____ enter test data.

2 A company manufactures electronic controls for central heating systems. What is the job title of the person who:
(a) decides what type of control systems are needed
(b) designs the control systems
(c) assembles the control systems
(d) sells the control systems?

3 The finance director of a company has a desktop microcomputer and her secretary has a word processor. The computers are compatible in the sense that they can exchange disks. Amongst the tasks of the finance director are using spreadsheets to analyse trading figures, and preparing reports based on these figures.
(a) Suggest a way in which the director and her secretary might share the work of preparing a report which includes figures from a spreadsheet.
(b) In what ways does this differ from the way it would have been done if the director did all her calculations on paper, and her secretary had only a typewriter?
(c) Comment on your answers.

4 A person with a university degree joins a company with a large computer installation as a junior programmer in the data processing department.
(a) Write down three possible career paths the graduate might follow.
(b) Estimate the number of years spent in each job.
(c) By looking at job advertisements in the computer press, estimate the salaries the person might earn in each job.
(d) Comment on this information.

Things to find out

1 A small company develops educational software. There are three people in the company. One markets the software, processes orders and keeps accounts. The other two design and write the programs, and produce the user guides to go with them.
(a) Suggest a suitable set of computer hardware for the company.
(b) Suggest a suitable set of software packages to run on the hardware.
(c) Find out or estimate the costs of the hardware and software, and calculate the total cost.

2 The computing industry is constantly changing. One aspect of this is the change in fortunes of IT companies. Look in some IT magazines and:
(a) Make a list of three IT companies which appear to be doing well at present. In each case, write down the reasons for the company doing well.
(b) Make a list of three IT companies which are not doing well, or which are closing down. In each case, write down the reasons for the company doing badly.
(c) Comment on your findings. In particular, look for connections between the reasons for the companies doing well, and those for the companies doing badly. Also comment on the effects on the jobs of the people working in the companies.

Points to discuss

1 OEMs, IT system manufacturers and software houses all operate in a highly competitive environment. Discuss the effects of this on the people who work in these companies and their customers.

2 A common problem in large organisations is the purchase of desktop microcomputers by staff in various departments for their own work, without reference to central management. These micros are often incompatible with the central computer system and with each other. Discuss the consequences of this, and suggest policies to overcome the problem.

25   Living with IT

Car assembly in about 1920. Every operation is done with the aid of simple hand tools.

Like jet engines, nuclear power and radar, electronic computers are a product of the Second World War. In the forty years since their invention, computers, together with control systems and telecommunications, have influenced almost every aspect of our lives. Information technology has been a force for change: changes in the way many people work, changes in the services provided by many organisations, changes in the capabilities of police forces, changes in the way people are governed. The pace of change is likely to speed up over the next few years, as computerised systems and electronic offices become the norm in all industrial countries and begin to be used to a significant extent in the Third World.

Most of the changes brought about by IT have been beneficial: more efficient services from banks, airlines, shops and many other organisations, better food distribution, higher quality goods at lower prices, etc. But some of the changes are causing concern. What about all the people put out of work by robots and electronically-controlled machines? What safeguards are there on all the personal information stored on computers? Can our money be stolen by people breaking into the banks' computer systems? What if the police were to use computers to store information about everyone? What about a war being started by accident through a computer error?

This chapter covers some general effects of the widespread use of IT. It draws some overall conclusions from the specific issues discussed at the ends of several of the applications chapters.

Car assembly in the 1980s. Robots are used for most of the repetitive work.

25A Employment and Unemployment

Looking for a job. Most jobs today involve the use of information technology in some way.

Almost every motor car manufacturer in the world faced the same problem during the late 1970s: falling sales as more cars were produced than were needed, rising costs from increases in wages, and dissatisfaction with the quality of the cars which were being produced. If something was not done about the situation, most car manufacturers would go out of business.

The cause was the same throughout the world: the technology being used to build motor cars was obsolete. Cars were being put together by large numbers of workers using simple hand tools. The jobs were monotonous, the workers wanted more and more pay to compensate for the boredom, and strikes were frequent. The solution, adopted in various ways throughout the world, has been the same. Traditional car production plants have been replaced by new ones which make extensive use of robots and electronically-controlled machines. In the process, millions of workers have lost their jobs. However, most of the car companies have survived, and the quality of cars is generally higher. Each company realises that its survival, and the jobs of all its remaining workers, depend on how well its cars sell in the world market. Unless quality can be kept up and costs can be kept down, the company will go out of business. IT is the key to higher quality and lower costs.

What has happened in the motor industry has been repeated, to a greater or lesser extent, in many other industries. A few leading examples are the steel industry, the newspaper industry, and the aircraft industry. Although the job losses have been less, the effective use of IT is the key to success in industries such as banking, insurance, retail shopping, and the travel business. The choices have always been similar: introduce new technology and new working practices, retrain some workers and make others redundant if necessary, or go out of business.

The loss of jobs with the introduction of IT has been offset by the creation of new jobs as the efficiency and greater productivity from the use of IT begin to take effect. The loss of traditional jobs and the creation of new jobs are beginning to balance out in most industrial countries, including the UK.

One problem is that the benefits and adverse effects of the change to new technology are not shared evenly. In the UK, the Midlands and northern England, parts of Scotland and Northern Ireland have suffered the worst effects of redundancies. The south, and certain areas in South Wales and Scotland have received most of the investments in new industries. Wages are higher in the prosperous areas, but so are prices, particularly house prices. It is difficult for someone who has been made redundant in an area of high unemployment to move to a more prosperous area.

The effects of redundancies also depend on age. The group most at risk is people in their 50s with about ten years to go before they retire. Retraining people for new jobs working with high-technology equipment is expensive, and younger people often adapt more easily to new work practices than older people. Accordingly, if redundancies are to be made, it is the older workers who are more likely to be chosen for redundancy, and they are the ones who find it most difficult to get jobs in a different line of work.

School leavers and university graduates also have difficulty finding work. Preference is often given, particularly for jobs in the IT industry, to people with some experience. Many young people cannot get a job without work experience, but cannot get work experience without a job.

The attitudes of British trade unions to the change to new technology have varied from cautious acceptance to strong opposition. The first wave of changes in the motor industry were bitterly opposed by the unions, but their opposition is now less outright. In the newspaper industry, there have been strikes, lockouts and mass redundancies. In a few newspapers, changes have been forced over the opposition of unions, and all the workers belonging to certain unions have been dismissed. In the banking and insurance industry, changes to IT have been more gradual. Opposition from banking unions has slowed the rate of introduction of IT, but agreement has eventually been reached. Most British trade unions are beginning to accept that the introduction of IT is in the long-term interests of their members, even though some redundancies are caused in the short term. They are also prepared to accept more flexible working practices than in the past. Union opposition is not generally an obstacle to the introduction of IT—the most serious delaying factor in many cases is the reluctance of managements to introduce new technology.

Questions

1 (a) Have the benefits and disadvantages of the introduction of IT been spread evenly throughout the United Kingdom?
 (b) What are some of the effects on different regions of the change to IT?
2 Give some examples of the different responses of trade unions in Britain to the introduction of new technology.
3 (a) Are trade unions the only obstacle to the introduction of IT?
 (b) What other obstacles are there? ·
4 In what ways does the introduction of IT lead to increased employment?

25B Privacy and Data Protection

In a few years' time, it is quite likely that you will have a bank account, a driver's licence, a television licence and an insurance policy. You may own a car, and have a mortgage on a house. You will be paid a salary, and probably pay gas, electricity, water and telephone bills. Information about every one of these is kept on computers. If you have a criminal record, there will be an entry in the criminal records index, which is held on computer. If you have been to hospital, the medical records may be on computer. If your company has a digital telephone exchange, every number which you dial from work, and the duration of the call, may be recorded.

All this is personal information. Computers have made it possible for thousands of millions of such items of data to be stored, accessed and sorted into categories very quickly. But how would you feel if the information about you was disclosed to other people? How would you like others to know how much you earn, or that your bank account was overdrawn, or that you have an endorsement on your driving

The UK Data Protection Act, 1984.

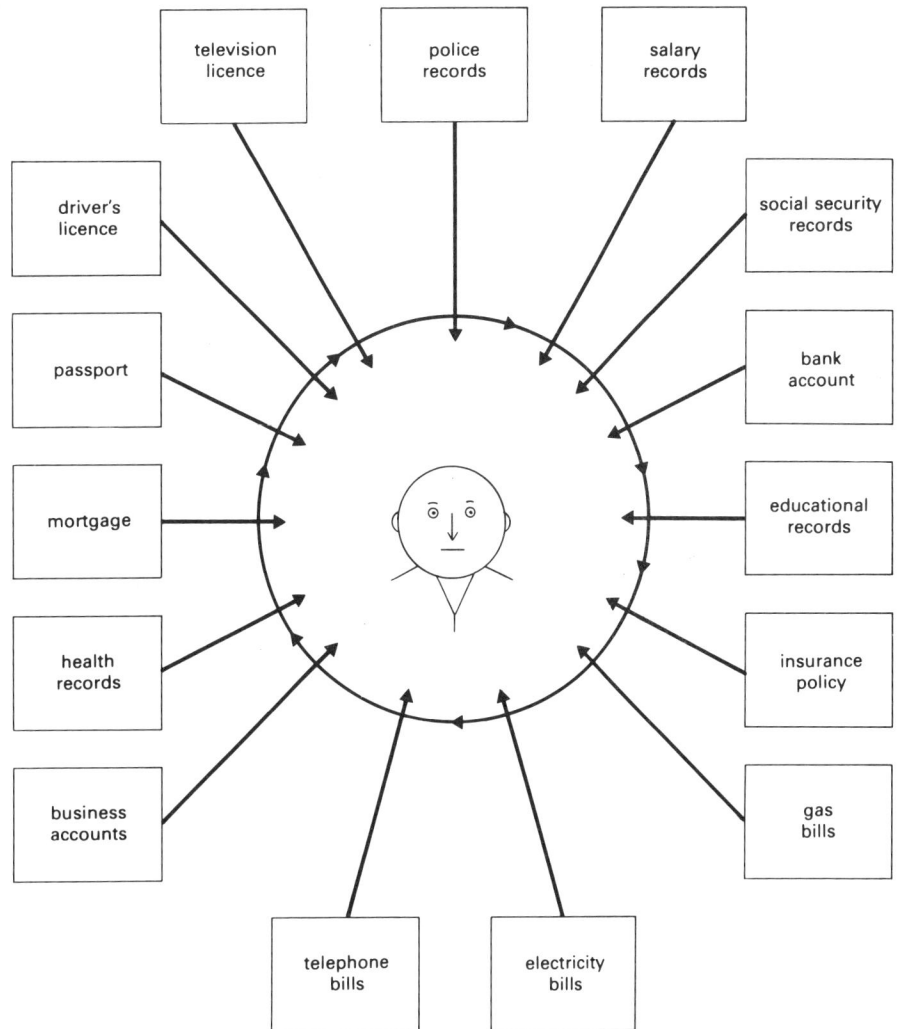

Figure 25.1   Network of computers storing information on all aspects of a person's private life

Application forms for registration under the
Data Protection Act.

licence? What if all these computers were linked, so that someone could find out all this information about you from a single computer network? See Figure 25.1. To protect you from this kind of thing, the **Data Protection Act** was passed in Britain in 1984. Most other countries in Western Europe and North America have similar laws.

In terms of the Data Protection Act, you are a **data subject**—a person about whom personal data is kept on computers. The banks, insurance companies, police and other organisations who keep the data are **data users**. All data users must register with the **Data Protection Registrar** in order to apply for permission to keep personal data on their computers. In registering, each organisation must state what data is kept, what it is used for, and who has access to it. It is against the law to use personal data for any purpose other than those which have been registered. Furthermore, data subjects have the right to see their own records, and to insist that any errors in them are corrected. Certain organisations are exempt from this provision, and some computer users such as the security services are exempt from the Data Protection Act altogether.

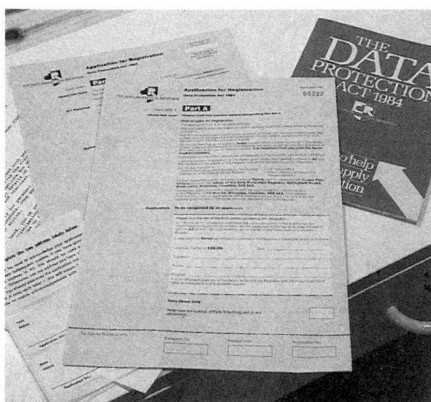

The Data Protection Act and similar laws in other countries prevent the organisations who keep personal data from abusing it. But there is another danger not covered by these Acts: the possibility of outsiders 'breaking into' computer systems in order to copy or alter information, or to carry out dishonest transactions. The greatest temptation is to use electronic funds transfer systems for fraud, a matter discussed in section 20C.

Viewdata systems such as Prestel and electronic mail systems have mailboxes which store incoming messages for users. There have been cases of these mailboxes being broken into by 'hackers', and messages altered. It is difficult to tell if a mailbox has been looked at and messages copied without any alteration.

As in the case of computer fraud, the extent of this problem is unknown. Some experts think that computer systems are often broken into for dishonest purposes; others think that the problem is rare. Very few people have been caught breaking into computer systems; even fewer have been prosecuted.

A number of measures are taken to ensure the security of data, many of them secret. The most common is a system of passwords. Users must identify themselves, when logging onto a computer system, by a code. They must then enter a password which must match the code. Some computer systems 'scramble' the data stored on disk or sent on a communications link. If an unauthorised person manages to gain access to the disk, or to intercept the communication, the data will not make sense. Other precautions include limiting access to the computer centre to a small number of staff, and ensuring that staff only use the computer for their own jobs: programmers may not operate the computer or enter data, operators may not write programs, etc.

A Prestel page on a computer screen. There have been cases of people 'breaking in' to the Prestel network, and interfering with other people's mailboxes.

1 List as many organisations as you can think of which store personal data on computers.
2 Explain the meaning of the term 'data subject', giving an example of its use.
3 What is the worst possible situation that could arise through the abuse of personal data stored on a computer?
4 List as many precautions as you can think of to prevent 'hackers' from copying or altering data on computer systems.
5 Suggest some reasons that passwords are not a foolproof security precaution for computer systems.

25D IT and Political Control

In Britain and many other Western countries, the government is accountable to the people. The actions of the police, the armed forces, the immigration authorities, the tax collectors and other government agencies can be questioned, in Parliament if nowhere else. However, this does not apply to every aspect of government, in particular to the

The UK House of Commons in session, 12th November 1986. In Britain and other democratic countries, laws are made through a process of public debates, by elected representatives of the people.

measures taken against terrorists, spies, and other organisations and persons which pose a threat to the security of the state. The extent to which these activities are secret varies from one country to another, but all countries have security services which operate mostly under cover.

One of the main weapons against terrorists, spies and other potential threats to the security of a state is information. The most valuable information is the whereabouts and movements of 'persons of interest', and the contents of messages sent between them. Electronic systems are one way of gathering this information and computers are used to decode it if necessary, and to store and analyse it. These computers and electronic systems are secret, and exempt from all data protection and similar laws. They have contributed greatly to the efficiency of security services, and helped combat terrorism in many countries.

The problem with IT in security services is where to draw the line. The computers are capable of storing data on millions of people. What is there to stop information being collected of legitimate opponents of governments, even on opposition members of parliament? Many governments in the world stay in power by limiting the activities of opponents in various ways. There is a danger of computers being used to assist in such practices, and exports of computers to certain countries are restricted in an attempt to prevent this happening.

25E IT at War

One of the driving forces behind the development of information technology has been the need for more sophisticated weapons. Many of the hardware and software systems now in use in offices, shops and homes were first developed for military use.

In the front line, guns of all sizes are aimed by computer. Rockets and torpedoes are guided by electronic systems, sometimes carried on board. Aircraft, tanks, ships and submarines have computers for navigation, defence against incoming missiles, and weapons guidance. Military supplies are administered by computer, and operations planned with the aid of computers. Nuclear missiles are controlled by computer once they have been fired. It is likely that detailed decisions in a nuclear war would be made by computer.

The **Strategic Defense Initiative (SDI)** at present under discussion in the USA aims to place defensive systems in space which can destroy incoming nuclear missiles. SDI systems are to be controlled entirely by computer, in real time. If any are built, they will need computers far more powerful than any at present in operation.

There are a number of problems with the widespread use of IT for military purposes. On the one hand it is not certain that sophisticated weapons with complex electronics are superior to simple, conventional weapons. On the other hand, new weapons systems are developed so quickly that a weapon system, developed at great cost, may be obsolete soon after it is taken into service. As computers are used increasingly in planning military operations and making decisions during them, there is the danger that a computer malfunction could start a conflict by mistake, or cause an operation to be a catastrophic failure.

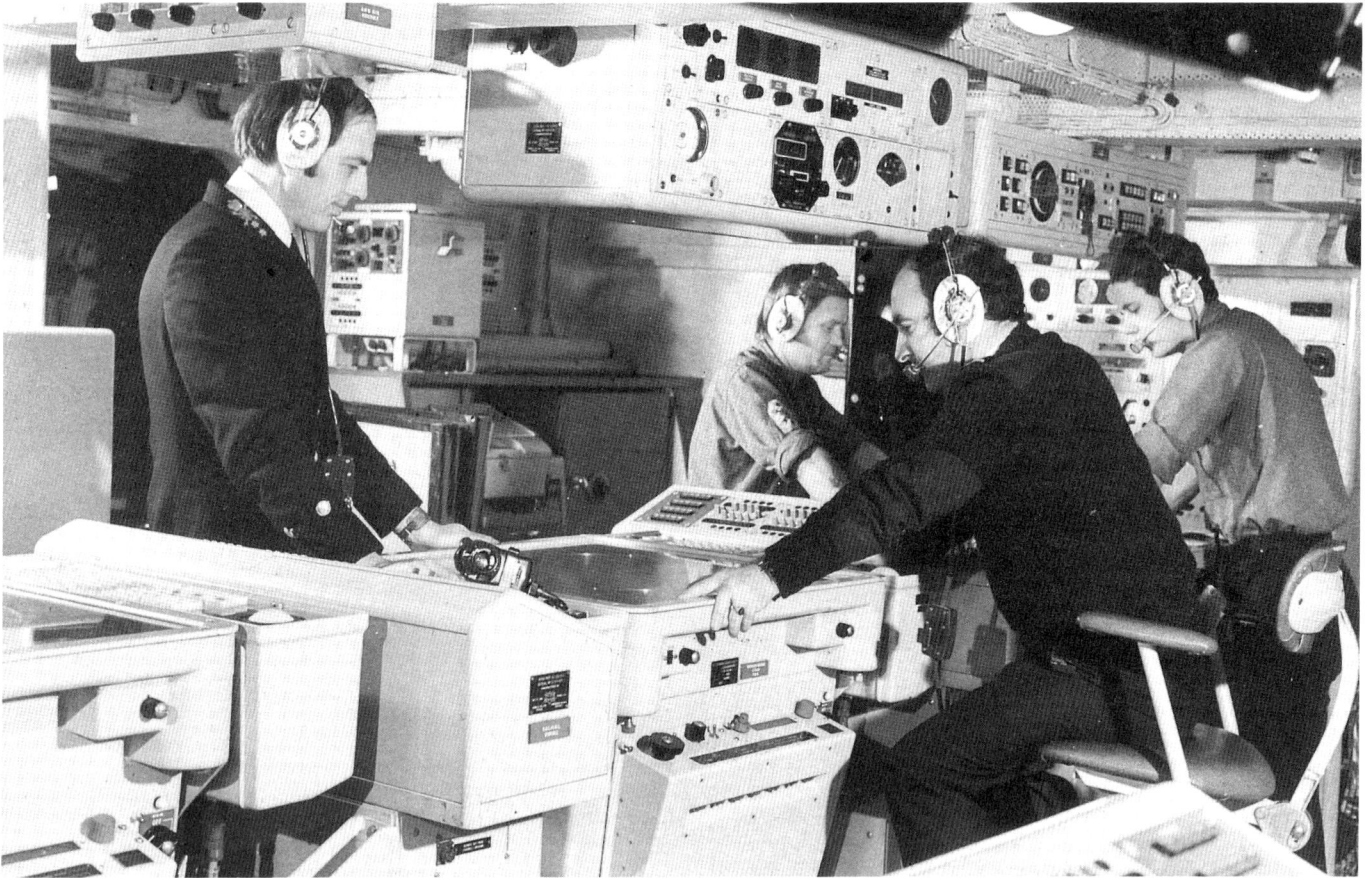

The weapons control centre of a modern warship. Electronic systems are used to guide weapons, and to detect other ships, aircraft and missiles.

Questions

These questions cover sections 25D and 25E.

1 In what ways can computers be used against spies and terrorists? For each application, state the possible problems if the system is used against an innocent person.
2 Give one reason for restricting the export of computers to certain countries.
3 In what ways are IT systems used in weapons?
4 What are the disadvantages of complex weapons systems controlled by electronics?
5 In what way is it intended to use computers for SDI systems?

25F End-of-Chapter Summary

The main points of this chapter are as follows:

- IT is a force for change—it is changing working practices, the services provided by many organisations and the way people are governed.
- Many companies have been faced with the choice between introducing IT or going out of business. Large numbers of jobs have been lost in the change to new technology, but the remaining jobs are more secure. Jobs are being created by the increased efficiency of organisations which use computers.
- The effects on employment of IT have varied from one region to another. Older workers have suffered more from redundancy than younger ones.

- In the past, trade unions have been strongly opposed to the introduction of IT. At present, union resistance is less of an obstacle to change than the reluctance of managements.
- Laws such as the UK Data Protection Act protect data subjects from unauthorised use of personal data about them.
- Measures taken to ensure the security of data include passwords, scrambling data, limiting access to computers, and strict segregation of the work done by computer staff.
- There is concern over the potential abuse of computers by security services in order to restrict the activities of opponents to governments.
- Military computer systems give rise to concern over the consequences of a computer malfunction during a conflict, and the possibility of a conflict being started by mistake by a computer error.

Exercise 25

1 A company which makes metal components for motor car engines has been losing money steadily over the last five years. The management decides that the only way to save the company is to replace all the existing lathes and machine tools with new equipment which is controlled by computer. This will involve a loss of 110 jobs from a workforce of 200. The remaining 90 staff will have to be retrained on the new equipment, and work flexible hours instead of the previous fixed-length shifts.
(a) Which of the workers are the most likely to be made redundant, and why?
(b) State the reasons which the management might give to the workforce when explaining the need for these changes.
(c) State the case which a trade union representative might make in opposing the changes altogether.
(d) State the case which a trade union representative might make in accepting the changes, but arguing for the best redundancy and retraining arrangements for the union members.

2 The following is *not* based on a true story:

Mrs Jones is telephoned by a representative of a credit agency.

"Mrs Jones, we haven't met, but I am representing a credit agency who might be able to be of assistance to you. We understand that you are having slight problems with your bank at present. We have checked up your salary, and can see that, given enough time, you might be able to sort things out. We have also checked with your insurance company, and see that you have a life policy which would do very nicely as a security against a loan. Therefore I am pleased to offer you a long term, low interest loan ..."

(a) What *three* offences have been committed against the Data Protection Act in getting the above information?
(b) As the law stands in the UK, the companies which keep the data are at fault, rather than the credit agency which is using it dishonestly. Suggest a change in the law which might remedy this situation.
(c) Comment on how Mrs Jones might feel after the telephone call.

3 Write a fictional story in which a computer is used to help trap a group of terrorists before they can detonate a bomb. Make the story as realistic as possible.

4 In the next few years, the passports issued by all EEC countries will contain a page of OCR characters which can be read into a computer. It will then be possible to log the movements of everyone with an EEC passport into and out of any EEC country, and store all these on a central computer system. (There is *no* plan to implement such a system at present.)
(a) State the potential advantages of such a system.
(b) State the potential disadvantages of a system of this nature.
(c) Give your opinion whether such a system should or should not be implemented. Indicate which reasons were the most important in coming to your conclusion.

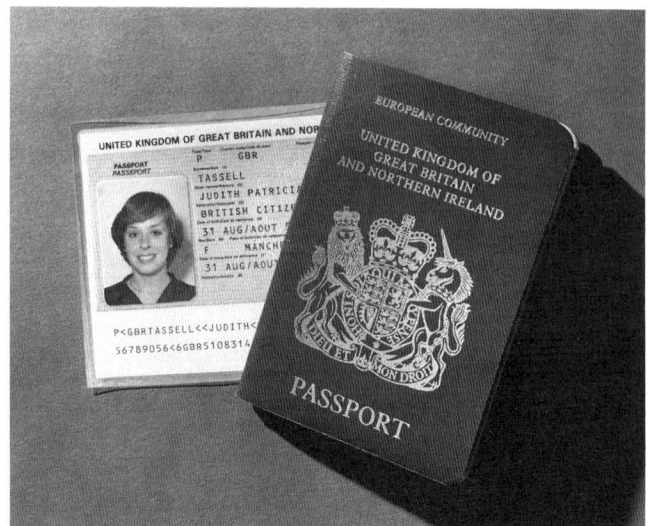

The machine-readable page of a British passport. The information on the page is printed in OCR characters.

Things to find out

1 Look in some local and national newspapers to see if you can find reports of any cases of fraud or similar crimes which have been committed with the aid of a computer. For any which you find:
(a) Briefly describe the nature of the crime.
(b) State whether the person(s) responsible were caught and charged.
(c) If they were charged, were they convicted? If so, what sentence did they receive?
(d) Suggest ways in which future crimes of this sort might be prevented.

2 Choose *one* of the following industries as a case study: the motor industry, the newspaper industry, shipbuilding, steelmaking, banking. Alternatively, choose a prominent local industry, with more than one company working in it.
(a) Find out what changes in technology have taken place in the chosen industry over the last twenty years.
(b) Find out what effects these changes have had on jobs in the industry.
(c) Find out what the attitude of trade unions in the industry has been to the introduction of new technology.
(d) Find out how much resistance there was from the unions to the changes.
(e) Find out whether any companies in the industry have gone out of business during the period you are investigating. If so, why did this happen?
(f) Comment on your findings.

3 One of the main factors influencing the outcome of the Second World War was the ability of the Allies to 'crack' the secret code used by the Germans to communicate with submarines in the Atlantic. An early type of electronic computer, known as a **Colossus**, was used.
(a) Find out how the secret German codes were set up, and how the codes were broken.
(b) Find out how important the activities of German submarines in the Atlantic were to the course of the war.

(c) Discuss the contribution made by these early computers and the people who designed and operated them to the outcome of the Second World War.

4 At least one British ship was sunk during the 1982 Falklands conflict because its electronic defence systems were inferior to the guidance systems used on a missile fired at it.
(a) Find out which ships were sunk during the Falklands conflict, and how they were sunk.
(b) Discuss the consequences of the inferior computer systems on the ships.
(c) Find out what changes have been made to British naval vessels since the Falklands conflict.

5 At the end of 1986, an **airborne early warning (AEW)** system for Britain which had been under development for nearly ten years was cancelled and an alternative one ordered.
(a) Find out what an AEW system is used for.
(b) Find out which company was developing the system, and which company supplied the replacement.
(c) Find out why the original AEW system was cancelled.
(d) Find out how much money was wasted on the development of the AEW system which was not implemented.
(e) In your opinion, should the original system have been continued, or was it better to cancel it and order a replacement? Give your reasons.

6* (a) Find out what weapons systems are proposed for the strategic defense initiative (SDI). What computer systems will be needed to control these weapons?
(b) Find out and summarise the case for developing defense systems of this nature.
(c) Find out and summarise the case against these systems.
(d) Give your opinion on whether or not the SDI should go ahead.

Points to discuss

1 The UK Data Protection Act only covers personal data held on computers. It does not deal with data held on paper files.
(a) Suggest some ways in which organisations might take advantage of this loophole in the law.

(b) Discuss the consequences of this limitation.
(c) Give, with reasons, your opinion on whether the Data Protection Act should be extended to cover all personal data, however it is stored.

26 Revision Exercise

The following questions are all taken from specimen GCSE examination papers in Computer Studies. The abbreviations for the Examining Groups are as follows:

LEAG   London and East Anglian Group
MEG   Midland Examining Group
NISEC   Northern Ireland Schools Examinations Council
SEG   Southern Examining Group

1 Figure 26.1 shows a bar code. Some supermarkets make use of these at their checkouts.
(a) Give *two* advantages to the supermarket of using bar codes.
(b) Why is the product's price not included in the bar code?
(c) Why is a check digit included?   LEAG Paper 1 Q8

5 010033 001344

Figure 26.1

2 Use the following list to complete the sentences:

laser scanner
microfiche
modem
mouse
OCR reader
OMR reader

(a) Bar code labels can be read by a ....
(b) Graphics design is easier using a ....
(c) Turnaround documents, e.g. gas bill, can be read by a ....
(d) Multiple-choice exam answer sheets can be read by a ....
(e) Computers can be linked by telephone, using a ....
(f) Details of books in a library can be stored on ....
                                          LEAG Paper 1 Q9

3 Figure 26.2 shows a customer's receipt, printed at a supermarket checkout. For each item listed below, write
    T if it is keyed in by the till operator
    W if it is worked out by the computer
    D if it is read from the disc storage.
(a) Code Number
(b) Description
(c) Price Each
(d) Quantity
(e) Total Price
(f) Final Total
(g) Amount Paid
(h) Change Given
(i) Would the information be stored on disc using **serial** or **direct** access?   LEAG Paper 1 Q12

Code	Description	Quantity	Price Each	Total Price
123	Baked Beans	4	0.19	0.76
227	Toilet Rolls	2	0.70	1.40
	Final Total			2.16
	Amount Paid			5.00
	Change Given			2.84

Figure 26.2

4 To send a letter with an electronic mail system, you would type it in on your keyboard and it would be sent to a central computer. Each time that you connect to the computer, you will be given a list of the letters waiting for you.
(a) Give *one* advantage of electronic mail compared with sending a letter by post.
(b) Give *one* advantage compared with using the telephone.
(c) Post Office workers are concerned over the widespread use of electronic mail. Give *one* reason for this concern.
(d) Give an example of an item which could not be sent by electronic mail.   LEAG Paper 1 Q15

The following text refers to questions 5 and 6.

An electricity board uses a computerised system to charge customers for the electricity they have used. The board has about a million customers each of whom has a customer account number. Details of each customer are stored in a CUSTOMER FILE in account number order. Each customer's electricity meter is read every three months and bills calculated from the readings are sent to the customers.

The meters are read by a meter reader who has a list of customers' names, addresses and account numbers and visits every house, shop, office and factory on the list. The meter reader copies the meter reading onto this list.

If the meter reader does not manage to read a meter, he or she leaves a card. The customer should then read the meter, complete the card and post it to the electricity board. If the card is not returned, the bill is estimated from the amount of electricity used in the same period of the previous year.

The meter readings and customer account numbers are punched by the data processing staff, and form the BILLING TRANSACTION FILE for any particular day. The BILLING TRANSACTION FILE is processed with the CUSTOMER FILE to produce the bills for the customers and information for the electricity board managers.

The bills include the account number and the amount owed and have a detachable slip to be returned with the payment. Customers pay their bills at the electricity showrooms, a bank or the post office, or by sending a cheque or postal order to the electricity board.

The returned payment slips for each day are collected together to form the PAYMENT TRANSACTION FILE which is processed against the CUSTOMER FILE and used to produce a list of those customers who still owe money.

5 The list which the meter reader uses contains the names of the customers he or she has to visit.
(a) State the *two* other items of information for each customer which will be on the list. Explain why each is needed.
(b) What piece of information does the meter reader copy onto the list?
(c) The list is used to produce the BILLING TRANSACTION FILE.
(i) The key field in the BILLING TRANSACTION FILE contains a check digit. Which is the key field? What is the purpose of the check digit?
(ii) Apart from the key field, only *one* other item of information is needed to complete a record in the BILLING TRANSACTION FILE. Which item is this? Explain why the other two items which appear on the list are *not* needed in the BILLING TRANSACTION FILE.
(iii) The two required items of information for each customer on the list are punched by the data processing staff. Describe a method of verification used to ensure that the data is correctly punched. LEAG Paper 2 Q1
6 Each record in the CUSTOMER FILE contains at least eight fields. Part of the record for Mr F Bloggs is shown below:

FIELD NAME	FIELD CONTENTS
ACCOUNT NO	128743182
CUSTOMER NAME	MR F BLOGGS
CUSTOMER ADDRESS	141 LOW ST
METER READING 3 MONTHS AGO	14276
METER READING 6 MONTHS AGO	14011
METER READING 9 MONTHS AGO	13780
METER READING 12 MONTHS AGO	13589
METER READING 15 MONTHS AGO	13301

(a) Which is the key field in the CUSTOMER FILE? Explain why this is the key field.
(b) One of these fields is the meter reading taken three months ago. Explain why this reading is needed.
(c) There must also be other meter readings for the last year. State *one* reason why these readings are needed.
(d) State *one* reason why the record must contain the customer's name and address.
(e) State *one* reason why this record must contain the customer's account number.
(f) Mr F Bloggs has just had his meter read. The reading is 14441. When the CUSTOMER FILE is updated, this meter reading is written in the field named METER READING 3 MONTHS AGO. Explain why this is the correct field name for the new meter reading.
(g) Show the field contents of the record for Mr F Bloggs after his record has been updated.

FIELD NAME	FIELD CONTENTS
ACCOUNT NO	
CUSTOMER NAME	
CUSTOMER ADDRESS	
METER READING 3 MONTHS AGO	14441
METER READING 6 MONTHS AGO	
METER READING 9 MONTHS AGO	
METER READING 12 MONTHS AGO	
METER READING 15 MONTHS AGO	

LEAG Paper 2 Q2

7 A small firm needs to use a computer system for information retrieval. It can either use a microcomputer with floppy discs or have on-line access to a main frame computer. State *one* advantage and *one* disadvantage to the firm if it uses a microcomputer. LEAG Paper 3 Q10
8 A library uses a computerised system to record which books have been loaned. When books are loaned the following data is recorded on computer files:
the borrower's code number
the code numbers of the books which have been borrowed.
(a) Suggest, with a reason, a suitable method of data capture.
(b) State *two* reasons why code numbers are used rather than the book titles.
(c) State *one* way in which a computerised library system might affect the privacy of a borrower. LEAG Paper 3 Q12
9 Use the following terms to complete the sentences below. You may not use a term more than once.

assembler; execution; high-level language; logical; machine code; object; source; syntax.

A compiler translates the whole of a ___ program into ___ before execution. The original program is the ___ code and the translated program is called the ___ code. An ___ translates a low-level language program into machine code.
The compiler detects ___ errors during compilation and ___ errors during the running of the program. ___ errors can only be detected by examining the results.
LEAG Paper 3 Q16

10 (a) Explain what real-time processing is.

(b) Describe an application where a computer system is needed for real-time process control.

(c) For this application of real-time process control, describe

(i) the data which is needed by the computer

(ii) how the data is captured, including how it is validated

(iii) the processing that is done

(iv) output signals from the computer and how these signals produce the necessary effects.   LEAG Paper 5 Q3

11 ACCARD is a credit card company. The company issues cards to individuals who use them to buy goods without cash. The company sets the credit limit for each individual, pays for the goods and later recovers the money from the card holder. All retailers offering ACCARD services to their customers have on-line ACCARD readers (with numeric keypads) connected to the ACCARD computer centre at Esshampton. The retailer is given an authorisation number for each· purchase which is beyond the shop's limit.

(a) Describe *two* of the data files that must be housed at the Esshampton centre.

(b) An individual tries to use an ACCARD card to make a purchase which is more than the shop's limit. Explain how the system would process this request for credit. (Give meaningful names to any data files that the system uses.)

(c) It would seem that computerised credit card systems offer an easy and convenient way of purchasing: yet many people voice opinions against such systems because of the personal nature of the information recorded. Briefly discuss whether this objection is valid.   LEAG Paper 5 Q4

12 List *three* items of data which would be input into a system which calculates a weekly wage.   MEG Paper 1 G8

13 For *each* of the following applications choose the correct method of processing.

Application	Method of Processing		
Chemical manufacturing process	Batch	On-line	Computer control
	Batch	On-line	Computer control
Company payroll	Batch	On-line	Computer control
Computerised theatre booking system	Batch	On-line	Computer control
Industrial robot			

MEG Paper 1 F12

14 Give *two* ways in which microprocessors have affected life in the home.   MEG Paper 1 E18

15 A newsagent uses a microcomputer, floppy disks and a printer to keep a record of papers and magazines ordered by the customers.

Write down *three* processes the system could carry out for the newsagent.   MEG Paper 2 D7

16 Copy the table and fill in each of the blank spaces with 0 or 1 as appropriate, to represent the outputs P, Q and R for the logic network in Figure 26.3.

A	B	C	P	Q	R
0	0	0	0	1	1
0	0	1	0	0	
0	1	0	0		
0	1	1	0		
1	0	0			
1	0	1			
1	1	0			
1	1	1			

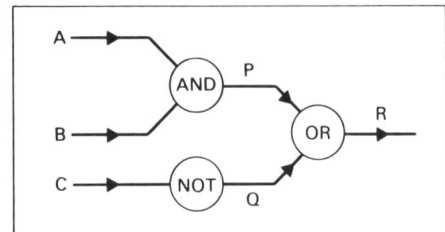

Figure 26.3

MEG Paper 2 C11

17 (a) Choose *three* applications in the list below which would be carried out using batch processing.

airline seat reservation
printing electricity bills
producing payslips
a warning system for 'seat belts not fastened' in a car
running an interactive program from a terminal
printing examination certificates
traffic control
monitoring a hospital patient's heart.

(b) Select *one* of the applications you have chosen and describe briefly the processing involved. MEG Paper 2 C13

18 A word processor automatically keeps the two most recent versions of each document, the versions of the document ARTICLE being stored as ARTICLE.NEW and ARTICLE.OLD. The current (most recent) version, ARTICLE.NEW, is loaded from disk and edited on the screen.

Explain carefully what operations take place when this new version is stored on disk.   MEG Paper 3 B5

19 Following a school general knowledge contest the results are to be input into the school computer. Each record is to consist of the pupil's name and initials, the pupil's mark and the initials of the pupil's tutor.

For example: SMITH R. M.
73
MFT

(a) Sketch a suitable screen layout for inputting the data.

(b) Describe the validation checks which might be carried out on each of the three items.

(c) Give *two* ways in which incorrect data might pass your validation checks.   MEG Paper 3 B6

20 A certain computer is to be used to monitor temperature levels at intervals of 1 second. It is also to be used to process data previously recorded. Interrupts are to be used to allow both tasks to be performed efficiently.

Explain what is meant by interrupts, with reference to the above example.   MEG Paper 3 A9

21 Choose any *three* of the following and for each write:
(i) where it might be used
(ii) what it might be used for
(iii) an advantage of its use.

1 teletext
2 robots
3 computer-aided learning
4 word processing
5 computer-aided design.   NISEC Paper 1 Q9

22 From the following list choose the one which best completes the sentence.

   program
   peripheral
   Cobol
   light pen
   immediate access
   real time

(a) _____ is a commercial programming language.
(b) A lot of instructions for a computer is a _____.
(c) Another name for the main store of a computer is the _____ store.
(d) A computer which continually updates its memory is said to be working in _____.
(e) A _____ is a device by which a user can write or draw on the computer screen.   NISEC Paper 1 Q12

23 Study the list of computer applications below and then answer the questions that follow.

   airline seat reservations
   traffic control
   electricity billing
   payroll
   monitoring a hospital patient's heart

(a) Write down *one* of these that must be 'real-time' processing.
(b) Explain why the application named in (a) must be done in 'real-time'.
(c) Choose another application from the list that is carried out using batch processing.
(d) For the application chosen in (c) name *three* items of input data. State how this data is input.
          NISEC Paper 2 A5

24 Describe the following pieces of hardware and state what each is used for. Diagrams may be used to illustrate your answer.
(a) magnetic tape unit
(b) acoustic coupler
(c) line printer
(d) floppy disc unit   NISEC Paper 2 A6

The following text refers to questions 25 and 26.

A mail order company sells a wide range of goods through the post to its agents. All of the items for sale are illustrated in a colour catalogue. A brief description of each item is given in the catalogue including size, colour and price. The catalogue also gives a catalogue number for each item.

When an agent wishes to order items she completes an order form and posts it to the company for processing.

25 The MASTER STOCK FILE holds information on all the stock in the warehouse. Each record contains at least 12 fields, e.g.

Catalogue number	DR5643
Page number	254
Price	42.89
Description	Office desk
Size	26
Colour	Ash brown
Weekly payment	2.15
Stock level	8
Reorder level	5
Reorder quantity	10
Supplier code	BHP
Location in warehouse	H27

The MASTER STOCK FILE is a sequential file sorted in order of catalogue number.
(i) Catalogue number is the key field but it is not unique. What other two fields are needed to identify a record uniquely?
(ii) Why is the description field not used to identify a stock record during order processing?
(iii) What information does the field 'stock level' contain?
(iv) What is meant by 'reorder level'?
(v) What is meant by 'reorder quantity'?
(vi) Who would use the information in the field 'location in warehouse'?
(vii) The code for the location in the warehouse is in two parts—a letter followed by a two digit number. Suggest a meaning for each part of the code.   NISEC Paper 2 B10

26 One report produced by the system goes to the warehouse so that the storekeepers can pick out each item required and parcel it for posting to the agent.
(i) List *five* pieces of information that should be on the list.
(ii) In what order would the items appear on this 'picking list'?
(iii) Some items may appear on this list that are not found in the warehouse although the computer record on the STOCK FILE says that they are there. How could this happen?   NISEC Paper 2 B13

27 Programmers often spend more time maintaining programs than writing new ones. Give *three* reasons why program maintenance is necessary.   NISEC Paper 3 B35

28 A program is executed and produces results which are found to be incorrect. List *three* different methods the programmer can use to locate a mistake in the program.   NISEC Paper 3 B37

29 The stages in producing a successful computer-based system include the following:
   implementation
   maintenance
   feasibility study
   problem identification
   system specification
   technical design
(i) Write down these stages in the order in which they would normally be carried out.
(ii) Describe what is involved in any *two* of the stages listed above and say why each is necessary.
          NISEC Paper 4 B9

30 (a) Networks are used to ensure the efficient exchange of information.
(i) With the help of diagrams describe *three* different network configurations.
(ii) State *two* disadvantages of using the public telephone system for networking.
(iii) What is a multiplexer and how may it be used to advantage in a network?
(b) Indicate the function of the Sequence Control Register and the Instruction Register in the CPU.
Describe a typical fetch-execute cycle in the execution of a program instruction, with reference to these two registers.   NISEC Paper 4 B10

31 (a) What is meant by a multi-access computer?
(b) Why do users of a multi-access computer usually have to have a user's password?
(c) Three levels of access to files held on a computer backing store are:
     read and write, read only, forbidden.
Give an appropriate situation for *each* of these.
(d) Give *three* actions that must be taken by the operating system of a multi-access computer to organise the work of everyone using it.   SEG Paper 2 Q8

32 Computer systems are now being used extensively in hospitals. Computers form part of life-support systems and medical records are kept in computer files.
(a) Blood pressure is a human physical response suitable for monitoring by computer. Suggest *two* others.
(b) Give *three* reasons why computers are used in life-support systems.
(c) Give *three* tasks for which human medical staff are more suitable than computers.
(d) Give *three* of the benefits gained by both hospital staff and patients in having medical records held in a computer file.
(e) It has been suggested that when personal data is held on file, people should have the right to see the contents of records which refer to them. Argue the case for and against the right of a patient to see his or her own records.   SEG Paper 2 Q12

The following text refers to questions 33 to 35.

An order processing system, including a stock control procedure, as used by mail order companies, has information stored in four files.

The STOCK file contains CATALOGUE-ITEM-NUMBER, ITEM-DESCRIPTION, QUANTITY-ON-HAND, RE-ORDER LEVEL and ITEM-PRICE.

The ORDER file contains ORDER-NUMBER, DATE-OF-ORDER, CATALOGUE-ITEM-NUMBER, QUANTITY-ORDERED and CUSTOMER-NUMBER.

The CUSTOMER file contains CUSTOMER-NUMBER, CUSTOMER-NAME, CUSTOMER-ADDRESS and CREDIT-LIMIT.

The RE-ORDER file contains CATALOGUE-ITEM-NUMBER, SUPPLIER-NAME and SUPPLIER-ADDRESS.

33 (a) Why does the CUSTOMER file contain a CUSTOMER-NUMBER?
(b) What information might be held in coded form in the CUSTOMER-NUMBER?
(c) How could the mail order company detect errors in the customer number?   SEG Paper 3 Q6

34 (a) What is contained in the RE-ORDER LEVEL field in the STOCK file?
(b) Show when and how this field is used in connection with the RE-ORDER file.
(c) What is the benefit of the RE-ORDER file to the main order company?
(d) Give *one* other field which must be included in the RE-ORDER file and which is not in any of the other files, to automatically produce a re-order for an item.
                              SEG Paper 3 Q8

35 Draw a systems diagram to show how a customer's order may be processed from receipt to dispatch of goods.
                              SEG Paper 3 Q9

27 Project Suggestions

This chapter contains a list of suggestions for GCSE projects, in addition to those found in most of the applications chapters. They can be done using the information retrieval, word processing, spreadsheet or other software packages described in chapters 11 to 20, or the control systems in chapter 21. A few of the projects involve the use of more than one package.

The degree of difficulty and the time taken on a project depend mainly on the amount of detail included in the project. The ideas given here can be implemented quite simply or in a fair amount of detail as required. It is better to set out to do a straightforward project and complete it successfully than to try something too ambitious!

1 Use an information retrieval system to keep records of the subscribers to a magazine. There is a record for each subscriber containing name, address and other details. The information is used for address labels to attach to the magazines, and to remind readers when their subscriptions are due. The operations on the information include:

- Entering new subscribers.
- Updating the records of subscribers when they change their address or pay their subscriptions.
- Printing address labels for all subscribers.
- Printing reminders to all the subscribers whose subscriptions are due.
- Deleting the records of subscribers who have stopped paying.

The reminder letters can be done on a word processor, if this has facilities to read data from an information retrieval system.

2 Set up a computerised diary based on an information retrieval system. Create a file for each year, with a record for each day and fields for the date, times of the day and notes. Include facilities to enable someone to:

- Enter appointments for any day.
- Look up the appointments on any day.
- Print the appointments on any day.
- Find an appointment by looking up a keyword in the appointment. For example, typing the keyword 'theatre' finds all the theatre bookings.

3 Set up a database of local amenities with a record for each amenity. Include sports centres, swimming baths, community centres, museums, art galleries, theatres, cinemas, youth clubs, discos, etc. Include at least the following information about each:

name and address
opening hours

admission prices
age restrictions (if any)
facilities for disabled people
how to get there by public transport

Include facilities to enter and edit data, to select groups of amenities (e.g. all those which are free) and to search for particular ones.

4 Use a word processor to write the script for a short film or video. Make use of the formatting facilities to set out the directions, narrative, commentary, etc. Some possible topics are:

- A documentary film about life in your local community.
- A film about an important local feature, such as a river, canal, harbour, public building or cathedral.
- A film on an extract from a set book or play.
- A children's film, based on a traditional story or nursery rhyme.

As the project progresses, a number of drafts of the script will be needed. Use the word processor to amend one version of the script in order to produce the next one.

5 A spreadsheet can be used to keep the accounts for a youth club. Use one spreadsheet for each month. Either set it out like the bank account spreadsheet in section 12B, or use separate columns for income and expenditure, as shown in Figure 27.1. Write a user guide, explaining how to:

- Open an account at the start of a month.
- Make an entry.
- Write the account to disk.
- Print the account.
- Close the account at the end of the month.

```
 _____1_____ ___2_____ ____3_____ ___4_____ ____5_____ ____6_____ ____7_____ ___8___
 1   Month:   January     Year:        1987
 2   --------  --------    --------    --------
 3
 4   Income                             Spending
 5    Date        Ref        Item      Amount     Date        Ref        Item      Amount
 6   *-------   --------    --------   -------*   *-------   --------   --------   -------*
 7   01/01/87              Balance     £87.33    03/01/97   C100135    Crisps      £7.43
 8   03/01/87   S029       Subs        £13.35    05/01/87   C100136    Coffee      £3.95
 9   03/01/87   C035       Canteen      £9.76    09/01/87   C100137    Equipmnt   £39.50
10   10/01/87   S030       Subs        £18.29    15/01/87   C100138    Record      £5.50
11   10/01/87   C036       Canteen     £10.23    16/01/87   C100139    Prizes      £6.50
12   17/01/87   R011       Raffle      £23.75    19/01/87   C100140    Drinks     £23.35
13   17/01/87   S031       Subs         £8.35    23/01/87   C100141    Repairs    £13.95
14   24/01/87   C037       Canteen      £7.37    25/01/87   C100142    Crisps      £6.95
15   24/01/87   S032       Subs         £5.38    30/01/87   C100143    Football   £13.50
16   31/01/87   C038       Canteen     £19.35
17   31/01/87   S033       Subs        £31.45
18
19                                    --------                                   --------
20   31/01/87              Total      £234.61    31/01/87              Total     £120.63
21                                    --------                                   --------
22                                              31/01/87              Balance    £113.98
23                                                                               --------
24                                                                               £234.61
25                                                                               --------
26
```

Figure 27.1 Spreadsheet for youth club accounts

6 Investigate the flow of traffic through a junction at various times of the day. With the help of some friends, count the number of cars travelling in each direction through the junction over one-minute or five-minute intervals. Enter this data in a statistical program, and work out the total number of cars flowing in the various directions and the average number of cars per minute. Produce graphs of these figures.

Write a report, including a diagram of the junction and the figures you have collected and analysed. Based on the figures, comment on how well the junction works and make suggestions for ways of smoothing the flows of traffic.

7 Pollution in the air consists of various kinds of smoke, particularly smoke containing lead particles, and gases such as sulphur dioxide, carbon monoxide and carbon dioxide (which is found naturally in small quantities). If you are able to borrow equipment to measure the levels of any of these pollutants, this can form the basis of a pollution monitoring project.

Set up the apparatus, and record the concentration of one or more pollutants over a period of time. If possible, leave the equipment running for several days at a time, logging the data automatically. Enter the data into a statistical program (if it cannot be transferred directly from the recording apparatus). Calculate the average concentrations at various times of the day, and see if you can find patterns in the data. Is there a daily pattern? If so, when are the highest and lowest levels? Is there a weekly variation on this pattern? If so, what are the highest and lowest days?

Write a report, giving details of the substances measured, the position of the measuring equipment, and present the results. Include a map of the area where the apparatus was placed. Try to find the causes of the pollution, and suggest how it might be reduced.

8 If you have set up one of the reservations systems described in chapter 16, a fairly simple project is to provide a ticket printing facility for the system. One possible method is to use a small spreadsheet as the basis of a ticket, with all the constant information on it. The date, time and ticket number are entered into appropriate cells, and the complete ticket is printed. A more advanced version, which may require a specially written program, is given the date and time and a range of seat numbers, such as B6 to B9, and prints all the tickets in the range.

9 Use a CAD system to produce the ideal design for your room in your house. Enter the outline of your room and store it as a basis for the design. Then draw in the built-in furniture, other furniture, light fittings, telephone, television and computer data links you would like in your ideal room. If the design contains movable partitions or folding tables, show the alternative arrangements. Either produce a plan and a number of separate elevations, or work in three dimensions on a single design.

10 Use a CAD system to design a house which will use as little energy as possible to be kept warm. Look in books and magazines to get some ideas, and get leaflets on energy savings from the gas board and other organisations. Some general principles of energy conservation are:

- The area of the outside walls and roof should be as small as possible. Square or circular houses are preferable to long and narrow ones.
- Most windows should face south, and be double glazed.
- The house can be built partly underground to reduce heat loss from walls.
- The heating system should be in the centre of the house.

Draw a plan and the elevations of the house from each side. Do *not* include too much detail.

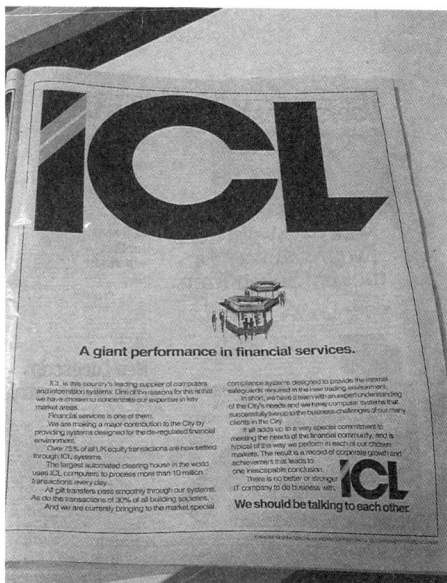

The logo of a computer manufacturer.

11 The manufacturers of computer systems use various symbols called **logos** to identify their products. A project can be based on these logos, as follows:

- Make a collection of the logos of a number of computer companies. Photocopy or cut them from magazines and brochures.
- Find out the effect of the logo on people. Either discuss them with others or carry out a survey. Find out how many people recognise each logo, and what kind of impression it creates on them.
- Use a CAD system to design a logo of your own for a range of computers. First decide who is to use the range of computers. Use what you have learned from the study of the other logos in the design. Write a report giving the reasons for your design, stating why it should appeal to the group of people who you hope will buy the computers.

12 Design some patterns for fabric, wallpaper or wall tiles using a CAD program or one for **tesselations**. Collect some samples of other designs before you start and look at the amount of detail in the design, the colours, etc. Discuss the designs with others to get an idea of their popularity and why people like or dislike them.

  Write a report giving the reasons for your designs and explaining how the CAD system is used to produce the designs.

13 The ideas behind the bus journey simulation in section 18A can be used to simulate the operation of a ferry crossing a river or lake. The ferry journey has three phases: loading, travelling and offloading. The loading and offloading times depend on the number of people and vehicles being carried. While the ferry is crossing, queues of people and vehicles build up at each side. Investigate the effects of

- a faster crossing
- faster loading and offloading
- a larger ferry

on the number of people and vehicles which can be taken across in a day.

14 The 'tree' structure of a local viewdata system, described in section 19B, is similar to that of a family tree. See Figure 27.2. There is one 'page' for each person, with links to their parents and children. It is a worthwhile project to use a local viewdata system for a family tree: either you own family tree or that of an important local family, or the Royal family.

Include as many records as you can find information for, and describe in your report how to:

- set up the viewdata system
- add pages for additional people
- view the pages
- print pages.

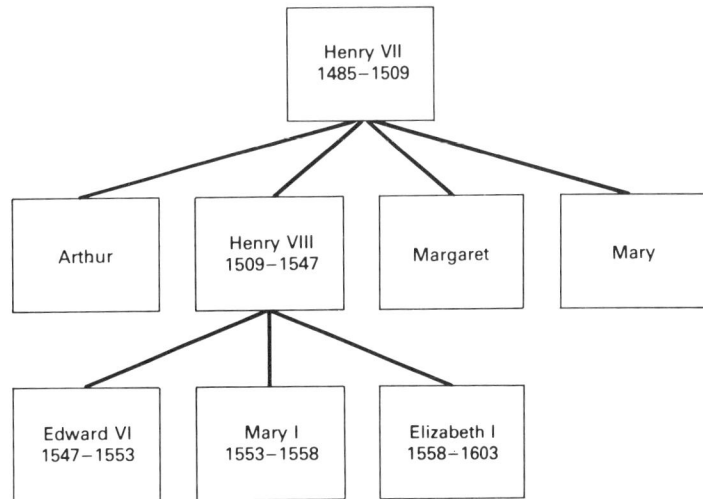

Figure 27.2 Viewdata family tree

15 If you can borrow some logic gates from an electronics kit and some items from a model train set, a number of projects are possible. One is to build an automatic level crossing, controlled by the movement of the train:

- When the train approaches the crossing, the warning lights flash. Use an electrical contact to detect the train.
- After a few seconds, if there are no cars still on the crossing, the barriers come down and a signal turns green to allow the train over. Use a light beam to detect cars on the crossing.
- If there is a car on the crossing, the signal stays red to stop the train. The signal stays red until the car is off the crossing.

A more complex control system can be built for a crossing over two tracks, with the trains running in opposite directions.

16 The items in an electronics kit can be used to make aids for disabled people. Some ideas to follow up are:

- A control system for a wheelchair based on head or eye movements.
- Systems for entering data into a computer based on head or eye movements, or a simple joystick.

Whichever project you choose, start by contacting a disabled person, or a group of disabled people, and find out what they need or what will be useful to them. Many aids for disabled people are not much use because they have been designed by able-bodied people who do not understand the needs of disabled people properly.

17 A number of introductory information retrieval packages store data on disk in a simple format, but have only limited facilities for processing the data. If you are able to write programs in Basic or a similar programming language, it is possible to plan a project which uses the information retrieval package for the entry, editing and storage of the data, and a program of your own to process the data. (You may need some help with the program modules which read the data from the files.) Some ideas are as follows:

- Use an estate agent's information system (section 10B), and write a program to count the number of houses in each category (using the Property Type field). Also calculate the total asking price and average price in each category. Print this data in a suitably laid out report.

  Other programs based on this information can group the properties by the length of time they have been on the file, or the length of time it took to complete the sale. The averages of these times can be calculated.
- Use a spreadsheet program for invoices, as shown in Figure 27.3. Then write a stock control program to take a set of invoices (representing a day's trading) and produce a report showing the total number of each item sold. Also calculate the total value of the invoices. Print the report in a suitable layout.

```
   _____1_____2_____3_____4_____5
 1 Invoice:   87013           Date: 23/01/87
 2 --------  --------        --------  --------
 3
 4      To:    Cash     Sale
 5
 6
 7 Quantity            Item    Price    Amount
 8 --------  --------  --------  --------  --------
 9        3  Writing     Pad    £1.35     £4.05
10        2     Pack  Envelope  £0.85     £1.70
11        2     Ring    File    £1.05     £2.10
12        1              Pen    £1.85     £1.85
13
14                                      --------
15                            Total     £9.70
16                                      --------
17
```

Figure 27.3 Invoice

- An ambitious project is to use the payroll master file (section 13A) and transaction file (section 13B) and write a program to produce payslips, as described in section 13C. Assume that the records in both files have been sorted in order, and that the records in each file correspond.
- Even more ambitious is a project for stock control, using the stock master file from section 14A and the movement records

from section 14B. This program reads transaction records and finds and updates the corresponding master records, as described in section 14C. It writes the updated master records back to disk, and displays messages if the stock level is below the minimum level.

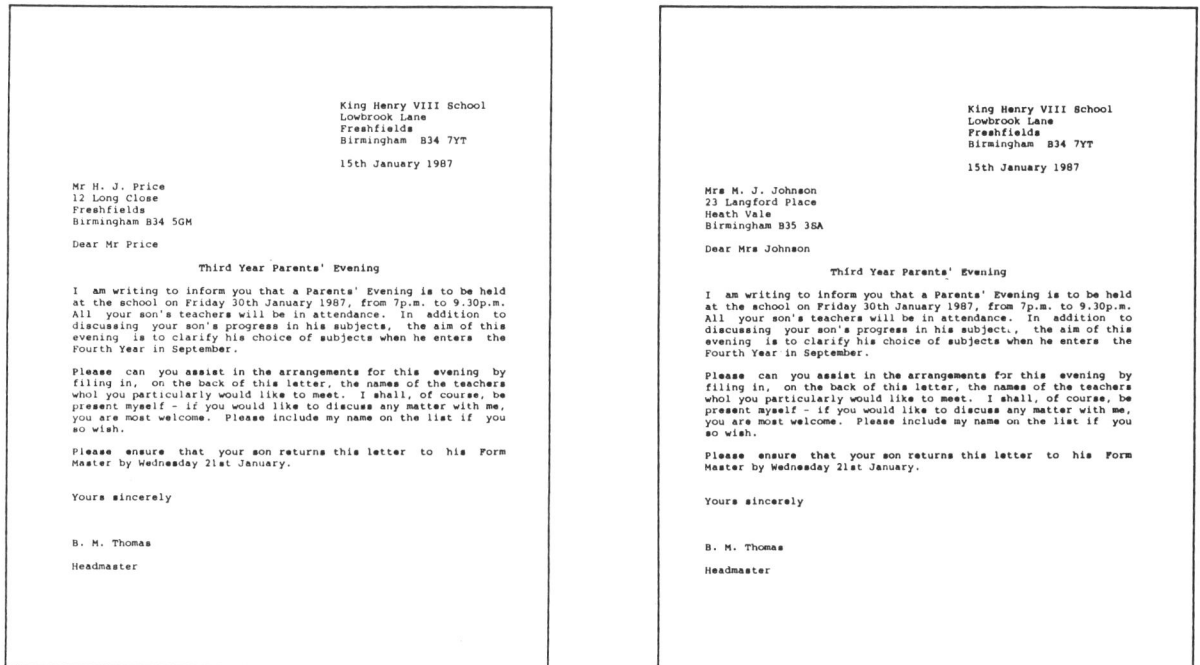

Figure 27.4   Letters produced using mailmerge

18   Some word processing systems have a **mailmerge** facility. This enables them to read data from a file (created by an information retrieval system) and copy it into documents. A common use for this is to read a set of names and addresses and copy them into a base letter to produce a set of letters, each individually addressed. See Figure 27.4. If you have access to a word processor with this facility and an information retrieval system which can create compatible data files, then a number of projects are possible:

- Use the club membership file created in chapter 9, and prepare a letter to be sent to all members advising them of a meeting or event to be held by the club. Produce a few personalised letters, individually addressed to members.
- Create a file of names and addresses of your friends, and write a Christmas letter to be addressed to each of them. Describe what you have done during the previous year in a way which is interesting to them all. Place the field names from the data file in the correct places in the letter, and print a few copies to show that the mailmerge system is working.
- Imagine that you have developed a software package suitable for small businesses using a microcomputer. Prepare a letter to a group of people who might be interested in buying the software package. Set up a data file with a suitable set of names and addresses, and produce a set of individually addressed letters.

19 If you have access to a **page make-up** program **which can** assemble the pages of a newspaper or magazine from **files of text** and graphics (Figure 27.5), then a number of **projects are** possible:

- A class newsletter or newspaper containing articles and drawings, with headings in large text, and lines ruled to improve its appearance.
- A newsletter for the club from chapter 9.
- A Christmas card or birthday card including text and graphics.

The details of the operation of pagemaker programs vary, but the general principles are the same:

- Create or edit the text on a word processing program.
- Create the illustrations on a drawing program.
- Use the pagemaker program to set out the design of the page(s). Allocate spaces for articles, headings and drawings, and rule lines to separate them.
- Copy the articles into the spaces for them. There are facilities for adjusting the length of the articles, and for making text flow from one column to another.
- Choose the typeface for the articles. Identify sections to be in larger or smaller type, and in bold or italics. Also choose the typeface and size for headings.
- Copy the drawings into the spaces allocated for them. They may be enlarged or reduced in size, or trimmed to fit.
- Print a 'proof' of each complete page. Check it carefully, and make any corrections or amendments needed.
- Print the final version of each page.

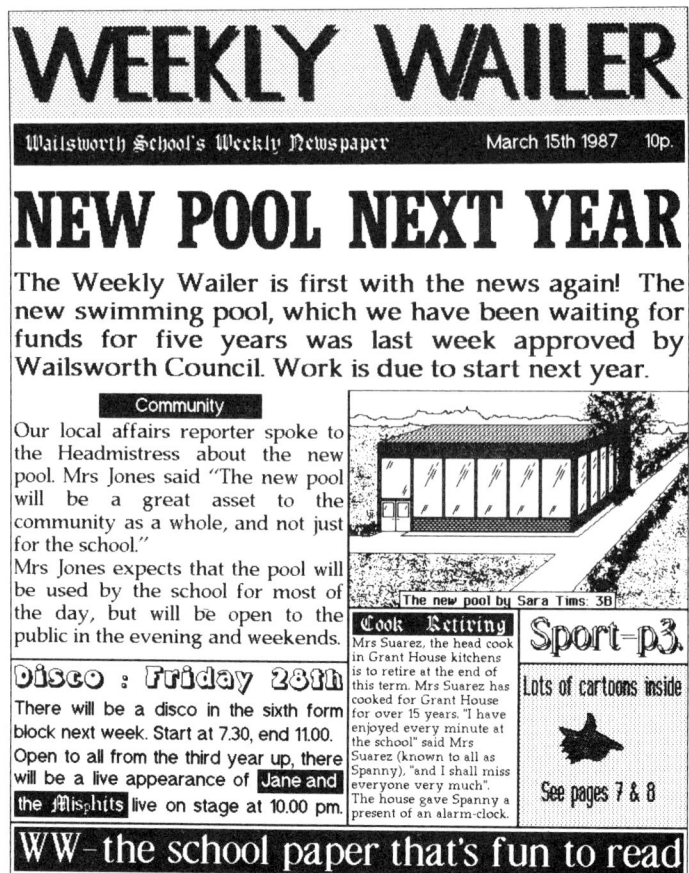

Figure 27.5 Page produced on page make-up system

Glossary of Terms

acceptance test   a test of a computer or program by its intending users.

accumulator (AC)   a register in a processor which holds the data item being processed at the time.

address   a number which identifies a cell in a computer memory.

algorithm   a description of the steps needed to carry out a task.

American Standard Code for Information Interchange (ASCII)   the character code used by most computers.

analogue device   a device which represents data by a physical quantity such as a voltage.

analogue-to-digital converter (ADC)   a device which converts from analogue to digital signals.

applications program   a program for a computer application.

artificial intelligence   the ability of a machine to copy some aspects of human intelligence.

artwork   the diagrams showing the layout of the layers of a chip or printed circuit board.

assembler   a program which translates programs from assembly language to machine language.

assembly language   a programming language which provides a symbolic form of the machine language of a computer.

backing store   storage for large quantities of data, accessible to a processor.

backup   a copy of a file, or the contents of a disk or tape, made for security purposes.

bar code   a code made up of a pattern of wide and narrow bars.

batch processing   a type of operating system where programs are run in batches, or a type of computer application where data is processed in batches.

batch total   a check total used in data validation.

binary   base two.

binary coded decimal (BCD)   a data code where each digit of a decimal number is converted separately to binary.

bit   a binary digit (0 or 1).

block   a unit of data stored together and transferred to or from a magnetic tape in one operation.

Boolean logic   the theory of mathematical logic which forms the basis of the design of computers.

byte   a set of eight bits.

cell   a storage space in a computer memory.

central processing unit (CPU)   the unit of a computer in which the processing of data takes place.

check digit   an extra number or letter placed on the end of a data item for checking purposes.

chip   the popular name for an integrated circuit.

communications satellite   a satellite used for data communications between ground stations.

compiler   a program which translates programs in a high-level language into machine language.

computer   a digital electronic information processing machine, under the control of a stored program.

computer architect   a person who designs computers.

computer bureau   a company which does data processing for other companies.

computer operator   a person who operates a computer.

computer output on microfilm (COM)   a method of photographing computer output onto microfilm.

computer-aided design (CAD)   the use of computers for design work.

computer-aided design/computer-aided manufacture (CAD/CAM)   an integrated computer system used to design and manufacture goods.

control character   a character in a file or message used for control purposes.

control total   see batch total.

cursor   a highlighted area on a computer screen which indicates where the next typed character will appear.

daisy wheel printer   a type of printer where characters are mounted on the spokes of a wheel.

data   information in a form which can be stored on and processed by a computer.

data capture   obtaining input information for use in data processing.

data controller   a person who supervises the collection and input of data.

data dictionary   a table which describes the properties of a data file.

data processing (DP) department   the department of an organisation which does the data processing for the organisation.

data processing manager (DPM)   the person in charge of a data processing department.

Data Protection Act   the law in the United Kingdom which governs the use of personal information on computers.

Data Protection Registrar   the person responsible for implementing the Data Protection Act.

data subject   a person about whom personal information is stored on a computer.

data user   an organisation which uses personal information on a computer system.

database   a large store of related data which is used by a number of computer applications.

database administrator (DBA)   the person in charge of a database system.

database system   a computer system centred on a database.

device   a piece of equipment which forms part of a computer.

diagnostic error message   a message which indicates the location and the cause of an error in a program.

digital   the representation of data as a set of digits.

digital plotter   an output device which produces graphs or drawings.

digital telephone exchange   an electronic telephone exchange which handles calls in digital form.

digitiser   an input device for graphics systems.

direct data entry (DDE) a method of data entry where input data is typed directly onto a magnetic disk or tape.

directive an assembly language instruction which is acted on directly by the assembler, and not translated into machine code.

disk drive a device which transfers data to and from magnetic disks.

distributed processing processing shared in a computer system between a number of processors and intelligent terminals.

dividend a sum of money paid to the holders of shares in a company.

documentation a written description of how a program works, or how it is to be used.

dot matrix printer a type of printer which forms characters as patterns of dots.

dry run carrying out each step of a program by hand, and writing down the results of each step.

electronic funds transfer (EFT) the transfer of money between banks by messages sent between their computers.

electronic funds transfer at point-of-sale (EFTPOS) paying for goods by electronic funds transfer as they are bought.

electronic mail a service which enables letters to be sent between computers via the telephone network.

encryption the use of a secret code for data.

end-of-file record a special record which marks the end of a file.

error message a message produced by a compiler, assembler or operating system when an error has occurred.

error report a list of all the errors in a set of input data.

expert system a computer system which can give reasoned advice in a particular field.

facsimile a system which transmits images of documents or diagrams from one place to another via the telephone network.

feedback monitoring the output of a control system in order to provide an input to the system.

fetch-execute cycle the cycle of operations by which a processor carries out one machine instruction.

fibre optics the use of fine strands of glass to carry signals in the form of light waves.

field a space in a file for one item of data.

field engineer a person who installs and maintains computer systems.

Fifth Generation computer a computer based on an inference processor operating on a knowledge base and with an intelligent user interface.

file a structured collection of related data.

file dump a copy of a file made on backing store.

file index a table of data which associates certain fields with the location of the records in a file containing the fields.

fileserver the device on a computer network which holds the backing store shared by the network workstations.

floppy disk a single flexible magnetic disk.

flow diagram a diagram consisting of a linked set of boxes, which describes the steps of a process.

formatting preparing a magnetic disk for data storage.

fourth generation language (4GL) a set of program development tools including data dictionaries, screen design modules and program generators.

frame the storage area for one character on magnetic tape.

games paddle an input device used for computer games.

gate a logic element which carries out a Boolean operation.

gateway a link between a viewdata network and another computer system.

generation when a file is updated, a new generation of the file is created.

gigabyte one million million bytes.

grandfather-father-son principle keeping the three most recent generations of a file, and updating it in a cycle.

graphics displaying diagrams and drawings on a computer screen.

ground station the place where signals are sent to and from a communications satellite.

hacker a person who breaks into computer systems.

hard copy printed output data.

hard-wired control describes a control system where the control is carried out entirely by hardware.

hardware the physical components of a computer, communications or control system.

hexadecimal base sixteen.

high-level language an application-oriented programming language, independent of the hardware of any particular computer.

high-resolution graphics (HRG) graphics which can show a fine degree of detail.

image file a file which stores a graphics image.

indexed sequential file a sequential file which has an index.

inference processor a processor which draws reasoned conclusions from a knowledge base.

information provider an organisation which supplies information to a viewdata network.

information retrieval system a type of computer application based on a store of information which can be accessed at any time.

information technology (IT) the combination of computers, communications and control systems, all based on digital electronic components.

ink jet printer a type of printer which forms characters by squirting ink from fine nozzles.

input data supplied to a computer system.

instruction register (IR) the register in a processor which holds the machine instruction currently being processed.

integrated circuit a solid-state device containing a large number of logic circuits.

integrated services digital network (ISDN) a single digital communications network for voice, data, television and other signals.

intelligent knowledge-based system (IKBS) a computer system which draws inferences from a knowledge base.

intelligent terminal a terminal which is capable of a certain amount of processing.

intelligent user interface a computer interface which is able to relate closely to the requirements of the user.

interactive processing data processing which involves a two-way exchange of information between the computer and the user.

interface a point of contact between one part of a computer system and another.

interpreter a program which takes a program in a high-level language and carries out the instructions in it.

interrupt a temporary halt in the processing of a program while some other operation takes place.

inverted file a file in which each record contains fields taken from a number of records in another file.

joystick an input device used for computer games.

key a field in a record which identifies the record for some operation such as sorting.

keyboard an input device containing a set of keys.

keypad a simple keyboard with a small number of keys.

kilobyte (K) one thousand bytes (precisely 1024 bytes).

Kimball tag a tag containing data as a pattern of punched holes.

knowledge base a collection of information and rules relating the information.

label a set of characters which identifies an assembly language instruction or data item.

laser printer a type of printer which uses a laser beam to form the characters.

library module a program module carrying out a common task which may be incorporated into a number of applications programs.

light pen an input device which draws lines on a display screen.

line printer a type of printer which prints an entire line in one operation.

listing a printout of a program or program module.

local viewdata system a viewdata system on a single computer or local network.

log file a file which contains records of all the instructions issued by an operator to a computer, and the messages sent by the computer in response.

logic circuit an electrical circuit made up of logic elements.

low-level language a machine or assembly language.

machine code a programming language which controls the hardware of a computer directly.

machine instruction an instruction in a machine code, which a computer carries out in one operation.

machine language *see* machine code.

magnetic ink character recognition (MICR) reading characters printed in a magnetic ink by a special input device.

magnetic strip a strip on a price tag or credit card which holds data in magnetic form.

mailbox the storage space on an electronic mail or viewdata system for incoming messages to users.

mainframe computer a large computer consisting of a number of separate units.

mark sensing input from marks pencilled in on forms.

master data data used for reference by a data processing system.

master file a file of reference data.

medium a material on which data is stored.

megabyte one million bytes.

memory the part of a computer system which stores the data and programs which are in use at the time.

memory address the part of a machine instruction which locates the data item to be processed.

merging combining two ordered files to produce a single ordered file.

microchip a common name for integrated circuit.

microcomputer a computer based on a single microprocessor chip.

microprocessor a single chip containing the processing hardware of a computer.

microwave radio radio used for medium-distance data communications links.

minicomputer a medium-sized computer contained in a small number of units.

mnemonic operation code a set of letters forming the operation code in an assembly language.

model a simple system (often on a computer) which simulates the behaviour of another system.

modem a device which links a computer or terminal to a telephone line.

module a part of a computer program which performs a specific task and has a precisely defined interface to the rest of the program.

monitor the display screen on a computer or terminal.

mouse a small input device which is moved on the surface of a desk to move a pointer on a computer screen.

multi-access a type of operating system which allows a number of terminals to have access to a computer at the same time.

multiplexer a device which shares a single communications channel among a number of terminals.

network a communications system linking a number of computers.

network administrator the person in charge of a computer network.

numerically-controlled (NC) machine a machine controlled by a computer.

on-line describes a computer system or terminal which has continuous access to a computer processor.

operating system a program which co-ordinates the overall running of a computer.

operation code the part of a machine instruction which specifies the type of operation to be carried out.

operation table a table showing the inputs and corresponding outputs of a logic circuit.

operations manager the person in charge of the running of a computer system.

operator documentation a set of instructions for use by a computer operator when running a program.

optical character recognition (OCR) reading printed characters by optical means on an input device.

optical disk a disk which stores data as small indentations on its surface, read by laser beam.

original equipment manufacturer (OEM) a company which makes computer components.

output the data which is printed or displayed by a computer after processing.

overflow error the error which occurs when a number is too large for a computer to represent.

packet switching sending data on a network of computers as a sequence of packets.

page one screenful of data on a viewdata system.

peripheral an input, output or backing store device.

personal identification number (PIN) a number which confirms the identity of a person using a cash terminal.

pixel one of the dots which makes up a computer graphics display.

place value the value of a bit or digit, depending on its place in a number.

point-of-sale (POS) system a computer system where sales are recorded at terminals as they are made.

portfolio a collection of shares in companies.

presence check a check to see that a data item has been input.

printed circuit board (PCB) a fibreglass board on which are mounted chips and other components, with metal tracks connecting the components.

primary key the most significant key in a search or sort.

probe a measuring device which produces an electrical signal.

process control a type of computer application, where computers are used to monitor and control equipment.

processor   the part of a computer where the processing of data takes place.

program   a set of instructions which control the operation of a computer.

program counter (PC)   the register in a processor which holds the address of the current machine instruction.

program documentation   a written description of the workings of a program.

program generator   a software development tool which enables programs to be specified, and produces the programs from the specifications.

program maintenance   making changes in a program in order to correct errors and keep it up-to-date.

programmable read-only memory (PROM)   read-only memory chips which can be loaded with data by users.

programmed control   a type of control system where the control is carried out by software.

programmer   a person who designs, writes, maintains and documents computer programs.

prototype   an initial working version of a computer system or program.

random access   the ability to access any part of a data storage medium equally quickly.

random access memory (RAM)   memory chips in which data can be read from or written to any location.

random access file   a file in which any record can be accessed individually.

random file   a file in which the records are stored in random order, with an algorithm for locating a record from its key.

random number   a number chosen at random.

range check   a check to see that a number lies within a certain range.

read-only memory (ROM)   memory chips which store data that can be read but not overwritten.

read/write head   the device which transfers data to or from a magnetic disk or tape.

real-time processing   computer processing which must keep up with some external event such as a chemical reaction, which it monitors or controls.

record   the unit of data in a file, containing a number of fields.

record locking   when a record is in use on a multi-access system, it is locked so that other users cannot access it.

register   a storage space in a computer for a data item for a particular purpose.

remote access terminal   a terminal linked to a computer from a long distance.

remote input device   an input device linked to a computer from a long distance.

resolution   the degree of detail in a graphics system.

robot   a device which carries out some physical process under the control of a stored program.

ROM cartridge   an exchangeable ROM chip mounted in a cartridge.

run-time error   an error which occurs during the running of a program.

screen design module   a software development tool used to design display screens for the input and output of data.

secondary key   the second most significant key used for sorting or searching a file.

sector   a unit of data stored together on a disk track and transferred to or from the disk in one operation.

sensor   *see* probe.

sequence control register (SCR)   *see* program counter.

sequential file   a file in which the records are in order of one or more keys.

serial access   access to a data storage medium in the order in which the data is written to the medium.

serial access file   a file in which the records are accessed only in the order in which they are written.

serial file   a file in which the records are in no particular order.

shift leader   the person in charge of the computer operators and other staff working on a shift.

silicon disk   a portion of computer memory used as if it were a disk.

simulation   the use of a simple system (often on a computer) to study the behaviour of a more complex system.

software   the programs which control the hardware of a computer.

software development tool   *see* fourth generation language.

software engineer   a person who designs, develops and maintains computer software in accordance with strict standards and schedules.

software house   a company which develops computer software for other organisations.

software package   a complete, ready-to-use item of computer software.

sort key   the field in a record used to sort the records in order.

source document   a document from which input data is obtained.

spreadsheet   a type of computer program which manipulates data in tables containing rows and columns.

statement   a document which shows all the transactions over a period of time and the balance of an account.

strategic defense initiative (SDI)   a defense system against incoming nuclear missiles, based on advanced weapons in space.

supercomputer   a powerful mainframe computer able to do large numbers of calculations very quickly.

Swift   the international electronic funds transfer network.

symbolic address   a sequence of characters representing an address in an assembly language.

syntax error   an error in the use of a programming language.

system maintenance   making changes to a data processing system to correct errors or bring it up-to-date.

systems analyst   a person who plans how work is to be done on a computer.

systems programmer   a person who writes systems software for computers.

team leader   the person in charge of the programmers and systems analysts developing a data processing system.

teletext   the broadcast of pages of information by television.

terminal   a device providing a direct link between a computer and a person using it.

test data   data used to test a program for errors.

text file   a file containing a set of text, such as a word processor document.

touch-sensitive screen   a display screen with input facilities activated by touch.

track   a circular area for storing data on a magnetic disk, or a thin metal conducting strip on a printed circuit board.

transaction data   the data in a transaction file.

transaction file   a data file used to update a master file.

transaction processing   a type of data processing where transactions are processed in real time.

truth table   *see* operation table.

Turing test   a test for artificial intelligence.

turnaround document   a document which is output from one data processing operation and input into another.
twos complement   a method of representing binary numbers where the most significant bit is negative.
type check   a check to see if a data item is a particular type: numeric, alphabetic or special.

updating   bringing a file or other set of data up-to-date.
user guide   a document which describes how to use a computer program.
user interface   the point of contact between a computer or program and the person using it.
utility program   an item of systems software used for a common process such as formatting disks.

validation   checking input data before using it for processing.
verification   checking input data while it is being entered.
viewdata   a system where users access data by telephone from a central computer for display on television sets or terminals.
visual display unit (VDU)   a terminal where input and output are displayed on a screen.

Winchester disk   a high-capacity fixed magnetic disk.
window   an area of a display screen showing the output from one program.
workstation   a computer keyboard and screen, generally on a network, at which one person works.

Index